MOVING
ENCOUNTERS

A VOLUME IN THE SERIES

Native Americans of the Northeast:
Culture, History, and the Contemporary

Edited by
Barry O'Connell and Colin G. Calloway

Moving Encounters

Sympathy and the Indian Question in Antebellum Literature

Laura L. Mielke

University of Massachusetts Press

AMHERST

LC   2007022045
ISBN 978-1-55849-631-6 (paper); 630-9 (library cloth)

Designed by Jack Harrison
Set in Monotype Dante with Viva display by dix!
Printed and bound by The Maple-Vail Book Manufacturing Group

Library of Congress Cataloging-in-Publication Data

Mielke, Laura L.
Moving encounters : sympathy and the Indian question in Antebellum literature /
Laura L. Mielke.
p.   cm. — (Native Americans of the Northeast: culture, history,
and the contemporary)
Includes bibliographical references and index.
ISBN-13: 978-1-55849-630-9 (alk. paper)
ISBN-13: 978-1-55849-631-6 (pbk. : alk. paper)
1. American literature—19th century—History and criticism.
2. Indians in literature.   3. Sympathy in literature.
I. Title.
PS217.I49M54   2008
810.9'352997—dc22   2007022045

British Library Cataloguing in Publication data are available.

To Scott and Henry

CONTENTS

ILLUSTRATIONS

ACKNOWLEDGMENTS

My work on this project began ten years ago in a graduate-level survey of early American literature at the University of North Carolina at Chapel Hill. There I first encountered the writings of William Apess and the scholarship of Philip Gura, and my intellectual life has never been the same. Since then Philip has been my chief advocate and most astute critic; without him this book would not be. Many other generous Carolinians left their imprint on this project, including Robert Allen, Charles Capper, Robert Johnstone, John Kasson, Joy Kasson, Timothy Marr, Theda Perdue, Richard Rust, Mark Simpson-Vos, Jane Thrailkill, and John Ware. Colleagues at Iowa State University who helped me refine my arguments and apply for much-needed funding include Christopher Curtis, Jane Davis, Sara Gregg, John Hagge, Charles Kostelnick, Leland Poague, Diane Price Herndl, and Amy Slagell. In the wider scholarly world, Joshua David Bellin, Matt Cohen, Philip Deloria, Glenn Hendler, Carolyn Karcher, Jon Miller, Susan Ryan, Priscilla Wald, and Hilary Wyss all offered advice, commentary, and encouragement at critical points in my research. Michael Everton has been an especially generous reader and friend whose knowledge of the period and impatience for sloppy prose pushed me to think harder and write better.

The chapters of this book benefited from audiences' tough questions and stimulating remarks at a number of conferences and symposiums between 2002 and 2006: the American Literature Association Conference, the Interdisciplinary Nineteenth-Century Studies Annual Conference, the American Studies Association Annual Meeting, the Chesapeake Chapter of the American Studies Association Conference, the American Art and American Life Symposium at UNC-CH, the Sequoyah Symposium on Southeastern Indians at Western Carolina University, the Geography of Americanism Conference at the Historical Society of Pennsylvania, and the Works-in-Progress Series at the McNeil Center for Early American Studies.

The American Association of University Women, the UNC-CH Royster Society of Fellows, the ISU College of Liberal Arts and Sciences, the ISU Center for Excellence in the Arts and Humanities, and the UNC-CH and ISU Departments of English gave necessary financial support. In addition, the ISU Vice Provost for Research Office supplied a publication subvention grant for which both the

University of Massachusetts Press and I are grateful. The UNC-CH and ISU Libraries, especially their Interlibrary Loan Services, Duke University's Special Collections, and the Library of Congress Manuscripts Division provided access to various materials. In particular, Barbara Bair and Evelyn Timberlake at the Library of Congress made my visit there miraculously productive.

At the University of Massachusetts Press, Clark Dougan carefully and kindly guided the manuscript and me through the stages of editorial review and revision, and Carol Betsch shepherded the project through editing and production. Renée Bergland, Barry O'Connell, and Colin Calloway offered invaluable commentary, and Deborah Smith meticulously copyedited the manuscript.

An earlier version of Chapter 1 appeared as "Sentiment and Space in Lydia Maria Child's Native American Writings, 1824–1870," *Legacy: A Journal of American Women Writers* 21.2 (Winter 2004): 172–92; an earlier version of Chapter 4 was published as "'native to the question': William Apess, Black Hawk, and the Sentimental Context of Early Native American Autobiography," *American Indian Quarterly* 26 (Spring 2002): 246–70. I thank the editors and reviewers of those journals for supplying both feedback and a wider audience in the early stages of the project; the University of Nebraska Press kindly gave permission to reprint those essays.

Finally, I am deeply grateful to David, Sue, and Matt Mielke, Thelma Barnes, Bob, Kathy, and Andrew Hanrath, and the rest of my family for their unwavering support and patience. I dedicate this book to Scott Hanrath, whose love, brains, and sympathy sustained me throughout the long process of writing *Moving Encounters*, and to our son Henry, whose arrival makes the conclusion of the process all the sweeter.

MOVING
ENCOUNTERS

INTRODUCTION

The Moving Encounter
in Antebellum Literature

In the three decades following the War of 1812, the United States developed a new answer to the Indian Question, the name given to the problem of American Indian presence within and just beyond the borders of the expanding young nation. The federal government implemented a policy of Indian removal whereby the republic sought to acquire American Indian lands east of the Mississippi River, to relocate those American Indians to the west, to undermine if not eradicate American Indian political sovereignty, and to initiate a process of acculturation at arm's length. In 1819, James Monroe signed the Civilization Fund Act, which set aside ten thousand dollars a year for the instruction of American Indian children in "reading, writing, and arithmetic" and American Indian adults in agricultural methods.[1] Politicians and members of benevolent societies increasingly argued, however, that such efforts to save American Indians from extinction through education were undermined by the pupils' proximity to the corrupting elements of non-Native culture. Thus, removal policy signaled a desire to secure land for eager settlers and to shore up U.S. territory in the wake of conflicts with France, Spain, and Britain and a rejection of the belief that American Indians could become "civilized" while directly contending with a rapidly expanding Euro-American population.[2] First proposed by Thomas Jefferson in 1803 and fleshed out by Monroe in an address to Congress in January 1825, removal was made official federal policy under Andrew Jackson through the passage of the Indian Removal Act of 1830. From the late 1810s through the 1840s, the United States negotiated land cession treaties with Ohio Valley, Southern, and Great Plains American Indian nations—including (among others) the Wyandots, Potawatomis, Ottawas, Ojibwes, Choctaws, Creeks, Chickasaws, Sioux, Sauks, Mesquakies, Ioways, Winnebagos, Menominees, and Miami—and fought legal and military battles over the legitimacy of treaties with the Seminoles, Creeks, and Cherokee.[3]

During these same three decades, non-Native readers and audience members across the country eagerly consumed a wide range of "Indian" texts and per-

1

formances, including romances, works of history, and theatrical melodramas recounting colonial conflicts; anthologies of American Indian biographies and the
first American Indian autobiographies; public appearances and demonstrations
by American Indian leaders and delegations brought east for political negotiation
or popular entertainment; elegiac and epic poetry lamenting the death of the Indian; and ethnographic collections detailing Native practices and oral traditions.[4]
These texts and performances recreated for audiences the charged meeting of
American Indians and Euro-Americans at the moment of first contact. That is,
they contained what I call *moving encounters*, scenes in which representatives of
the two "races," face-to-face in a setting claimed by both, participated in a highly
emotional exchange that indicated their hearts had more in common than their
external appearances or political allegiances suggested. The moving encounter
proposed the possibility of mutual sympathy between American Indians and
Euro-Americans, of community instead of division. Essential to such scenes was
the sentimental intermediary who provided necessary translation—linguistic,
cultural, affective—and attempted to minimize the emotional volatility that so
quickly led to confrontation and violence. In antebellum ethnography, the author offered himself as an intermediary to audiences of written works and public demonstrations. In fiction and drama one character often took on this role
of broker, but the writer or performer of the moving encounter also necessarily acted as a sentimental intermediary for the audience, who encountered the
portrayed Indian at a safe distance. When "real" Indians performed in museums
and theaters and spoke from podiums, when they provided their own accounts
of American Indian culture and asserted national sovereignty and civil rights,
managing showmen and eager journalists often stepped in to provide delimiting
commentary.[5]

From our perspective today, the prominence in works of the 1820s to 1840s
of the moving encounter—one managed by the intermediary but nonetheless thrilling for eager non-Native audiences—appears on the surface to be at
odds with the federal policy of removal under which performances and texts
(negotiations and treaties) assume a deep-seated difference between Natives and
non-Natives and ensure the segregation of the two groups until similarity can
be attained, if ever. Yet the relationship between removal policy and a fascination with Indian-white relationships in this period is not so easily summarized.
In the nineteenth century, natural and social scientists described human societies as advancing through stages of development related to the primary means
of subsistence (hunting, herding, farming) and their tendency toward related
progress: "progressive (civilized); stationary (semi-civilized); and nonprogressive
(savage or completely 'barbaric')." Categories of historical determinism were
readily linked to racial groups and used to assess their present and future position within a natural hierarchy of peoples. Supposedly stalled in the nonprogressive stage, American Indians appeared either doomed to disappear or destined to

be degraded by the worst aspects (such as alcohol) of the dominant progressive society.[6]

American Indians' affective lives, ethnographers and racial scientists argued, exacerbated this situation. Whereas Caucasians were characterized by reflective sympathy and self-control, and Africans by childlike, whole-hearted devotion, American Indians were distinguished by their emotional repression, except in the context of warfare and the hunt. What ethnographers of this period, from Henry Rowe Schoolcraft to Lewis Henry Morgan, uncovered to the delight of readers was the hidden affective life of the "child of nature"; appearing at first to be a self-sufficient, stoical, and unreflective resident of an often harrowing natural world, the Indian was also unused to restraining himself or herself in accord with the social expectations of civilization. For this reason, and as evidenced in their oral traditions, he or she could erupt in expressive displays of intense love, anger, grief, or pride, particularly in the context of familial relationships. In a review of Schoolcraft's 1839 *Algic Researches*, a collection of (primarily Ojibwe) oral traditions, H. Whiting expresses representative surprise in the face of such analysis: "War, the chase, these alone were supposed to arouse them, to excite and employ their faculties. But we now see that they have lively fancies, which can invest bird and beast, and even inanimate objects, with social qualities, that may surround them, even in solitude, with many of the charms of life." Descriptions of American Indians' best traits—which Schoolcraft elsewhere identified as fortitude, endurance, bravery, eloquence, hospitality, and faithfulness—suggested to Whiting "that there are happy methods of softening affections which we feared were unchangeably obdurate, and that untaught and grovelling minds may occasionally be led into deep thought, giving them, though all unconsciously, perhaps, a new enlargement and elevation."[7] Antebellum authors regularly represented the Indian as a man of feeling, a family man and a chivalrous hero who defended the honor of young women and judged the valor of young men; likewise, the image of the Indian maiden or wife as a sacrificing protector, the symbolic mother of the nation, took root. Without the tools or behaviors of the civilized, savage groups faced degradation and oblivion; they needed to submit to the plow and to a regulation of feelings. The emotions they shared with non-Native counterparts, according to these accounts, could prove detrimental to civilizing efforts if left unchecked and excessive.

The moving encounter in literature of this period therefore often, though not always, ended with the failure of sympathy to overcome the persisting differences of the two parties and the historical conditions leading to the distrust and hatred between them—and for this reason, sentimental portrayals of American Indians of this period have since been read as reinforcing removal ideology. In these works, what the sentimental intermediary attempted to arbitrate, be it past transgressions, future schemes, or simple misunderstandings, reasserted itself with great force, and common emotion evaporated in the presence of inexorable conflict between the types of humankind. In the antebellum United States the need for authors to serve as intermediaries confirmed that the intense exchange of feeling represented in the moving encounter was inherently unstable, potentially false, possibly dangerous, and in many accounts, mercifully short-lived. While most politicians and intellectuals agreed that American Indians would disappear unless benevolent Euro-Americans intervened on their behalf, many authors likewise depicted sympathy with the Indian as doomed. What moved the participants in the moving encounter was not just the threat of Indian disappearance but also the impending termination of Indian-white intimacy; sympathy and doom existed in a symbiotic relationship that indulged audience desire for affective connection in a temporally circumscribed fashion. In this way, the moving/affective qualities of the Indian-white encounter bled into the moving/displacing force of the narrative. The "inevitability" of Indian departure and the end of the encounter was a necessary condition for an essentially unsustainable interracial, transcultural sympathy. Sympathy, in this construction, could alleviate wrongs but not solve them because it could not provide sufficient basis for peaceful coexistence.

But sentimental portrayals of American Indians in the antebellum period were not exclusively allied with the cause of removal or the historical narrative of Indian disappearance; scenes moving in the affective sense and in the sense of literal dislocation also migrated all over the ideological map. While the poignant prospect of American Indian extinction played an important role in federal promotion of removal policy, many activists, American Indian and Euro-American alike, never lost faith in the power of sympathy to overcome the greed and prejudice fueling the dispossession of American Indian nations. Like their abolitionist contemporaries, authors defending Native rights appealed to audience members' emotions through portrayals of how Euro-Americans harmed American Indian families and, as a result, harmed their own souls. Also like their abolitionist peers, these authors struggled to transform audience members' interest in the exotic Other into political motivation—into a conviction that they were not simply passive spectators of unalterable tragedy.

Thus, a period of land-cession treaties, violent warfare across the frontiers, and conflict in courtrooms also produced a politically adaptable literature stressing a strong, emotional connection between American Indians and Euro-Americans. When portrayals emphasized the ephemerality of the moving encounter, they echoed a tension within Jacksonian removal policy between declarations of benevolent paternalism and refusals to enforce federal laws and treaty agreements in the name of states rights. (The President was, on the one hand, a Great Father obligated to guard and protect wayward red children and, on the other, a stubborn supporter of those unruly settlers and defiant legislatures who posed the greatest threat to American Indian livelihood and sovereignty.)[8] Whether lamenting the Indian fate or challenging abuses, moving encounters also captured the spirit of a transitional moment. Conflicts from the mid-eighteenth century through the early nineteenth century, including the Seven Years' War, the Revolutionary War, battles in the Ohio Valley, the first of multiple wars with the Seminoles and Creeks, and the War of 1812, effectively secured U.S. hegemony in the Trans-Appalachian region and eliminated a previous system of negotiation and accommodation between American Indian nations and European colonial and postcolonial governments. A system of negotiation was replaced with the contested rule of an imperial power that wrapped its territorial gains in the mantle of disinterested goodwill.[9] As a representation of Indian-white exchange often cut short by death, the moving encounter appealed to those audience members nostalgic for former times and those who accepted the new order as a sign of historical progress, as well as those who resisted all attempts by the United States to establish authority over American Indian nations.

Richard White, in his account of relationships among the French, American Indian, and British groups of the *pays d'en haut*, or the Great Lakes region, from the late seventeenth century through the turn of the nineteenth, famously argues that during a period in which neither American Indian nations nor French colonial forces could secure control over the region, residents created a "middle ground" in which they developed "new systems of meaning and of exchange" from the fragments remaining after the seventeenth-century Iroquoian wars.[10] Since the publication of White's *The Middle Ground*, critics note, the work's central interpretive metaphor has been abstracted from its chronological and geographical specificity and applied to any frontier in which the historian or cultural critic identifies elements of cultural exchange—a development White cautiously endorses. While some consider such analyses of the frontier as "the birthplace of cultural pluralism" to be a product of turn-of-the-twenty-first-century romanticism, the depiction of the North American frontier as a lost opportunity for compromise between indigenous and colonizing peoples first appeared in the cultural productions of turn-of-the-nineteenth-century United States.[11] The middle ground of the Great Lakes country was politically dismantled through a series of conflicts in the second half of the eighteenth century that culminated in the Treaty of Ghent (1815), which secured U.S. authority over the region. Between the start of the Seven Years' War and first half of the nineteenth century, writes R. Douglas Hurt, "the frontier as an inclusive, intercultural borderland gave way to subjugation by the Americans who absorbed those frontiers into their national boundaries and made the previous frontiers exclusive regions for their own use and determination."[12] Removal policy, as proposed by Jefferson and solidified by Monroe and Jackson, reflected the sea change in the relations between Natives and non-Natives in the larger Trans-Appalachian region and the declaration of U.S. authority over the territories and the American Indian occupants. In response, authors of the period enshrined in literature the Indian-white exchange that characterized a region many declared already forever transformed and others embraced as representing the potential for the peaceful coexistence of the United States and American Indian neighbors.

Recognizing these historical developments and responding to the cultural nationalism of 1820s United States, James Fenimore Cooper set his first three Leatherstocking Tales, *The Pioneers* (1823), *The Last of the Mohicans* (1826), and *The Prairie* (1827), in the period between the Seven Years' War and the Louisiana Purchase (of the two installments published in the 1840s, one is set before this period). These historical romances retrospectively dramatize the decline of an Indian-white middle ground through a series of moving encounters. One notable instance comes in the final paragraphs of *The Last of the Mohicans*. In the aftermath of the deaths of Cora Munro and Chingachgook's son, Uncas, Chingachgook despairs that he is the last of his race and thus all alone. Cooper's hero Natty Bumppo, or Hawk-eye, interrupts and assures him that he is not without companionship:

> "No, no," cried Hawk-eye, who had been gazing with a yearning look at the rigid features of his friend, with something like his own self-command, but whose philosophy could endure no longer; "no, Sagamore, not alone. The gifts of our colours may be different, but God has placed us as to journey in the same path. I have no kin, and I may also say, like you, no people. He was your son, and a red-skin by nature; and it may be, that your blood was nearer;—but if ever I forget the lad, who has so often fou't at my side in war, and slept at my side in peace, may He who made us all, whatever may be our colour or our gifts, forget me. The boy has left us for a time, but, Sagamore, you are not alone!"
>
> Chingachgook grasped the hand that, in the warmth of feeling, the scout had stretched across the fresh earth, and in an attitude of friendship these two sturdy and intrepid woodsmen bowed their heads together, while scalding tears fell to their feet, watering the grave of Uncas, like drops of falling rain.[13]

This "burst of feeling" on the part of two stoic woodsmen forges a new family in the presence of a son's resting place. Their hands stretched across the grave recall (or presage, given the date of the novel's action) the image on the Thomas Jefferson Peace Medal of an American Indian hand and a Euro-American hand clasped in friendship, and their tears sanctify the site of their renewed relationship. But this "warmth of feeling" is framed by death and departure; not only has the last of Chingachgook's line died but the reader of the Leatherstocking Tales also knows from *The Pioneers* that Chingachgook will die a degraded alcoholic, his history eclipsed by the Christian name Indian John. The emotional scene of union across "colour" and in spite of death concludes with the reassertion of Indian decline by none other than the Lenape prophet Tamenund, who declares, "Go, children of the Lenape; the anger of the Manitto is not done. Why should Tamenund stay? The pale-faces are masters of the earth, and the time of the red-men has not yet come again."[14]

Readers have long seen Cooper's *The Last of the Mohicans* and other antebellum treatments of the doomed Indian myth as articulations of imperial desire shot through with guilt.[15] At one level, Leatherstocking, in his role as intermediary, cries on behalf of a nation unsettled by its own imperial actions, but at another he represents an expiring form of relationship with American Indians and, by extension, the expiring Indian as well. Cooper's historical romances chronicle the passing of a world in which a white scout could spend his formative years among Moravian Delaware Indians and then enjoy a lifelong friendship with a Mohican chief. Natty Bumppo represents the last of his own race—white intermediaries—and as the Indian embraces his fate, fulfills his own historical role by mourning that loss. Thus the moving encounter that captures the heart of Natty's actions, in both senses of the word, cannot exist without the death of Uncas and the voluntary removal of Tamenund's people. According to the Leatherstocking Tales, Indian-white intimacy has become unsustainable, even untrustworthy, and those moments in Indian country that move the sympathetic Natty, and the reader through him, also ensure the movement of American Indians away from frontiers rapidly becoming the United States. The moving encounter flowers in this period as a recreation of the lost middle ground and in works like Cooper's historical romances indicates a stirring memorial to what has passed, a memorial much like Uncas's grave.

While the moving encounter often portrayed the balance between affective intimacy and permanent division in antebellum assessments of the relationship between Native and non-Native residents of the United States, the figure also revealed how easily that balance was disturbed or even inverted. Thus, the image of Indian-white emotional intimacy and commonality performed a wide variety of political and cultural work in the decades surrounding the passage of the Indian Removal Act. The instability and eventual failure of Indian-white sympathy took on a very different meaning in the autobiographies of William Apess or Black Hawk than in the proslavery fiction of William Gilmore Simms or Mary Howard Schoolcraft, for example. The failure of sympathy in the former pointed to a horrible moral failing on the part of the United States. Even in Cooper's Leatherstocking Tales, the moving encounters indicated a deep unease over Indian policy. The pervasiveness of moving encounters across antebellum literature suggests that non-Native audiences experienced a cycle of sympathetic identification and its dispersion. They could never put doomed sympathy or the doomed Indian to rest.[16]

The multivalence and pervasiveness of sympathy in the antebellum period, I propose, can best be explained through a delineation of a well-discussed though often elusive critical term: sentimentalism. The loss of a perceived middle ground in western territories corresponded with the development of an American literature of sentimentalism (or sensibility), which was influenced by British and European romanticism and molded by the rise of liberal Protestantism in the early nineteenth century.[17] While critics use the word *sentimentalism* to identify a particular literary genre and rhetorical mode, it more accurately identifies a social philosophy that influenced aesthetic and persuasive texts in the period. Within the sentimental worldview, bonds between members of society were created through common emotion; the ability of the individual to sympathize with another overcame the selfishness that destabilizes community. Within sentimental culture, moral judgment rested with the heart rather than the head, with the conscience rather than external law, in accord with liberal Protestantism's emphasis on a loving Christ's atonement and establishment of a New Covenant. Indeed, the Christian family in its ideal form was a manifestation of the sentimental social model: the rule of the father, like that of the government and other public institutions, was softened by his benevolence and checked by the effusive love of the mother, the angel of the private realm, and both were blessed by the presence of children whose innocence (or separation from society) ensured unclouded consciences. In the antebellum United States, when various calls for social reform captivated public attention, sentimental works addressed the distance between the familial model and the reality of a modern market society. The sentimental mode played a crucial role in the discourses of the temperance movement, debates over slavery, calls for educational and penal reform, the women's suffrage movement, and deliberations over the Indian Question. In each of these contexts, appeals to the heart did not produce a common answer any more than they guaranteed common action. Instead, sentimentalism provided the larger reform culture with the terms of debate: a set of rhetorical appeals and literary or theatrical figures widely and variously employed.[18]

The social philosophy of sentimentalism and its related literary and rhetorical modes represented an essential discursive context for the moving encounter as a type of scene and as an experience evoked by an author or performer. Because the moving encounter sprang from sentimentalism, it was infused with pathos—and all the tensions critics have identified as inherent in antebellum sentimentalism. Sentimental texts and performances stirred the emotions of the audience through the spectacle of suffering and of responses to that suffering, providing examples of both commendable compassionate responses and lamentable hardhearted reactions. Displays of emotion, like expressions of faith, can be deceptive, so sentimental texts and performances depicted images that awakened readers' feelings and characters whose callousness, emotional disingenuousness, and religious hypocrisy indicated the source of human sin and divisiveness. Within the logic of sentimental works, then, the honest expression of heartfelt sympathy could appear to be a morally sufficient response to others' suffering.[19] One recalls that Harriet Beecher Stowe's *Uncle Tom's Cabin* concludes with the death of the hero and the migration, or removal, to Africa of other independent African Americans. One recalls as well that the tears Natty Bumppo and readers of *The Last of the Mohicans* first shed over Uncas's grave in 1826 came one year after President Monroe urged Congress to "act with a generous spirit" by adopting a policy of removal.[20]

Another relevant criticism of sentimentalism arises from the inherent hierarchy in and tenuousness of the relationship between the sympathizer and the object of sympathy, especially in the context of a familial-based social model. The most common characters in sentimental texts—slaves, orphans, animals, those unjustly punished, and dead or dying loved ones—are essentially helpless, defined through their dependence on a kindly parental figure and by a narrator who often pleads directly with the audience for sympathy. At the same time, as Glenn Hendler emphasizes, within sentimentalism "any culturally marked or affirmed difference can become an insurmountable obstacle to sympathetic identification." The very "impossibility of complete sympathetic identification," Susan M. Ryan elaborates, makes charity possible.[21] That one's attempt, through feeling, to overcome the dissimilarity with another will always conclude with a confirmation of that person's absolute difference suggests sentimental texts often are complicit in the nineteenth-century concept of racial hierarchy. Accordingly, Maureen Konkle argues that Euro-Americans' sympathetic rhetoric combined with an emphasis on Native difference repressed American Indian sovereignty. If the paired emphases of sympathy and difference disempowered American Indian political leaders, the combination of sympathy and doom demarcated a distinct endpoint for emotional connection and personal responsibility. The disappearing Indian caused Euro-Americans to cry while disappearing sympathy relieved them of responsibility.[22]

Whereas "doom" infected much of the discourse of Indian-white sympathy, it did not, however, taint all instances, as seen in congressional deliberations over removal policy. President Andrew Jackson, promoting removal policy in his first inaugural address of December 8, 1829, emphasized, "Our conduct toward these people is deeply interesting to our national character. Their present condition, contrasted with what they once were, makes a most powerful appeal to our sympathies." Once the Indians were relocated outside of the corrupting white society, he continued, "the benevolent may endeavor to teach them the arts of civilization, and, by promoting union and harmony among them, to raise up an interesting commonwealth, destined to perpetuate the race and to attest the humanity and justice of this Government."[23] A leading voice of opposition to the Indian Removal Act, Senator Theodore Frelinghuysen of New Jersey, countered with similar language in a speech to the Senate on April 9, 1830: "I believe, sir, it is not now seriously denied that the Indians . . . have a place in human sympathy, and are justly entitled to a share in the common bounties of a benignant Providence." Yet he proceeded in the lengthy speech to replace the description of Indian disappearance and U.S. intervention with a catalogue of unconscionable acts on the part of pitiless settlers and politicians that the nation needed to redress.[24] The Cherokee leaders and citizens who entered the congressional debate through memorials challenged the terms, and by extension the honesty, of Euro-American sympathy; for example, the December 18, 1829, Memorial of the Cherokee Citizens conjured up a moving encounter between the authors and the congressmen—"As weak and poor children are accustomed to look to their guardians and patrons for protection, so we would come and make our grievances known"—only immediately to question whether the self-interested and dominant politicians would ever feel for the petitioners. Dropping the hierarchical version of sympathy, they concluded with a bold assertion of Cherokee sovereignty and replaced the sentimental simile of a weak child with that of a brother demanding recognition of his right to God-given, father-bestowed land.[25]

These three examples from 1829 to 1830 illustrate how the national reaction to the plight of the doomed Indian was taken as an indication of the moral decency of the United States by those on all sides of the Indian Question. They also demonstrate the ideological adaptability of sentimental rhetoric and figures, including and especially the moving encounter. I assert that when one reads such words from a modern vantage point and rejects all appeals to sympathy as essentially complicit in an imperial worldview, one resurrects the language of doomed sympathy and invokes the discourse of extinction.[26] That is, an utter refusal of nineteenth-century sentimentalism and early twenty-first-century intercultural criticism condemns all parties, regardless of ethnic or national affiliation, to a failure of imagination and heart. It revives the belief that one's inability truly to know someone else's feelings indicates deep-seated differences that will always sustain the harmful legacies of colonialism. It also suggests all future attempts to feel someone else's pain or even simply to conceive of an emotional life distinct from one's own will be futile, even dubious.

Another approach is possible. This book dissects the moving encounter as a sentimental trope and a register of the major shift in Indian-white relations in the early nineteenth century and reconstructs a critical middle ground between a naive acceptance of sentimentalism and a prejudiced dismissal of all sympathy as suspect.[27] Through close readings of fiction, poetry, ethnography, travel writing, melodrama, and autobiography, I raise the possibility that by attending to the antebellum fascination with physical encounter and mutual emotion we may better understand the complex history of colonial and national relations between American Indians and Euro-Americans, as well as African Americans. Thus, *Moving Encounters* begins with a chapter on the Indian writings of the author-activist Lydia Maria Child, who worked mightily during the nineteenth century to refine the moving encounter and in particular the role of the sentimental intermediary in order to develop a literature of feeling that moved readers to action on behalf of American Indians. Child's Indian writings provide an overview of the many forms the moving encounter could take and the ways in which antebellum authors consciously revised the figure in the light of the myth of doomed sympathy and debates over slavery.

Chapters 2 and 3 treat works by James Fenimore Cooper and William Gilmore Simms, historical romancers whose portrayal of Indian-white colonial relations in New York and the Southeast are often contrasted. What critics have overlooked, however, is their respective engagements with the discourse of sympathy and more specifically the sentimental intermediary. In *The Prairie* (1827), Cooper's Natty Bumppo, a product of a youth spent among Delaware Indians and a manhood spent fighting in the Seven Years' War, the Revolution, and the Ohio Valley conflicts of the 1790s, is a sentimental intermediary whose time has come and gone. The instability of both Indians' and settlers' emotions leads to the demise of Natty and frontier exchange, and in this way Natty personifies the fleeting middle ground. Thus the novel, which begins with a celebration of U.S. expansion and settlement in the antebellum period, concludes with the scene of Natty's death at the start of the nineteenth century. Rather than trace the tragic demise of sympathy, Simms's stories in *The Wigwam and the Cabin* (1845) portray the foolishness of the sentimental intermediary and the need for a white patriarch who, clear headed and clear hearted, will rule over the childlike African and the degenerate Indian. In Simms's works, then, the moving encounter is replaced with an established relationship between benevolent master and wayward slave, and we see the intricate relationship between the southern rejection of Indian sovereignty and defense of slavery.

In Chapter 4 I examine the first American Indian autobiographies, arguing that works by or as-told-by William Apess, Mary Jemison, and Black Hawk demonstrate how American Indians adapted sentimental rhetoric and the moving encounter to protest Euro-American claims of American Indian inferiority. Because audiences were drawn to textual encounters with American Indians and readily consumed such works, Euro-American reviewers and editors responded quickly to take over the role of intermediary, to control through commentary and editing the dangerous, direct complaint of the American Indian. Even so, we should not dismiss the language of sympathy that pervades early American Indian autobiographies as an editorial imposition but consider it evidence of how American Indians adopted and adapted the sentimental terms of the debate surrounding the Indian Question. In Chapter 5 I argue that the possibility of an Indian's serving as intermediary—translating for Euro-Americans the meaning of their mutual encounter—fascinated Margaret Fuller and Henry David Thoreau who, in their transcendental travel writing, considered various forms of mediation between the individual and Nature. Fuller's moving encounters with American Indians in the Great Lakes region and Thoreau's relationships with Penobscot guides in the Maine woods convinced these idealists that the American Indian who negotiates the changing frontier may offer the best model for how individuals can bridge the gap between Me and Not-Me. Whereas Chapter 4 considers attempts on the part of Euro-American reviewers and editors to control the sentimental rhetoric of early American Indian autobiography, Chapter 5 traces two Euro-American authors' gradual, tentative acceptance of American

Indian authority on the link between the material world and what Ralph Waldo Emerson called the Over-Soul.

The emphasis that sentimental culture placed on affective understanding informed scientific empiricism in the antebellum period as those studying human societies drew upon their own sympathy and familial relationships to measure and contrast the emotional lives of American Indians and African Americans.[28] Chapter 6 explores the early collaborations of the Indian agent and ethnographer Henry Rowe Schoolcraft and his métis wife, Jane Johnston Schoolcraft, as well as George Catlin's ethnographic writings and paintings of the 1830s and 1840s, all of which bear the stamp of sentimentalism. Catlin practiced what I call a "full-bodied empiricism" in that he employed all his senses—including his sense of the heart—to gather information about western American Indian nations, and as a result, put himself in harm's way. He argued that the intensity and explosive nature of encounter in the West and the harmful impact of "civilization" (specifically alcohol, guns, and other manufactured goods) on American Indians necessitated the maintenance of a preserve, or national park. The ethnographer, in Catlin's sentimental perspective, saved American Indians from degradation by offering re-creations of his moving encounters for public consumption through texts, paintings, and performances. In the decade just prior to Catlin's travels, Henry and Jane Schoolcraft collected Ojibwe oral traditions and produced poetry that used their relationship as a model of sentimental marriage and as a metaphor for the proper association between American Indians and their Euro-American civilizers. As a result, their foundational ethnographic work framed the study of cultures as a civilizing act modeled after familial relations. However, as prejudice against racial intermarriage heightened in the 1830s and Henry sought to increase his reputation among federal officials as an invaluable scholar of the Indian, their marriage and ethnographic collaboration deteriorated. Doomed sympathy became a biographical reality for the Schoolcrafts and for Catlin.

Certainly Henry Rowe Schoolcraft's second wife, the South Carolina plantation heiress Mary Howard Schoolcraft, rejected racial intermarriage, and in Chapter 7 I look ahead to mid-century to consider her fictionalized treatment of Jane Johnston Schoolcraft within the context of her proslavery novel, *The Black Gauntlet* (1861). Like Mary Eastman, whose *Aunt Phillis's Cabin* (1852) was the most popular of the anti-Tom novels, Mary Howard Schoolcraft drew on the Old Testament story of Noah's curse against son Ham and grandson Canaan to reassert a divinely ordained racial hierarchy in which whites serve as parental authorities over Africans and American Indians—but not as their spouses or actual fathers. In this way, Schoolcraft and Eastman, like Simms, represented the southern response to what they saw as New England's misguided plans for the Indian and the African. Yet more immediately, both Eastman and Mary Howard Schoolcraft were married to men who had served as Indian agents and fathered children with American Indian women, a fact that certainly informed their revision of sentimental ethnography and their biblically inspired defense of slavery. Eastman insisted white women should focus their efforts on ameliorating the condition of Indian women, and Schoolcraft fashioned herself Henry's true wife and ethnographic collaborator, roles she, like Jane Johnston Schoolcraft before her, insisted were inherently allied.

This book concludes with a narrative of the evolving moving encounter in the theater. The treatment of Child's American Indian writings in Chapter 1 foreshadows the manifestations of the moving encounter considered in Chapters 2 through 7. Chapter 8, then, summarizes themes in previous chapters and indicates the fate of moving encounters in the subsequent age of realism. Popular Indian melodramas of the 1820s and 1830s staged Indian-white encounters, recreating for audiences the experience of poignant contact with the noble savage of America's past. Yet by the 1840s, Indian-hater fiction influenced stage productions, and the playwright Louisa Medina turned the theatrical moving encounter on its head as she redirected audience sympathy to victims of wanton Indian violence. Subsequent parodies of the Indian melodrama by the Anglo-Irish playwright John Brougham did not suggest sympathy had been misdirected but rather that it had been manipulated to such an extent that audiences could no longer distinguish between fiction and the political realities in a nation whose colonial past and imperial present depended on the conquest of Indian lands and African bodies. In Brougham's raucous burlesques, the audience faced only the stereotypes of racial melodrama and thus the absurdity of the moving encounter that disguises greed as munificence. In this way, Brougham's 1855 *Po-Ca-Hon-Tas* signaled the late stage of the antebellum moving encounter and the rise of a much more pessimistic post-bellum portrayal of Indian-white relations.

Brougham did not get the final say on this matter, however, as sentimental portrayals of American Indians persisted through the end of the nineteenth century and on to the present. Indeed, works by Simms, Mary Howard Schoolcraft, Medina, and others that portray Indians as emotionally immature or, worse yet, as wolflike dissemblers represent one half of a long-standing dichotomy in portrayals of American Indians and the Euro-Americans who sympathize with them: the sentimental versus the cynical. But as Herman Melville highlights in *The Confidence-Man* (1857), the Indian-lover and Indian-hater alike dehumanize American Indians as either pathetic objects of benevolent programs or the atavistic perpetrators of unspeakable violence against white America.[29]

Again, the analyses in *Moving Encounters* suggest that a third possibility must exist. Many authors in the antebellum period—in the aftermath of the late eighteenth-century and early nineteenth-century territorial conflicts and the in the midst of the formulation and implementation removal policy—struggled to create a literature based on the emotional commensurability of American Indians and Euro-Americans that did not, finally, promote the subjugation of

American Indians or assume their degradation and disappearance inevitable. Works by such authors as Child, Apess, Thoreau, Catlin, and Jane Johnston Schoolcraft presage and inspire our emphasis at the start of the twenty-first century on living American Indian cultures and a shared history of the Americas. We can and should contemplate not just the legacy of the moving encounter but also how we might refashion it in the present and reclaim or even refine the language of fellow-feeling in the interest of social justice.

1

The Evolution of Moving Encounters in Lydia Maria Child's American Indian Writings, 1824–1870

In her 1824 children's book *Evenings in New England*, Lydia Maria Child (then Lydia Maria Francis and writing as "An American Lady") includes the dialogue "Personification," in which Aunt Maria helps her nephew Robert interpret a personification of North America: a "young female, clothed in a robe all covered with stripes and stars, carrying a cap upon a high pole, around which an eagle is fluttering; and occasionally looking back upon an Indian, who is aiming his bow and arrow at a wild deer." [1] Aunt Maria, Child's alter ego, offers a straightforward interpretation: "For several hundred years after America was discovered, it was inhabited only by Indians. Now the country is mostly filled by Europeans, and we look back to the savage state as to what we have been." The tableau of America makes manifest the progressive, deterministic narrative of history wherein the civilized European figuratively and literally takes the place of the savage American Indian and neglects, or perhaps denies, the plurality of the young country.

In *A Romance of the Republic* (1867), published forty-three years later, Child provides her audience another tableau of America, drawing on common republican symbols, such as the flag and liberty cap; in this text, however, the personification is decidedly interracial and intercultural: "Under festoons of the American flag, surmounted by the eagle, stood Eulalia, in ribbons of red, white, and blue, with a circle of stars round her head. One hand upheld the shield of the Union, and in the other the scales of Justice were evenly poised. By her side stood Rosen Blumen, holding in one hand a gilded pole surmounted by a liberty-cap, while her other hand rested protectingly on the head of Tulee's Benny, who was kneeling and looking upward in thanksgiving." [2] Cousins Eulalia King and Rosen Blumen are the daughters of biracial mothers fluent in English, Spanish, and French and fathers of Anglo and Germanic extraction, respectively, and Benny is the child of freed slaves. Performed for the birthday of Mr. King, a Civil War veteran who lost a leg fighting for emancipation, this tableau celebrates what Child saw as the ideal outcome of the North's victory: a national family unified across race, ethnicity, and region through the diffusion of culture within a nurturing domestic setting. These disparate national tableaux, framing Child's long and varied career, depend on radically contrasting definitions of national membership. Between 1824 and 1867, Child's image of America shifted from a people defined by their historical and geographic distance from noble but ill-fated savages to a multiracial and multicultural citizenry united by familial bonds.

Published the same year as *Evenings in New England*, Child's historical romance *Hobomok, A Tale of Early Times* (1824) also dramatizes the succession of the races, as critics have noted. But in subsequent works Child develops a radical defense of American Indian rights bearing a strong resemblance to her arguments in favor of abolition. In writings from *An Appeal in Favor of that Class of Americans Called Africans* (1833) to *A Romance of the Republic*, Child conjures moving domestic scenes, such as the separation of families, the abuse of slaves at the hands of both masters and mistresses (supposed parental figures), and the enforcement of improper sexual relationships. Like Harriet Beecher Stowe, Child most often inspires the sympathy of the reader by converting the slave from chattel to endangered child. Her domestic-familial arguments on behalf of American Indians also infantilize the group, but in slight contrast, reflect Child's attention to the endangerment not of bodies but of habitations. In a variety of genres, from short stories and children's literature to journalistic essays and a political tract written between 1824 and 1870, Child describes and analyzes American Indian difference and Euro-American sympathy in terms of travel or migration between and within spaces—forests, communities, public buildings, private dwellings—strongly associated with one group or another. Stopping briefly, the parties in her early works experience moving encounters (affective tableaux, if you will) often overseen by a maternal or auntlike sentimental intermediary and always curtailed by external forces of history. Yet Child's later American Indian writings do not portray moving encounters doomed to end but instead present images of lasting reconciliation between American Indians and Euro-Americans within the Euro-American home. Here sympathy begins with the traversing of great distance and results in the national family's incorporation of American Indians within the domestic setting, through familial love and material consumption.[3] Acculturation takes place not at a distance, as proposed by removal policy, but within the domestic nation. In Child's Indian writings the moving encounter must literally be brought to rest to achieve and sustain intercultural community.

Admittedly, Child's challenge to the progressive narrative of history and prevailing racial hierarchy through her revision of the moving encounter and role as intermediary resonates with arguments for racial segregation and "civilization" efforts.[4] While I do not intend to dismiss Child's legacy as an eloquent activist for the rights of racial minorities in the nineteenth-century United States, I acknowledge that in a period framed by federal policies of removal and allotment, Child's American Indian writings problematically associated cultural-racial categories with distinct spaces (lands and buildings), fetishizing difference and naturalizing segregation but also denying American Indian sovereignty. Her association of difference and place indicates a failure not just of Child's vision but of her literary strategy: to inspire sympathy by underscoring first difference and then the maternal mediation of it. Child alternately portrayed difference as the impetus for sympathetic identification and the target of reform. Through analysis of the evolving moving encounter in works that span close to fifty years, I show how Child used this figure for moral instruction, political argumentation, and transcendental meditation; how she tapped sentimental discourse to decry Euro-American hypocrisy and promote a family-based social model; and how she highlighted the moving encounter's relevance to historical determinism and to the emergence of racial science and popular ethnographic displays. I show, that is, how over the course of a lifetime of writing about Indians, Child continually revised the moving encounter to suit her political and aesthetic goals. Reading beyond her 1824 works, we find in Child's American Indian writings evidence of a lifelong struggle to refine a powerful but problematic sentimental figure—and to imagine sustained Indian-white sympathy.

The Structure of Sympathy in *Hobomok*

Just as "Personification" positions the Euro-American in the foreground "looking back" on the American Indian, *Hobomok* represents the dispossession of American Indians as a geographic and chronologic distance formed between the savage and the republican female. The title character's movement westward is implicitly, inextricably linked to a permanent disappearance of American Indians from the region in which Child's novel was written, set, and primarily consumed. The penultimate chapter brings the title character's declaration that, for the sake of Mary, "Hobomok will go far off among some of the red men in the west" and concludes with the affirmation that he "forever passed away from New England." [5] In this manner, *Hobomok* dramatizes the succession of races in the movement toward civilization and claims as readers' cultural-spiritual forefather a hunting Indian, rather than a stern Puritan. But first the novel asserts the inevitability of Euro-Americans' and American Indians' dissociation after close contact, the historical failure of their emotional bonds despite the ascendance of a maternal ethics based on sympathy. [6] Child uses a variety of narrative strategies that bring the Euro-American heroine into emotional and physical intimacy with the American Indian hero then destroy or repress that intimacy. In doing so, she transports the sympathetic Euro-American reader into the historical and emotional world of this relationship, and thus into an uneasy and short-lived moving encounter with a representative national savage.

One of Child's narrative strategies involves a proliferation of mediating "authors." The preface is written by Frederic, a supportive friend of the unnamed author who encouraged "him" to publish the novel, and the author informs us that he did not produce the tale from thin air but began with "an old, worn-out manuscript, which accidentally came in my way" and with which, he says, he has "take[n] the liberty of substituting my own expressions for his [the manuscript author's] antiquated and almost unintelligible style" (H 6, 7). Like the narrator of Hawthorne's "The Custom-House," the "author" of *Hobomok* demonstrates the ability of an artifact to transport him to a period thought to be beyond historical and emotional reach and to inspire him to compose another artifact that will transport his readers in turn. In the colonial world Child's narrator makes accessible, storytelling promotes a peaceful relationship between American Indians and Euro-Americans through an emphasis on maternal bonds and the sympathetic responses they elicit. Hobomok first became enamored of Mary when she successfully "administered cordials to his sick mother" (H 33), and in turn Mary, whose own mother was sick, "found a welcome relief in unlocking all her hopes, fears, and disappointments to her untutored friend" (H 36). Once united by their common attachment to their mothers, the two grow closer through Hobomok's recounting of Iroquois history (H 98). Ultimately, Hobomok's loyalty to Mary leads him to warn the settlement of Corbitant's impending retributive strike and her to choose him as a husband. Child emphasizes that, in sharing their stories and with them their feelings, the American Indian and Euro-American may form a peaceful and productive relationship.

Child also promotes a sympathetic relationship between the American Indian and Euro-American through repeated references to the necessary authority of conscience in society and the rule of the heart in marriage, an emphasis intrinsic to the work's elevation of maternal figures and its attack on patriarchal Calvinism. Child contrasts in particular the stern Mr. Francis Higginson—who preaches, "Liberty of conscience is the gilded bait whereby Satan has caught many souls"—with Mary's saintlike mother, who proclaims, "I have lately thought that a humble heart was more than a strong mind, in perceiving the things appertaining to divine truth" (H 65, 76). In the realm of conjugal relationships, Hobomok's courtship of and marriage to Mary represents how unchecked sympathy and generosity affect another's heart. Mary weds Hobomok when, after the reported death of her fiancée, Charles, Hobomok comforts her at her mother's grave and expresses his desire to make her happy. Here Child infamously emphasizes Mary's temporary mental instability—the "partial derangement of [her] faculties" and the "chaos in [her] mind" (H 120, 121)—and the absence of the mother who might halt her fatal actions. Once they are married, however, Hobomok becomes Mary's motherly caregiver, showing his wife only a "tender reverence" in sharp contrast to the actions of her father. As a result, Child writes, "Mary by degrees gave way to [his love's] influence, until she welcomed his return with something like affection," even telling Sally, "Every day I live with that kind, noble-hearted creature, the better I love him" (*H* 135, 137). The reader witnesses the potential of sympathy, as modeled by mothers and practiced by their children, to unite American Indians and Euro-Americans and (temporarily) sanctify interracial familial and sexual bonds.[7]

Boldly incorporating Puritan belief in and fear of the occult, Child traces how witchcraft and portents bring Mary and Hobomok together and constitute an argument for the inevitability (if not the naturalness)[8] of their marriage. Mary first faces the possibility of breaking the racial taboo when Hobomok's unexpected arrival during her observance of a bloodletting ritual indicates that he and not Charles will be Mary's bridegroom (*H* 13). Charles also appears on the scene because a bad dream has warned him that Mary is in danger—the first of two portents concerning Mary's inexorable movement toward racial intermarriage. The second, a cloud that bears an uncanny resemblance to a ship, appears to Mary and others in the community shortly before they learn of the shipwreck of Charles's vessel (*H* 115, 117). The portents push Mary in the direction of marriage with Hobomok, a union initiated by a ceremony reminiscent of their earlier rites in the woods (*H* 124–25). In addition to highlighting Mary's temporary insanity, the novel produces its own sorcery (or sleight of hand) to convince the reader that racial intermarriage is unavoidable even if aberrant.

Critics note that marriage proves the uncomfortable turning point in the novel's construction of Mary and Hobomok's attachment, their gradual procession to Hobomok's wigwam. Once the sympathetic moments and the occult occurrences bring about a wedding in chapter 17, the novel quickly dismantles their relationship in the remaining three chapters, underscoring, in Ezra Tawill's terms, "the more fundamental property of race."[9] Mary and Hobomok's home is troubled; for Mary the birth of a son is "entwined with many mournful associations," and the child contracts the illness of which Hobomok's mother dies (*H* 136, 137). The final chapter completes the repression of the Indian-white family as Charles returns, Hobomok departs, Mary and Charles marry, and the latter adopts young Charles Hobomok Conant as his own (*H* 149). Euro-America reincorporates the offspring of racial intermarriage, and the moving encounter concludes with physical estrangement: when the son grows up, "his father was seldom spoken of; and by degrees his Indian appellation was silently omitted" (*H* 150). Mary always remembers Hobomok, just as the country remembers his service in preempting an attack on an exposed colony, affirming a willed physical absence but symbolic presence of the American Indian. As in "Personification," the republican female, author, and reader look back on an American Indian participation in the national family, a contribution that has been pushed from the foreground into history.

Maternal Guides and Childlike Sympathy in the *Juvenile Miscellany*

Child's increasing involvement in reform movements in the 1820s led her to reject the myth of the doomed Indian and to revise the national tableaux in *Hobomok* and *Evenings in New England* accordingly. While Aunt Maria of *Evenings in New England* discourages her nephew's desire to aid American Indians by explaining, "It is probable that in the course of a few hundred years, they will cease to exist as a distinct people," the mother in *First Settlers of New England* (1829) declares, "It is, in my opinion, decidedly wrong, to speak of the removal, or extinction of the Indians as inevitable; it surely implies that the people of these states have not sufficient virtue or magnanimity to redeem their past offences."[10] From the mid-1820s to the mid-1830s, as Child became increasingly involved with abolitionism and the defense of American Indians, she also focused her authorial attention primarily on the production of children's literature. The dialogues and stories of this period reflect Child's faith in the transformative power of sentiment and familial ties with regard to the race problems facing the United States. She embraces the moving encounter, representing sympathy as cyclical travel between Euro-American and American Indian spaces and emphasizing the guidance of mother figures. Simultaneously she encourages children to treat American Indians humanely and assigns American Indians to distinct geographic and domestic locales.

In Child's day, the prevailing culture of reform, the fear of social upheaval in a fledgling democracy, and an idealization of the child contributed to the formulation of an American children's literature that was extremely didactic and moral in focus. Textbooks and books for home instruction placed facts and concepts at the service of character development; in *The Mother's Book*, for example, Child advised that children "should be taught to love knowledge for the sake of the good it will enable them to do others, not because they will gain praise by it."[11] By the time Child published *First Settlers*, which appeared during her tenure as editor of the *Juvenile Miscellany* (1826–34), she had begun to agitate for American Indian rights, and the topic provided perfect material for her pedagogical goals. *First Settlers* contains a series of mother-daughter dialogues in which the mother argues that Puritanical Calvinism led to American Indian genocide (specifically of the Pequots, Narragansetts, and Pokanokets) and that the contemporary victimization of the Cherokees is a legacy of colonialism. Child hopes that *First Settlers* "will impress our youth with the conviction of their obligation to alleviate, as much as is in their power, the sufferings of the generous and interesting race of men whom we have so unjustly supplanted." The mother reads the prominent chronicles of the Pequot War by John Winthrop and William Hubbard to her daughters, Caroline and Eliza, and is pleased when this historiographic lesson prompts Eliza to declare, "As Caroline and myself have so deeply felt for the suffering aborigines of our country, we shall feel it to be our duty to engage the sympathy of others, by relating the wrongs they have sustained." The girls' mother has stirred their emotions and prompted them to seek others' affective responses, modeling a proper pedagogy for which an implied parallel exists in the readers' world.[12]

Child's mother and aunt figures in the *Miscellany* are sentimental intermediaries, navigating for children the physical or temporal divide between Euro-American and American Indians, challenging prejudices and received stereotypes, promoting productive citizenship through sympathy, and transforming children's hearts. For example, the first tale in the first issue, "Adventure in the Woods," subverts the standard Indian captivity tale through the operations of maternal intermediaries. Benjamin and Rachel Wilson, British children newly arrived in colonial Boston and terrified of Indians, become lost in the woods, and an old American Indian woman to whom their mother once gave food "tak[es] the weary little girl in her arms as if she had been an infant" and escorts her and her brother to their family. Rather than forced bondage, the children experience maternal care, and rather than remaining in the supposed realm of the violent savage, they are promptly returned to their loving home. Their adventure has been a journey across cultural-racial lines and the discovery that sympathy—their mother's for this woman, this woman's for them—makes the process safe and productive.[13] In two other anticaptivity tales by Child in the *Miscellany*, Anglo-American boys held in captivity far from home find themselves well treated by Natives in accord with a recognizable moral code and briefly appreciate life-changing intimate relationships. The protagonists' travel between these habitations dramatizes the moral action of sympathy but also its link to the ideology of removal: geographic segregation in accord with cultural-racial hierarchy as overseen by benevolent Euro-Americans.[14]

Child always joins moral instruction with the dismantling of racial prejudice, using the sentimental defense of American Indians to promote industrious as well as sympathetic citizenship. The narrator of "The Indian Boy," another stand-in for Child, navigates for her audience the distance between her familiar home and munificent position and the poverty and need of the title character's dwelling. Alexis is a picturesque little Penobscot boy with eyes "as bright as jet buttons," a blue cap with a red tassel, and a blanket tied with yellow strings. Left behind with his sick grandmother and sister while the men go off to hunt, he comes to the narrator to beg for flour. The narrator is concerned, or perhaps suspicious, because she has given him flour recently, so after supplying his needs she travels the following day to his home to check on the living conditions. Once she has entered Alexis's home and he has given her a promised basket, she determines that the boy has been very conscientious in caring for his grandmother. He then becomes, in addition to an object of charity, a model for the reader: "Alexis could tell little white boys a great many things they never heard of; and he was as kind to the old and sick, as ever any child was in the world." But the sympathy the narrator demonstrates through her gifts and her movement into Alexis's world is paralleled only by the attractive child's repeated movement into her world for food; they have established the relationship of dependence Jefferson and subsequent politicians insisted would lead to acculturation. The tale concludes with the narrator's promise that "if he is [the chief of the Penobscot tribe], I will write what coat and cap he wears, when he goes to Washington, to ask the President about hunting moose and deer." Alexis's future entails other trips to Euro-Americans in quest of subsistence; he will continue to supply opportunities for moving encounters, chances for them to enjoy his charming appearance, sympathize with him, civilize him, and send him on his way.[15]

"Buffalo Creek," the last American Indian tale Child wrote for the *Miscellany*, fuses an example of sentimental pedagogy with an encounter between Euro-Americans and American Indians and in so doing conveys the usefulness, the thrill, and the vulnerability of sympathy. The mother of nine-year old Henry Kirby promises that the family will cross Lake Erie to visit Buffalo Creek Reservation if he will study for four hours a day for an entire month. After Henry's trials and errors, the Kirby family travels to the reservation, where they find an appropriate reflection of Henry's lesson in the "tall fine looking" Seneca leader Red Jacket and in the progress the Seneca nation has in becoming civilized. Mrs. Kirby and a family friend, Lucy, the narrator of the story, call on the wigwam of an industrious woman who, like little Alexis with his grandmother, makes baskets for sale as she tends her sick husband. As Mrs. Kirby and Lucy select their purchases, "the celebrated Miss Brandt, who was educated in England, and is the daughter of a most cultivated, intelligent Indian," enters and offers medical services to the old man. Later Lucy romanticizes Miss Brandt, as well as a lone musician she observes, and the Kirby family patiently corrects her foolishness: "'Oh Lucy, Lucy,' said Mrs. Kirby, smiling, 'will real life ever dissolve your wild visions and romantic notions?'" True sympathy with the American Indians is better represented by practical business and social interactions, for the Kirby family seeks to encourage the moral development of the Seneca people the same way they do the development of young Henry. At the expense of Lucy—perhaps a stand-in for the author of *Hobomok*—Child promotes the careful pairing of sympathy with character instruction rather than romantic emotional excess. She does not, however, envision a lasting connection between the Seneca people and their Euro-American neighbors; the Kirbys return to their home, leaving a lake between themselves and Buffalo Creek Reservation. This seemingly final departure of the representative Euro-American family is ironic because of the fate of the Buffalo Creek Reservation after 1817, the year in which the story is set. When Child published "Buffalo Creek" in 1833, the Ogden Land Company had begun to acquire Seneca land through controversial treaties, and in the 1840s, Seneca inhabitants left Buffalo Creek Reservation entirely.[16]

As an author and editor of children's literature, Child sought to foster lives governed by sympathy, in particular by performing the role of a maternal intermediary who gently leads children to reject removal and other practices based on racial prejudice. Yet Child's children's literature presents sympathy as the movement across fixed difference, and insofar as the writings link the moral development of readers to proper sympathy, they construct a pedagogy wherein American Indians serve the development of the Euro-American child's moral sense or faculty. This pedagogy becomes clear later in "Anti-Slavery Education," a brief piece in the June 3, 1841, *National Anti-Slavery Standard*, edited by Child, in which a young Euro-American boy's benevolent actions toward American Indians are the precursor to his work as an abolitionist. The child, who provides food and affection to starving American Indian children because "they looked *so* poor," represents "a spirit to regenerate the world!"[17] This anecdote may hint that Child identified the Indian Question as central in her own development as a reformer-author, for *Hobomok* was her first publication and *First Settlers* preceded *An Appeal in Favor of That Class of Americans Called Africans*. "Anti-Slavery Education" certainly reflects the shift of national attention by the early 1840s from the Indian Question to the slavery debates. Whether the piece grew out of Child's personal experience or the historical context, it insists that to become a benevolent adult bent on destroying the institution of slavery the white child must first learn to pity the poor Indian.

Harmonizing the Material and the Spiritual in the New York Letters

Child dedicated herself full-time to abolition, and in May 1841 she assumed the editorship of the *National Anti-Slavery Standard*, the official organ of the American Anti-Slavery Society. There her effort to reach (and hopefully persuade) a larger audience with the abolitionist message by increasing the amount of literary or pleasure reading in the periodical led to complaints from prominent American Anti-Slavery Society members who believed the periodical was losing its zeal. Their complaints ultimately contributed to her resignation as editor in 1843.[18] The resistance Child encountered to her literary promotion of abolition appears to have informed her ongoing investigation of the tensions within and among sentimentalism, reform, idealism, and transcendentalism, as evidenced by the popular series of New York literary sketches she published in the *Standard* from 1841 to 1843. Collected as *Letters from New-York* shortly after Child left the *Standard* in May of 1843, and supplemented in 1845 by *Letters from New York, Second Series*, these popular sketches explore the physical restraints placed on ideal sympathy.[19] Through the language of sentiment they attempt to unite the transcendental pursuit of truth and the reformist goal of social perfection within the challenging context of commercial culture. Child's musings on the tension and the relationship between physical and spiritual forms and pursuits suggest at least a passing awareness of the contradictions in the moving encounter that doomed intimacy at the start.

In *Letters from New-York*, specific areas of the city spark reflections on topics ranging from democracy and religious pluralism to immigration, abolition, and the Indian Question. In the first letter (August 19, 1841), Child struggles to balance such reform commitments with romantic and artistic inclinations: "Blame me not, if I turn wearily aside from the dusty road of reforming duty, to gather flowers in sheltered nooks, or play with gems in hidden grottoes. The Practical has striven hard to suffocate the Ideal within me; but it is immortal, and cannot die. It needs but a glance of Beauty from earth or sky, and it starts into blooming life, like the aloe touched by fairy wand." [20] The tension between pragmatic reform and artistic expression partook of a transcendental dilemma Child had come across particularly in the work of Ralph Waldo Emerson, whose developing conception of reform inspired her, as Bruce Mills argues, to value writing that "did not easily harmonize with the strident rhetoric of reform societies." By using the appeal of literature to promote abolition to a wide audience, Child, in the Standard, infuses the rhetoric of organized reform with that of an individual's love for another, much as Ralph Waldo Emerson does in "Man the Reformer." [21] Child attempts to bring about a wholesale change in her readers' relationship with the downtrodden—immigrants, workers, African Americans, American Indians, the poor—by modeling a divine, transformative love.

Yet Child's letters convey, in Stephanie A. Tingley's words, "her activist's impatience with theory that is divorced from application and action." [22] As she echoes and models Emerson's call for loving social reform, Child similarly translates transcendental pursuits for public reformers. Both series of her New York letters employ bodily metaphors that link the perception of truth—the individual's discernment of universal order and spiritual force—with social action. In an April 7, 1844, entry in *Letters from New York, Second Series*, Child describes the cosmic relation between the perception of truth and social action as akin to the human circulatory system and imagines her postmortem reform efforts: "I will come in the deep stillness of the starry midnight, and whisper it to gentle, child-like souls.... The mystical word will pass from God's free atmosphere into the lungs of society, and renovate the spiritual blood, which, having completed its course, will return to the centre. And day by day the whole body will be slowly changed, so that no little veinlet or bone will remain as it was, before the despised mystical word was uttered." [23] In what amounts to a spiritual conversion, Child disembodies herself, the reformer-author, and detextualizes the reform essay but at the same time embodies society through a metaphor. Reimagining divine truth as the oxygen necessary to life and the truth-speaker as a part of a larger biological system (wherein she finds *Child*-like souls), Child underscores the necessity of personal as well as collective reform. Moreover, in bold, poetic language she demonstrates the capabilities of the individual genius even as she subordinates genius to the will of God. By fusing the spiritual and the material, the ideal and the political, she emphasizes the ultimate goal of reform: the transformation of the individual as well as her or his actions. In the earlier entries of *Letters from New-York*, death provides Child radical possibilities for social unity and reform, primarily through reflections on burial sites of recent immigrants as indicative of cross-cultural sympathy within the evolving, expanding U.S. social body.[24] Child does admit that the reconciliation of the spiritual and the material, the ideal and the political, and even the aesthetic and the practical may not be entirely possible. Reflecting on the graveyard of the quarantine grounds at Staten Island, she expresses her longing for a physical trace of the dead immigrant's thoughts, declaring, "O, how rich in more than Shakspearean [sic] beauty would be the literature of that quarantine ground, if all the images that pass in procession before those dying eyes, would write themselves in daguerreotype!" (*LNY* 92).

Child, like Margaret Fuller and Henry David Thoreau after her, confronts the roadblocks to spiritual and material reform through a moving encounter with American Indians. In a letter dated March 1843, she reports having seen fifteen "Sacs, Fox, and Iowas" (Sauks, Mesquakies, and Ioways) at Barnum's American Museum (*LNY* 161). She emphasizes at the start of the letter the ridiculousness of racial science, attacking the correlation of facial angles with innate racial superiority and affirming that physical differences among the races "are the *effects* of spiritual influences, long operating on character, and in their turn becoming *causes*."[25] Child rejects racial science and argues that only observation of "The LAW OF LOVE" will bring all races to the civilized spiritual and physical state. Further, she mourns the disregard Euro-Americans have for the law of love, as suggested by physical and emotional segregation: "We stand apart from them, and expect them to feel grateful for our condescension in noticing them at all. We do not embrace them warmly with our sympathies, and put our souls into their soul's stead" (*LNY* 163). Though Child literally stands apart from the two women on display, No-Nos-See (the She Wolf) and Do-Hum-Me (the Productive Pumpkin), she strives to put her soul in their souls' stead: "I would suffer almost anything, if my soul could be transmigrated into the She Wolf, or the Productive Pumpkin, and their souls pass consciously into my frame, for a few days, that I might experience the fashion of their thoughts and feelings. Was there ever such a foolish wish! The soul *is* Me, and *is* Thee. I might as well put on their blankets, as their bodies, for purposes of spiritual insight" (*LNY* 164–65). This passage at first appears to announce Child's pessimism regarding sympathy; the American Indian women's souls seem autonomous and unknowable so that Child longingly asks, "In that other world, shall we be enabled to know exactly how heaven, and earth, and hell, appear to other persons, nations, and tribes?" Yet Child's complaint that "these children of the forest do not even give us glimpses of their inner life" assumes that their souls, though obscured by cultural and physical difference (blankets, bodies, cranial angles, religious practices, residences, and so forth), partake of a common spiritual realm. In fact, her sympathy depends on this commonality, and she recognizes as both the German intellectual Johann Gottfried von Herder and the Ioway prophet Wa-Con-To-Kitch-Er do, "that matter is only the time-garment of the spirit" (*LNY* 165). Her task is to sympathize, to use physical encounter as an opportunity for transcending the material casing, or what Walt Whitman called "this necessary film."[26]

Child the reformer points out that commercial culture hijacks the "universal want" to know how American Indians think and feel (*LNY* 165). This act is particularly egregious because of the primary reason for that want: the belief that American Indians' relation to nature and their spiritual insights are not fettered by the materialism of civilization. As Child asks earlier in *Letters from New-York* (May 26, 1842), "Should I have learned more of the spirit's life, could I have wandered at midnight with Pocahontas, on this fair island of Manhattan? I should have, at least, learned *all*; the soul of Nature's child might have lisped, and stammered in broken sentences, but it would not have muttered through a mask" (*LNY* 78). Barnum's display reminds Child that nature's children—humans of all races—readily become civilization's victims. No-Nos-See, Do-Hum-Me, and their compatriots, "set up for a two-shilling show, with monkeys, flamingoes, dancers, and buffoons!," exemplify the tragedy of the individuals debased through a submission to antebellum capitalism, who irrevocably alter their appearance, habits, location, and health to attain currency that leads to further market participation. Barnum's display is a grotesque sample of Euro-American popular culture that would consume the "authentic Indian" as a moving spectacle through ethnographic displays and "playing Indian." When Child comments, "I might as well put on their blankets," she signals the absurdity not of the impulse for transmigration but (to pick one example) of actor Edwin Forrest's costume in the lead role of *Metamora; or, The Last of the Wampanoags* (1829).[27] Physical difference springs from but does not heighten spiritual difference, and Child happily observes, "In their imperturbable countenances, I thought I could once or twice detect a slight expression of scorn at the eager curiosity of the crowd" (*LNY* 164).

Thus Child conceives of No-Nos-See and Do-Hum-Me as Henry David Thoreau does the Indian basket-maker in *Walden* (1854): as representative of, concurrently, the dignified individual with an autonomous vision of truth and the victim of capitalism whose exploitation by market forces results in the degradation of her or his soul.[28] Both authors draw on two versions of the Native in this period—the noble savage and the degraded Indian—to create a composite symbol for transcendentalism's target and ideal. "The Indian" could be associated at once with the gallant and the brutal, the idyllic and the degraded, the spiritual and the vulgar, the past and the present, the dead and the living, and the stoic and the effusive. Like Thoreau, Child describes American Indians who have been self-sufficient but are forced into commercial relationships with Euro-

Americans. American Indians embody the tension between the real and ideal, and they suffer physical and spiritual side effects.

At the end of Child's letter on the American Indians at Barnum's museum, the physicality of the American Indians reasserts itself in their demonstration of the "war-dance," bringing Child temporarily to admit, "I was never before so much struck with the animalism of Indian character." She continues by emphasizing that their song represents "mere brute vengeance"; it "clove the brain like a tomahawk, and was hot with hatred." In a few paragraphs, Child moves from a desire for complete sympathy with two American Indian women to a detailed and sensational vision of a frontier mother's confrontation with blood-thirsty savages. The physical manifestation of American Indian culture and beliefs temporarily challenges her adherence to the Law of Love. "But instantly," she writes, again shifting perspective, "I felt that I was wronging them in my thought. Through paint and feathers, I saw gleams of right honest and friendly expression; and I said, we are children of the same Father, seeking the same home." Child affirms that their dance, costume, and former violence cannot accurately reflect their souls, and all animalism, all revenge, will melt away "before the persuasive power of Christian love!" (*LNY* 166). In the postscript Child reports that Do-Hum-Me and No-Nos-See have since died in the unpleasant urban conditions but that this reinforces her faith in love's ability to see through unpleasant physical markers. "Do-Hum-Me was but nineteen years old, in vigorous health, when I saw her a few days since," Child recalls, "and obviously so happy in her newly wedded love, that it ran over at her expressive eyes, and mantled her handsome face like a veil of sunshine" (*LNY* 167). Suddenly finding Do-Hum-Me's emotions accessible, Child employs a simile to unite the spiritual and material worlds; a sunshine veil illuminates rather than obscures the face and the act of blushing (implied by the verb *to mantle*)[29] translates emotions into a physical sign. A palpable shroud or pall of affection replaces the "blanket" that reveals nothing of Do-Hum-Me's inner life. The spiritual influence of love witnessed in the moment of encounter has made the woman's physical appearance temporarily legible to the sympathetic Child.

I use the words *shroud* and *pall* above to emphasize that the force of affective translation in this instance stems from death as well as from love. Just as the graves of immigrants far from their homelands stir Child's sympathy and bridge the barrier of religious and linguistic differences, so the improperly located grave of Do-Hum-Me—situated "among the trees, in Greenwood Cemetery; not the trees that whispered to her childhood"—provokes Child to cry, "Alas, for the handsome one, how lonely she sleeps here!" Now that Child finds ready sympathy with the displaced band, she romanticizes their removal, or proper relocation, to "their own broad prairies in the West" and, indeed, to "their 'fair hunting grounds' beyond the sky" (*LNY* 167). Child converts Barnum's gross display of sensationalized difference within the museum into a celebration of Christian love and a transcendental meditation on the union of souls. But her vision of spiritual and physical transformation achieved through moving encounter depends on American Indians' deaths. The American Indians Child so desires to understand she abstracts to signify, among other things, the unknowable Other, the savage warrior, the victim of market forces, the resistant primitive, and the tragic lover. The exit of the American Indian representatives at the end of Child's letter—their physical departure and their death—makes certain that this complex signification stands.[30]

A Final Appeal to the Family

After the Civil War, however, heightened cynicism about the possibility of American Indian acculturation and a flare-up of Indian wars inspired Child to return to the moving encounter. She wrote her 1868 *Appeal for the Indians* in response to a report by the recently established Indian Peace Commission, decrying past treatment of American Indians by the United States and calling for their immediate civilization through education. Even as she welcomes the commission's willingness to admit past wrongs, Child challenges its plans for aggressive acculturation and calls for a more gradual cultural assimilation of American Indians. In doing so, she uses a familiar familial metaphor: "How *ought* we to view the peoples who are less advanced than ourselves? Simply as younger members of the same great human family, who need to be protected, instructed and encouraged, till they are capable of appreciating and sharing all our advantages."[31] Thus, Child suggests, missionaries and teachers should draw on American Indians' language and cultural practices to aid their acquisition of English language and culture. Her pedagogy literally makes of all American Indians children to be nurtured and trained by patient and disciplinary (not punitive) parents.

An *Appeal for the Indians* echoes Child's most famous abolitionist work, *An Appeal in Favor of that Class of Americans Called Africans*, in argumentation as well as title, for Child once again builds a sentimental defense of the victimized from examples of their admirable family relations and Euro-Americans' barbarous behavior. "I cannot say," she emphasizes, "that Indians are the worst savages" (*AI* 224). Child notes that the Seminole leader Osceola was acting as any husband would when he "fought like a tiger" because his "beautiful wife had been torn from him and sold into slavery" (*AI* 223). Likewise, she tells the story of a Kennebec man whose neighbors "habitually treated him as an outcast," ignoring him even as he grieved the death of his only child (*AI* 226). Child lauds American Indians by noting that they "never strike children" (*AI* 229)—a claim quite appealing to the many who favored character building over corporal punishment—and that "their affections are very strong," as evidenced "by their tender memories of the dead, and their longing to rejoin them" (*AI* 230). While American Indians "never...offend the modesty of female captives," "soldiers and agents have often treated the Indian women as overseers are accustomed to treat negro slaves" (*AI* 229, 224). The piece even ends with an anecdote about one American Indian who hears of hell and responds, "If there is such a place, it must be for white men only," a comment she believes displays "some latent sarcasm" (*AI* 232). Child's sarcasm is far from latent when she refers to "civilized" Euro-Americans' hypocritical treatment of American Indians to undermine their assumed position of moral and racial superiority and to bring the two groups into a more harmonious relationship.

Carolyn L. Karcher convincingly links *An Appeal for the Indians* to Child's *A Romance of the Republic* and the short story "Willie Wharton," arguing that *An Appeal for the Indians* translates Child's "ideal of interracial marriage and cultural fusion"—the subject of the two fictional works—"into political terms."[32] "Willie Wharton," which appeared in the *Atlantic Monthly* in March 1863, offers the most explicit demonstration of Child's strategy for civilizing American Indians. The title character, a six-year-old resident of the western prairie, brings home to his surprised parents a young American Indian girl, Wik-a-nee (little small thing), who has become lost. The girl's grateful parents soon reclaim her. A few months later, Willie himself becomes lost on the prairie and, unbeknownst to his family, an American Indian family adopts him. After many years and the death of Mrs. Wharton, Willie is reunited with the Wharton family through the efforts of his brother Charles. Now, however, Willie is an acculturated American Indian and has married A-lee-lah, the grown-up Wik-a-nee. Using careful, measured inducements, the Wharton family brings the young couple to live in the fashion of Euro-Americans, and the tale ends with a description of their bright, fully acculturated child.

"Willie Wharton" is a remarkable story not simply because it depicts a marriage between a Euro-American and American Indian but because it does so optimistically; the moving encounter between white and Indian lovers lead to a sustained, productive partnership. Early historical romances such as *Hobomok*, Catharine Maria Sedgwick's *Hope Leslie; or Early Times in the Massachusetts* (1827), and James Fenimore Cooper's *The Wept of Wish-ton-Wish; A Tale* (1829) established the figure of a tragic interracial family bound for familial estrangement or death. Between 1828 and 1846, Child published three versions of a story in which a white Frenchman in the mid-eighteenth century marries a Sioux woman to gain her father's land and as a result leads her and their family to destruction.[33] In "Willie Wharton" Child returns to the interracial family with an unusually affirmative perspective and underscores the contrast with *The Wept of Wish-ton-Wish* by echoing the alliteration of Cooper's title and the novel's emphasis on the lost child's grieving mother and diligently searching father. Like *Hobomok* and her children's literature, "Willie Wharton" associates sympathy with mothers' and children's travel between Euro-American and American Indian spaces, and Child achieves in this story the unity of spiritual and material worlds she contemplated when viewing Do-Hum-Me and No-Nos-See. Yet this unity is achieved through cultural adaptation, and for this reason the short story is subject to a common criticism of *A Romance of the Republic*: it promotes racial reconciliation "through a renaturalization of the practices and relations associated with a (white) heterosexual and familial order."[34] As the culmination of Child's American Indian fiction and its exploration of fleeting Indian-white intimacy through the moving encounter, "Willie Wharton" communicates at once Child's radical idealism for the future of an interracial United States and her ingrained commitment to the erasure of American Indian culture.

Like "Adventure in the Woods," "Willie Wharton" includes the reversal of expectations for the entry of American Indians into Euro-American space. When Willie finds Wik-a-nee and leads her to his family's house, the worried parents conclude that their care for her will bring them no harm. "Nothing but justice and kindness," Mr. Wharton concludes, "is needed to render these wild people firm friends to the whites."[35] More important, he affirms his wife's natural role as sentimental intermediary: "Your gentle eyes and motherly ways are a better defence [sic] than armies would be." The Whartons welcome Wik-a-nee into their home, and as she and Willie sleep that night they form a "charming picture" of untroubled Indian-white relations: "The little white boy of six summers and the Indian maiden of four slept there as cozily as two kittens with different fur" (WW 258). When Wik-a-nee's parents arrive, they gratefully give Willie and Mrs. Wharton baskets, and Willie's basket becomes a prominent household object, "brought forward" for every visitor. In return, Willie gives Wik-a-nee a box of guinea peas that delight her, and Child celebrates the exchange: "Blessed childhood, that yields spontaneously to those attractions, ignoring all distinctions of pride or prejudice!" (WW 260). The care that Mrs. Wharton, Willie, and the whole family show Wik-a-nee creates a happy ending illustrative of ideal sympathy.

An interlude in the story uses death—as Child's New York letters do so often—to re-empower the maternal intermediary and provide a material link between American Indian and Euro-American worlds. Once Willie disappears, Indian captivity appears to be a brutal reality; the prairie homes become "haunted by a little ghost,...an accusing spirit," and the small red and yellow basket that Wik-a-nee gave Willie becomes a charged symbol of their perhaps superior behavior in protecting the Indian visitor (WW 267). Mrs. Wharton wastes away but finds comfort in a deathbed vision: "Our Willie!" she cries; "Don't you see him? Wik-a-nee is with him, and he is weaving a string of Guinea-peas in her hair. He wears an Indian blanket; but they look happy, there where yellow leaves are falling and the bright waters are sparkling" (WW 269). This second image of Willie and Wik-a-nee's intimacy again creates a new American family through captivity as the lost child is incorporated into a domestic scene. This time the mother acts as intermediary from the deathbed, supplying a glimpse of Willie but also prompting Willie, who has his own vision from deep within Indian territory, to determine, "I *must* go to my mother!" (WW 270). Charles then reads in the newspaper an article about an Indianized white man who has set out looking for his mother, and soon he finds Willie.

Child emphasizes the acquisition of culture rather than the inheritance of physical traits, as Karcher notes, yet she also ties cultural knowledge and practice to a biological structure, the family.[36] Willie's potential for reincorporation lies with his familial attachments, and A-lee-lah's potential lies with her attachment to Willie, and through him his family. From the moment Willie and A-lee-lah arrive at the Wharton home, Child's narrative promotes the kind of gradualist civilizing project she describes in *An Appeal for the Indians*. Through the family's warm greeting—"Welcome home, brother! Welcome, sister!"—the occult overtones of interracial union that Child developed in *Hobomok* disperse: two who enter as "strange apparitions" immediately become children of the family (WW 282). With her emphasis on female sentimental intermediaries, Child goes on to imagine an American Indian woman aiding a Euro-American man's reincorporation into his family. As the story's voice of reason, Uncle George, explains: "[Willie's] love for her [A-lee-lah] safely bridges over the wide chasm between his savage and his civilized life. Without her, he could not feel at home among us; and the probability is that we should not be able to keep him." The Wharton family also indulges the couple's "Indian dialect," understanding that "it was thus they had talked when they first made love" and any attempt to forbid their discussions would shift their romantic attachment in opposition to acculturation (WW 284). Willie and A-lee-lah's romantic relationship testifies to the affective equality of American Indians, but it also becomes the means of bringing them into a superior culture. Child emphasizes that to overcome cultural-racial division, to stop captivity and other violent incursions on the national family, one must cultivate and recreate the attachments and habits of the (biological) family unit.

The remainder of the narrative focuses on A-lee-lah's adaptation to the Wharton household, emphasizing the role of familial love in the civilizing process and the expression of that love in the exchange and consumption of domestic objects.[37] Yet even as the narrative promotes a gradual, affective-material strategy for acculturating A-lee-lah, it is punctuated by biological metaphors. As in *A Romance of the Republic*, "Child merges the discourse of race into the discourse of flowers in order to interrogate what is 'natural' about Reconstruction racial ideology,"[38] suggesting that the successful incorporation of a racial minority requires literal as well as metaphorical cross-fertilization. Uncle George sums up his philosophy of gradual acculturation through familial love: "Wildflowers, as well as garden-flowers, grow best in the sunshine" (WW 282). When the family persuades A-lee-lah and Willie to have a Christian wedding, A-lee-lah's "wedding-finery" represents "a becoming *hybrid* between English and Indian costumes" (WW 285; emphasis mine). Indeed, the bride is so attractive that Mr.

Wharton declares "She is handsome as a wild tulip." A-lee-lah, then, represents the site of cultural and biological mixture that will produce beautiful, cultivated descendents. Charles's description even associates her cultural adaptation with biological transformation: "The grub has come out of her blanket a brilliant butterfly" (WW 286). A story that begins with movements across "the wide, flowery prairie" (WW 253) ends with the human world's successful imitation of biology's lesson: flowers may be domesticated to greater beauty.

A-lee-lah's slow adoption of Euro-American culture is also keyed to a concept prominent in nineteenth-century ethnography and defenses of imperial actions: the evolution of human types through social stages, from savage to civilized. Child associates her botanical refinement with progress from a barbarous American Indian wardrobe to a semicivilized Arabesque one. A-lee-lah's beautiful, "hybrid" wedding garments and hair ornaments, an improvement over her traditional blanket and the "mass of straight black hair" over her forehead (WW 282), still bear little resemblance to what the Wharton women wear: "Loose trousers of emerald-green merino were fastened with scarlet cord and tassels above gaiters of yellow beaver-skin thickly embroidered with beads of many colors. An upper garment of scarlet merino was ornamented with gilded buttons, on each of which was a shining star.... At the waist, it was fastened with a green morocco belt and gilded buckle.... The braids were fastened by a comb with gilded points, which made her look like a crowned Indian queen" (WW 285). The amount of scarlet and gold in A-lee-lah's outfit, the similarity of her pants to East Indian Bloomers, the appearance of stars on her buttons, and the adjectives "morocco," "Guinea," and even "Indian" all contribute to the orientalizing of A-lee-lah, as does her earlier comparison with a tulip.[39] Her tastes also will continue to progress; we learn that later in life "she ceased to delight in garments of scarlet and yellow," and "consented to wear a woman's riding-hat with a drooping feather." Like her fashion sense, A-lee-lah's musical preference alters as she becomes more civilized: "She never attained to Italian embroidery of sound, still less to German intonations of intellect"—the hallmarks of superior European music—"but the rude, monotonous Indian chants gave place to the melodies of Scotland, Ireland, and Ethiopia" (WW 287). Embracing folk music, A-lee-lah demonstrates her incorporation into, if not high European culture, the democratic culture of the United States.[40]

Because acculturation depends on familial love, domestic consumption, and biological processes, the story ends with a paragraph on A-lee-lah and Willie's daughter Jenny. Jenny's biological inheritance includes her father's "mind" and "her mother's beautiful eyes," while her cultural inheritance comes from the village and extended family wherein she is raised, as indicated by her bearing her paternal grandmother's name (WW 287). As critics note, Child's privileging of Euro-American culture limited an otherwise revolutionary vision of an integrated nation. More strikingly, Child never considered American Indian national sovereignty a possibility. Her association of racial and cultural difference prevented her from conceiving of an incorporated American Indian who retains any Native element.

"This subject is painful and wearisome to me"

Child's literary tableaux portray moving encounters between Euro-Americans and American Indians that produce economic and familial relations. In doing so, they support, even prophesy, particular national models and facilitate within the reader a change of heart leading to moral action. The convergence in the forest of Mary Conant, Hobomok, and Charles Brown during Mary's occult ceremony, for example, prefigures the relationships they will have throughout the novel. In "Buffalo Creek," Mrs. Kirby and Lucy watch Miss Brandt tend a sick man, exemplifying American Indian uplift through Anglo education and hard work. The American Indians on display at Barnum's American Museum suggest to Child the capacity of sympathy to overcome physical difference. And in "Willie Wharton," the dying Mrs. Wharton's vision of Willie and A-lee-lah predicts the interracial family of the frontier as realized in the couple's picturesque wedding. Like the tableau vivant, Child's American Indian writings represent abstract concepts in physical and spatial terms, specifically through the perpetual reworking of the moving encounter. By portraying sympathy as travel or migration, however, Child naturalizes racial segregation, and by locating American Indians' future solely within Euro-American families and homes, she insists on erasing American Indian culture and sovereignty even as she sustains Indian-white sympathy.

In an 1870 letter to Charles Sumner, Child expresses her hesitation about her role as sentimental intermediary in the light of American Indians' violent opposition to Euro-American "civilization": "I have no romantic feelings about the Indians. On the contrary, I have to struggle with considerable repugnance toward them; and something of the same feeling I have toward all *fighters.* War, even in its best aspects, is a barbarism; and sooner or later, the world will outgrow it. But though my efforts for the Indians are mere duty-work, I do it as earnestly, as I should if they were a people more suited to my taste." [41] Sympathy gone, desire evaporated, Child in this passage has no wish to have her soul transmigrate into the body of a distasteful fighter, and she relocates the pathos of her argument with all victims of violence. That same year, Child's last published piece on American Indians, "The Indians," appeared in the inaugural issue of *The Standard,* the short-lived successor to the *National Anti-Slavery Standard.* In response to the Piegan Massacre of January 1870 in which U.S. cavalrymen attacked an unprotected Piegan camp and killed 173 men, women, and children, Child argues that the U.S. armed forces have, ironically, met American Indian barbarism with barbarous violence, almost sneering as she notes, "Now the approved method of teaching red men not to commit murder is to slaughter their wives and children!" "The plain truth is," Child insists, "our influence has made the Indians worse, instead of better, than we found them." Her solution to the problem of Indian degradation involves a campaign of assimilation much more aggressive than those she previously promoted. In addition to instituting "laws at once strict and impartial," discouraging the traffic in alcohol, encouraging "agricultural and mechanical labor" and land possession, rewarding the acquisition of English, and promoting Christianity, Child recommends that the United States disband the American Indian nations.[42] The solution of acculturation through the dispersal of national authority, coupled with private land ownership, resonates with the Dawes General Allotment Act of 1887 through which millions of acres were transferred from American Indian possession and control. Child's long association of cultural-racial difference with geographical locations and sympathy with travel leads her, in the postbellum era, to accept the "civilization" of American Indians through real estate—an ultimately destructive strategy.[43]

Child's American Indian writings created moving encounters for Euro-American readers, bringing them into vicarious contact with humanized American Indians, and occasionally into accord with Child's political views. That they also reinforced the concept of difference and the centrality of property to American Indian claims for equality seems to have troubled Child enough to prompt her continual revision. Perhaps this process is behind Child's expression of frustration in the final paragraph of "The Indians":

> This subject is painful and wearisome to me; and there is so much prejudice and passion in the field, that I write with little hope. But when I think of the good monk Telemachus, his example inspires me with fresh courage. When enslaved gladiators were killing each other, upon compulsion, for the entertainment of the Roman populace, he sprang on the arena and loudly proclaimed that the custom was wicked, cruel, and brutalizing. The populace were accustomed to think that gladiators had no rights or feelings which Romans were bound to respect, and the man who pleaded for them was killed on the spot. But the words he had uttered sank into some hearts, and took root there; and the fruit they bore was the abolition of these barbarous gladiatorial shows. Would that my weak voice could do something to arrest the insane and cruel disregard of Indian rights and feelings.[44]

Child conjures a national tableau quite appropriate for the tumultuous period of Reconstruction's demise and violent actions against American Indians: an endangered reformer shouts to a roaring, bloodthirsty mass and its degraded victims. After decades of voicing her adamant opposition to the abuse of American Indians, Child reveals her fear that American Indians, like African Americans, are trapped in a cycle of violence not readily broken by the discourse of "rights and feelings." Yet at the same time she insists, or perhaps pleads, that the kernel of her message, her assertion of the dignity of all humanity, remains in the heart of her beloved nation. Child's mixed assessment of her reform work, I believe, results from her perception of physical impediments to sympathy. Her revision of the moving encounter over the course of the nineteenth century testifies to her tireless attempt to transform impediments into enabling metaphors, to imagine unity through difference.

2

Doomed Sympathy and *The Prairie*
Rereading Natty Bumppo as a Sentimental Intermediary

Like Lydia Maria Child in her antebellum Indian writings, James Fenimore Cooper used deathbeds and gravesites to inspire reader sympathy and to close the Indian-white encounter with the fulfillment of Indian doom. At the conclusion of *The Pioneers, or the Sources of the Susquehanna; A Descriptive Tale* (1823), readers join Natty Bumppo, Judge Templeton, Oliver Effingham, and Elizabeth Temple at the graves of Major Effingham and Chingachgook, or Indian John, whose "faults were those of an Indian and his virtues those of a man." *The Last of the Mohicans; A Narrative of 1757* (1826) concludes with the interment of the dark beauty Cora Munro, whose mother was of West Indies and British ancestry, and her lover Uncas, Chingachgook's son, "the last warrior of the wise race of the Mohicans."[1] In the final pages of *The Pioneers* and *The Last of the Mohicans*, the graves of Chingachgook and Uncas, with their proximity to the graves of a loyalist officer and a mixed-blood heroine, respectively, symbolize the lost possibility of union between whites and Indians in the American setting. Within the frontiers depicted in the Leatherstocking Tales, characters of various racial and national affiliations repeatedly participate in moving encounters: they come into contact with one another, respond emotionally, erupt into violence, and witness the victory and ascension of one party over the others. The concluding funerals of Cooper's first two Tales retrospectively reenact these encounters, moving the spectators and readers to tears but also promulgating the impossibility of sustained relationships between living and breathing Indians and the white nation.

In these concluding burial scenes, Natty translates for the grieving parties, correcting the inaccurate inscription on Chingachgook's grave—he tells Oliver, "'Gach, boy; —'gach-gook; Chingachgook; which, intarpreted, means Bigsarpent. The name should be set down right, for an Indian's name has always some meaning in it"—and rendering Colonel Munro's expression of a universal, or rank- and color-blind, salvation into what he insists will be a more comprehensible expression of gratitude to the Delaware women who arrange the burial of his daughter. Indeed, by the end of *The Last of the Mohicans*, Cooper has clearly established this hero not only as a guide for Euro-Americans through frontier spaces but as a cultural intermediary who oversees and facilitates Indian-white encounters.[2] Natty is uniquely positioned to serve in this role as a man who lived among the Delaware Indians in his youth and who remained loyal to his white "blood" through national service, fighting in the Seven Years' War, the Revolutionary War, and finally in the Ohio Valley campaigns led by General "Mad Anthony" Wayne. In *The Prairie; A Tale* (1827), the third and intended final installment of the Leatherstocking Tales, Cooper depicts an elderly Natty who, in the words of Kay Seymour House, has embraced his "role as a disinterested mediator among four warring factions."[3] In the aftermath of eighteenth-century wars and contemporary with Lewis and Clark's expedition, Natty, no longer battle ready and reduced to trapping for subsistence, embodies the lost hope for and future demise of Indian-white accommodation in the West.

Henry Nash Smith and subsequent critics point out that because of Natty's attachment to nature and aversion to civil law, there is irony as well as tragedy in his role as frontier guide. Natty aids what many, including Cooper in the preface to *The Prairie*, identify as national and moral progress by guiding settlers to "uncultivated" land; however, the novels portray the immoral actions central to the settlement process and ask whether they undermine the national and religious justifications of domestic imperialism. Richard Drinnon frames the doubts haunting the Leatherstocking Tales in this way: "How could a system of justice in the clearings be built upon a record of injustice in the wilderness? A society of Christian brotherhood erected upon its denial? Respect for law and order based on broken treaties, bribery and debauchery, and a thoroughgoing contempt for the natural rights of natives?"[4] Natty's cultural mediation, as seen in the graveside scenes, often results in preservation of words or memories rather than people. He facilitates meetings that almost always conclude with burials, mediating between cultural representatives who cannot, or will not, be reconciled to one another. This intermediary brings cultural conflict to a boil, spurring the process that will dismantle his world, an Indian-white crossroads in which "a man without a cross" of American Indian blood may reside with his Mohican friend or live within the Delaware or Pawnee communities.[5] *The Prairie* presents an elderly Natty fully aware of his paradoxical role.

As the first two Leatherstocking Tales conclude with touching graveside memorials for fallen noble savages and their white counterparts, the third ends with the burial of Natty alone, making *The Prairie*, in D. H. Lawrence's words, "a strange, splendid book, full of sense of doom."[6] In the autumn after their adventures with the old trapper, Paul Hover and Duncan Uncas Middleton return to the Pawnee village in which Natty has been living, only to find him at death's door. Seated, facing west, with the body of his beloved dog, Hector, nearby, surrounded by a large circle of villagers and flanked by a dozen Pawnee chiefs, Natty delivers his final request to Middleton and his final blessing to his adopted son, Hard-Heart. Then, just as the dying Chingachgook in *The Pioneers* "raised himself, as if in obedience to a signal for his departure, and stretched his wasted arm towards the west," Natty answers God's call: "Middleton felt the hand which he held, grasp his own, with incredible power, and the old man, supported on either side by his friends, rose upright to his feet. For a moment, he looked about him, as if to invite all in presence to listen, (the lingering remnant of human frailty) and then, with a fine military elevation of his head, and with a voice that might be heard in every part of that numerous assembly he pronounced the word—'Here!'"[7] This spectacular deathbed scene represents the culmination of a novel in which the hero dwells on his lost prowess, his former adventures, his current weakened state, and his impending death; he even admits a desire to have died alongside Chingachgook back east: "if I were to choose a change it would be to say, that such as they who have liv'd long together in friendship and kindness...should be permitted to give up life at such times, as when the death of one, leaves the other but little reason to wish to live" (P 250). Natty Bumppo of *The Prairie*, reduced to "the trapper" as Chingachgook was to "Indian John," appears subject to the myth of doom that in the first two Tales condemns the last two Mohicans. Like Uncas, his story and his name have been and will continue to be passed along. Duncan Uncas Middleton tells Natty that three members of the Heyward-Middleton family bear the name Nathaniel, and the narrative informs us that Middleton "is the source from which we have derived most of the intelligence necessary to compose our legend" (P 115, 376). Also like Uncas, Natty appears to be the last of his race.

What does it signify that Natty, the frontier guide and sentimental intermediary, succumbs to a poignant death in a Pawnee village? Why is the Leatherstocking of this final installment, in the words of the critics, "peculiarly withered, almost mummified," and "already a member of the living dead"?[8] Has the "man without a cross" become so Indianized as to share the noble savage's fate? Notably, Natty's physical decline coincides with the convergence of various parties in the once barren prairie and the misunderstanding and violence that arise despite his best efforts, pointing to the larger historical-geographical context for the novel. The second half of the eighteenth century and the first years of the nineteenth century witnessed a series of wars, treaties, and U.S. territorial gains that changed forever the relationships between Native and non-Native communities in the trans-Appalachian region. Through the Treaty of Ghent and the formulation and implementation of removal policy in the first three decades of the nineteenth century, a region that had been a "middle ground," or site of political and cultural negotiation between whites and Indians, came under the dominion of the United States. Cooper's dying intermediary in the period of Lewis and Clark links the paradoxical narrative of the Indian' demise to the deterioration of frontier accommodation in the opening decades of the nineteenth century. As a white man who finds his calling far from settlements and his best friend among the Indians, Natty shares the fate of American Indians but more immediately of the middle ground.

Although critics now recognize the operation of sentimental discourse across gender in the antebellum period, few have been willing to consider Natty Bumppo (a.k.a. Deerslayer, Hawk-eye, Leatherstocking, Pathfinder, etc.) as particularly sentimental. Instead, Natty and Cooper's other heroes, white and Indian, are associated with the masculine response to or protest against a feminine culture of domesticity.[9] I maintain that Cooper's use of sentimental discourse and the moving encounter in *The Prairie* does not so much attack feminine discipline as declare, with regret, the irrelevance and the failure of sympathy in the frontier context. Natty's remarkable death and the marker erected by Middleton associate him with his Mohican friends and link the doomed-Indian myth—an emotional narrative underwriting Euro-American violence and passivity—to the wasted potential of a multicultural continent. Fading from the start of the novel, Natty serves as a noble sentimental intermediary who demonstrates the potential and the impossibility of sympathy-inspired mutual accommodation among the occupants of the West.

Setting the Stage

The Prairie is the only Leatherstocking Tale not named for an individual (*The Last of the Mohicans, The Pathfinder, The Deerslayer*) or group (*The Pioneers*) and the only one of the five novels not set in New York—facts that prompt one to consider the historical significance of the western land on which Natty Bumppo plays out the final scenes of his life. Ironically, Cooper completed this tale of the American prairie while in Paris and never visited the region in which it is set. Perhaps it is not surprising, then, that *The Prairie* does not locate the plot in a specific latitude or longitude, though the narration does refer to the Mississippi River as five hundred miles away (*P* 17). Smith argues that the novel portrays the prairie as less an actual place than "an Elizabethan stage, a neutral space where any character may be brought at a moment's notice without arousing in the audience a desire to have the entrance accounted for." [10] Yet the description of this setting as a neutral space echoes the account of the Great Plains found in Cooper's primary sources, *The History of the Expedition under the Command of Captains Lewis and Clark*, 2 vols. (1814), and Edwin James's *An Account of an Expedition from Pittsburgh to the Rocky Mountains; Performed in the Years 1819 and '20, . . . under the Command of Major Stephen H. Long* (1823).[11] Cooper depicted the adaptable prairie as the next frontier for American settlers after the rapid changes in the Old Northwest, an opportunity created through the Louisiana Purchase and subsequent expeditions. The land to which Natty has fled provides the void in which the hero may for the last time confront the social institutions and hierarchies he has challenged his entire life. That void is as much the unlimited frontier contemporary audiences saw in the western lands as it is the theatrical neutral space. Having abandoned the East for open territory, Natty moves to a region that, in the first years of the nineteenth century, represented the next staging ground for the nation's future.

The nation's future appeared uncertain because of the questions of national membership raised by westward expansion. The Louisiana Purchase brought various Native and Creole populations into the nation and initiated a century-long conflict over the relative position of American Indian nations and African Americans, enslaved and free, with respect to white citizens of the United States.[12] (This conflict was a legacy entirely appropriate for Jefferson, a slaveholder whose first draft of the *Declaration of Independence* included criticism of chattel slavery and a sympathetic student of American Indian history and culture who formulated the concept of removal.) In the years immediately following the acquisition of the land, many in the United States expressed fear that the immense territory would prove divisive as well as unmanageable.[13] Complicating this fear was the increasing sense that the continent of North America, settled by Euro-Americans beginning on the coast of the Atlantic Ocean and pushing ever westward, contained a range of communities representing the various stages in the progressive development of human society, from the hunting to the agricultural economies (from savage to civilized). As the frontier moved slowly from east to west, and Indian was joined or superseded by fur trader, soldier, frontiersman, and settler, the progressive development of human society could be mapped on an east-to-west axis—as could the visible diversity of the nation.[14] The opening narrative of *The Prairie* celebrates the acquisition of the land for having "placed the countless tribes of savages, who lay along our borders, entirely within our controul [*sic*]," and, within a generation, for having resulted in Missouri statehood: "Most of those who witnessed the purchase of the empty empire, have lived to see already a populous and sovereign state, parcelled [*sic*] from its inhabitants, and received into the bosom of the national Union, on terms of political equality" (*P* 9, 10–11). Even if the rest of the territory becomes an independent nation, the years of U.S. rule will prove stabilizing: "If ever time or necessity shall require a peaceful division of this vast empire, it assures us a neighbour that will possess our language, our religion, our institutions, and it is also to be hoped, our sense of political justice" (*P* 9). According to Cooper, the primary benefit of the Louisiana Purchase appears to be the United States' subsequent ability to manage, if not erase, conflicting societies on the continent.

Cooper's novel, nonetheless, presents the nation's continental sweep as far from manifest because of the imperfection of humanity. In a telling exchange with Dr. Obed Battius, Natty links the barrenness of the prairie to the abuses of previous tenants: "Now if man is so blinded in his folly as to go on, ages on ages, doing harm chiefly to himself," Natty declares, "there is the same reason to think that he has wrought his evil here, as in the Countries you call so old" (*P* 240). Selfishness and carelessness lie at the heart of human history and imprint themselves on the earth; the prairie is barren because of the wastefulness of previous, ancient populations, and God's judgment upon them. In this way, Steven Conn notes, Cooper resists the progressive narratives of western settlement in this period and complicates the triumphalism that justified wrongs perpetrated against Native inhabitants.[15] Natty Bumppo is neither R. W. B. Lewis's "individual emancipated from history" nor a figure of the nation's inexorable ascendance but an individual who, in an attempt to flee history, experiences the tumultuous turn of its wheels across the continent.[16] The prairie on which he lives out his final years bears witness to the distance between a society divinely ordered and one corrupted by human conflict.

Thus the prairie and Natty both bear the marks of history, corrupted by unavoidable forces yet sustained by a divine order not yet realized. In this paradoxical site—which is settled and unsettled and which holds the hope for the nation's future and the threat of its disunity—Natty makes his last, noble attempt to mediate between diverse peoples employing emotional language and appeals to sympathy. Natty marches (slowly, yes) toward his inevitable death as he strives to fend off misunderstanding and violence among the parties that converge on the prairie. But the parties' differences and self-interest make this an impossible task, and the tensions inherent in the historical narrative of western progress condemn Natty to a prairie grave. Natty the trapper is a former solider who eschews his gun, a loner on whose path multiple people converge, an environmentalist who assists tree-cutters, and a sentimental intermediary destined to witness misunderstanding and violence. Like Chingachgook and Uncas, he dies a victim of inexorable U.S. imperialism, and like the prairie in which he is buried, he represents the promise of mediation overwhelmed by violent conflict.

Encounters, Translation, Ethnography

The "unguarded territory" of the West, proclaims the opening paragraph of chapter 10 in *The Prairie*, was teaming with "white adventurers," "the metiffs or half breeds," and "Indian tribes" long before the Louisiana Purchase. "It was, therefore," the narrative continues, "no unusual thing for strangers to encounter each other in the endless wastes of the West" (*P* 107). Instead of the future prairie Cooper envisions with neighbors who "possess our language, our religion, our institutions, and it is also to be hoped, our sense of political justice," the turn-of-the-century prairie contains multiple groups of peoples with multiple languages, religious faiths, practices, and senses of justice. The prairie stage provides the setting for a series of moving encounters between the region's constituent groups and wayfarers.

Those wayfarers and conflicts are representative. Natty's early years among the Delaware Indians and later years fighting in the Ohio Valley associate him at once with the benevolence of the Moravian missionary John Heckewelder and the ruthless fighting of General Wayne. The family of Ishmael Bush, like its patriarch's namesake, wanders the land after fleeing civilization; specifically, the Bushes left Kentucky because Ishmael was suspected of murdering a sheriff's deputy (P 58). The Bush men also seek ransom for a captive, a young Spanish Creole woman from Louisiana, Inez de Certavallos, whom Abiram White, Esther Bush's brother, kidnapped on her wedding day. Duncan Uncas Middleton, descendent of Duncan Heyward from *The Last of the Mohicans*, pursues his new wife into the territory, with military in tow and the authorization of President Jefferson (P 111). Meanwhile, a young woman taken in by the Bush family, Ellen (Nelly) Wade, offers Inez comfort in her captivity and chafes against the brutish life of her host family. Ellen also has a lover in hot pursuit: the rustic beekeeper Paul Hover follows the Bush family from Kentucky to the prairie, ready to rescue and marry Ellen. Attending the Bush family is the clownish Dr. Obed Battius, a naturalist whose passion for classification leads him to make ridiculous observations, even mistaking his own donkey, Asinus, for a marvelous prairie monster. Natty, the Bush family, Paul and Ellen, Middleton and Inez, and Dr. Battius all encounter representatives of the good (Pawnee) and bad (Sioux) Indians of the region. The Pawnee band is led by the noble young Hard-Heart, who seeks revenge on his sworn Sioux enemies, headed by Mahtoree. Mahtoree and his band successfully raid the Bush camp for livestock and capture Natty's assembled party.

The volatile moving encounters of various people on Cooper's prairie occur because of conflicts and violent disagreements, some initiated elsewhere and some located in the immediate vicinity. Most obviously, the Pawnee and the Sioux who occupy Cooper's prairie clash over proprietorship of hunting grounds, and in chapters 3 and 17 their reconnoitering brings them to encounter the white characters. Again, the Bush family heads west because of the trouble they have raised in challenge to property laws and because they deal in human flesh; fleeing one violent frontier for another, they carry human bondage along with them. Ishmael and Abiram's kidnapping of Inez spurs Middleton's pursuit, suggesting the inevitability of a military solution to increasing turmoil over the future of slavery in the nation and reminding readers that they gain imaginary access to western territories and their indigenous inhabitants through military actions, including the documentation of western lands and people by Long and Lewis and Clark. *The Prairie* fittingly represents the convergence of multiple groups in the frontier space and the related development of close and even procreative relationships as the result of conflict.

In the many scenes when these various parties, and in particular the Euro-Americans and the American Indians, encounter one another, Natty is a governing force, translating words, revising expression, offering environmental information, distinguishing between cultures and races, and always illuminating the larger significance of their interactions within this region. His activities as an intermediary are registered in the names he has accumulated over his long and storied life, including Deerslayer, Hawk-eye, La Longue Carabine, Leatherstocking, and Pathfinder. He tells Paul, "Lord, lad, I've been called in my time, by as many names, as there are people among whom I've dwelt." While on earth, Natty is himself translated by the accumulated parties of the prairie between and among whom he moves. His subsequent words to Paul (and the subsequent plot) reflect how Natty's cultural relativism extends to the end of his life: "But little will it matter when the time shall come that all are to be muster'd, face to face, by what titles a mortal has play'd his part; I humbly trust I shall be able to answer to any of mine, in a loud and manly voice" (*P* 171). The intermediary's identity will be fixed, refined through death.

The emphasis on translation in *The Prairie* suggests just how crucial aural assessments are to parties encountering one another in this western desert, even within a novel noted for its attention to visual representation. The Bush family's first encounter with Natty at sunset, as critics point out, is spectacular: "In the centre of this flood of fiery light a human form appeared, drawn against the gilded background, as distinctly, and seemingly as palpable, as though it would come within the grasp of any extended hand. The figure was colossal; the attitude musing and melancholy, and the situation directly in the route of the travellers. But embedded, as it was, in its setting of garish light, it was impossible to distinguish its just proportions or true character." Natty stands as the unavoidable and overwhelming occupant of this frontier zone who is prepared to lead migrants through the gradations of society to their destiny. The image appropriately fills Ishmael Bush with "superstitious awe" (*P* 14–15). But soon his actual physical state is apparent, suggesting the toll that mediation has taken on Cooper's hero and an inner force that will not allow Natty to cease his toil: "His form had withered, but it was not wasted. The sinews and muscles, which had once denoted great strength, though shrunken, were still visible; and his whole figure had attained an appearance of induration, which, if it were not for the well-known frailty of humanity, would have seemed to bid defiance to the further approaches of decay" (*P* 16). Withered but not wasted, Natty perseveres on "this hungry Prairie" through instinct and words rather than by his rifle or brute strength. The passage of time has reduced a man formerly identified by his marksmanship (Deerslayer, Hawk-eye, La Longue Carabine) to his essence: the intermediary.

At this point begins the exchange of words on which the future of the region depends.

[Ishmael asks Natty,] "And what may you name the district, hereaway?"

"By what name," returned the old man, pointing significantly upward, "would you call the spot, where you see yonder cloud?"

The emigrant looked at the other, like one who did not comprehend his meaning and who half suspected he was trifled with.   (P 17)

Though they soon find a common understanding of Natty's obligation to advise any stranger, Natty and the Bush family have an uneasy relationship due to their differing conceptions of the prairie (natural space versus territory to be claimed). The tension between them prompts Natty's first expression of a historical vision at odds with that established in the opening pages of the novel. He declares, "I often think the Lord has placed this barren belt of Prairie, behind the States, to warn men to what their folly may yet bring the land!" (P 24). The Bush family does not heed this warning—one Abiram first heard in the settlements[17]—and, moreover, distrusts the messenger. Because, as the narration later explains, "the gradations of society . . . are to be traced from the bosom of the states . . . to those distant and ever-receding borders which mark the skirts," this distrustful, peripatetic family stands closer to "barbarity" than to the "refined" and thus distrusts and rejects the advice of the prairie's mythic resident and caretaker (P 66).

After Natty leads them to an appropriate campsite, the Bush family immediately chops down the few trees in the vicinity, which Natty observes with "a melancholy gaze" and "a bitter smile" (P 19). As the family continues to set up camp, the solitary trapper's curiosity, and perhaps loneliness, draws him to the mysterious tent in which Abiram and Ishmael conceal the captive Inez. Chastised by Ishmael for snooping, Natty apologizes by highlighting his isolation and explaining, "I did not know, but there was something behind the cloth, that might bring former days to my mind" (P 20). This hope for connection to his former life through domestic items or residents remains strong in the old trapper. Later, after the Sioux band raids the Bush camp, Natty again watches closely as the family departs the site and the two elders pack up the tent and its secret contents. This act of observation wins an even sterner rebuke from Ishmael: "Stranger, I did believe this prying into the concerns of others, was the business of women in the towns and settlements, and not the manner in which men, who are used to live where each has room for himself, deal with the secrets of their neighbors" (P 82). The "feminine" behavior of Cooper's frontier hero suggests the paradox of his life: his simultaneous attraction to and repulsion from the white community, his desire to flee white families and his irresistible urge to recall and even recapture his former position within one.

Ishmael's rebuke and distrust of Natty also of course arises from his desire to conceal Inez, to keep the flap down on Pandora's tent, if you will. Daughter of the wealthy Catholic Don Augustin de Certavallos of Louisiana, Inez represents the union of regions and colonial-European cultures within the United States through her marriage to Middleton. Her kidnapping threatens that union, as the lawlessness of her captors does more generally. Because her identity and story are not revealed until chapter 15, Inez also represents the specter of slavery within the newly acquired territory, a role at first similar to Cora Munro's in *The Last of the Mohicans*, though unlike Cora, Inez does not actually have "tainted" blood. Nonetheless Abiram White, "a dealer in black flesh" and "'a regular translator of the human body from one State to another," with his conspicuous surname and murderous inclinations, readily turns his greedy eyes on the dark-skinned "Louisianian Lady" (*P* 92, 166, 156). Though the Bush family transports a captive rather than a slave into the prairie, Abiram's past and the mystery surrounding Inez suggest that slavery threatens the future of the territory, undermining potential unions and supporting the chaos of a mob democracy.[18] This secret tent so carefully, so religiously tended to by the Bush family patriarchs resembles at first the Ark of the Covenant, but once its true contents are revealed, it represents instead the distance of these settlers from moral law.

Ishmael's insinuation of Natty's unnatural proclivity to domesticity and gossip underscores as well the tensions inherent in Natty's role as sentimental intermediary. Natty's regular philosophizing suggests his respect for emotion and for its ability to overcome differences, a trait acquired through his early encounter and communion with Delaware Indians and their Moravian missionaries. Natty tells Battius that he reads the Bible because it "speaks in every line according to human feelings and therein according to reason" (*P* 197). His respect for this book and its faithfulness to human feelings stems from a cross-cultural experience : "Many is the long winter evening that I have passed, in the wigwams of the Delawares, listening to the good Moravians as they dealt forth the history and doctrines of the elder times to the people of the Lenape" (*P* 239). Yet Ishmael Bush gets it wrong when he comments, with suspicion, to Natty, "It seems that your heart is with the red-skins" (*P* 76). Natty's heart lies with the prairie, seemingly between the Indians and whites, and through emotions he attempts to bring those around him closer together.

As translator, Natty uses his cross-cultural sympathy as well as his ethnographic knowledge to help parties understand each other. Eric Cheyfitz and others have argued that Natty's translation regulates race, enforcing distinctions and segregation rather than bridging difference or building coalitions. A reading of translation in *The Prairie* attentive to the series of moving encounters and Natty's role as sentimental intermediary suggests, however, that his translation, like his body and the land on which he lives, has been doomed to degeneration in the context of human greed and violence. He is not so much a "border guard," as Janet Dean concludes, but a figure of sympathy whose attention to difference is in the interest of peace.[19] Mahtoree explains, "Mahtoree has but one tongue, the gray-head, has many....He can talk to the Pawnee, and the Konza and the Omahaw, and he can talk to his own people" (*P* 282). Natty speaks in the Sioux tongue to Mahtoree and in Pawnee to Hard-Heart. Significantly, Natty's translations are not word-for-word; he emphasizes that to understand the Other, one must also interpret his emotions. This is particularly true during the captivity of Natty, Ellen, Paul, Inez, and Hard-Heart by the Sioux. We are told that in the exchange between Mahtoree and Paul, Natty alters the words of each to appeal to the other's sensibility so that Mahtoree says of Natty, "My father will make what a poor Indian says, fit for a white ear'" (P 283). Paul recognizes Natty's negotiation of the two cultures when he requests, "Harkee, old trapper,... speak such words to the ears of that damnable savage, as become a white man to use, and a heathen to hear" (P 284). Similarly, Natty tells Mahtoree that if he wishes to woo Inez and Ellen, he must change his language even before Natty translates it: "Teton,... the tongue of a red-skin must be coloured white, before it can make music in the ears of a Pale-face" (P 290). Because Natty translates emotion as well as language for the Indian and white characters, he feels implicated by the messages he shares. So when Hard-Heart asks Natty to translate a spiteful message for the Sioux regarding the number Hard-Heart has slain, Natty responds, "Pawnee, I love you, but being a Christian man, I cannot be the runner to bear such a message" (P 279). Bridging a cultural gap cannot be done objectively, and Natty's effectiveness and his ineffectiveness with translation are related to his ability to translate subjectively and his interest in maintaining social balance.

Natty's failure to bridge linguistic and emotional difference in the encounter—the next step in the deterioration of his identifying roles—leads to the violence of *The Prairie*. As Ishmael refuses to recognize any law other than that derived from the Old Testament, he also refuses to entertain others' uses of language and even their emotions. Angered by Mahtoree's captivity of Ellen, Inez, and Natty and determined to win them back, Ishmael demands of Natty: "Look you here, old gray-beard,... you'll play linguister, and put my words into Indian, without much caring whether they suit the stomach of a redskin, or not" (P 295). Natty ignores Ishmael's request, and Ishmael's unwillingness to sympathize with Mahtoree and thereby to reason with him leads to the Bush family's angry departure from the Sioux camp. Whereas the ignoble settler refuses translation and a multicultural frontier, the noble Pawnee Hard-Heart refuses translation and reconciliation with the Sioux. With Hard-Heart's torture and death imminent, an ancient Sioux, Le Balafré, approaches him and asks, "Does my son speak with the tongue of a Teton?" The narrator then tells us that although Hard-Heart does know the old man's language, "he was far too haughty to communicate his ideas, through the medium of a language that belonged to a hostile people" (P 311). Refusing to speak in the Sioux language prefaces Hard-Heart's refusal also to join the tribe as Le Balafré's adopted son, emphasizing his inability to move between the tribes: "[Le Balafré] has never seen a buffaloe [sic] change to a bat. He will never see a Pawnee become a Sioux!" (P 312). And soon after this, Hard-Heart kills Weucha and engages Mahtoree in a bloody battle. The intimacy of residents in the frontier zone collapses, despite the possibility of translation. Translation in *The Prairie* is linguistic and affective, with the power both to bridge difference and to enforce it, and the sentimental "linguister" appears trapped in an unavoidable cycle of violence.

Natty is not the only one. *The Prairie* describes multiple characters whose encounters with other cultures, and more specifically their observations of domestic situations, exacerbate rather than ameliorate tensions on the prairie. Antebellum America witnessed the emergence of ethnography, or the comparative study of human cultural, social, and linguistic practices (as I discuss in Chapter 6). *The Prairie* portrays ethnographic observation, like translation, as a promising intercultural activity that nonetheless results in cultural and physical violence. In a dramatic scene in chapter 4, Mahtoree enters the Bush family campsite at night to reconnoiter. As the family sleeps unsuspectingly, Mahtoree snoops and even gains access to the secret tent in which Inez is imprisoned (*P* 52). In chapter 25, we follow Paul, Ellen, Inez, and Natty into the Sioux village where they are held captive and observe "the daily exhibition of an encampment confident in its security" (*P* 272). Only through captivity may they see the Indians in their daily pursuits. Late in the novel, as part of the denouement, Paul's interest in the Pawnee village again leads to further study: "Paul when he saw an armed sentinel in the uniform of the States, pacing before its entrance, was content to stray among the dwellings of the 'redskins' prying with but little reserve into their domestic economy, commenting sometimes jocularly, sometimes gravely and always freely on their different expedients, or endeavoring to make the wondering housewives comprehend his quaint explanations of what he conceived to be the better customs of the whites" (*P* 366). Once there is a Euro-American military presence, Paul comfortably observes the practices of the Pawnee firsthand and suggests cultural improvements, ways of "civilizing" their practices. Indian-white conflict or its military resolution puts Paul in close proximity to the Pawnee people, and it also empowers him to act as a cultural authority (however humorous the scene may be). *The Prairie* reveals ethnography, which would provide one group with intimate knowledge of the other's life, to be an integral part of invasive military and cultural work.

In retrospect, Ishmael's suspicion of Natty's prying eyes and flexible tongue seems well-founded. The intermediary's work in *The Prairie* proves self-defeating as each effort to create productive encounters, to bridge differences and thereby save lives, fails. Just as sympathy can be subsumed by curiosity and manipulated by authors, mediation on the frontier can be co-opted by those who seek to "assure[] us a neighbour that will possess our language, our religion, our institutions, and it is also to be hoped, our sense of political justice" (*P* 9). Natty, who moves so quickly from a colossal form to a withered old trapper, must accept the unintended results of his well-intentioned words.

Exclusions, Remains

In "Experience" (1844), Ralph Waldo Emerson alludes to the pleasure he and other antebellum readers derived from the characters and machinations of Cooper's *The Prairie*. "The imagination," he writes, "delights in the wood-craft of Indians, trappers, and bee-hunters. We fancy that we are strangers, and not so intimately domesticated in the planet as the wild man, and the wild beast and bird. But the exclusion reaches them also."[20] Hard-Heart's camouflage in the thicket, Mahtoree's reconnaissance work in the Bushes' camp, Natty's strategy for surviving a prairie fire and a bison stampede, Paul Hover's description of bee-lining—all these forms of wood- or prairie-craft, Emerson suggests, highlight through contrasts the reader's perceived distance or exclusion from the natural world. Yet, Emerson continues as Child did in *Letters from New-York*, humans and animals alike suffer from the distance between the physical world and the spiritual world of which it is a sign. Even the frontiersmen who harness the force of nature realize that control is but an illusion. One recalls Natty's warning to the Bush family that the prairie represents God's warning to his decadent, belligerent children. The novel concludes with the decimation of Mahtoree's Sioux community and the departure of the two Euro-American couples from the prairie. Natty's concluding death indicates the exclusion reaches him also.

Set in 1805 and published in 1827, *The Prairie* places the myth of the lost middle ground in the context of Jefferson's Louisiana Purchase and his influential proposal of Indian removal taken up by Jackson. The moving encounters of the novel remind the reader of Cooper's star-crossed Indians in the preceding Leatherstocking Tales, but even more so, they emphasize the fleeting hope for a stage on which American Indians and Euro-Americans may live free from the violent (though necessary) imposition of U.S. rule. Cooper assigns to the prairie location all contact and communication among disparate peoples that signals the possibility of sentimental understanding and union. He also controls and contains this plot with prefaces and an opening narrative that declare, in almost celebratory retrospect, the demise of this possibility. *The Prairie* condemns Natty the linguister, observer, philosopher, and adoptive father from the beginning, establishing the conditions for his failure to mediate difference.

Why does Natty fail? Distrust and revenge thwart sympathy time and again as translation and ethnography lead to prejudice and migration to murder. Though he is the novel's representative good Indian and Natty's adoptive son, the appropriately named Hard-Heart exhibits all the human characteristics that lead to violence in the prairie. He spends the first half of the novel tracking the Sioux band for revenge, and as mentioned earlier, rejects Le Balafré's offer to become his adopted son. Moreover, after escaping torture and sure death, the skeptical Hard-Heart refuses Mahtoree's offer to form a pan-Indian alliance against the white settlers (P 334–335). Still, this hardened youth does not reject Natty's offer of adoption, recognizing perhaps the trapper's almost Christ-like status as a failed intermediary (P 313). In the midst of long-standing feuds, struggles for land, cultural pride, and simple blood lust, the ineffective Natty again achieves a mythic stature. As the novel proceeds, he comes to embody an ideal at odds with national "progress"—and the other characters venerate him for it (though the Bushes do so grudgingly). "That the attitude toward the universe which the trapper affirms ought to animate the lives of those who follow him is clearly the meaning of the three books," writes Donald A. Ringe. "That human nature being what it is, men will not follow his moral path is equally certain."[21]

The rejection of an ideal life represented by Natty, the inability or unwillingness to feel right, leads Ishmael and Abiram to steal Inez, Abiram to kill his nephew Asa Bush, the Sioux band to capture Ellen, Paul, Natty, and Hard-Heart, and the Sioux and Pawnee people to fight. Although Ishmael comes to recognize Natty's innocence (he neither killed Asa nor conspired with the Sioux), and the loss of Asa and Abiram chastens the Bush family for their greed, the characters do not create a new, united community in this region. Unlike *The Pioneers* and *The Last of the Mohicans*, *The Prairie* ends with the departure of white characters from the frontier space rather than with the death or retreat of its central noble American Indian character (in this instance, Hard-Heart). By closing the novel with white rather than Indian removal, Cooper suggests that the Bush family and their ilk are not ready yet for the intercultural, sentimental frontier; however, by ending the novel with Natty's death, he reminds the reader that the goal of an intercultural frontier has been abandoned since the first years of the century. In the 1849 preface to the novel, Cooper declares the nation's success in establishing authority over the region: "Since the original publication of this book, however, the boundaries of the republic have been carried to the Pacific, and 'the settler,' preceded by the 'trapper,' has already established himself on the shores of that vast sea" (P 6). Whereas Cooper's Leatherstocking Tales as a whole chronicle the disappearance of the Indians that stock their pages, *The Prairie* confirms the impossibility of the sustained community long ago rejected in the east and points to the success of subsequent imperial efforts to the west.

Natty's death, appropriately, prompts the novel's many players to return to the prairie stage and commemorate his life. This intermediary who has seen and even caused so much violence remains contradictory, representing isolation and community, noble savagery and aspiring civilization, national progress and human depravity, and natural and civil law.[22] He dies on the geographical incarnation of the sentimental intermediary's paradoxical position: a sparsely populated desert of God's design in which moving encounters are nonetheless common, potentially productive, and inevitably violent, taking place beyond civil control but remaining essential to the extension of national rule and culture. When Natty cries "Here!" as he dies, he does more than answer God's roll call or summons to judgment. Natty calls out the only name he has for this space where Hard-Heart and Middleton come together to mourn the same man. That is, Natty indicates the stage on which a new kind of community might have begun had not encounter itself been so moving, so vexed, so unstable—had the intermediary not been destined to fail from the start.

Thus, Natty's gravestone commemorates what many Euro-Americans believed to be an impossible dream of a nation united across difference through emotion. It is a physical marker of this space and of Natty's attempt to mediate between its residents and wayfarers. One can imagine the marker, like Natty's figure in chapter 1, thrusting upward from "the crest of the nearest wave of prairie," a "colossal" form backlit by the western sunset (P 14, 15). Encounter has fostered sympathy but ended in violence, promised familial union but led to separation and murder, prompted intercultural observation and translation but concluded with declarations of insurmountable difference, and represented national union but also uncovered the sources of disunion. Indian-white sympathy, like Natty and the Mohican men whom he loves, has been ill-fated from the first page of the Leatherstocking Tales. On what was intended to be the final page of the saga, Cooper, through Middleton, reverentially inters the promise of moving encounter in the prairie. Perhaps desirous finally to suppress the paradox at the heart of U.S. history and its narrative of the doomed Indian, he inscribes the gravestone with a veiled threat: *"May no wanton hand ever disturb his remains"* (P 386). The cycle of sympathy and death make this epitaph meaningless. Just over a decade later in *The Pathfinder, or The Inland Sea* (1840), Cooper resurrected Natty to record his failure to marry and establish a home.

3

"Be man!"

Emasculating Sympathy and the Southern Patriarchal Response in the Fiction of William Gilmore Simms

The Indian Question was crucial to the beginnings of a distinct identity for the American South before the Civil War. In the development and passage of the Indian Removal Act of 1830, the federal government "bow[ed] before southern state pressures" and then pointed to the resultant "confusion and despair among the southern Indians...as a justification for removal."[1] Georgia's and President Andrew Jackson's disregard for the Supreme Court decision in *Worcester v. Georgia* (1832), which denied Georgia's authority over the sovereign Cherokee nation, and the subsequent sacrifice of American Indian land rights for Southern states' rights, indicated the extent of the region's influence on federal policy but also its willingness to defend its political-economic system to the detriment of federal power. The adoption of this Southern policy strengthened the cultural identity of the region, reinforcing its commitment to concepts of biological and social hierarchy that underpinned the Southern economy and Southern intellectuals' assertions of Euro-American superiority. The racialist defense of removal, like the racialist defense of slavery in this period, was part of an effort "to provide a system of beliefs that would impart meaning to the regional way of life and in so doing to establish an essential role for thought in the South."[2] The American School of racial science emerged from the consideration of the Indian's low position within the racial hierarchy, and its most prominent defender, Josiah Clark Nott, came from Alabama. Moreover, the whole of Southern states benefited economically from removal as the lands vacated or soon-to-be vacated by southeastern tribes were settled by swarms of Euro-Americans from Virginia and the Carolinas.[3]

Indian removal was so important to the emerging expression of Southern political power and intellectual culture, as well as to the perpetuation of the Southern economic system, that even the politically ambiguous expressions of sympathy for the Indian in literature from New England and the mid-Atlantic were suspect in the South. Critics have pointed, for example, to the controversy caused by an 1831 performance in Augusta, Georgia, of John Augustus Stone's otherwise popular melodrama based on King Philip's War, *Metamora; or, The Last of the Wampanoags*. The play, which provides its Indian hero multiple speeches damning white colonizers, had to be cancelled because Augustans took it not as a sentimental display of the doomed Indian or the compelling recreation of short-lived Indian-white exchange but as "a direct indictment of their own treatment of Indians."[4] The depiction of cultural encounters in the Southern frontiers, as this incident indicates, required translation in accord with sectional visions of American expansion. In the South, the Indian-white encounter took on a very different form because it reflected a commitment to an agricultural economy and race-based patriarchal society. To the South Carolinian author William Gilmore Simms, the Southern frontier was "a center of cultural confrontation, a battleground where various cultural identities confront each other and where the American cultural identity is defined and eventually solidified."[5] During the 1830s and 1840s, in the context of the Second Seminole War (1835–1842) in Florida, which for many Euro-Americans linked American Indian military resistance with slave rebellion, and Choctaw, Creek, Chickasaw, and Cherokee removal from Mississippi, Georgia, Alabama, and North Carolina, Simms contributed to national literature a depiction of Indian-white moving encounters in the neglected setting of the Southern frontiers and asserted that American Indians performed a defining role in the nation's past and present.[6]

In 2003, the University of South Carolina Press published *An Early and Strong Sympathy: The Indian Writings of William Gilmore Simms*, a hefty anthology edited by John Caldwell Guilds, Simms's biographer, and Charles Hudson, a historian of southeastern Indians. Guilds and Hudson take the suggestive title and a lengthier epigraph for the collection from a letter Simms wrote to the ethnographer Henry Rowe Schoolcraft in 1851 in which he expresses regret that no one, including himself, is truly qualified to review the first volume of Schoolcraft's *Historical and Statistical Information Respecting the History, Condition and Prospects of the Indian Tribes of the United States* for the *Southern Quarterly Review*. Simms does assure Schoolcraft, however, that he has a personal and ethical interest in the subject matter: "An early and strong sympathy with the Red Man, in moral and literary points of view, have rendered me in some degree a fit person to insist upon their original claims and upon what is still due them by our race."[7] Attempting through his introduction and various headnotes to revive interest in the neglected author, Guilds in effect resurrects the nineteenth-century moving encounter through an emphasis on Euro-Americans' curiosity and attraction to American Indians, Euro-Americans' principled sympathy for the diminished group, the emotional intensity of the Indian-white meeting, and the production and consumption of a commendable literature that recreates encounter. According to Guilds, Simms's authentic sympathy and extensive travel, which produced in him an almost obsessive desire to write about American Indians, make his works authoritative. In contrast, Hudson's introduction, "An Ethno-historical View," emphasizes Simms's distorting focus on "racial identity," such that he "never came close to attaining the standard of evidence modern anthro-pologists require of firsthand field observations." "Despite his interest in Indian culture," Hudson concludes, "Simms lacked the knowledge and skills to understand its complexities."[8] Although Simms did not produce a literature that provides a reliable account of American Indian life, his work does have much to teach us about the Indian Question in the Southern context of this period—how an author now neglected as a slavery proponent created works revealing the contribution of the South to the national consideration of American Indian policy.[9]

Most significantly, Simms revises the sentimental impulse of antebellum literature, embracing at the outset not the equalizing force of common emotion but the inequality created in the act of sympathy. In an insightful review of *An Early and Strong Sympathy*, Thomas M. Allen emphasizes that Simms's works use sympathy to unite, often in unsettling or even obscure ways, section and nation, diversity and union. In this way, Simms creates a national history countering Northern "racialist nationalism" and promulgates his vision of national virtue. Allen writes: "Simms clearly believed that whites could extend sympathetic identification across racial lines, at least some of the time. He returned to the possibilities of such a practice again and again in his fictional recountings of the history and folklore of the South and then applied this hierarchical but multiethnic view of North American history, as it played out in the portions of the continent that would become the South, to the problem of fabricating national identity for the US of America in the present and future."[10] Sympathy in Simms's American Indian writings has little to do with the pleasurable, poignant acceptance of historical progress as dramatized by the doomed Indian (though there is certainly a strain of this in his works) or the sentimental protest against removal (though his critique of colonialism partakes of this rhetoric); rather, sympathy in Simms's American Indian writings is above all part of a cycle of contact and violence crucial to social cohesion and national unity. Simms's strong sympathy, if you will, keeps in mind the diversity of U.S. society and the often irresistible violence brought on by interracial encounter. Simms writes fiction rooted in Southern history to correct what were in his view the emasculating and asocial, and thus immoral, effects of a romantic or Cooperian approach and to establish a patriarchal system for the protection of women, Indians, and blacks within the South and within the nation as a whole. This approach is particularly apparent in *The Wigwam and the Cabin* (1845), Simms's finest collection of short stories. Whereas Cooper's sentimental intermediary, Natty Bumppo, dies as a symbol of the lost middle ground, the Southern patriarch of Simms's tales emerges as the linchpin for a hierarchical society in which racial violence is held in check only through his sympathetic authority.

"The Two Camps" as the Key to *The Wigwam and the Cabin*

Simms's determination to offer a Southern contribution or corrective to national history and literature contributed then and contributes now to his isolation as a sectional author. Yet Simms's patriarchal, Southern revision of the moving encounter, based on his belief that violence in the frontiers of his home region contributed to national unity, deserves rereading for its elucidation of the relationship between the Indian Question and the slavery debate that divided the nation. From the mid-1830s, Simms could alternately be described as an established and an embattled author. *The Yemassee* (1835), his historical romance based on a 1715 Indian war in South Carolina, was immensely popular, going through three printings in its first year. Yet over the next few years the Panic of 1837 and the increasing ease and cost effectiveness of publishing paperbacks and transporting proof sheets from Britain so damaged the market for two-volume novels that Simms grudgingly turned to other genres.[11] Likewise, Simms's fruitful trip to New York City in 1832—during which he met such luminaries as William Cullen Bryant, Edwin Forrest, James Kirke Paulding, and James Lawson (with whom he shared a lifelong correspondence)—accompanied the demise of his newspaper, the *Charleston City Gazette*, which was due to his unpopular support of Jackson during the Nullification Crisis.[12] Simms's affinity with the Young America project, and in particular his relationship with Evert Duyckinck, led to the publication of *The Wigwam and the Cabin* but also to public criticisms of Simms's style by Whiggish writers. Beginning in the 1840s, Simms moved away from a section-informed national literature to expressions of Southern nationalism in response to increasing attacks on Southern society, and he did so in part through explicit revision of the moving encounter both within and portrayed by his works. Simms's Southern nationalism ultimately prompted his break with Young America and his exclusion from the mainstream American literary canon. Louis D. Rubin writes, "Simms *was* a Jacksonian Democrat; he *became* an apologist for the plantation system. In that transaction is to be found much of the meaning of antebellum Southern literature."[13]

Simms composed the thirteen stories of *The Wigwam and the Cabin* in the context of conflicting calls for a national literature made by the Knickerbocker circle and Young America,[14] experiments in sectional literature (such as southwestern humor), national discord regarding the place of racial minorities within a democracy, and financial crises personal and national. Simms continued to write short stories in the years 1842–51, perhaps because they still sold in the tough economy, yet he struggled to find a publisher for *The Wigwam and the Cabin* and subsequently failed to find one for a companion work.[15] After asking numerous publishers, Simms's friendship with Duyckinck helped him place the two-volume collection with Wiley and Putnam in their Library of American Books, a series that includes Edgar Allan Poe's *Tales* (1845) and Nathaniel Hawthorne's *Mosses* from an Old Manse (1846). The first volume, or series, of *The Wigwam and the Cabin* appeared in October 1845, the second in February 1846, and they received positive reviews in the *Democratic Review* and the *Broadway Journal* (by Poe) but a scathing one in the *Knickerbocker*.[16] Simms's stories expose the violent interactions of people of different races, cultures, genders, and classes in the humble and transient abodes of the region, and their publishing history highlights the controversy surrounding the production of uniquely American literature in a nation struggling to make sense of the racial violence within its borders.

The second story of the collection, "The Two Camps. A Legend of the Old North State," provides an excellent introduction to Simms's vision of the Southern frontiers, such that Guilds suggests, "The story probably surpasses all others in *The Wigwam and the Cabin*, when measured in terms of artistic accomplishment and the significance of its insight into life on the American frontier."[17] It also provides a key to Simms's larger revision of the moving encounter within the Southern context. Originally published in 1843 in *The Gift for 1844*, "The Two Camps" is set in the mid-eighteenth century, around the time of the Cherokee War when a preemptive strike on the Cherokee by Carolina forces in 1759 led to two years of warfare that concluded with a large Cherokee land cession. However, the tale's focus on Cherokee factionalism resonates with the violence among the displaced Cherokee people after forced removal from Georgia in 1838–39, and in particular the retributive assassinations of Major Ridge, John Ridge, and Elias Boudinot, prominent signers of the June 22, 1839, Treaty of New Echota.[18] The tale also uses the comic hero of southwestern humor to puncture sentimental spectatorship in the presence of violence, suggesting that rapid change in the region requires manly vigor and the ascendance of white authority.

Daniel Nelson, an old frontiersman, tells the story "in his own words," after an introduction in which Simms/the narrator tells us that unlike other stories folks have shared with him, this one reports no "mere brutality" but instead an eerie and stirring experience of conflict between and among Cherokee and Euro-Americans "on the southern borders of North Carolina."[19] One night, on suspicion that local Indians are "becoming discontented," Daniel sets out, leaving his wife, Betsy, and his children in their cabin. He soon comes across the blood-chilling scene of a young white woman held captive by Indians at their campfire (WC 34). Hurling himself toward the captors, Daniel finds that the image is only an illusion. Inevitable conflict apparently haunts this land and does not take long to materialize. On the way home, Daniel stumbles upon another ghastly scene that is only too real: an unconscious young Cherokee boy with a bloody head wound. Daniel, compelled to intervene, uses his great strength to haul the boy home on his back (the subject of a prominent illustration in the collection), and the Nelson family nurses the boy, Lenatewá, back to health. This rescue is fortuitous, for Lenatewá's presence in their home thwarts a retributive attack by the party of Lenatewá's father, who mistakenly believes that whites have killed his son. Years later, during the Cherokee War, Daniel's daughter Lucy is taken captive, and Daniel discovers her in a camp mirroring his vision of years earlier, only "this time," Daniel comments, "it was a raal one" (*WC* 48). Lenatewá helps Daniel rescue Lucy by distracting the bulk of her captors, and subsequently Lenatewá courts the young woman. But the story closes with the murder of Lenatewá by a rival Cherokee party as he walks in the woods with his young love. Southwestern North Carolina is a violent land in which even lovers are not immune to the conflict between inhabitants, but more important, in which Indian-white attachments are destined to fail. In an oddly displaced lament for the departure of Cherokee, Simms emphasizes the necessity to embrace an active response to violence rather than a passively emotional one.

The rough-and-tumble Daniel Nelson, who saves Lenatewá, otherwise appears overwhelmed by his discoveries of brutality, describing them as moments of passive sentimental spectatorship reminiscent of Lydia Maria Child's experience viewing American Indians at Barnum's American Museum.[20] Daniel reports that when looking upon the first of the two camps, the illusory one, he "was weak as any child" and further that he "cried like a child." Shaken to the core by the spectacle of the white woman captive, Daniel tells us that he "never was in such a fix of fear and weakness in my life," and finally that he acts only from "a sort of madness growing out of my scare" (*WC* 38–39). Daniel's emasculated behavior—his overwhelming emotions and subsequent incapacity for action—makes sense in the context of the dreamlike vision, which brought on a temporary madness. Yet years later upon seeing the "raal" camp where Lucy is held, Daniel responds similarly. "That was a sight for a father," he declares. "I can't tell you—and I won't try—how I felt. . . . I lay so for a good half hour, I reckon, without stirring a limb; and you could only tell that life was in me, by seeing the big drops that squeezed out of my eyes now and then, and by a sort of shivering that shook me as you sometimes see the canebrake shaking with the gust of the pond inside." Daniel realizes he can "do nothing by looking," voicing a common criticism of sentimental spectatorship, but it takes Lenatewá to stir him with the harsh words, "Be man!" (*WC* 49). The spectacle of his suffering daughter literally unmans Daniel Nelson, a hero who earlier wrestles a bear, in the manner of Daniel Boone. In fact, before encountering either spectacle of captivity, Daniel describes himself as "wolfish" when faced with the possibility of Indian attacks (*WC* 36, 47). In this portrayal, Simms employs the characteristic comedy of popular southwestern humor pieces through his creation of a frontier hero who is both aggressive and sensitive. But he also uses Daniel as another example of faction in this region: the races battle, but so too do the individual's emotions. Sympathy and fear unman the frontier hero, and his Cherokee companion understands that he must subdue his tears to protect Lucy.[21]

Yet Daniel continues to act as a sentimental observer in the presence of Indians and violent dissent, recalling the carefully observant Natty Bumppo of *The Prai-*

rie, whom Ishmael rebukes as partaking in "the business of women in the towns and settlements."[22] When Lenatewá's party receives the long-lost son in front of the Nelson household, they celebrate his unexpected return and angrily respond to the news that the boy's uncle, "the black chief" of a related but smaller party of Cherokee, has betrayed Lenatewá. Throughout these exchanges, Daniel eagerly watches through the "loop-hole" of his cabin, a militarily strategic opening in the façade also associated with vision afforded by artistic retreat.[23] From this perspective at once defensive and contemplative, he excitedly recounts for the reader the black chief's assassination: "He had not got twenty steps when a dozen arrows went into him, and he tumbled for'a'ds, and grappled with the earth" (*WC* 44). Years later Daniel watches through the very same loop-hole as Lenatewá courts Lucy, and again the vision stirs him: "Then I thought, if there is any picture in this life more sweet and beautiful than two young people jest beginning to feel love for one another, and walking together in the innocence of their hearts, under the shady trees,—I've never seen it! I laid the rifle on my lap, and sat down on the floor and watched 'em through the loop until I felt the water in my eyes." Daniel again puts aside his masculine potential for violence in a moment of overwhelming sympathy, resembling nothing so much as the spectator of a melodrama. But "in the twinkle of an eye" the tender scene changes as Oloschotte and the treacherous Cherokee party emerge from the woods and kill Lenatewá with tomahawk blows, "once, twice, three times" to the head (*WC* 55). The graphic intratribal murders Daniel views from his home indicate that in this land where people wage war for existence, homes will become battlefields, burly men will weep over teenage romance, and the Cherokee nation will continue to suffer from murderous division.

Referring most obviously to the two scenes of white female captivity, the title "The Two Camps" also indicates the proliferation of opposing forces throughout the region. The spiritual world holds sway over material man, Euro-Americans and American Indians battle for living space, domestic Lucy wins the heart of savage Lenatewá, and Lenatewá and Oloschotte lead conflicting Cherokee bands. These oppositions clearly extend through the loophole, into the home, and deter the perpetuation of families; before Lenatewá's murder, Betsy Nelson rejects the possible marriage of Lucy and Lenatewá, and afterwards Lucy refuses ever to marry, her heart broken by the loss of her true love. Throughout the story, Simms depicts the conflict of emotions as well: individuals experience quick fluctuations between sympathy and hatred, aggression and compassion, and violence haunts individuals as well as the land itself. This conflict occurs because the rampant discord of the region impinges on the domestic space, which Simms celebrates throughout his oeuvre as the sanctuary of communal, familial sentiments. As its first chapter emphasizes, "The Two Camps" does not offer an ordinary story of violence by any means because Daniel "breathes life into his deeds" so that "in lieu of the dead body of the fact, we have its living spirit—

subtle, active, breathing and burning, and fresh in all the provocations and associations of life" (WC 33). Simms claims to resurrect the victims of the story
through the emotional and even ridiculous narration of Daniel, the sentimental
intermediary who brings the reader face-to-face with them. At the same time, he
dramatizes how father, mother, daughter, guest, home, and all associated feelings are subject to violence, and for this reason, the passive sentimental response
is naïve, unmanly, and dangerous. Sympathy is not doomed in this region, it is
dooming—and must be controlled.

Simms, National History, and the South

In a recent reconsideration of Simms's work, Sean R. Busick asserts, "Simms can
only be understood when he is understood as a historian. He certainly thought
of himself as a historian." Without doubt the tales of *The Wigwam and the Cabin*
illustrate Simms's theory of history, and more specifically of historical progress
and the moral function of historiography. Like many of his contemporaries,
Simms assumed that the passage of time brings material progress to human
society, but only through occasional conflict. David Moltke-Hansen explains,
"Simms's philosophy of history revolved between two poles: progress and order.
In his view, political, social, and cultural progress required political, social, and
cultural stability. He held the converse to be true as well: social, cultural, and
political stability required social, cultural, and political progress. Revolutions oc-
curred when stability was maintained at the expense of progress or *vice versa*."[24]
Progress, in this Hegelian perspective, arises from the synthesis of, or compromise between, competing systems or actors; however, a process depending on
synthesis, Simms held, "must be mediated by reason and moderation," and more
specifically, overseen by those endowed with greater reason and restraint to
whom others properly submit. Yet because human reason is not failsafe, because
even those endowed with remarkable intelligence and leadership make mistakes,
Simms "separated moral from material advancement" and concluded that "morality might spin in revolutions between progress and decline while wealth and
technology continued to flourish."[25] In the context of a larger historiographic
and ethnographic discourse that described American Indians and African Americans as exemplifying the earlier stages of human development, Simms came to
ask whether leaders, the guardians of moral progress, were properly governing
American Indians and African Americans to the benefit of the greater society.

The military conflicts, interracial communities, and burgeoning plantation
system of the Southern frontiers naturally informed and embodied Simms's vision of historical progress on the North American continent. He continually re-
conceptualized the Euro-American patriarch who would emerge to bring order
to the region and examined those who already served as leaders.[26] As my reading of "The Two Camps" shows, Simms was also interested in the evolution of

domestic and patriarchal cultures in the region, avoiding the simple romance of the "vanished Indian," or even the romantic hero, and depicting instead a region characterized by factionalism at every level. His works point to his search for those who brought order to events, who made history through the assertion of a moral, manly leadership.

In 1846 and 1847, Simms published the two-volume *Views and Reviews in American Literature, History and Fiction* under the auspices of the Wiley and Putnam Library of America. *Views and Reviews*, which Hugh Holman calls "a virtual manifesto in the Young America literary wars of the 1840's," contains journal essays by Simms promoting literary nationalism and assessing the current state of American literature.[27] In the lengthy "Epochs and Events of American History," Simms argues that one best examines historical process in literature because the literary artist "unites the parts in coherent dependency, and endows, with life and action, the otherwise motionless automata of history." "It is by such artists, indeed," Simms confidently declares, "that nations live." It is by such artists that nations, moreover, learn what is right, for literature dramatizes moral decision-making, proper social relations, admirable faith, and ideal national life. Simms's desire to restore a Southern element to national history springs from his moral project; he offers Southern historical examples for the edification of readers and defends his increasingly embattled position as a proslavery intellectual.[28]

Simms was particularly committed to recovering the Southern role in the founding of the United States. Between 1850 and 1866, Simms published five novels set in the region during the Revolutionary War, each of which found a parallel between past and present, "the Compromise of 1850, the Fugitive Slave Act, Secession, and, following the Civil War, the Lost Cause."[29] In his novels, political writings, and oratory of this era, Simms challenged Northern assertions that slave-holding South Carolina had been dominated by loyalists during the war; specifically, he responded in an 1848 article and an 1853 book to Lorenzo Sabine's damning account of South Carolina during the war, *The American Loyalists* (1847), and in 1856 set out on a lecture tour in the North in which he would defend his home state's reputation. In this period of sectional tension, he asserted that only through bloodshed does a nation achieve affective unity. Starting in abolitionist New York State, Simms was surprised to face hostile audiences and soon ended the tour; nonetheless, he persisted in his endeavor to restore Southern history and sectional conflict to their vital positions in national history.[30]

This philosophy Simms applied in the decade before the Civil War took root in his fiction of the removal era, and in this way the figure of the moving encounter contributed to his theories of history and a section-based literary nationalism. Set during the Yamassee War, a 1715–17 conflict in South Carolina between Anglo-American colonists and an alliance of American Indians, *The Yemassee* presents stock characters of the American historical romance—the bigoted Puritan minister, the rosy-cheeked virgin, the eloquent Indian, and the disaffected romantic youth—along with figures representing the variety of communities in the region—American Indians, Irish settlers, Spanish pirates, African slaves, and Anglo aristocrats. These characters, with their Southern qualities and social roles, lend more than local color to the work; their presence fleshes out the novel's social vision of a natural aristocracy attentive to racial difference and the project of civilization. Compare Simms's vision (as many do) to New Yorker Cooper's.[31] The hero Natty Bumppo dwells on the outskirts of both savagery and civilization as a friend of endangered American Indians and rescuer of white women he will not marry. In the first three Leatherstocking Tales, as I argue in the previous chapter, Natty Bumppo represents the passing of the middle ground through the failure of his sympathetic mediation and his burial on the prairie. Although the hero of *The Yemassee*, Gabriel Harrison (a.k.a. Lord Governor Charles Craven), similarly makes settlement possible through his valiant actions, he has every intention of leading the colonial civilization. Craven serves as an engine of historical progress—he is, in Simms's words, one of the "few minds always in advance, and for ever preparing the way for society, even sacrificing themselves nobly, that the species may have victory."[32] Simms has no illusions about the nature of this historical agent's power, identifying Craven as a member of the class of men who "become the tyrants of all the rest, and, as there are two kinds of tyranny in the world, they either enslave to cherish or to destroy" (*Y* 201). Enslaving to cherish—that is, to "civilize"—and asserting individual authority to protect collective liberty, Craven resembles not the maternal or avuncular intermediaries of Child's and Cooper's fiction but the Southern patriarch Andrew Jackson. Craven demonstrates, that is, the proper moral action of the American leader who would welcome conflict and bring about resolution with his own sword if necessary.[33]

Craven additionally demonstrates his patriarchal role, his governance of a world in which families are the building blocks of nations and the nation itself is a family. While Natty Bumppo hunts with Chingachgook and comforts him after the loss of his son Uncas, the relationship of Craven and his slave Hector resembles that of father and son. Craven's mastery of Hector encompasses the slave's heart and affections, and Craven declares, "He's the very prince of body servants, and loves me, I verily believe, as I do my mistress" (*Y* 105). Evidence of the effectiveness of Craven's rule lies in his ability to secure the proper devotion of his charge. Family relations are without a doubt important throughout the romance as a sign of cultural and national unity, for Simms believed that the history of familial relations, and in particular the history of "the patriarchal life—the first life of civilization," provided excellent material for romances. In "The Epochs and Events of American History," he asks to this end, "Where now are those glowing pictures over which our eyes have glistened—those holy traits of unbending patriotism and of undying love—of maternal courage, and of filial sacrifice—of a valor that knew not self, and of an endurance that confessed no pain?"[34] Such "glowing pictures" all exist in *The Yemassee*, calculated to make readers' eyes glisten and readers' hearts accept the authority of Simms's model patriarch.

Conflict in *The Yemassee* arises from and within American Indian and Anglo-American families. Thus, the Reverend and Mrs. Matthews disagree whether their daughter Bess should marry Harrison/Craven; the brothers Hugh and Walter Grayson disagree over the benefits of individualism and collectivism; the trader Granger and his wife have conflicting notions of military strategy; and most significantly, the warlike Yemassee chief Sanutee will not heed the pleas of his wife, Matiwan, to forgive their drunken son, Occonestoga, for his alliance with the Anglo-Americans. Occonestoga's punishment for treachery is simultaneously familial and national—and thoroughly heart-wrenching: "Go,—" the young Yemassee women chant during the ceremony of his punishment, "thou hast no wife in Yemassee—thou hast given no lodge to the daughter of Yemassee—thou hast slain no meat for thy children. Thou hast no name—the women of Yemassee know thee no more" (*Y* 195). Yet Matiwan uses her authority as mother to circumvent national justice when, rather than witness the removal of his Yemassee tattoo and his subsequent death-in-life (without the tattoo, he will no longer be a Yemassee or have access to the afterlife), she drives a tomahawk into his head. "He is not lost—he is not lost," she cries. "They may not take the child from his mother. They may not keep him from the valley of Manneyto. He is free—he is free" (*Y* 200). Matiwan later saves Craven from imprisonment and subsequent execution with similar maternal care, asking him, "The chief of the English—the pale mother loves him over the water?" (*Y* 281). He reassures her that she does, and that he loves his mother in return. Because family life exemplifies public life and family life requires and perpetuates cultural practice, South Carolinians cannot unite as a family until cultural-racial difference is controlled by the father figure. After the Reverend Matthews prays for "one flock of all classes and colours, all tribes and nations" united under Christ, Craven responds with the reasoning of Thomas Jefferson, "Until they shall adopt our pursuits, or we theirs, we can never form the one community for which your prayer is sent up; and so long as the hunting lands are abundant, the seductions of that mode of life will always baffle the approach of civilization among the Indians" (*Y* 134). If families are dismantled, orphaned members either disappear or, adopted by the governing patriarch, step into the victorious nation-family. Indian-white sympathy is not so much doomed as it is reformed by patriarchal benevolence. Hence, after the death of Matiwan's husband and son and the majority of the Yemassee, Craven and attending slaves "bore her tenderly away" (*Y* 413). The moving encounter of readers with Simms's representative Yemassee family ideally concludes with the readers' parallel commitment to tending feminized Indian charges.

From Simms's perspective, *The Yemassee* is not an exclusively South Carolin-

ian or Southern novel any more than Cooper's Leatherstocking Tales pertain
solely to the history of New York or the mid-Atlantic region. Simms believed
his attention to the local served national ends, and what we might call his increasing sectionalism from the 1830s to the 1850s resulted from his conviction
that the Southern social structure was best for American progress and from the
very real sense that it was embattled. The stories of *The Wigwam and the Cabin,*
written or revised during the decade following the publication of *The Yemassee,*
directly report Simms's developing theories regarding race relations in the South
and the proper solution to the Indian Question and the slavery debate in the nation. Simms dramatizes historical conflict and its solution, proposing that in the
rough-and-tumble world of the Southern frontiers one could find the essence
of America—a proposal Poe accepted in his review of the collection, declaring, "This is one of the most interesting of the Library [of American Books]
yet published—and decidedly the most American of the American books." [35] In
The Wigwam and the Cabin, even more so than in *The Yemassee,* Simms traces historical progress as emerging from conflict between factions and from the strong
sympathy of the Southern patriarch.

No Happily Ever After

Despite his concern with historical accuracy, Simms included in *The Wigwam
and the Cabin* "Indian" stories that resemble fairy tales, echoing the treatment
of Native oral traditions in Schoolcraft's collection *Algic Researches* (1839). [36]
These tales that establish local legends and lessons about human relationships
imagine national unity achieved through American Indian *genius loci* and bring
Euro-American audiences into direct encounters with exotic American Indians.
Yet even fables set in Indian country contribute to Simms's larger project of establishing the proper control of the white patriarch; these tales encourage the
reader to associate the relationship between American Indians husbands and
wives with that between the United States and the American Indians "within"
its borders.

"Jocassée: A Cherokee Legend" originally appeared in *The Gift for 1837* (1836)
and recounts a commonly popularized North American Indian legend of star-
crossed lovers whose demise imprints the landscape. [37] A young woman named
Jocassée and the handsome youth Nagoochie fall in love, thwarting the enmity
of their respective warring Cherokee parties, the Occonies (Brown Vipers) and
Estatoees (Green Birds). Their courtship occurs as Jocassée nurses Nagoochie
back to health after a hunting accident on Occony hunting grounds. When
Nagoochie kills the most ferocious wolf at a great Cherokee wolf hunt, he is told
to select a bride from the group of Cherokee women and enrages the Occonies
by choosing Jocassée (*WC* 178). Subsequently, the Occonies pick a fight with
the Estatoees and a vengeful Occony warrior strikes down Nagoochie while he

is disadvantaged in battle. Upon hearing the story of the Occony victory and Nagoochie's death, Jocassée falls over the side of her boat ("whether by accident or design") and drowns in the river (*WC* 184).

Readers of Simms's story, much like Daniel Nelson of the "Two Camps," gaze upon the young lovers' deaths with tear-filled eyes, again mourning the victims of Indian faction. But unlike Lucy and Lenatewá, Jocassée and Nagoochie are reunited in the spiritual world; legend tells us, writes Simms, that the lovers live in "a beautiful lodge" in "one of the most select in the valleys of Manneyto" (*WC* 185). The violence of their earthly separation leaves a direct historical trace as the river in northwest South Carolina becomes the Jocassée. This story is one of Simms's "literary myths of place" through which he sought "to provide a kind of mythical charter for Indian place-names" and consequently harnessed the myth of the doomed Indian for national purposes. Simms used the story of Jocassée as representative of Southern history in his failed 1856 lecture tour; thus, writes John D. Kerkering, "a personification that initially marked the absence of the Cherokee nation comes, in Simms's later writings, to mark the identity of a specific people, Southerners." [38] The authenticity and accuracy of this "Cherokee legend" are not as clear as Simms would have them be; Peter G. Murphy suggests that Simms may have borrowed elements of the tale from Henry Rowe Schoolcraft and Jane Johnston Schoolcraft's "Leelinau, or The Lost Daughter," a transcription/translation of an Ojibwe oral tradition that reflects the intricacies of the ethnographers' marriage and professional collaboration. Simms crafts the tragic tale of thwarted love—one of his many narratives of star-crossed lovers in prose and poetry—as another piece in his moral-historical narrative of a region marked by conflict. [39]

In contrast to Jocassée, who exemplifies the generous, feminine caregiver, Macourah, from another Indian "legend," "The Arm-Chair of Tustenuggee. A Tradition of the Catawba," exemplifies "the virago wife" who would repel men from familial connections and domestic life and thus upset national order. Macourah's husband, Conatee, and his handsome young hunting partner, Selonee, develop a close "intimacy" that does not disturb Macourah because she is attracted to her husband's friend (*WC* 94). On one excursion, Conatee swims across a river to pursue a boar-wolf he has wounded while Selonee kills a ferocious she-wolf. When Conatee does not return, Selonee pursues him. He does so in vain, however, for "Tustenuggee, the Grey Demon of Enoree" has encased Conatee within a tree (*WC* 107), and as this "Arm-Chair of Tustenuggee" holds Conatee captive, Selonee faces charges of murder. Unable to acquit himself, Selonee accepts a fate worse than death: marriage to Macourah, who "was now doubly hateful to him as his own wife" and fills him with "a loathing sensation of disgust" (*WC* 108–9). One fateful day Macourah pursues Selonee through the woods and stops to rest on the Arm-Chair. Tustenuggee swaps prisoners, Macourah replaces Conatee within the wood-prison, and Conatee returns to the village without revealing Macourah's captivity. Years later his son innocently chops apart the Arm-Chair "until the entire but unconnected members of the old squaw became visible" (WC 113). As in "Rip Van Winkle," marriage is a domestic prison—captivity by armchair—so the hen-pecked man takes refuge in a forest, and the nagging wife's anger leads to her own demise. "The Arm-Chair of Tustenuggee" may very well be a homage to Washington Irving's tale or a reworking of a Knickerbocker story in a Young America–inspired, American Indian vein.

Also as in "Rip Van Winkle," though more explicitly, Simms draws a connection between hunting and the masculine escape from the feminine realm. As Conatee fatefully pursues the boar-wolf, Selonee grapples with the she-wolf, finally driving a knife from her belly up to the breast bone. Simms offers a graphic description of Selonee's subsequent actions: "It was then, while she [the wolf] lay writhing and rolling upon the ground in the agonies of death, that he tore the heart from the opening he had made, and hurled it down to the cubs, who seized it with avidity. This done, he patted and caressed them, and while they struggled about him for the meat, he cut a fork in the ears of each, and putting the slips in his pouch, left the young ones without further hurt, for the future sport of the hunter" (WC 98). After brutally killing the she-wolf, the soon-to-be-unhappily-married Selonee perverts parental roles by feeding nurslings their mother's heart and marking (or circumcising) them only in preparation for later death. For many readers then and now the violence of the story is apparently absorbed by the comic treatment of the virago wife; it first appeared in 1840 in Godey's Lady's Book, a purveyor of domestic fiction, and Guilds calls it "a delightful comic story that gently mocks human foibles." [40] But the story dwells on the wife who tortures rather than attends her husband and the husband who, in response, imprisons and destroys the wife rather than suffer constraint. Even the story's punch line emphasizes the necessity of controlling the nagging woman: Conatee realizes that Selonee has told his beloved wife about the Arm-Chair and concludes, "Had he been a wise man he would have kept his secret, and then there would have been no difficulty in getting rid of a wicked wife" (WC 114). The two camps in this Simms story are gendered, as emasculation incites violence and marital propriety requires the assertion of masculine control. Likewise, foolish, inactive sympathy with American Indians upsets the racial hierarchy of a nation unified through conflict. As with Daniel Nelson of "The Two Camps," sometimes men need reminding.

"With a guiding hand and unyielding sway"

Multiple tales in The Wigwam and the Cabin convey Simms's formulation of the proper relation between the white patriarch and his charges through the depiction of interaction between slaves and Indians in the plantation setting. Clearly inspired by his 1824–25, 1826, and 1831 trips to an old Southwest "inhabited by Choctaw tribesmen, African slaves, fortune-seeking whites, renegades of all races, and exotic animals,"[41] these tales exhibit Simms's desire to record historical struggles on the way to social stability. Simms's attention to the diversity of the region had roots in his impulse toward realism and in his conviction that the progress of racially inferior groups depended on the willingness of Euro-Americans to enslave them. In "Miss Martineau on Slavery" (1837), a widely heralded a response to the British abolitionist Harriet Martineau's condemnation of Southern slavery in *Society in America* (1837), Simms maintains that labor and property drive civilization and that "the slaveholders of the south," who compel members of inferior cultures to cultivate rather than hunt, "are the great moral conservators, in one powerful interest, of the entire world."[42] (In *The Yemassee*, even the slaves recognize this truth; Hector pleads to remain Craven's slave, "De ting aint right; and enty I know wha' kind of ting freedom is wid black man? Ha! you make Hector free, he turn wuss more nor poor buckrah" [*Y* 397].) Slave owners help maintain a society structured through inequality and should extend their control over American Indians. For, Simms contends, "The inferior people must fly from the presence, or perish before the march of approaching civilization." Because the Indians of his region avoid labor even to the point of making their women menials, Simms concludes, "It is no less the duty, than the necessity, therefore, of civilization, to overcome these tribes;—to force the tasks of life upon them—to compel their labor—to teach them the arts of economy and providence; and with a guiding hand and unyielding sway, conduct them to the moral Pisgah, from whence they may behold the lovely and inviting Canaan of a higher and holier condition, spread out before them, and praying them to come." From this providential perspective, "removal is but a small and partial evil, in comparison with the many evils which must follow upon their stay," and all cultural-racial inferiors remaining in the region should submit physically to the Euro-American master.[43] Indeed, in "Literature and Art among the American Aborigines"—a positive review of Schoolcraft's *Algic Researches* (1839) and *Oneóta, or The Red Race of America* (1845) included in *Views and Reviews*—Simms names as "the secret cause of the moral improvement of the Cherokees" the fact that Creeks "whipt them into close limits, where they were compelled to labour, —and labour, —a blessing born of a penalty, —is the fruitful mother of all the nobler exercises of humanity." In addition, the Martineau review concludes with the observation that slavery has made blacks intellectually superior to Indians in the Carolinas.[44] Simms's proposal to take control of American Indian laborers both depends on and obscures the history of American Indian slavery and slave ownership in the southeastern United States. The federal government ended the Indian slave trade only after the Revolution, and American Indian societies participated in a variety of "'incorporation' and 'subordination'" processes, including servitude and slavery. Most prominently, by the nineteenth century many members of the Cherokee nation adopted plantation agricultural modes, including the use of slaves, and Cherokee slaves were removed alongside their masters. By the removal era Cherokee and Creek cultures distinguished between themselves and African Americans and adopted the concept of a racial hierarchy.[45] Perhaps in recognition of these developments, Simms explicitly places whites at the top of the heap.

Two stories in *The Wigwam and the Cabin* emphasize the necessity of slavery or removal to resolving the Indian Question.[46] "Oakatibbé, or the Choctaw Sampson" tells a story about Choctaw blood revenge that Simms heard during his 1824–25 trip to lower Mississippi and worked on for decades, first in poetry and later in prose, publishing the story in *Family Companion* in 1841 and subsequently in *The Wigwam and the Cabin*.[47] Set in the "great south-west" during the 1820s, when the Choctaw Confederation signed a removal treaty (*WC* 139), "Oakatibbé" begins with a Simms-like character and host, Colonel Harris, discussing the latter's experiment on his "new but rude plantation settlements": he "turn[s] to account the lazy Choctaws by whom he was surrounded," by hiring them as supplemental laborers for cotton picking (*WC* 140, 141). Harris, who serves as the guide to this region for the narrator as well as the reader, plans not just to profit by this arrangement (it will prevent him from buying more slaves and selling them later at a loss) but to reform the Choctaws. Harris and the narrator agree that American Indians will not become civilized until they are made to labor regularly and, more specifically, the men made to labor at least as much as the women (*WC* 143). But in Harris's experiment, only the Choctaw women, children, and elderly work—with the exception of one man, Oakatibbé. For this reason, the black slaves who work alongside the Choctaw people "felt their superiority in nearly every physical and intellectual respect, over the untutored savages" (*WC* 142). The narrator insists that without communal change, without coercion of the entire Choctaw nation, no individual will be civilized. "It cannot be tried upon an individual: it must be tried on a nation—at least upon a community,...under the full control of an already civilized people," he argues (*WC* 145–46). In making his case, he corrects Harrison's reading of Philip Freneau's "The Indian Student: or, Force of Nature" (1788), a poem that recounts the return of an Indian boy to his Indian life after education at Harvard because, the narrator insists, his isolation within civilization increased his attraction to Indian life.[48] We do observe Harris's effective use of his authority in chastising Loblolly Jack, an unruly Choctaw man who attempts to interfere with the weighing of the pickers' cotton, and Oakatibbé, who threatens to fight Jack; but Harris's control is sadly temporary. As the narrator insists, "They were not subordinate; they were not subdued," and this makes all the difference (*WC* 151).

Not surprisingly, because of Simms's theory, the isolated Oakatibbé fails to become a leader of the Choctaw people, and Harris's experiment tragically fails. As the only Choctaw man in his prime who seeks employment on the plantation,

Oakatibbé is subjected to Loblolly Jack's ridicule but not to Harris's guidance at the trader's shop where liquor is sold. When Jack harasses a drunken Oakatibbé, a fight ensues and Oakatibbé kills him. In what Hudson confirms is an accurate portrayal of Choctaw blood revenge,[49] the community immediately condemns Oakatibbé to die. He briefly rejects this tradition by accepting Harris's offer of a horse to flee the night before the execution, but the guilty man returns the next morning ready to accept Choctaw justice rather than Euro-American benevolence. "Custom," the narrator points out, "is the superior tyrant of all savage nations" (*WC* 160). The would-be tyrants, the benevolent Euro-Americans, become sentimental spectators at the execution, "with a degree of emotion which I would not now seek to describe" (*WC* 165). This emotional elision—so similar to Daniel Nelson's insistence, "I can't tell you—and I won't try—how I felt"— signals a lack of strength, a sympathetic response devoid of manly action. While one critic argues that Oakatibbé's return is heroic and signals a strain of cultural relativism in Simms's maturing social philosophy, in the eyes of the narrator and Harris, the Choctaw Sampson repeats the mistake of his Biblical namesake and of Freneau's Indian student.[50] Oakatibbé betrays the Choctaws by yielding to his weakness and then observing their forms of justice. Until Harris takes absolute control of his American Indian neighbors, their culture will never progress and they will never produce their own leader. The story concludes with the narrator's frustrated observation, "under other more favouring circumstances, [Oakatibbé] might have been a father to his nation" (*WC* 165).

"Caloya; or, the Loves of the Driver" provides a more involved comparison of American Indians and African slaves in the Carolinas of twenty years earlier.[51] Without the oversight of Euro-Americans, the Catawba Indians lead an itinerant life of peddling, coming to the Carolina coast annually so the women may dig clay and make culinary pots to sell locally. A nostalgic young planter, Colonel Gillison, allows one Catawba couple, Richard Knuckles, or Enefisto, and his wife, Caloya, to set up camp on his land because, he says, "the 'Red Gulley' is the place where they have been getting their clay ever since my grandfather settled this plantation" (*WC* 295). Gillison's black driver, Mingo Gillison, at first opposes this kindness but softens as soon as he sees Caloya, "one of the comeliest squaws that had ever enchanted the eyes of the Driver" (*WC* 299). A womanizer, Mingo pursues Caloya vigorously and plies Knuckle with Gillison's liquor and meat. *Mingo*, as Simms learned on his travel in Choctaw country, is both Choctaw for tribal leader and a derogatory term for Indian among whites, and as Moltke-Hansen notes, its resemblance to *Mandingo* possibly points to the driver's West African origins.[52] The irony of the driver's multivalent name is twofold: this African slave seeks to usurp the place of a degraded Indian, and his Indian label makes him subject to two forms of racist derision. Though "no Desdemona could have been more certainly true to her liege lord"—though no wife could more appropriately fill her role—soon Knuckles becomes intensely jealous and constructs a plot to murder this lord in slave's clothing (*WC* 302). The situation of Indians and blacks in the plantation system leads to violence because Mingo has been entrusted by his decidedly naïve master with great authority and Knuckles, as "a borderer of the white settlements," has become "a most wretched dependent, and that, too, upon his women" (*WC* 303). The tension between the races stems, Simms argues through the dialect-laden speech of Mingo, from the fundamental differences in their labor practices and economic status. "How you show you got freedom," Mingo asks Knuckles, "when here you expen' 'pon poor woman for work your pot, and half de time you got not'ing to put in 'em. Now, I is free man! Cause, you see my pot is always full, and when I does my work like a gempleman,—who cares? I laughs at mossa jist the same as I laughs at you" (*WC* 309). A driver and trickster in one, Mingo argues that Knuckle's freedom is illusory in an economy dependent on steady agricultural work. Mingo embraces another key element of "freedom" for the minority in this culture: accepting plantation ideology and cultivating a relationship with the Euro-American patriarch.

Just as he notes the failure of Colonel Harris in "Oakatibbé" to intervene successfully on behalf of the Choctaw Sampson, Simms underscores the foolishness of Gillison for giving any slave, even one as intelligent as Mingo, such leverage on the plantation.[53] The presence of the Catawba couple, and in particular of the degraded Knuckles, threatens Mingo's remaining subservience. Mingo's pride—its high point coming when he declares to Knuckles, "I'm the master!" (*WC* 301)—leads him to steal from Gillison's stores with impunity and finally to "trampl[e], with the ingenious pains-taking of a willful boy," the many pots Caloya has made (*WC* 319). Knuckles assaults Mingo at the close of the story and undermines the driver's claims of superiority. Although at the beginning of the story Mingo "trod the earth very much as its Lord" (*WC* 292), during the fight he oversees his own enslaved body and fuses the African and Indian races, crying, "Oh you d—n black red-skin, you kill mossa best nigger!" (*WC* 340). Further, the appearance of Mingo's wronged and furious wife, Diana, who proceeds to attack Caloya, belies Mingo's assertion all along that "a black Gentleman is always more 'spectable to a woman than an Indian" (*WC* 307). The marital chaos is part and parcel of racial chaos on the plantation. During the course of the story and Mingo's increasing ridiculousness, blacks and Indians become theoretically aligned and the story's denouement reestablishes the dichotomy necessary to the plantation society: white over color.

Only the reassertion of Gillison's control—he pays for Caloya's lost pots and demotes Mingo—halts a chaotic orgy of violence in the wigwam. Though he does not enslave the Catawba couple and their people (such enslavement is not a possibility in the historically grounded story, even if it is Simms's ideal) Gillison celebrates Caloya's escape from an unhappy marriage upon the death of Knuckles. The white master oversees a world in which slaves and Indians understand their inferior place in the plantation society and where, through his intervention, women occupy their proper marital role. When "Caloya" first appeared in the Southern journal *Magnolia* in 1841 it stirred controversy among readers for depicting a black overseer's courtship of a married American Indian woman. In a response printed in the magazine, Simms insisted that the story enlightened as well as entertained, implying that angry readers denied their own innate impulses: "There is nothing surely very attractive in Negroes and Indians; but something is conceded to intellectual curiosity; and the desire is a human, and very natural one, to know how our fellow beings fare in other aspects than our own, and under other forms of humanity, however inferior." [54] Like the contemporaries Child, Cooper, George Catlin, and William Apess, Simms wrote in response to readers' longing to encounter American Indians—and in this instance, African Americans as well.

Moving encounters in *The Wigwam and the Cabin* begin and end with clearly defined racial, social, cultural, and gender factions. Though essential to historical progress, such tension must not be allowed to undermine social progress all together—thus the necessity of one who would enforce racial and gender relations even in the context of violent conflict. As seen in "Oakatibbé" and "Caloya," only the white patriarch, who should be sympathetic and active but who often falls short of this ideal, can contain the violence of the encounter. This view explains Simms's otherwise inexplicable emphasis at the close of *The Yemassee* on the brutality shown by the armies of loyal slaves toward the defeated Indians. Under the rule and influence of their white masters, black slaves enact the violence necessary to subject Indians to the same authority, "scouring the field of battle with their huge clubs and hatchets, knocking upon the head all of the Indians who yet exhibited any signs of life" (*Y* 412). [55] For Simms, no amount of intimacy or sympathy could hold off the violence necessary to the progress of American history and the project of enlightening the "inferior" races. He provided one region's picture of such progress, a moral vision based on a local history but proclaimed national in reach.

4

Containing Native Feeling

Sentiment in the Autobiographies of William Apess, Mary Jemison, and Black Hawk

An anonymous review of William Apess's 1831 revised edition of *A Son of the Forest* in the *American Monthly Review* expresses frustration over an "error" Apess commits in describing his ancestry. Apess, a Pequot Indian, claims his grandmother was the granddaughter of King Philip—the (in)famous Wampanoag leader and namesake of the 1675–76 war between Algonquin Indians and New English colonists—and misidentifies Philip as a Pequot.[1] The reviewer concludes by voicing a concern that Apess's future attempts to write American Indian history will be inaccurate: "If Mr. Apes[s] should undertake the work he proposes, we recommend to him great diligence, discrimination, and accuracy, otherwise he will suffer imposition, and unawares impose upon others. He must enlarge the boundaries of his knowledge of Indian history, and not allow himself to be carried away by every slight and imperfect tradition."[2] Through the word *tradition*, a term associated at this time with the oral transmission of facts, beliefs, or social codes, the reviewer strongly implies that Apess's attempt to write his personal and tribal history is tainted by Indian sources.[3] Indeed, earlier in the text he dismisses Apess's genealogical claims with the offhand comment, "It does not appear that there is any authority for this statement, other than the tradition of the natives themselves." The reviewer assumes, as did Henry Rowe Schoolcraft and others in this period, that American Indians' historical narratives are exclusively oral and innately variable.[4] Such unstable stories lie outside the realm of discriminating and accurate historiographic pursuits; the Indian's knowledge (even this literate Indian's knowledge) is circumscribed by the culture of his race. In the vision of this reviewer, American Indian traditions have a volatile and dangerous presence in the writing of history, and unless the writer, or in this instance the reviewer, supplies the reader with proper historical sources treated with proper historical rigor, all will "suffer imposition."

After this charge, and after two pages of discounting and correcting Apess's "native tradition," the review ends with the suggestion that, should Apess suc-

70

ceed in "enlarg[ing] the boundaries of his knowledge of Indian history," his Indian-ness may still benefit his writing: "In this way we trust, from the other advantages of his situation, being *native to the question*, he will make an authentic and valuable book."[5] Through this italicized pun, the reviewer underscores what his presumed audience defines as and values in an "authentic" book: personal investment and expression. To be native to a question is to be personally involved and implicated in an issue, and to be Native in the age of the Indian Question is to be socially and politically restricted because of one's cultural and racial identity, and therefore to have an unavoidably subjective opinion regarding American Indian rights. Ultimately the review calls on Apess to unite a historian's (allegedly) disinterested, rigorous research with the perspective of an orphaned son of the forest who decries the continuing dispossession of his fellow Indians. Producing a text that communicates the Indian's authentic feeling proves valuable in the 1820s and 1830s when curious white readers seek the thrill of hearing the savage's voice. For this reason, the reviewer deems Apess's Indian qualities— otherwise detrimental for the historian and citizen of Jacksonian America—"the other advantages of his situation."

This rich, suggestive review of *A Son of the Forest* provides entrée for a reconsideration of the emergence and cultural work of the American Indian autobiography in the context of the antebellum moving encounter, through which authors supposedly brought the Native to the Question. Nina Baym's description of the prescriptive work of the mid-nineteenth-century fiction review holds here; this review provides us insight into a public taste for the authentic American Indian narrative and the perceived dangers of such texts.[6] The attraction of Apess's autobiography lies in the veracity of his American Indian identity, his emotional response to the related hardships, and his impassioned complaint— the ways in which his non-Native reader comes face-to-face with a "son of the forest." The complaint, however, imperils the reader in a period when the Indian Question embroiled the nation and spurred American Indian resistance. The reviewer attempts to defuse Apess's condemnation of U.S. Indian policy and widespread prejudice by placing Apess in an authorial double bind: while the value of *Son* for a Euro-American audience lies in Apess's Indian-ness—his "being *native to the question*"—his Indian-ness indicates the text is historically inaccurate. Put another way, the reviewer acknowledges that this work may stir the reader's sympathy but declares that emotion an unreliable basis for an institutional indictment. The review's simultaneous praise and derision for Apess's Indian identity constitutes one of many attempts in this period to contain the attractive and potentially incendiary personal testimony of the American Indian autobiography through what Michelle Burnham identifies as "a double strategy of bestowal and retraction"—a tactic in which editors and reviewers identify the cultural hybridity of an American Indian autobiography (which is the product of either multiple authors or a literate, and therefore tainted, Indian) as both the condition of publication and the negator of textual authenticity. By claiming the ability to assess the authenticity of American Indian life stories, editors and reviewers asserted themselves as the true intermediaries of Indian-white textual encounter—those few capable of identifying what was truly Native and of controlling misleading emotion.[7]

Because sentimental discourse has been characterized as exclusively Euro-American, critics have either down played the relationship of early American Indian autobiographies to contemporary Euro-American works or portrayed the sentimental elements of early American Indian autobiographies as inauthentic and even corrupting. Instead, I suggest that we view the emergence of American Indian autobiographies as inextricably linked to sentimental culture and the popularity of the literary moving encounter, that we consider what happens when American Indians, who in this period were so often the objects of the sentimental gaze in literature, artworks, ethnography, and political discourse, composed in what was recognized as sentimental language, effectively taking on the role of intermediary in the Indian-white moving encounter. One result is the reactionary declaration of white control through reviews and, in as-told-to autobiographies, the careful balancing of the subject's voice and the editor's craft. Three American Indian autobiographies of the 1820s and 1830s, Apess's *A Son of the Forest* (1831, 2nd edition), James Everett Seaver's edition of *Narrative of the Life of Mary Jemison* (1824), and J. B. Patterson's edition of *Life of Ma-Ka-Tai-Me-She-Kia-Kiak or Black Hawk* (1833), bear the marks of literary sentimentalism, especially in their claims to the superiority of American Indian familial bonds and emotional expression. Although the sentimentalism of these texts, particularly of *Narrative* and *Life*, might signal editorial imposition, and authenticity in this period was publicly conferred or denied by white editors and reviewers, these works present American Indian subjects who themselves declare that the encounter between the Euro-American and the American Indian demands along with the audience's tears its recognition of American Indians' equality and rights, if not their full national sovereignty. The texts' comparisons of American Indian and Euro-American emotional authenticity produce some expressions of essentialism, but the overall effect is to raise the possibility of a moving encounter facilitated by the American Indian that is not doomed from the start, that does not conclude when overwhelming emotion necessitates segregation and the disappearance of American Indians.[8]

Sentimental Culture and the Emergence of American Indian Autobiography

Sentimental readers valued, as the review of Apess's autobiography suggests, the "authentic" text, the one that "really proceed[ed] from its reputed source or author."[9] Authentic texts, many believed, prompted genuine feeling in the presence of genuine expression, employing sentimental tropes but promising that the thrilling or touching exploits of the narrator could be located in a real subject. When Lydia Maria Child observed the "Sacs, Fox, and Iowas" appearing at Barnum's American Museum in 1843, she asked herself, "In that other world, shall we be enabled to know exactly how heaven, and earth, and hell, appear to other persons, nations, and tribes?" Her subsequent response reveals the function of life writing in a sentimental culture: "I would it might be so; for I have an intense desire for such revelations. I do not care to travel to Rome, or St. Petersburg, because I can only look *at* people; and I want to look *into* them, and *through* them; to know how things appear to *their* spiritual eyes, and sound to *their* spiritual ears. This is a universal want; hence the interest taken in autobiography, by all classes of readers." [10] The authentic autobiography appeared to provide a window into its subject's soul. The "universal want" Child describes represents a widespread impulse in a period when individuals sought, through the identification of common human emotions, to know and understand the subjective experience of others.

As Ann Fabian and Stephen Carl Arch show, late eighteenth- and nineteenth-century American audiences eagerly read personal narratives that treated experiences of religious fervor, dangerous exploits, jarring captivity, and tremendous suffering—the experiences of those subject to external forces. Tracing the emergence of the American autobiography from "'self-biographical' narratives," Arch emphasizes that the autobiography as we know it "developed in the United States from within the space occupied by marginalized, oppressed groups." [11] To be sure, the "personal" narratives from this period are often more readily referred to as slave, captivity, and conversion narratives. In the face of social upheaval, participants in an affective culture consumed portraits of those subject to crueler circumstances and established at once their similarity to victims and their distance from extreme suffering. American Indians were no exception.

Autobiographies written or narrated by American Indians and reflecting their difficult position in the face of acculturation and removal found a ready audience within a literary culture that pursued sympathetic understanding and, more specifically, valued authentic personal narratives of the downtrodden. Nonetheless, Arnold Krupat notes, this "interest in the Indians' own perspective" provided American Indians an opportunity to express resistance in texts. [12] The bestseller of 1824 was Seaver's *Narrative of the Life of Mary Jemison*, an as-told-to narrative of a Scotch-Irish American woman's life as an acculturated Seneca. In the subsequent fourteen years, autobiographical writings by Hendrick Aupaumut (1827, Mahican), Apess, Black Hawk (1833, Sauk), Paul Cuffe (1839, Pequot), and George Copway (1847, Ojibwe) also appeared, as did additional autobiographies of acculturated American Indians. [13] In addition, and most likely reinforcing the popularity of the autobiographies, American Indian biographies sold well in the antebellum period; for example, in 1832 both B. B. Thatcher and Samuel Gardner

Drake published successful collections titled *Indian Biography*.[14] The Indian's life story acquired tremendous value in the antebellum United States for the emotional power it wielded.

As suggested by the 1832 review of *A Son of the Forest* in *American Monthly Review*, the question of an American Indian autobiography's authenticity was complicated by the characterization of American Indian culture as exclusively oral; while Euro-Americans pointed to American Indian illiteracy as proof of cultural inferiority, the literate Indian was dismissed as a paradox or even as non-Indian. Illiteracy functioned as a racial as well as a cultural indicator, which directly impacted the reception of American Indian autobiography in a sentimental culture seeking an authentic Native personal narrative. In a review of *Life of Ma-Ka-Tai-Me-She-Kia-Kiak or Black Hawk*, William Joseph Snelling, author of *Tales of the Northwest* (1830), declares the text to be "the only autobiography of an Indian extant, for we do not consider Mr. Apes[s] and a few other persons of unmixed Indian blood, who have written books, to be Indians." *Son*, according to Snelling, literally pales in comparison with an autobiography recorded directly from the mouth of a full-blooded, unacculturated American Indian. He explains: "If he [the Indian] writes, it is in the character of a white man. But here is an autobiography of a wild, unadulterated savage, gall yet fermenting in his veins, his heart still burning with the sense of wrong, the words of wrath and scorn yet scarce cold upon his lips, ('If you wish to fight us, come on,') and his hands still reeking with recent slaughter."[15] Through his distinction between Apess and Black Hawk, Snelling unwittingly reveals the desired authenticity of the American Indian autobiography to be a Euro-American construct. He characterizes Black Hawk, his quintessential "real" Indian, as a noble primitive and reduces to a macho dare his complex narrative of resistance to imperialism. In naming the as-told-to autobiography as authentic, Snelling denies that Black Hawk's mediating transcriber and translators write in the character of white men but instead simply make accessible the experience of a noble savage.

The distinction between written and dictated personal narratives remains significant in considerations of American Indian autobiographies. Krupat refers to the two kinds as autobiographies by Indians and Indian autobiographies, respectively, taking into account differences in authorial control and philosophy.[16] As Snelling's review suggests, in the antebellum period the perceived authenticity of a personal narrative could depend on who wielded the pen. In addition, differences between the authorship of *Son*, *Narrative*, and *Life* lead to different uses of sentimental language and figures, including the moving encounter. Apess, I argue, responds intentionally to the hypocrisy of a culture that forwards the dispossession of American Indian populations through images of Indian-white sympathy by claiming sentimental authority himself. *Life* and *Narrative* are what Krupat terms "*original bicultural composite composition*[s]," each registering the encounter of an American Indian and a Euro-American in the voice of the former transmitted by the latter.[17] Black Hawk and Jemison's indictment of Euro-American actions and affirmation of human equality are likely translated into the terms of sentimental America by Euro-American recorders. Nonetheless, the encounters in their texts reform the language of sympathy and, as in Apess's work, reveal the hypocrisy of a comparatively callous society. The sentimental context of early American Indian autobiography permeates *Son*, *Narrative*, and *Life* as they anticipate and meet, but also subvert, reader expectations. Written in the language of sentiment, these early American Indian autobiographies facilitate moving encounters between reader and author, giving the lie to cultural or racial "authenticity" as they challenge the emotional authenticity of readers who seek the thrill of confrontation with "a wild, unadulterated savage" but do not respond productively to the Indian's complaint.

Apess's " 'affecting' tale"

When one considers the length of and use of sources in Apess's appendix to *Son*, the accusation that Apess depends on inaccurate American Indian tradition appears absurd. In a head note to the appendix, Apess tells his reader that he "has somewhat abridged 'his life' " in order to provide extensive scholarly background, sacrificing personal narrative to historical narrative.[18] Roumiana Velikova's study of the appendix shows, moreover, that the mistake regarding King Philip's tribal affiliation originates with Elias Boudinot's *Star in the West* (1816). The shaky historiographic tradition that supposedly misleads Apess and his readers is, in fact, a Euro-American's, and in this way, the review of Apess's text ultimately exposes the questionable elements of Euro-American historiography to a culture that would deny American Indians the ability to construct historical narratives.[19] The review also demonstrates how the early American Indian autobiography contains a struggle for control over the textual moving encounter between Native subject and non-Native reader. Just as early American Indian autobiography includes moments of resistance to a readership that desires emotional intimacy with American Indians yet devalues their challenges to cultural-racial hierarchy, the reviews and editorial apparatuses of those autobiographies expose their white authors' attempts to harness the authority of the American Indian autobiographer for economic and political purposes.

Critical assessments of Apess's writing since the 1992 appearance of *On Our Own Ground: The Complete Writings of William Apess, a Pequot*, edited by Barry O'Connell, have focused in particular on how literacy, Euro-American historiography, and Christianity—all forces of assimilation—actually contribute to Apess's indictment of geographic and cultural imperialism, concluding that Apess and his work, as the title of an article by Gordon Sayre suggests, defy the forces of assimilation and confound the concept of authenticity.[20] In this way, the elements of Apess's writing that would threaten his text's authenticity in the eyes of antebellum Euro-American readers become his most effective tools for criticizing those readers. Through the characteristics of personal narratives and sentimental literature, Apess taps the popular moving encounter as he brings his Euro-American readers in contact with a suffering American Indian: himself. *Son* is punctuated by moments of physical and emotional pain aimed to bring the reader to sympathize with the plight of an Indian estranged from himself, his family, his culture, and his God. Apess illustrates the extent of his childhood poverty by recounting experiences such as his grandparents' alcohol consumption, the near death of his sister by starvation ("Young as I was, my very heart bled for her," he tells us [*S* 5]), and the kindness of white neighbors who offered charity to his family. He recalls numerous occasions on which he was whipped or beaten for minor misdeeds or actions he never committed. For example, a severe beating by his grandmother prompted his removal to the guardianship of the town, but he received many unwarranted floggings at the hands of his foster father, Mr. Furman, and subsequent guardians.[21] Apess presents his younger self as the pitiable object of both violence and benevolence.

Additionally, Apess illustrates his youthful introduction to particularly moving situations in sentimental terms. His first exposure to the church begins at the graveyard: Mrs. Furman, a model of sentimental parenting, directed Apess's attention to the graves of children, and, he reports, "[she] told me that I might die" and offered "pious admonitions" (*S* 9). Apess's account of military service during the War of 1812 consists primarily of his emotional responses to the spectacles of brutality, within and between the opposing armies. He witnessed the execution of a court-martialed soldier and the near execution of another who "wept like a child"; regarding the latter, Apess comments, "To me this was an awful day—my heart seemed to leap into my throat" (*S* 26). Of battle he writes, "The horribly disfigured bodies of the dead—the piercing groans of the wounded and the dying—the cries for help and succor from those who could not help themselves—were most appalling. I can never forget it" (*S* 29). Apess brings the reader into his own memories of suffering, prompting emotional response through the ready expression of his own feelings. During the time of his first conversion he dreams of a hell that, though not unique to Euro-American religious experience, resonates with other sensationalist depictions: "I thought I saw a world of fire.... I was greatly in fear of dropping into that awful place, the smoke of the torment of which ascendeth up forever and ever" (*S* 20). Of his first time speaking at a meeting, he notes, "I was now in my proper element, just harnessed for the work, with the fire of divine love burning on my heart" (*S* 41). Just after, Apess includes an account of his getting lost in a swamp while traveling to his father's home, an occasion that quickly became a religious experience for the young enthusiast (*S* 42). Depictions of extreme duress and extreme emotion, intended to extract the reader's tears, punctuate *Son*, especially in those moments leading to Apess's religious and what we might call his racial awakening.[22]

Apess draws on sentimental literature apart from personal narratives as well, openly demonstrating his fluency in the language of the culture in which and to which he writes. Through the reference to King Philip and the title, which uses the romantic vision of the pantheistic Indian, Apess associates himself with the characteristic Indian of literature. He even incorporates Washington Irving's "Traits of Indian Character" in his appendix, following Elias Boudinot's lead.[23] In this sense, his life story presents an Indian in many ways familiar to sentimental audiences. At the same time, Apess includes evidence that he intentionally challenges the sentimental acquiescence to denials of Indian equality and sovereignty in sentimental terms. In particular, Apess recollects when, as a teenager, he escaped indentureship and traveled with a confidence man (or boy) named John who, having heard a group of soldiers' "affecting" tale, "concluded to incorporate a part of it with his own" (*S* 24). This story implicates Apess in the act of autobiographical dishonesty, and by extension further unsettles the "authenticity" of *Son*, but it also underscores his strategic employment of sentimental language and the critique involved in this act.

Apess's narrative, as Cheryl Walker has commented regarding the body of Apess's writing, exhibits a strategic combination of irony and mimicry.[24] Apess foregrounds his emotion and explicitly courts the reader's sympathy but simultaneously delivers a harsh appraisal of Euro-American sentimentalism. This combination of pathos and criticism is fitting, for sentimental literature indicts the hard-hearted, but it is terribly ironic as well, for the object of "pity" levels the charge at the sentimental spectator (reader included). For example, Apess ends the moving account of his childhood sufferings at the hands of alcoholic grandparents by blaming whites—the very group who responded sympathetically and intervened in the abuse—"inasmuch as they introduced among my countrymen that bane of comfort and happiness, ardent spirits" (*S* 7). Apess declares he has chosen the romantic label "a son of the forest" to emphasize his explicit rejection of "Indian" as "a slur upon an oppressed and scattered nation" he believes was "imported for the special purpose of degrading us" (*S* 10). Apess at once meets and challenges readers' expectations, asserting authorial control over sentimental language and tropes in the light of sympathy's abuse by those who deny American Indians' agency and predict their disappearance.

Apess's fluency in sentimental expression stands in sharp contrast with what he depicts as Euro-Americans' failure to sympathize with him or, at the very least, to recognize the force of his sentimental message. While wandering after his service in the war, Apess found that many whites "would forget the dignity of human nature so far as to blackguard me because I was an Indian." Although he wished to respond with violence, he practiced a benevolent control that reversed the direction of race-based pity: "It appeared to me as if they had not the sense and wisdom of the brute creation" (*S* 36). This appraisal of Euro-Americans' sympathy extends in particular to Christians. As an American Indian, Apess could not receive a license from the Methodist Episcopal Church. He was reprimanded for preaching anyway and finally joined the Methodist Protestant Church, which ordained him in 1829. The first edition of *A Son of the Forest* contains scathing commentary on the Methodist Episcopal Church, and the second retains more general accusations of racism. (O'Connell admits we do not know much about how or even where Apess published *Son*, but he speculates that Apess at least began the project as part of his drive for ordination by the Methodist Conference.)[25] But in both editions, Apess uses the story of a violent response to his preaching to highlight the failure of a white audience to sympathize with or even hear his Christian message. On only his second night of preaching, Apess tells us, "I found a great concourse of people who had come out to hear the Indian preach, and as soon as I had commenced, the sons of the devil began to show their front—and I was treated not with the greatest loving kindness, as one of them threw an old hat in my face, and this example was followed by others, who threw sticks at me" (*S* 44). Through such bitter accounts of his dealings with the hard-hearted, Apess demonstrates how Euro-Americans consume the Indian as circumscribed by stereotype and law but will not sympathize with the actual, and even Christian, American Indian they encounter every day.[26] This passage asks whether Euro-Americans really want an assimilated American Indian, or indeed *any* American Indian in flesh and blood. Apess's use of sentimentalism in his autobiography reveals that the "authentic" Indian readers wish to encounter is a literary construct.

"Just as we feel, we are": Mary Jemison's Dangerous Family Narrative

Mary Jemison, the daughter of Scotch-Irish immigrants who had settled in south-central, frontier Pennsylvania, was captured by a small French and Shawnee band during an attack on the Jemison home on April 5, 1758. She was adopted by Seneca sisters, then went on to marry American Indian men, bear eight children, and on multiple occasions reject repatriation to Euro-American society. Jemison's acculturation puzzled many and prompted the publisher Daniel W. Banister to employ James Everett Seaver to record her narrative in 1823 when Jemison was in her seventies. As Seaver writes in the introduction to the first edition of *Narrative of the Life of Mary Jemison*, he spent three days in the presence of Banister and Jemison's trusted friend and adviser at the house of Jennet Whaley in Castile, New York, "taking a sketch of her narrative as she recited it."[27] *Narrative* appeared in 1824 with Seaver listed as author, and it quickly became the year's bestseller. Jemison died September 19, 1833, having survived two daughters, three murdered sons (two at the hands of brothers), and the dispersion of much of her real estate, but the story of her life persisted in the national imagination.[28] During the nineteenth and early twentieth centuries, Seaver and subsequent editors produced a string of *Narrative* editions, providing curious readers with appendixes concerning the events of Jemison's life, ethnographic data on the Iroquois, and historical accounts of Euro-American and American Indian conflicts.[29]

Today the genre and the authorship of this important antebellum work appear indeterminate; Deborah Larsen used it as a basis for her 2002 novel *The White*, which attempts to fill in the gaps of Jemison's account as created by white editors, and a recent PBS documentary on the French and Indian War cites Jemison's account as a captivity narrative.[30] Prominent critical treatments of captivity narratives include discussions of *Narrative* because its opening chapters recount the surprise attack on the Jemison home, Mary's departure from her mother, the violent disposal of her fellow captives, and her adoption by the Seneca people, events typical of captivity narratives of the seventeenth, eighteenth, and early nineteenth centuries. However, others point out, *Narrative* does not include the crucial ending of the captivity narrative, the return and reincorporation of the captive, and therefore it remains on the margins of the genre.[31] Susan Walsh convincingly argues that Jemison's place within the Seneca tribe and her own family suggests that the text should be read not as a captivity narrative without redemption but simply as the as-told-to autobiography of "a Seneca woman" (re)named "Dehgewanus." She goes so far as to declare: "the Seaver/Jemison *Narrative* may well be 'the first Indian autobiography to reach publication.'"[32] Perhaps we can say that to read *Narrative* in the 1820s was to encounter encounter, to confront liminality embodied in a white female member of a Seneca community.

As a culturally composite text, *Narrative* contains a depiction of human sympathy that draws on various, and at times conflicted, understandings of the role of emotion in overcoming difference. The argument that Euro-American women who became acculturated into American Indian society demonstrated the admirable, white trait of sympathy was commonplace in narratives of "white Indians." In contrast, American Indian societies used emotional displays to bridge the cultural and racial difference between themselves and captives, successfully "transform[ing] their hostile or fearful white captives into affectionate Indian relatives" by generously clothing and feeding them, teaching them survival skills, respecting their sexual autonomy, and simply being kind.[33] *Narrative* testifies to differing cultural perceptions and uses of feeling in the context of Indian-white encounter, and as a result, emotion appears to breech difference and reinforce it in alternate moments of the text.

As critics often highlight, Jemison—by whom I now mean the narrator-function created by Seaver's record of Jemison's tale—connects her incorporation into the Seneca community as facilitated by immediate, strong bonds with family members who do not recognize Indian-white difference as absolute. Immediately after the Seneca sisters who adopt Jemison publicly mourn for the brother whom Jemison replaces, "joy sparkled in their countenances, and they seemed to rejoice over me as over a long lost child" (*N* 38). She finds and returns much love with her first husband, Sheninjee, a Delaware. Jemison admits, "The idea of spending my days with him, at first seemed perfectly irreconcilable to my feelings," but she confesses that, "his good nature, generosity, tenderness, and friendship towards me, soon gained my affection; and, strange as it may seem, I loved him!" (*N* 44). Consequently, after four years with her adoptive family and husband, Jemison reports feeling, "with them was my home," and further, upon visiting her adopted sisters she finds, "I loved them as I should have loved my own sister had she lived, and I had been brought up with her" (*N* 46, 54). This statement is followed by a specific example of the adopted mother's deep affection and sympathy for Jemison: when one of the sisters wishes Jemison to accompany her to the execution of a captive, her mother chastises her, "Oh! how can you think of making her bleed at the wounds which now are but partially healed?" (*N* 57). The mother's and sisters' love for Jemison secures reciprocal love and Jemison's willing membership in their family. The story of Corn Planter and Old John included in *Narrative* further illustrates American Indian familial love. When an expedition of Seneca attacks frontier settlements and captures John O'Bail, the white father of the Seneca leader Corn Planter, the son reveals his identity to his father, declares, "I respect you, my father," and grants him his wish "to return to [his] fields and live with [his] white children" (*N* 78). Like Jemison's loved ones, Corn Planter demonstrates the generosity of his feelings toward family members of any race or culture.

Narrative contrasts Corn Planter's benevolence toward his estranged white father with the extreme violence of Ebenezer Allen, a disaffected Pennsylvanian who takes up residence among the Seneca, toward all American Indians.[34] Though Jemison once protected Allen, she enumerates the ways in which he flaunts his disrespect for family and home, particularly through his marriage to three women, two white and one Indian. In addition, Allen betrays the trust of the Indians and his mixed-blood daughter by requesting land on her behalf and then selling it for his own profit. Jemison concludes with an account of an atrocity he committed while scouting: he killed a father and infant as the mother watched. The narrative further underscores the narrowness of Euro-American hearts through descriptions of Jemison's own hardships as a mother. Jemison refuses to return to Euro-American society because, she writes, "I had got a larger family of Indian children, that I must take with me; and that if I should be so fortunate as to find my relatives, they would despise them, if not myself; and treat us as enemies; or, at least with a degree of cold indifference, which I thought I could not endure" (*N* 93). Here Jemison emphasizes that, unlike the Seneca, Euro-Americans allow race to overwhelm family ties. Most likely this prejudice, and the memory of her having been swindled by land-hungry whites, contributed to her hesitancy to speak with Seaver. He points out in the introduction that Jemison's primary fear during the interview was "that she should say something that would be injurious to herself or family" (*N* xiii). As the mother of an interracial family, Jemison knew that she need not say much to prompt harsh judgment.

In addition to providing an unflattering contrast between Euro-American prejudice and American Indian familial love, *Narrative* represents the Euro-American who overcomes prejudice through feeling. Jemison can respond to her adoptive family's and her husbands' generous affection only by loving them in return. Even stronger is the love Jemison has for her children, whose mixed heritage does not sicken her (as it does her white relatives) but instead drives her to protect them from prejudice. Throughout *Narrative*, her maternal love overwhelms adversity as well as difference, most notably during the hardships of the war. In the fall of 1779, American forces under General John Sullivan destroyed Seneca property, leaving them homeless and hungry. Jemison declares in the narrative, "I immediately resolved to take my children and look out for myself, without delay" (*N* 74). She and her five children removed to Gardow flats, where she husked corn for two runaway slaves and secured enough for her family to survive the winter. To her contemporary reader, this image of a white woman feeding her "half-breed" children by working for blacks would have been shocking. Yet according to the narrative, Jemison's resourcefulness made her proud; she and her children survived a winter, she emphasizes, in which "many of our people barely escaped with their lives" (*N* 75). Jemison stayed on in Gardow flats and prospered. At the end of *Narrative*, Jemison summarizes the wealth of her family: "I have been the mother of eight children; three of whom are now living, and I have at this time thirty-nine grand children, and fourteen great-grand children. . . . I live in my own house, and on my own land." (*N* 143). *Narrative* offers the life of a loving woman as proof that the history of Indian-white hostilities has little significance in the presence of strong familial attachments and difficulties.

For all of the recent sophisticated descriptions of sentiment in *Narrative*, the fact remains that the expressions of Jemison's attachment to her American Indian families are often marked by assertions of cultural-racial essentialism, prompting one critic to conclude that sentimentalism "masks, although it does not erase, Jemison's Indianness beneath the conventions of nineteenth-century white womanhood."[35] The origin of the expressions of essentialism (whether in Jemison's words or Seaver's transcription) is not always identifiable. Moreover, those expressions become more prominent with each succeeding nineteenth-century edition, and for some readers, they overwhelm any ideological or cultural dialogue.[36] The final chapter of *Narrative* supplies fodder for these readings, for it suggests that, in looking back on her life, Jemison considered her survival of captivity and acculturation as her "reduction from a civilized to a savage state" (*N* 139). As various critics have pointed out, the nineteenth-century editorial and critical apparatuses point to Jemison's emotional attachments to her Seneca families as evidence not of Jemison's acculturation but rather of her persisting whiteness. In his foreword to the 1918 facsimile of the first edition, Charles

Delamater Vail declares, "Amidst the hardening surroundings of barbaric life, she preserved the sensibilities of a white woman" (*N* h). He continues, "Her natural tender emotions were never extinguished; the atrocities of the uncivilized people among whom it was her destiny to live always shocked her. She cherished a lively sympathy for the sufferings of others, and never failed to minister to the needy and unfortunate according to her resources." Hence, Vail suggests, Jemison's refusal to return to Euro-American society was not the result of her conversion to barbarism but of her inherent, civilized, feminine sympathy. Jemison sustained her whiteness even as she married fierce warriors and birthed children—or, better yet, she gave proof of her racial purity through her willingness to submit to an interracial family.

Vail's interpretation of Jemison's persistent whiteness is reinforced by chapter 11 of *Narrative*, which shares a detailed biography of Jemison's second husband, Hiokatoo, complete with his physical attainments and the atrocities he committed in war. The biography begins with Jemison's supposed admission that although "he uniformly treated me with tenderness" and "was a man of tender feelings to his friends," "his cruelties to his enemies perhaps were unparalleled, and will not admit a word of palliation" (*N* 104). Yet, as Seaver admits and subsequent critics note, Seaver received the account of Hiokatoo's life not from Mary Jemison but from George Jemison, an impostor cousin who lived on her land for a number of years and tricked her at one point into selling him a large tract. That Mary Jemison would not provide an account of Hiokatoo's life makes some sense because, as Walsh points out, a Seneca wife would not have told her husband's exploits, let alone expressed disapproval of them to a visitor.[37] Nonetheless, Seaver interprets the situation in the introduction and chapter 11 through the assumption that "The thoughts of his deeds, probably chilled her old heart, and made her dread to rehearse them." (*N* xiv). Though written as if narrated by Jemison, this chapter represents a clear and direct case of substantial content revision to an as-told-to narrative; the editor, in the role of a sentimental intermediary, imposes feelings on the Native subject for the edification of the non-Native reader.

Expressions of cultural-racial essentialism are not limited to narrative or editorial commentary but potentially dramatized by emotional scenes in *Narrative*. Most notably, the parting words of Jemison's mother provide instructions for how the young girl may retain not only her life but also her Christian, Anglo-American heritage. After a Shawnee captor replaces the young Jemison's shoes with moccasins, her mother understands she will be spared and addresses her: "Alas, my dear! my heart bleeds at the thoughts of what awaits you; but, if you leave us, remember my child your own name, and the name of your father and mother. Be careful and not forget your English tongue. If you shall have an opportunity to get away from the Indians, don't try to escape; for if you do they will find and destroy you. Don't forget, my little daughter, the prayers that I have learned you—say them often; be a good child, and God will bless you. May God bless you my child, and make you comfortable and happy" (*N* 27–28). Seaver's *Narrative* provides evidence that Jemison remembered this injunction. Though Jemison joins and creates a Seneca family, Seaver tells us that, "She speaks English plainly and distinctly," and she admits even her happy life with the Seneca was "marred" by "the recollection that I had once had tender parents, and a home that I loved" (*N* xi, 48). This emotional scene, resonant with the captivity narrative and sentimental novel, animates feelings and cultural commitments Jemison appears never to have jettisoned in her life as a white Indian.

More important, a later writer and editor used this scene to revise the arc of Jemison's story. Laura Wright, a missionary on the Buffalo and Cattaraugus reservations, provides a chapter in the 1877 edition of *Narrative*, edited by William T. Letchworth, in which she describes Jemison, on the approach of death, haunted by her lost family and religion. Having told Wright that her mother's last instruction was that she never forget "the prayer which you have always repeated with your little brothers and sisters"—a directive almost identical to that reported in *Narrative*—Jemison admits sorrowfully "now I do not know how to pray" and, as a result, she cannot sleep for crying (*N* 209–10). Wright tells us, "I then repeated the Lord's prayer in English. She listened, with an expression both solemn and tender, till near the close, when suddenly it was evident a chord had been touched which vibrated into the far distant past, and awakened memories both sweet and painful. She immediately became almost convulsed with weeping, and it was some time before she could speak" (*N* 211). In this account, Jemison has remembered but not kept the maternal commandment reported in *Narrative*. Still, a recitation of the foundational Christian prayer by a surrogate mother figure spurs Jemison's emotional recollection of the faith and relationships denied her in captivity. Wright provides a dramatic distillation of Jemison's reported conversion under the tutelage of her husband, the Reverend Asher Wright, and in doing so, supplies an apocryphal, but nonetheless effective, conclusion echoing Jemison's mother's parting words.[38] Put another way, through a scene of moving encounter with an Indianized Jemison, Wright brings *Narrative* to its generic fruition, granting the captive's religious redemption in a moving dramatization of the victory of her "civilized" identity despite years of residence among the Indians.

Seaver, Vail, Wright, and others' intrusions come under the guise of providing the reader with the most accurate and appropriate embodiment of Jemison's story. In the introduction, Seaver promotes biographical writing as "the greatest and best field in which to study mankind, or human nature," for it "is a telescope of life, through which we can see the extremes and excesses of the varied properties of the human heart" (*N* iii). Seaver's use of the word *biography* rather than *autobiography* may be linked as much to his lack of familiarity with the latter term as to his authorial agency.[39] Still, it seems significant that, through his metaphor,

Seaver describes his subject as valuable yet distant and places the crucial authorial instrument in his control. The importance of biography lies in the revelation of human emotion, detectable only through the author's careful manipulation of the textual lens—a philosophy that appears to inform even Larsen's twenty-first-century understandings of Jemison's experience. Seaver continues with a comparison: "the biographical page," he argues, is more worthy of our consideration than the "gilded monument," for the former teaches "pity...benevolence...and compassion" and excites "all the sympathies of the soul" (N iv). In the author's carefully constructed text, one gains access to the depths of human emotion and sympathetic understanding and in the sculptor's finished form one finds embodied those great actions already known and publicly celebrated. Seaver admits, even promotes, the fact that he has altered the received words to ensure their moral clarity, but then he continues: "Strict fidelity had been observed in the composition.... Without the aid of fiction, what was received as matter of fact, only has been recorded" (N v). He considers his authorship a form of sentimental mediation that makes Jemison's heart visible to his audience in the private act of reading.[40] Perhaps, then, Seaver would have accepted Leonard Bliss Jr.'s metaphor for writing American Indian biography not as sculpting and gilding an ornate monument but as "rearing, with the cold and scattered hearth-stones of their once cheerful homes, a monument to their memory."[41]

Immediately after referring to her "reduction from a civilized to a savage state," Jemison, in the final chapter *of Narrative,* names one source of her strength while living with the Seneca: her willingness to accept her condition. From this Jemison extrapolates a moral: "As every one knows that great exertions of the mind tend directly to debilitate the body, it will appear obvious that we ought, when confined, to exert all our faculties to promote our present comfort, and let future days provide their own sacrifices. In regard to ourselves, just as we feel, we are" (N 140). On the surface, Jemison promotes the captive's stoic repression of fear, melancholy, hatred, and desire for freedom in the interest of self-preservation. Indeed, *Narrative* ascribes her physical strength to her willing acceptance of the hardships of Seneca life.[42] But this biological claim resonates at another level. If one's constitution is strengthened by positive feelings, by one's acceptance of and even love for American Indian society, could not these same feelings have an impact on one's very identity? In a text preoccupied with Euro-American and American Indian difference, this is a revolutionary suggestion. The case of Jemison suggests that social contentment and familial love work on the body and its very identity. If this is so, the following might be a corollary: A commitment to a progressive narrative of history and racial essentialism work on the body, augmenting, if not entirely creating, identity. Now Jemison's reported words sound accusatory: "just as we feel, we are." This is the compelling (though often muddled or compromised) social criticism leveled by

American Indian autobiographies in the antebellum period that Seaver and others stifled through sentimental editing.

Black Hawk's "sorrow fresh"

In 1832, the Sauk military leader Black Hawk and remnants of his "British Band" surrendered to U.S. officers after their armed resistance to removal of the Sauk from territory in Wisconsin and Illinois. In the winter of 1832–33, Black Hawk and ten others leaders in his group were held at Jefferson Barracks in St. Louis, and in April 1833, after five were released, Black Hawk and the remainder were taken to Washington, DC, to meet with President Jackson. From there they were transported to Fortress Monroe in Old Point Comfort, Virginia. Much to their dismay, this was not the last of their travels before returning to Iowa. Departing Virginia on June 3, 1833, Black Hawk and the other prisoners were required to tour the eastern portion of the United States, stopping in Baltimore, Philadelphia, New York, Boston, Albany, Buffalo, and Detroit, so that, as President Jackson was reported to have told them, "You will see that our young men are as numerous as the leaves in the woods. What can you do against us?" [43] Just as congregations gaped at Apess and white Pennsylvanians spoke fondly of the "White Woman of the Genesee," crowds in each city swarmed to view the combatants of the Black Hawk War. Spectators' eagerness, paired with the obvious subject position of the Sauk men, prompted the actress Fanny Kemble Butler to comment, "That men . . . should be brought as strange animals at a show, to be gazed at the livelong day by succeeding shoals of gaping folk, struck me as totally unfitting." The spectacle of Black Hawk and his fellow prisoners was also presented in the popular media. In each city the band visited, newspapers and pamphlets distributed "bits of gossip about what the men said and did," referring to these largely fabricated anecdotes as *"Blackhawkiana."* [44] Whether fitting for military captives or not, the exhibition of Black Hawk in cities and newspapers across the northeastern United States fed and fueled Euro-Americans' desire to encounter the "real" Indian and led to the production of a textual equivalent.

After Black Hawk's return to Iowa, he told the story of his life to Antoine LeClair, a mixed-blood U.S. interpreter for the Sacs and Foxes, and John B. Patterson, a newspaperman from Virginia who had briefly edited a newspaper in Galena, Illinois, during the Black Hawk War. The narrative appeared later that year as *Life of Ma-Ka-Tai-Me-She-Kia-Kiak or Black Hawk,* with the words "DICTATED BY HIMSELF" prominently displayed on the title page with no mention of Patterson or LeClair. [45] With its claim to be Black Hawk's authentic production, the text answered the demands of a public still eager to come in contact with the fallen leader. As a result, it went through five editions in its first year of publication. Two reviewers in addition to Snelling heralded it as an anomaly in

American literature: "the only autobiography of an American Indian" and even "the first published production of an American Indian." [46] The crowds seeking first a glimpse and then the words of Black Hawk could believe that they were getting the real thing and furthermore that Black Hawk's *Life* provided access to the feelings of a representative opponent to civilization.

In all likelihood Patterson had banked on the success of the tour when he determined to edit *Life*, and according to a prefatory note by LeClaire, Black Hawk dictated his account in response to the tour. Black Hawk wanted to share his story, LeClaire reports, "that the people of the United States, (among whom he had been travelling, and by whom he had been treated with great respect, friendship and hospitality,) might know the causes that had impelled him to act as he had done, and the *principles* by which he was governed." [47] Black Hawk had seen swarms pressing to get a look at him and, according to this account, consequently determined to take advantage of the spotlight. He would vindicate his actions to an audience intent on studying them though predisposed to interpreting them as savage. Patterson and Black Hawk both took advantage of the demand for Black Hawk when they created a text through which eager audiences could encounter him.

Like *Narrative of the Life of Mary Jemison*, *Life of Black Hawk* is the product of Indian-white collaboration; it points to the encounters between the Sauks and the Euro-American settlers and soldiers, between Black Hawk and the spectators in the northeastern United States, and between LeClair, Patterson, and Black Hawk. It reflects as well the widespread desire of Euro-Americans to experience their own moving encounter with the infamous American Indian, through his textual performance. Insofar as Black Hawk sought to exploit this desire on multiple levels (commercially, politically, and morally), *Life* responds to the audience's desire in a variety of ways (with generosity, anger, and even judgment). Black Hawk's autobiography, like Jemison's and Apess's, provides curious, sentimental Euro-America with touching moments and a criticism of a culture that would consume the Indian narrative but disparage its contribution to the debate over the rights of American Indians.

Critics have analyzed the discourses of savagism, irony, and resistance in *Life*, but few have considered the presence and source of sentimentalism in the text, the way in which it attends to and values feelings, prompting readers to focus on them. [48] I suggest that though LeClair and Patterson may have used the language of their eager audience in translating and shaping Black Hawk's narrative, the sentimental elements of the text are not entirely conservative. As Scheckel and others argue, the sentimentalism of *Life* abuts and blends with the discourse of savagism, challenging the readers' expectations. While the appeal to sympathy often depends on the portrayal of Black Hawk as a noble but doomed primitive railing against inevitable progress, *Life* conveys Indian resistance in the form of a sentimental analysis. Through sentimental rhetoric and literary figures, it draws on feeling to make moral and political arguments against the United States' treatment of the Sauk people and other American Indians, often by demonstrating American Indians' superiority in sympathy.

Like Apess's *Son* and Jemison's *Narrative*, *Life* includes several sentimental situations familiar to the audience, many of which focus on men grieving the loss of children. The Black Hawk of *Life* describes mourning the deaths of his eldest son and youngest daughter by fasting and removing himself and his family from the rest of the community for two years (*L* 47). Earlier, in an Indianized death-bed scene, he speaks with an *"old friend,"* the father of his adopted son, who has brought himself to the verge of death after whites murder that son (*L* 27). Once the old man has recounted the mistreatment of his people, he dies an exceedingly romantic, tragic death: "I took the hand of my old friend in mine, and pledged myself to avenge the death of his son! It was now dark—a terrible storm commenced raging, with heavy torrents of rain, thunder, and lightening. I had taken my blanket off and wrapped it around the old man. When the storm abated, I kindled a fire, and took hold of my old friend to remove him near to it—but *he was dead!* I remained with him the balance of the night" (*L* 28). In addition to his old friend's sad tale, the text relates the heart-rending story told him by Gomo, a Pottowatomie chief, of his men being murdered by whites while out hunting for the "war chief at Peoria" (*L* 39). The tale concludes with Black Hawk's self-censorship: "I could relate many similar ones that have come within my own knowledge and observation; but I dislike to look back and bring on sorrow afresh. I will resume my narrative" (*L* 40). The reader, however, realizes that this narrative contains a string of such stories, seemingly compiled to spur just such fresh sorrow. Here the composite narration protests too much, thereby underscoring the sentimental power of Black Hawk's tales and (like Apess before him) flaunting his fluency in sentimental language, conveying what Neil Schmitz calls the "ironic biculturality" of *Life*.[49]

Every heartbreaking tale in *Life*, like that of Gomo, stems from specific malevolent action on the part of white Americans. Having offered these examples of horrific crimes committed against American Indians, the text declares Black Hawk's suspicion that Euro-Americans lack "any standard of right and wrong" (*L* 55). This claim depends on the reader's ability and willingness to apply an understood standard and to find the subjects of Black Hawk's complaint guilty. The implication is that, rather than lack a standard, Euro-Americans simply fail to observe the existing one, and further, that their failure is readily apparent even to this so-called savage. The Black Hawk of *Life* claims the authority to apply a standard of right and wrong and, through example, to promote its observation. The textual Black Hawk's censure of white Americans has an overtone of moral instruction: "Bad, and cruel, as our people were treated by the whites, not one of them was hurt or molested by any of my band. I hope this will prove that we are a peaceable people—having permitted ten men to take possession of our corn-fields; prevent us from planting corn; burn our lodges; ill-treat our women; and *beat to death* our men, without offering resistance to their barbarous cruelties. This is a lesson worthy for the white man to learn: to use forbearance when injured" (*L* 52).

Insisting that *Life* contains "a cross-culturally produced 'Indian' voice that is responding to white voices in the language of whites," Mark Wallace associates its criticism of Euro-American hypocrisy with that spoken by American Indian characters in the work of James Fenimore Cooper and other American authors.[50] Yet in those works, the American Indian critic's moral judgment does not reverse the future disappearance of American Indians, for he asserts the inexorability of the culture he critiques. In contrast, *Life* attempts—through harsh criticism and behavioral modeling—to alter the readers so drawn to Black Hawk. This American Indian insists on white responsibility for Indian tragedy, denying that the destruction of American Indian lives and cultures occurs as part of an irreversible and inevitable succession of races, and then instructs the audience members to change their behavior accordingly. As *Life* presents the defeated Black Hawk's complaint and defense, *Narrative* recounts Jemison's captivity and hardships, and *Son* tells of Apess's degradation as a youth, all three autobiographies also offer living, breathing members of American Indian societies as moral exemplars for a culture whose military success has not guaranteed ethical progress. These literary Indians exist and persist in the flesh.

Like the other autobiographies, *Life* offers American Indians as affective as well as moral exemplars, openly questioning the authenticity of white Americans' sentiment. One scene in particular appeals to sentimental readers' reverence for familial attachments to reveal the hypocrisy of Euro-America's treatment of American Indian families. A Sauk, who has been captured by the British and accused of killing a Frenchman, visits with his wife and six children before his execution. "I cannot describe their *meeting* and *parting*, to be understood by the whites"; the narrative comments, "as it appears that their feelings are acted upon by certain rules laid down by their *preachers!—whilst* ours are governed only by the monitor within us" (*L* 21). Again the Black Hawk of *Life* sarcastically insists on eliding sentimental content, though this time with the additional aim of attacking the quality of Euro-American feeling. This comment has grave implications for a sentimental culture in which liberal Christianity, with its focus on emotion and individual expression of faith, was rapidly gaining in popularity. Black Hawk accuses whites of valuing justice over mercy and Christians of valuing the head (theology) over the heart (that internal monitor).

The narrative undermines the commitment of sentimental culture to right feeling by accusing whites of placing profit before people. In one particular passage, Black Hawk declares the hardest aspect of removal to be the inability "to visit the graves of our friends, and keep them in repair for many years." The narrative continues to describe this Sauk "custom" as if white readers are un-familiar with mourning, explaining, "The mother will go alone to weep over the grave of her child! The brave, with pleasure, visits the grave of his father, after he has been successful in war, and repaints the post that shows where he lies!" The statement that "this hardship is not known to whites" not only under-scores whites' control over land but also suggests that these mobile, land-hungry people are not attentive to ancestral graves (*L* 42). The textual Black Hawk ac-cuses sentimental America, despite its marked attachment to the deathbed and the cemetery, of showing little respect to the dead of either race. Time and again he reverses the known order of savagery and civilization, challenging the ethno-graphic description of American Indians as subject to emotional extremes; Black Hawk's subjects practice forbearance, prize their families, value emotion, and revere burial grounds, following the recognized Christian ethic more faithfully than do their Christian enemies. The curious, sentimental readers who seek an intimate encounter with the noble, defeated Indian find an angry, judgmental American Indian who would advise them to reform their ways.

For all the strategic use of sentimentalism in Black Hawk's *Life*, reviewers and subsequent biographers resisted a Black Hawk who would manipulate senti-mental language or substantially challenge the inevitability, not to mention the morality, of removal. In his review of *Life*, Snelling expresses difficulty accepting as authentic the text's sentimental expressions (a complaint that resonates with recent attempts by critics to distinguish LeClair/Patterson's words from Black Hawk's). "The only drawback upon our credence," Snelling complains, "is the intermixture of courtly phrases, and the figures of speech, which our novelists are so fond of putting into the mouths of Indians. These are, doubtless, to be attributed to the bad taste of Black Hawk's amanuensis."[51] The reviewer from *New England Magazine* concurs that Patterson was channeling literary sources as he recorded Black Hawk's words: "The interpreter should not have made the unlettered narrator quote from the English poets." Interestingly, he denies that Black Hawk is an exemplary man: "As heroism is getting cheap," he sarcastically notes, "we may be allowed to call Black Hawk a hero." The journal *Hesperian; or, Western Monthly Magazine* engages this opinion twice. The reviewer of Benjamin Drake's *The Life and Adventures of Black-Hawk* (1838) agrees with Drake, who "does not regard Black-Hawk as being a great man," but a later memorial for Black Hawk reconsiders this judgment: "Though, when compared with PHILIP and RED-JACKET, and TECUMSEH, not a very great man,... in the catalogue of Aboriginal Chieftains, he [Black-Hawk] deserves most honorable mention."[52] Black Hawk stands on the edge of a pantheon created by such biographers as Benjamin Drake, Samuel Gardner Drake, and B. B. Thatcher, and his placement there comes at the discretion of white readers and writers rather than as a result of his own claims.

Denying the subversive sentimentalism of *Life*, Snelling's review and one in *American Quarterly Review* reinforce Black Hawk's admirable traits as those of a noble savage and his outraged narrative as inconsequential to the Indian Question. In doing to, they appear eager to contain Black Hawk's active challenge to removal. The reviewer for *American Quarterly Review* takes the timing of Black Hawk's tour—it was concurrent with President Jackson's visit to many of the same cities—as an opportunity to criticize Jackson as a white barbarian whom Black Hawk supposedly referred to as a "brave": "Now, if a military man, or a *great brave*, as the Indians denominate such, be, in the view of a savage, the proper man to be raised to the presidentship of this great nation, is not that very circumstance calculated to make *civilized persons* hesitate in adopting the same estimate?"[53] Similarly, Snelling deflates Black Hawk's moral judgments as part of his "rude feeling of chivalry" and treats the text's revelations as niceties: "Yet it is pleasant and honorable to human nature, to see that these savage warriors are sometimes compassionate and magnanimous." According to Snelling, none of *Life* provides sufficient proof of a broader guilt or depravity among Euro-Americans or their policies; the men who committed the horrible acts against Black Hawk's people simply prove that "white savages are to be found on the frontier, as well as red." Although Snelling does acknowledge the power of Black Hawk's testimony, he concludes with an observation intended to mitigate its future effect: "We are persuaded that, could Black Hawk and his counsellors have been permitted to plead their own cause on the floor of Congress, attended with a competent interpreter, all the misery, expense, and bloodshed which ensued, might have been prevented."[54] That is, had this textual encounter been actual—had Black Hawk given his account directly to legislators in a timely fashion—his moving words would have made a difference. The Black Hawk War is the result of misunderstanding, not wrong intentions, and Black Hawk's complaint is relevant to federal Indian policy only insofar as we can imagine the events leading to his capture having taken another direction.

Black Hawk's *Life*, then, responds to the desire of an audience that would encounter the real savage who dares challenge the progress of civilization in the young nation. In doing so, this composite text supplies readers with both the romantic figure they seek and a challenge to their consumption of that figure. The Black Hawk of *Life*, like Apess of *Son* and Jemison of *Narrative*, takes up sentimental language and situations in ways suggesting that American Indians feel right and act right but their civilized dispossessors do not. Editors and reviewers of the period attempt to displace this challenge by taking back the role of intermediary. Thus, if we attend to the sentimental context of early American Indian autobiography—the popularity of personal narratives, the widespread desire to sympathize with the victimized, the common romanticizing of the Indian, and the consideration by reviewers of textual authenticity—we can trace a struggle for control over the discourse of sympathy in an era of removal.

"Facts, plain facts"

Unlike the figure of William Apess, who disappeared from memory, the figure of Black Hawk, like that of Mary Jemison, had lasting popularity and was restrained and reformed through the efforts of editors and historians. Beginning in 1834, a proliferation of other texts concerning Black Hawk and his "war" with the United States corrected and contained the narrative of the captured Sauk. This continuing interest had to do in part with the prominence of its white participants; as William T. Hagan notes, "The subsequent rise to fame of Abraham Lincoln, Jefferson Davis, Zachary Taylor, and a host of others... cast a nostalgic glamour over the miserable little campaign." Texts of particular importance included the militiaman John A. Wakefield's *History of the War Between the United States and the Sac and Fox Nations of Indians* (1834); Benjamin Drake's *The Life and Adventures of Black Hawk* (1838), for which Drake interviewed participants in the war; and Elbert H. Smith's epic *Ma-Ka-Tai-She-Kia-Kiak; or Black Hawk and Scenes in the West, a National Poem* (1848). Hagan concludes that "the net result of this body of literature was the creation of a war which never took place." Insofar as "it served to divert attention from the operation of the federal Indian policy during a vital thirty-year period," the literature on the Black Hawk War in the 1830s and 1840s may be said to have countered *Life*'s challenge to curious, sentimental Euro-America.[55]

An 1838 review of Benjamin Drake's *The Life and Adventures of Black-Hawk* in the *Hesperian* declares that "several volumes have been published, professing to be 'Lives' of the brave old warrior.... But until the present book, we had but little like an accurate and comprehensive account of that contest."[56] Like the 1832 review of Apess's *Son*, this one approaches the life writing of an American Indian as untrustworthy, though interesting for its rarity and for the thrills of its "authenticity." For a presentation of things as they actually are, Thatcher argues, one must go to the work of the Euro-American historian or biographer. In 1832 in the *North American Review*, he makes the explicit link between finding a solution to the Indian Question and the pursuit of Indian biography: "A great crisis has arrived in the relations existing between the tribes of that remarkable race, and the civilized and Christian population, which presses upon their borders.... In this discussion, their original constitution, moral and intellectual, and especially their collective and individual competency for civilized life, are involved; and here it is, that history and biography should be made to render their services. It is not speculation or theory that is needed,—but facts, plain facts."[57] With these words the author of *Indian Biography* practices self-promotion. (The next sentence of this review even emphasizes that "the latter of the two departments of Indian literature just named, has been singularly overlooked.") Thatcher reins in the subversive potential of the emerging genre of American Indian autobiography in this period of "great crisis." The testimony of American Indians had the

potential to undermine the ethical status of removal, and the writing and transcription of their narratives threatened to topple a sentimental culture's faith in
its own affective knowledge and civilized behavior—but editors, reviewers, biographers, and historians made every effort to defuse Native words.

The following year, O. W. B. Peabody, also writing in *North American Review*,
praises Thatcher and his work for containing the threat of sympathy with American Indians:

> There is much to awaken interest and sympathy in the character of this unfortu-
> nate race, who, with manners and habits essentially savage, exhibited some traits
> of refined and elevated feeling, and who, when brought into direct contrast with
> cultivated men, were, in some respects, able to put civilization to shame....But
> to carry this feeling so far, as to express regret that civilization has extended; to
> maintain, that it would have been better that the country should still be a hunting
> ground, instead of being divided into cities and villages; to speak, as if the acci-
> dental vices of civilized life are so many and great, that barbarism would be bet-
> ter, is carrying this sympathy much farther than good sense and reason would be
> disposed to go. Wherever civilization comes in conflict with barbarism, we mean,
> with a race which has no active principle of improvement within it, it is the order
> of nature that barbarism shall give way.[58]

Euro-American biographers, the arbiters of facts, could not, would not allow
sympathy to override the natural course of history. The popular demand for
moving encounters that opened the door to American Indian autobiographies
did not reverse federal Indian policy. Being Native to the Question provided an
audience but did not guarantee one's answer would be heeded. Through editorial
and other means, Euro-Americans endeavored to control narratives of American
Indian experience because those narratives harnessed the language of sympathy
to create a forceful challenge to federal Indian policy. We are left to attend to the
ways in which the autobiographies of Apess, Jemison, and Black Hawk reshaped
the encounter and employed (in often subtle or compromised ways) sentimental
language in opposition to racism and removal.

5

The Book, the Poet, the Indian

Transcendental Intermediaries in Margaret Fuller's *Summer on the Lakes* and Henry David Thoreau's *The Maine Woods*

Transcendentalism originated from dissent within Unitarianism over, among other things, the perceived danger of an empirical approach to spiritual truth. George Hochfield explains, "It was very simple and the transcendentalists saw it: if you relied on the senses, you could never believe in miracles; and if faith depended on miracles, there could be no faith." Transcendentalists' emphasis on the necessity of intuition to religious faith extended to all of human understanding. Emerson's *Nature* (1836) most clearly outlines how Nature "stand[s] as the apparition of God," its elements corresponding with spiritual truths that must be intuited by the individual who enters Nature for this purpose. Perceiving the correspondence, the transcendental subject "penetrates the illusion of separation between internal and external, nature, man and God, visible and invisible, the particular and the universal." [1] To illustrate this point, Emerson offers readers his famous image of the transcendental pilgrim as eyeball: "Standing on the bare ground,—my head bathed by the blithe air, and uplifted into infinite space,—all mean egotism vanishes. I become a transparent eye-ball. I am nothing. I see all. The currents of the Universal Being circulate through me; I am part or particle of God." [2]

Like Emerson, Margaret Fuller and Henry David Thoreau rejected a Lockean sensationalism that would ignore the primacy of intuition and the spiritual significance of its subject matter, and they affirmed the divinity of humanity as achieved through an ideal perception of Nature. Insofar as the corrupting influences of social institutions alienated individuals from Nature, Fuller and Thoreau sought in sojourns to "uncivilized" lands—the Great Lakes region for Fuller, the Maine wilderness for Thoreau (among other locations in New England)—the means to overcome the perceived distance between "civilized" humanity and what Thoreau termed the Wild—or all that is the uncultivated and available as a resource for the expression of the soul. In their transcendental travel narratives, Fuller and Thoreau communicated the rather personal development of their minds in this context, the "process of growth, unfolding and ripening,"[3] and their intuited truths that could serve as guideposts for the readers' own journeys. More specifically, in *Summer on the Lakes, in 1843* (1844) and *The Maine Woods* (1864), respectively, Fuller and Thoreau transformed the well-known western sojourn into highly personal testimony regarding humanity's place within an organic universe. In the process, both authors considered the place of American Indians within the transcendental vision of Nature; whether judging the American Indians to be unsullied noble savages or the degraded victims of imperialism, Fuller and Thoreau felt compelled to ask what particular role they played in their (at once personal and universal) quest to transcend the false divisions between the material and the spiritual.

In the antebellum period Euro-Americans attempted to gain control over American Indian writing—and by extension, society—by applying a standard of Indian authenticity that declared the literate American Indian inauthentic and that precluded American Indian oral traditions from the categories of history and literature, unless Euro-American authors recorded those traditions in their own medium.[4] As Euro-American authorities assessed the authenticity of the American Indian autobiographer's identity, they also reclaimed the role of the intermediary who gives meaning to the encounter between the Native and non-Native within the work and at the moment of its consumption. Avid readers of all Indian works in this period, Fuller and Thoreau were familiar with contemporary American Indian autobiographies and, more broadly, with the figure of the moving encounter and the literary role of the sentimental intermediary. By necessity, they attempted in their narratives to assess the authenticity of the works they read and the Indians they met, but they also recorded how their experiences with American Indians made them reconsider their own transcendental authorship.

Although "they tried to move from the idea of a past savage perfection to one of a future civilized perfection,"[5] Fuller and Thoreau, like Lydia Maria Child, James Fenimore Cooper, and William Apess, responded to a cultural fascination with the sympathetic doomed Indian and the sentimental intermediary. As *Summer on the Lakes* and *The Maine Woods* dramatize the centrality of Nature—and more specifically of the individual's observation of it—to spiritual insight, they also depict the Indian-white moving encounter as an occasion for earthly transcendence. Fuller's and Thoreau's travels among American Indians, experienced and reported in the context of antebellum literary culture, allowed them to reflect on how humans and texts mediate difference and bridge the earthly and the spiritual realms. Exploring the textual and human mediation of difference within a sentimental culture, both authors catalogued their linguistic, rhetorical, and ideological resources, including the discourse of sympathy. Ultimately, Fuller and Thoreau revised the sentimental intermediary in such a way that the moving encounter between Indians and whites came to signify all mediation.[6]

Fuller, Thoreau, and the Moving Encounter

Fuller's *Summer on the Lakes* records a trip she took in 1843 just after submitting "The Great Lawsuit: Man versus Men, Woman versus Women" to her publisher.[7] Using money paid her by Sarah Shaw for language lessons, Fuller joined the family of her friends Sarah and James Clarke on a lengthy tour of the Great Lakes beginning May 23. Starting at Niagara Falls, a vastly popular tourist destination in this period, Sarah, James, and Fuller proceeded to Buffalo and then, by a five-day lake voyage, to Chicago. After two weeks in the city, Fuller joined Sarah, William Hull Clarke, and Rebecca Hull Clarke for a tour on the prairies, a seventy-mile trek to the small towns of Oregon and Belvidere, Illinois. Once they had returned to Chicago, Fuller and Sarah Clarke traveled to Milwaukee. Fuller ended her trip with nine days at Mackinac Island, where the annual Ojibwe and Ottawa encampment was under way. She then went home to Cambridge by way of New York.

Thoreau's *The Maine Woods*, a collection of essays published posthumously, treats excursions Thoreau and his companions took to the wilderness of Maine between 1846 and 1857.[8] "Ktaadn," first published in *Sartain's Union Magazine* in July through November 1848 as "Ktaadn, and the Maine Woods," is Thoreau's account of a journey he and his cousin George Thatcher made to North Twin Lake and Mount Katahdin in August 1846. In September 1853 he, Thatcher, and their Penobscot guide, Joe Aitteon, took a moose-hunting trip to Chesuncook Lake, an experience captured in "Chesuncook," first published in 1857 by James Russell Lowell's *Atlantic Monthly*. Thoreau was working on the third essay, "The Allegash and East Branch," when he died in 1862. At twice the length of the other two essays, it recounts his July through August 1857 canoe trip with Ed Hoar and their Penobscot guide, Joe Polis, on the west and east branches of the Penobscot River. Thoreau's sister compiled and published *The Maine Woods*, fulfilling what appears to have been Thoreau's original intent for the pieces, which reflect Thoreau's developing attitude toward American Indians.[9]

On the surface, to associate *Summer on the Lakes* and *The Maine Woods* with standard antebellum travel narratives, texts on American Indians, or sentimental works is to ignore the many ways in which transcendental authors positioned their writings in opposition to popular literature and called for artistic experimentation in accord with artistic self-reliance. Critics such as David Reynolds, Richard F. Teichgraeber III, and Paul Gilmore, however, have shown that the relationship of transcendentalism and popular culture, including the discourse of sentimentalism, was not solely hostile but in many ways mutually enriching.[10] Just as transcendentalists harnessed the reform impulse to promote the reform of the individual, Thoreau and Fuller harnessed antebellum literary practice to forward their social and philosophical arguments. In these particular travel narratives, the moving encounter provides fodder for metaphysical speculation.

In the penultimate chapter of *Summer on the Lakes*, however, Fuller assures her readers:

> I have not wished to write sentimentally about the Indians, however moved by the thought of their wrongs and speedy extinction. I know that the Europeans who took possession of this country, felt themselves justified by their superior civilization and religious ideas. Had they been truly civilized or Christianized, the conflicts which sprang from the collision of the two races, might have been avoided; but this cannot be expected in movements made by masses of men. The mass has never yet been humanized, though the age may develop a human thought.[11]

In addition to supporting Ann Douglas's description of Fuller as the heroine of tough thinking in an age of intellectual flabbiness,[12] this paragraph conveys Fuller's acknowledgment of the pervasive sentiment in literary treatments of American Indians. Though Fuller unselfconsciously employs the myth of the doomed Indian, she appears fully aware that her own account of encountering the Indian and viewing frontier space uses the popular language of sympathy. As critics have noted, oppression of the disadvantaged—be they women, Indians, children, or animals—is a primary theme of *Summer on the Lakes*, providing the strongest suggestion that Fuller's sojourn after the publication of "The Great Lawsuit" contributed directly to her subsequent composition of *Woman in the Nineteenth Century* (1845).[13] Further, the dialogue in *Summer on the Lakes* between "Free Hope" and "Self-Poise" pits a social and sympathetic Fuller (the former) against an isolated, corpse-cold Emerson, making a strong case for free and open expression of emotion (*SL* 148–49). Fuller candidly states her desire to avoid sentimentalizing the American Indians she encountered in the Great Lakes region, but she also emphasizes her sympathetic response to the spectacle of oppression, reclaiming and revising the affective language used to portray Indian-white encounters.[14]

Throughout *Summer on the Lakes*, Fuller, in the role of sentimental intermediary, recounts and recreates moving encounters. Fuller's narrative persona experiences intimate interaction with American Indians, expresses sympathy, critiques the impulse for encounter, then proceeds to her next destination. In chapter 5, for example, Fuller describes how she, her female companions, and the guide took shelter in an Indian encampment at Silver Lake, Wisconsin, during a rainstorm. She praises their hosts' "gentle courtesy, which marks them towards the stranger, who stands in any need"—a courtesy heightened by their own "extreme poverty." Despite the damp and dirt, Fuller becomes absorbed in the details of the lodge in which the women tourists huddle as well as in the actions of an "old theatrical looking Indian" and the agitated ponies outside. She is, nonetheless, keenly aware that her spectatorship makes their hospitality that much more impressive for, "it was obvious that the visit, which inconvenienced them, could only have been caused by the most impertinent curiosity" (*SL* 141).[15] The theatrical context for this scene is important for another reason: beyond encounter, Fuller figures herself as audience and her hosts as performers.

Fuller recognizes that, despite her access to the domestic life of American Indians, a great distance remains between them. "They seemed to think we would not like to touch them," she writes; "a sick girl in the lodge where I was, persisted in moving so as to give me the dry place; a woman with the sweet melancholy eye of the race, kept off the children and wet dogs from even the hem of the garment" (*SL* 141). Fuller's language resonates with one of Jesus's miracles: when Jesus heals a woman who has approached him in a crowd with the belief, "If I may but touch his garment, I shall be whole." In the midst of a poor and sick Indian family, Fuller's unsullied hem operates at once as a symbol of sentimental potential, or the white woman's sacrifice on behalf of the lowly, and a rebuke to her inaction. It suggests that the narrator desires to heal this group, that she, like Jesus, is aware of her power within this context, and finally, that the presence of sympathetic women within the American Indian home may very well lead to healing. The allusion shows up again in *Woman in the Nineteenth Century* as Fuller figures the greatness of such women as Sappho and Héloïse: "Across the ages, forms lean, trying to touch the hem of their retreating robes." [16] In *Summer* the momentarily Christological Fuller also moves forward in time, leaving this "extremely destitute" Potawatomi encampment and commenting that she and her fellow travelers have received "a picturesque scene for memory" (*SL* 142). Like Child's letter on the American Indian group at Barnum's museum, this passage exposes Fuller's capitulation to the commercial consumption of the sympathetic degraded Indian but also shows how she imagines the moment of encounter (despite the context of tourism) as potentially facilitating transcendence.

Thoreau in *The Maine Woods* likewise enters Indian country in pursuit of first-hand encounter, though his account carries a stark criticism of tourism's effect on American Indians. In the essay "Chesuncook," Thoreau's initial attitude toward his Penobscot guide, Joe Aitteon, is one of condescension; having hired him "mainly that I might have an opportunity to study his ways," Thoreau finds those ways disappointingly bastardized. [17] In Thoreau's view, Aitteon is another degraded Indian who has lost the admirable traits of his race while gaining only the basest elements of civilization. Aitteon whistles "O, Susanna," employs such colloquialisms as "Yes, Sir-ee" and "Sartain," cannot live off the resources of the woods, and facilitates the group's moose hunt to which Thoreau responds: "I already and for weeks afterward felt my nature the coarser for this part of my woodland experience, and was reminded that our life should be lived as tenderly and daintily as one would pluck a flower" (*MW* 107, 120). But at the posthunt campsite, where the hunters have begun to fire-cure their meat and near to which three more American Indian men camp, Thoreau experiences revelatory intimacy with the so-called degraded Aitteon and his compatriots. Thoreau does not join this group of men in their conversation but remains the quiet observer who (like the reader) encounters them from afar. It pays off; what Millette Shamir identifies as Thoreau's distant intimacy with American Indians and their cultural practice bridges the historical expanse between himself and what he considers to be the authentic savage.[18] Of the meat-curing process, he writes, "Altogether it was about as savage a sight as ever was witnessed, and I was carried back at once three hundred years" (MW 135). He even notes that, when nearly "roasted out" by the campfire, he recalled "the sufferings of the Jesuit missionaries, and what extremes of heat and cold the Indians were said to endure" (MW 136). Aitteon, the degraded Indian, becomes a vision of unspoiled savagery as Thoreau sits by the fire.

In addition, the men's use of "unaltered Indian language," which contrasts with their otherwise degraded habits, suddenly supplies "startling evidence of their being a distinct and comparatively aboriginal race." Until this point, Thoreau remains dependent on accounts he has read, underscoring that the Indian guides "knew but little of the history of their race, and could be entertained by stories about their ancestors as readily as any way" (MW 136), but their use of Native language reverses his judgment. Thoreau's fascination with language in general stems from his belief that "the extraordinary similarities among languages themselves might reveal the final meaning of the Logos as expressed through both them and the world they reflected."[19] For this reason, the American Indian language at the camp startles Thoreau and even supersedes his arrowhead gathering and his reading as sources of Indian knowledge. Thoreau writes with retrospective ecstasy: "These Abenakis gossiped, laughed, and jested, in the language in which Eliot's Indian Bible is written, the language which has been spoken in New England who shall say how long?...I felt that I stood, or rather lay, as near to the primitive man of America, that night, as any of the discoverers ever did" (MW 136–37).[20] It literally transports him back in time to a moment when Indian-white encounter (aborigine and missionary or explorer) represented the convergence of distinct cultures.

Like Fuller at Silver Lake, Thoreau comes into a surprising and charged intimacy with American Indians but then returns to his sojourn. Unlike Fuller, Thoreau does not, at this point in the work, consider even briefly the limits of his approach to American Indians as spectacle; "Chesuncook" concludes with Thoreau's promotion of "national preserves...in which the bear and panther, and some even of the hunter race, may still exist," envisioning, as the ethnographer George Catlin did, a western reserve for the benefit of Euro-American spectators as well as primitive man (MW 156). Thoreau, that is, promotes further consumption of the exhibited American Indian, hypothesizing a space that would work, in effect, like a museum.[21] In this way, Fuller and Thoreau conclude these encounters with reference to the picturesque, yet in subsequent sections of their works, they problematize the moving encounters in the context of their common study of the book of Nature.

The Text as Intermediary

Summer on the Lakes and *The Maine Woods* record their authors' intense awareness of contemporary depictions of American Indians, including moving encounters, and their active efforts to personalize and transform these depictions.[22] These works also represent Fuller's and Thoreau's conscious contributions to the very popular genre of the travel narrative. In the antebellum period, as western exploration and settlement rapidly increased, travel narratives proliferated. Lawrence Buell links the emergence of an eager readership to a number of factors, including the romanticism and didacticism of contemporary American literature, the vast areas yet to be explored by whites, and European curiosity about the new nation. Writing travel narratives in this context, Thoreau and Fuller not only supply reader demand but revise the form to philosophical, aesthetic, and political ends.[23] Assuredly significant differences exist between their two texts, not the least of which are the contrasting geographic and social foci: Fuller tours the Great Lakes region (including Niagara Falls, the Illinois prairie, and Mackinac Island) and contemplates the proper place for women in marriage and on the frontier; Thoreau traverses northern Maine and considers how best to balance Nature and Culture. Yet these differences confirm the breadth of both transcendental reform and the travel narrative genre, and they remind us that the transcendental experimentation with literary forms took place within a market that rewarded authors of the most popular genres.[24]

Even as they express a deep distrust of sentimental convention, Fuller and Thoreau consider the ways in which texts containing popular encounters may provide models for the intermediary. The authors' reading and travel experiences situate *Summer on the Lakes* and *The Maine Woods* in the rapidly expanding American library of books about Indians. Like many of the volumes in this collection, these books communicate factual information or personal reflections and what the authors perceive to be the national and spiritual significance of American Indian presence. Fuller's and Thoreau's narratives explicitly, intentionally mediate difference between American Indian and Euro-American culture and bring the non-Native reader into vicarious encounter with Natives. The authors' faith in texts and their own insights leads them to offer their narratives as sympathetic intermediaries between the American Indian and Euro-American and between the individual and Nature, the earthly and the spiritual. Paradoxically, though in a manner common for transcendental works, these works celebrate simultaneously the individual's immediate experience in Nature and the effectiveness of textual mediation.

Fuller's busy and varied tour of the Great Lakes region was framed by two library sojourns that had a great impact on her travel narrative. While in Chicago for two weeks, Fuller reports in *Summer on the Lakes*, "I read all the books I could find about the new region," including "all the books about the Indians" a fact proven through her discussion of works by George Catlin, Sir Charles Augustus Murray, Henry Rowe Schoolcraft, Anna Jameson, Washington Irving, and Thomas McKenney in chapter 2 (*SL* 87). Once she returned to Cambridge, she secured permission to use the Harvard library, where she continued to read widely in literature on the region.[25] Indeed, Fuller's account of her travels has long been noted (and often negatively) as highly text-focused, incorporating book reviews, poems, and letters, including ones not authored by Fuller, and two passages comprising what we might call a literature review of Fuller's research subject. Though her text is full to brimming with others' words, Fuller laments that she cannot include more: in "To a Friend," the opening poem of *Summer on the Lakes*, she announces, "I give you what I can, not what I would, / If my small drinking-cup would hold a flood" (*SL* 69–70); and in closing she declares, "I wish I had a thread long enough to string on it all these beads that take my fancy; but, as I have not, I can only refer the reader to the books themselves, which may be found in the library of Harvard College, if not elsewhere" (*SL* 216). What critics have described as Fuller's exploitation of "the polyphonic model of travel writing," or her inclusion in *Summer on the Lakes* of "multiple voices," also indicates a deep faith in textual mediation. *Summer on the Lakes* confronts the reader with the catalogue of experiences and voices emerging from frontier regions.[26]

Chapters 2 and 6, which Stephen Adams contends share a "series of cross-references, parallels, and contrasts," in particular expose Fuller's dependence on texts and her profound optimism regarding the textual record of American Indians.[27] Taken as a whole, Fuller's discussion of books in these two chapters hints at the kind of text she hopes to produce and helps us further to understand her authorial choices in *Summer on the Lakes*. In her analysis and comparison of recent travel narratives and works on American Indians, she appears to value most those texts that maintain a tension between sympathetic and objective observation, manifesting what William W. Stowe notes as "the disparate aspects of her consciousness: the appreciative and the analytic, the intellectual and the aesthetic, the conventionally masculine and feminine."[28] Fuller singles out those authors who express sympathy for American Indians and achieve linguistic and rhetorical accuracy in their translations of Indian words.

Fuller assumes the necessity of reading in preparation for encounter with American Indians; in chapter 2 she comments that the works she engaged with in Chicago "aided me in judging of what I afterwards saw and heard of the Indians" (*SL* 89). She declares that "Catlin's book [*Letters and Notes on the Manners, Customs, and Conditions of North American Indians* (2 vols., 1841)] is far the best," though others who have previously traveled in the region have told her "that he is not to be depended on for the accuracy of his facts." Her explanation under-scores affect as the key category of judgment: "They admitted, however, *what from my feelings I was sure of*, that he is true to the spirit of the scene, and that a far better view can be got from him than from any source at present existing, of the Indian tribes of the far west, and of the country where their inheritance lay" (*SL* 87; emphasis mine). Fuller insists that "the Indian cannot be looked at truly except by a poetic eye." From the context it appears she grants Catlin's eye this status because he produces writings that are first and foremost accurate in their depiction of spirit, the immaterial yet essential characteristics of American Indians and their land. Fuller places Henry Rowe Schoolcraft's *Algic Researches* (1839) in stark contrast with *Letters and Notes* and, in doing so, distinguishes between Catlin's intuitive powers and Schoolcraft's sentimental language. In Schoolcraft's translations of American Indian mythology, "the flimsy graces, common to the style of annuals and souvenirs, [have been] substituted for the Spartan brevity and sinewy grasp of Indian speech." His use of sentimental language creates an image of degradation Fuller draws, no doubt, from Catlin's 1832 portrait "Wi-jún-jon, Pigeon's Egg Head (The Light), Going to and Returning from Washington" (see fig. 3): they resemble "the Brave whom the bad taste of some white patron has arranged in frock-coat, hat, and pantaloons." As Irving's *A Tour on the Prairie* (1835) has "a stereotype, second-hand air" (*SL* 88), so Schoolcraft's (and Anna Jameson's) use of a popular style creates stale and inaccurate accounts. Fuller does not reject the use of feeling and intuition to bridge the gap between herself and the people whom she studies; rather, she refines the sentimental mode by rejecting all figures and expressions that, in her estimation, convey only second-hand emotion. Fuller claims for herself a new sentimental authorship that mediates without muddying the waters of genuine feeling.

Fuller argues that readers must pursue proper sympathy through literature by taking up those works that proceed in accord with genuine expression of emotion (Catlin's letters) rather than the careful employment of sentimental convention (Schoolcraft's tales). Texts that are poetic and faithful to the spirit of their subject matter actually mediate between the reader and the subject matter, approximating first-hand experience and enriching subsequent first-hand experience. Fuller, like a man she meets from Geneva, Illinois, precedes her trek to the prairies with extensive research, "thus realizing Wordsworth's description of the wise man, who 'sees what he foresaw'" (*SL* 91). In chapter 6, Fuller bases her criticism of texts by such authors as Jane Johnston Schoolcraft, Anne MacVicar Grant, Jonathan Carver, and Thomas McKenney and James Hall, as well as her disavowal of sentimentalism quoted earlier, on the careful and heartfelt readings that inform her authorship. Fuller follows her criticism in chapter 2 of School-craft's translations with her own translation of a myth titled "Muckwa, or The Bear" which tells the story of a man who marries a bear but must leave her and one of their children after his desire to hunt leads him mistakenly to kill his sister-in-law (*SL* 193–94). The tale is Fuller's commentary on Schoolcraft's translation practices as well as "the sorrows of unequal relations."[29] Indeed, Fuller declares that the tale is "poetical," "pathetic," and moral and that it reveals "the *savoir faire*, the nonchalance, and Vivian Greyism [witticism and whimsy][30] of Indian life"—the "spirit" of Indian life (*SL* 194–95). Fuller admits that American Indian culture possesses "a kind of beauty and grandeur, which few of the every-day crowd have hearts to feel" (*SL* 189).

Just before the "Muckwa" tale, Fuller offers a positive image of another Euro-American authorial intermediary in the poem "Governor Everett Receiving the Indian Chiefs, November, 1837," treating the Massachusetts governor's greeting to members of the Sac and Fox nations visiting Boston in 1837 (she includes the speech just after) (*SL* 182–87). Fuller praises Edward Everett as we watch him,

> Assume the very hue of savage mind,
> Yet in rude accents show the thought refined;—
> Assume the naiveté of infant age,
> And in such prattle seem still more a sage.   (*SL* 185)

To Fuller, Everett's speech has the traits Schoolcraft's myths lack, for it represents the proper communication of (decidedly immature) American Indian material by a Euro-American. Yet Everett's original audience, the Sac and Fox delegation, was not the same as Schoolcraft's. Everett assumes the ability, as Natty Bumppo does in *The Prairie*, to take on the American Indian point-of-view and translate cultural expression. Calling the speech "the happiest attempt ever made to meet the Indian in his own way, and catch the tone of his mind," Fuller misses the implication that Everett's welcome has been cloaked in an Indian-ized version of Euro-American sentimental rhetoric.[31] As proof of its effectiveness, we are told that the leader, Keokuk, "did actually shed tears" upon hearing Everett's reference to fatherhood (*SL* 186), but this response suggests more a victory for Everett's political language, his wisdom and authority before an emotive Indian. Fuller's determination to pair sympathy with objective observation falls aside in the context of a poetic meditation on the sway of supposedly heartfelt composition.

The story "Muckwa" proves significant to Fuller's conception of the textual intermediary in that it represents one of the "genuine fragments" of Indian life, a collection of which Fuller believes "will indicate as clearly their life, as a horse's head from the Parthenon the genius of Greece." *Summer on the Lakes*, with its numerous scraps of American Indian lives and cultural practices, presumably contributes to such a collection. Fuller also actively supports a broader, national collection of fragments: "We hope, too, there will be a national institute, containing all the remains of the Indians,—all that had been preserved by official intercourse at Washington, Catlin's collection, and a picture gallery as complete as can be made, with a collection of skulls from all parts of the country. To this should be joined the scanty library that exists on the subject" (*SL* 211). This pro-posal is in keeping with Fuller's literature reviews in *Summer on the Lakes*, her extensive inclusion of Indian material, her consistent praise for the work of Catlin, and her comparison of Indian stories to the Grecian horse's head. Yet one is surprised when Fuller—quite casually, quite suddenly—gives credence to racial scientists' study of remains, and more specifically to Samuel George Morton's collection of Indian skulls on which he based his 1839 work *Crania Americana* and his conclusion that American Indians, with their comparatively small cranial capacity, stand at the bottom of the racial hierarchy. Not just carved horse's heads but preserved Indian heads are necessary for the national institute. As Fuller pushes for an "accurate" sympathetic text, one free of the canned sen-timentalism for which she falls in the "Governor Everett" poem, she embraces the racial-scientific collection. Fuller's promotion of textual intermediaries finds her alternating between extremes that, in the eyes of today's reader, neglect the American Indian culture she means to illuminate or translate. Luckily in other chapters, which I will turn to in a moment, Fuller considers alternatives.

By 1850 and the second of his Maine excursions, Thoreau had begun his exten-sive research in "natural history, early American history, and the history of North American Indians before contact with Europeans." Thoreau's notes on the sub-ject eventually filled eleven notebooks (or twelve if one includes the notebook on Canadian topics). In the "Indian Books," Thoreau took notes primarily on first-hand accounts of Indian-white contact, avoiding literary works and eventually favoring compendiums such as the *Jesuit Relations* and Henry Rowe Schoolcraft's *Historical and Statistical Information Respecting the History, Condition and Prospects of the Indian Tribes of the United States*. Like Fuller's studies, Thoreau's were enriched by access to the Harvard library, which he gained through special peti-tion in 1849.[32] And like Fuller's studies, Thoreau's studies signal his faith in rev-elation arising from the textual compilation or cataloguing of facts. Thoreau's "Indian Books" make manifest the transcendental value placed on "*Contact! Con-tact!*" as well as on written accounts of first-hand experience (*MW* 71)—a value readily expressed in the figure of the moving encounter.

Informed as it is by Thoreau's reading, *The Maine Woods* only occasionally nods to other texts. As a result, Thoreau studies the promise of textual media-tion through a meta-narrative quite different from Fuller's. Thoreau foregrounds his ambivalence about bringing the process of writing and printing to the Maine woods;[33] but in so doing, he emphasizes the importance of texts to the popu-lar understanding of American wilderness. Thoreau similarly betrays an am-bivalence about the written record of the sojourn in the wilderness in *Walden*, dismissing his interest in travel narratives yet declaring, "A written word is the choicest of relics."[34] "Ktaadn" includes descriptions of multiple encounters with print in the midst of the forest and the author's often disgusted response. At Katepskonegan lake, he and Thatcher find "a large flaming Oak Hall hand-bill, about two feet long, wrapped round the trunk of a pine" such that "even the bears and wolves, moose, deer, otter, and beaver, not to mention the Indian, may learn where they can fit themselves according to the latest fashion, or, at least, recover from of their own lost garments" (*MW* 50). Here the presence of print is solely commercial and, as a result, ludicrous in a wilderness Thoreau insists is primarily traversed by Indians and wildlife rather than lumbermen and tourists such as himself.

More admirable sources of print exist in the woods of "Ktaadn" but in incomplete form and in seemingly inappropriate communities. Thoreau and Thatcher meet a Scotsman named McCauslin who, Thoreau argues, proves that "the deeper you penetrate into the woods, the more intelligent, and, in one sense, less countrified do you find the inhabitants; for always the pioneer has been a traveller, and, to some extent, a man of the world" (*MW* 22). McCauslin's intelligence and understanding of the region, oddly enough, stem from his travels rather than his reading material, which consists of "the Wandering Jew, cheap edition, and fine print, the Criminal Calendar, and Parish's Geography, and flash novels two or three" (*MW* 25). This wise man's library of popular texts finds its strange counterpart in the collection of odd fragments of slightly more highbrow material at the logger's camp: "some genealogical chapter out of the Old Testament; and . . . Emerson's Address on West India Emancipation . . . ; also, an odd number of the Westminster Review, for 1834, and a pamphlet entitled History of the Erection of the Monument on the Grave of Myron Holley." Thoreau's tongue-in-cheek reference to these "well thumbed and soiled" pieces as "the readable, or reading matter" reminds us of the scarcity of valued texts in the woods (*MW* 34). On viewing the burnt lands, Thoreau writes, "Talk of mysteries!—Think of our life in nature,—daily to be shown matter, to come in contact with it,—rocks, trees, wind on our cheeks! the *solid* earth! the *actual* world! the *common sense! Contact! Contact! Who* are we? *where* are we?" (*MW* 71). Thoreau's reversion to the language of the romantic sublime and his uncharacteristic dependence on italics and exclamation marks indicate, Ann E. Lundeberg writes, "a central gap or silence where determining the significance of experience has become impossible."[35] An essay in which Thoreau is unable to give full expression to the wilderness portrays the Maine woods as retaining only handbills, pulp novels, and scraps of the Old Testament. The failure of his language mirrors a failure of texts.

The last essay of *The Maine Woods*, "The Allegash and East Branch," and the subsequent appendix exhibit a greater faith in the influence of writing in the wilderness and of writing making the wilderness available to readers, a faith apparently springing from Thoreau's productive relationship with his guide, Joe Polis. Thoreau and Polis's conversations provide the reader vicarious intimacy and also data, or a substantial portion of Thoreau's record of American Indian vocabulary. Their conversations begin with a pact into which both enter willingly: Thoreau reports, "I told him that in this voyage I would tell him all I knew, and he should tell me all he knew, to which he readily agreed" (*MW* 168). In appendix 7, Thoreau includes a list of "Indian Words" that distinguishes vocabulary by source, indicating the fruitfulness of this pact (*MW* 320–25).[36] Thoreau takes a cue in appendix 6 from the Maine travel narratives he read in preparation for his trips and advises the reader, "An Indian may be hired for about one dollar and fifty cents per day" (*MW* 320). The juxtaposition of these appendixes, along with information on trees, plants, birds, and animals of the region, highlights *The Maine Woods*'s generic task of facilitating the reader's imaginative and actual travel to the same territory and showcases its ability to bridge the reader's and the Indian guide's worlds.

Fuller and Thoreau wrote travel narratives that use the notion of collection to transform the popular travel narrative into a transcendental text facilitating the reader's meditation on Nature. Fuller's anthology and Thoreau's appendixes provide readers with tales and facts through which they may intuit correspondence and thereby divine truth. Fuller, who sifts the entire range of texts on the Indian, and Thoreau, who seeks to transcribe Nature's language, conduct scholarship that forwards the text as the most successful intermediary between author and Nature, reader and Nature, Native and non-Native. In the process, however, they must define the role of the text's author as intermediary.

The Poet as Intermediary

In "The Poet" (1844), Emerson moves from the transcendental theory of correspondence between Nature and Spirit to a vision of literary experimentation and cultural nationalism. "The world being thus put under the mind for verb and noun," he explains, "the poet is he who can articulate it." Anticipating the arrival of Walt Whitman's *Leaves of Grass*, Emerson optimistically declares, "Yet America is a poem in our eyes; its ample geography dazzles the imagination, and it will not wait long for metres."[37] In *Summer on the Lakes*, Fuller also establishes her poetic calling as the creation of meaning from her observation of the natural world and of a society in flux: "I trust by reverent faith to woo the mighty meaning of the scene, perhaps to foresee the law by which a new order, a new poetry is to be evoked from this chaos, and with a curiosity as ardent, but not so selfish as that of Macbeth, to call up the apparitions of future kings from the strange ingredients of the witch's caldron" (*SL* 86). Fuller embraces the nationalism inherent in the Poet's project with her reference to Macbeth; in addition to creating from the frontier a new poetry, she would also describe the future of American settlement and governance in this place. *Summer on the Lakes* repeatedly presents such reflections on the poet's project, for Fuller insists, "What I got from the journey was the poetic impression of the country at large; it is all I have aimed to communicate" (*SL* 109). Yet neither Fuller nor Thoreau in their travel narratives assumes that Nature is primarily "a symbol, in the whole, and in every part"; rather, they adapt the theory of correspondence to their respective projects.[38] Fuller and Thoreau travel through a natural world that signifies the greater web of relations but also has immediate physical importance and impact on the observer. Though they revise the Emersonian theory of correspondence, they depend on a figure similar to Emerson's Poet, one who announces the significance of Nature, liberates the reader, and creates a peculiarly American form of expression.[39]

The narrators' respective poetic visions in these works make them effective intermediaries between the reader and the wilderness and between the reader and the resident American Indians, a fact emphasized by the contrast between the narrators and other inadequate and even ridiculous intermediaries. *Summer on the Lakes* implicitly compares Fuller favorably with "a 'guide to the [Niagara] falls,'" introduced early on in the work. Fuller sarcastically notes that "one might as soon think of asking for a gentleman usher to point out the moon." The sublime falls, overdetermined through their constant description in tourist guides of the period, should instead speak directly to the viewer. Fuller's complaint comes at the outset of her treatment of the region, distinguishing her own travel narrative from that of the commercially oriented, superfluous guide to the falls. Continuing, "Yet why should we wonder at such, either, when we have Commentaries on Shakespeare, and Harmonies of the Gospels?" (*SL* 75), Fuller associates the productions of Poets (the Bard and the Saints in this instance) with natural phenomena and, by extension, dissociates herself and her narrative from the common "guide." Similarly, Thoreau presents himself as possessing poetic powers of description quite distinct from those of other Maine travelers. For example, he complains that a lumberman thinks the highest praise for a tree is that its remaining stump is capable of holding a yoke of oxen (*MW* 229). The "Anglo American," he complains, "ignorantly erases mythological tablets in order to print his handbills and town meeting warrants on them" (*MW* 229). In contrast, as he writes in an earlier essay, "it is the poet, who loves them [pine trees] as his own shadow in the air, and lets them stand.... It is as immortal as I am, and perchance will go to as high a heaven, there to tower above me still" (*MW* 122). In contrast with the lumberman, Thoreau reads the mythological tablets of living trees rather than the width of their remains. Thoreau and Fuller present themselves as Poets whose narratives facilitate the reader's intuitive response to Nature and remain divorced (as much as is possible, given their positions within a tourist trade and a literary market) from the American commodification of Nature.

In theorizing and modeling their particular versions of the Poet, Fuller and Thoreau propose an ideal intermediary between Emerson's ME and NOT ME, or between the Soul and Nature, and between the Me and Other, the Native and non-Native, the civilized and the savage.[40] *Summer on the Lakes* and *The Maine*

Woods mention such failed intermediaries as the Niagara guide and the lumber-man but also the degraded Indian and racist Euro-American. Fuller-as-Poet appreciates picturesque scenery and domestic tranquility, affinities that help her encourage an understanding of and sympathy for the American Indians she encounters in the Great Lakes region. Thoreau-as-Poet relates first and foremost with the pine tree and the moose, yet his quest for understanding Nature leads him (as apparent over the course of *The Maine Woods*) to become judge and aficionado of American Indian culture. Both reject commodification as humanity's best approach to Nature, so both offer their own actions and authorship as the model and source for Euro-Americans' relation with American Indians. Doing so, they revise the sentimental intermediary as well as the travel narrative.

Promoting herself as Poet, Fuller outlines the inadequacies of those intermediaries who claim Euro-American and American Indian allegiance alike. The Ojibwe and Scotch-Irish writer Jane Johnston Schoolcraft provides Fuller "eloquent contradiction" of her assumption that American Indian women occupy an "inferior position"; however, Fuller rejects this opinion for that of the Scottish essayist Anne MacVicar Grant who, Fuller insists, "looked more at both sides to find the truth" and thus saw the women's subservience (*SL* 175, 177). As the reviewer of William Apess's *A Son of the Forest* questions the reliability of a Native historian, Fuller rejects Jane Johnston Schoolcraft's defense as false despite and because of her Ojibwe heritage.[41] Noting American Indian women's "coarse and ugly" appearances as well as their "peculiarly awkward gait, and forms bent by burthens," Fuller concludes, "it is impossible to look upon the Indian women, without feeling that they *do* occupy a lower place than women among the nations of European civilization" (*SL* 175, 178). Fuller wishes of course to make an argument for the necessity of challenging patriarchy (which she proceeds to do in this passage),[42] but her unfavorable cultural comparison, paired with her rejection of a part-Indian source, reinforces a cultural elitism favoring the Poet.

Just as she rejects the guide to the Niagara Falls, Fuller rejects particular Euro-American intermediaries who do not approach their tasks with sympathy. The Christological Fuller we find at Silver Lake embodies the potential for sympathy in contrast with other members of the touring party. The group's guide tells the women about a local man who quietly observed a pensive American Indian, and when the latter became aware he was being watched he "gave a wild, snorting sound of indignation and pain, and strode away." As Anne Baker points out, Fuller reveals her "deep misgivings about a 'tyrannous' mode of perceiving the world," when she exclaims, "What feelings must consume their heart [sic] at such moments!" (*SL* 138).[43] Though she gazes long on the scenery of the region, she offers descriptions primarily of American Indians with whom she interacts. That she can do this suggests her sympathy far surpasses that of other women travelers. Fuller writes, in the context of Indian women's "inferior position," "I have spoken of the hatred felt by the white man for the Indian: with white women it

seems to amount to disgust, to loathing. How I could endure the dirt, the peculiar smell of the Indians, and their dwellings, was a great marvel in the eyes
of my lady acquaintance" (*SL* 181). Fuller enters the home at Silver Lake and
the campsite at Mackinac with the goal of resisting both prejudiced repulsion
and blind sympathy, of refusing to "either exalt the Red man into a Demigod or
degrade him into a beast" (*SL* 175). Instead she serves as the intermediary who
brings her feelings and skills of observation equally to bear on her interactions
of American Indians and her textual translations.

The so-called degraded Indian informs Fuller's and Thoreau's definitions of
the intermediary. When Thoreau considers the failed intermediary in *The Maine
Woods*, he turns to the Indian whose growing dependence on Euro-American
commercial goods (particularly alcohol) has estranged him from his natural environment. In "Ktaadn" and "Chesuncook," Thoreau contrasts the Indian guide
directly with himself, suggesting that the Poet stands closer to Nature than the
Indian victimized by contemporary life. At the start of "Ktaadn," Thoreau expresses his distaste for the appearance of "a short shabby washerwoman-looking
Indian" and "shabby, forlorn, and cheerless" homes (*MW* 6). He comments in
disgust, "I even thought that a row of wigwams, with a dance of pow-wows, and
a prisoner tortured at the stake, would be more respectable than this" (*MW* 7).
Nor does he find a noble savage, or for that matter, a cruel savage, in his guide
Louis Neptune. Neptune and his companion do not meet with Thoreau and
Thatcher as planned but instead go on a drinking binge. Coming across them
at the close of the trip, Thoreau describes the men as similar to "the sinister and
slouching fellows whom you meet picking up strings and paper in the streets
of a city," for "in the progress of degradation, the distinction of races is soon
lost" (*MW* 78). Thoreau might add that in the context of wilderness travel the
same distinction is lost, for as Poet, Thoreau accesses the vision of Nature otherwise associated with "the red face of man." He has experienced the sublimity
of Katahdin, and he can see "an age not yet described by poets." Thoreau, in
contrast with the actions and the figure of Neptune, bridges cultural difference
and centuries to bring the reader a vision not of degradation but of "a still more
ancient and primitive man, whose history is not brought down even to the former" (*MW* 79).

In "Chesuncook" Thoreau expresses his anger over moose hunting, an activity he associates with the American Indian who cannot make a graceful transi-
tion between the Native and the Euro-American cultural worlds. Although he
begins by admitting a desire to see Indians hunting a moose despite "some com-
punctions," Thoreau offers only a harsh condemnation after the hunt: "What
a coarse and imperfect use Indians and hunters make of nature! No wonder
that their race is so soon exterminated" (*MW* 99, 120). Irate and self-righteous,
Thoreau pushes a condemnation of all hunters to a pronouncement of Indian
fate, a metaphysical justification of American Indian genocide. This "reporter or

chaplain to the hunters" can see the improper relations between American Indians and Nature, an impropriety linked directly to improper relations between
Euro-Americans and American Indians. His subsequent remarks on seeing "a
true Indian dandy," who dons urban finery after moose hunting, have a thematic
resonance (*MW* 144): hunting commodifies Nature and, taken to its logical end,
situates American Indians in degrading market relationships. "Alas for the Hunter
Race!" cries Thoreau, "the white man has driven off their game and substituted
a cent in its place" (*MW* 146). Indian displacement ends the encounter and the
Poet proves more sympathetic to Nature.

   Fuller also acts as a judge and offers herself as the Poet whose eye for natural beauty and affinity for domestic scenes enable her to "feel acquainted with
the soul of this race" (*SL* 222). Baker rightfully emphasizes that *Summer on the
Lakes* "is a book in which Fuller carries on an extended conversation with herself
about the best ways to see, as well as about the moral implications of seeing."[44]
The scenery around the Rock River in Illinois captivates Fuller, who must find
its correspondence to what she calls "the scene of some of the latest romance
of Indian warfare," the Black Hawk War (1832). Considering the magnificence
of the former land of the renegade Sauk leader, Fuller declares, "No wonder
he could not resist the longing, unwise though its indulgence might be, to return in summer to this home of beauty" (*SL* 94). Pages later, the picturesque
land damns Black Hawk's actions; after traveling on Black Hawk's Trail, Fuller
asks with incredulity, "How could they let themselves be conquered, with such
a country to fight for!" (*SL* 98). But she soon returns to praise for their taste of
scenery: "I will ever believe that the men who chose that dwelling-place were
able to feel emotions of noble happiness as they returned to it, and so were the
women that received them" (*SL* 100). Like Thoreau's consideration of hunting
in "Chesuncook," Fuller's rumination on Black Hawk's scenic country leads her
to blame American Indians for their victimization—they did not fully appreciate
what was wrested from them—even as she praises their relationship with Nature. Fuller naturalizes, poeticizes the "inevitable, fatal" dispossession of American Indians in the region: "Still, in travelling through this country, I could not but
be struck with the force of a symbol. Wherever the hog comes, the rattlesnake
disappears; the omnivorous traveller, safe in its stupidity, willingly and easily
makes a meal of the most dangerous of reptiles, and one whom the Indian looks
on with a mystic awe. Even so the white settler pursues the Indian, and is victor
in the chase" (*SL* 96–97). In both texts, the Poet's testimony to the proper relationship between humanity and Nature includes a correspondence of American
Indian defeat with a lack of sustained vision.

   In addition to looking upon the landscape, Fuller observes the domestic relations among American Indians that she might better understand them. Her
visit at the Potawatomis' encampment at Silver Lake leaves her with "a picturesque scene for memory" (*SL* 142), and at Mackinac she enters an encampment

and finds "a scene of ideal loveliness." In contrast with their elders, the young women appear to represent domestic nurturing and resistance to domestic servitude in the midst of a dying culture. "Here and there lounged a young girl," she writes, "with a baby at her back, whose bright eyes glanced, as if born into a world of courage and of joy, instead of ignominious servitude and slow decay." Other girls who are cutting wood, a chore associated with the drudgery of an Indian woman's life, Fuller describes as "talking and laughing, in the low musical tone, so charming in the Indian women" (*SL* 174). Finally, Fuller insists that "the Indian wigwam is the scene of the purest domestic pleasures" wherein she has "witnessed scenes of conjugal and parental love . . . from which I have often, often thought the educated white man, proud of his superior civilization, might learn an useful lesson" (*SL* 176). By encountering American Indians in their family roles and in their living space, Fuller momentarily finds an image contradicting the narrative of degradation and death. After declaring, "I feel acquainted with the soul of this race," she continues, "I read its nobler thought in their defaced figures. There *was* a greatness, unique and precious, which he who does not feel will never duly appreciate the majesty of nature in this American continent" (*SL* 222). This Poet finds her vision of Nature and the Indian domestic space interdependent and unique. Like the Emersonian Poet, she teaches her readers how and what to see, locating traces of the Soul in "defaced figures," transcending (momentarily) what she emphasizes as the inexorable historical racial decline. Though Fuller resists sentimentalism explicitly, she clearly resembles the sentimental intermediary whose sympathy is doomed.

Doom overshadows Thoreau's first two essays in *The Maine Woods*. In "Chesuncook," he describes his Poet's task in the context of the men among whom he travels in Maine: "The poet's, commonly, is not a logger's path, but a woodman's. The logger and pioneer have preceded him, like John the Baptist; eaten the wild honey, it may be, but the locusts also; banished decaying wood and the spongy mosses which feed on it, and built hearths and humanized Nature for him." Thoreau comes after forces associated in "Ktaadn" with crude commercialism, but here those same forces are linked to John the Baptist, the bombastic, if unsavory, predecessor to a literally liberating god. Like Fuller in her account of Silver Lake, the Poet associates himself with Christ the God-man, the bridge between heaven and earth, and by implication the Poet still acts as the intermediary between readers and Nature. Thoreau continues: "Not only for strength, but for beauty, the poet must, from time to time, travel the logger's path and the Indian's trail, to drink at some new and more bracing fountain of the Muses, far in the recesses of the wilderness" (*MW* 156). Like the logger, the Indian also humanizes Nature for the Poet; however, in this essay the Indian is the pathfinder while the Poet is the divine truth-sayer. Thoreau reconsiders this relationship in his final essay.

In "The Allegash and East Branch," Thoreau revisits his allusion to John the

Baptist and the related conception of the American Indian as he reconceives his role as Poet. Finding phosphorescent wood near a campsite, Thoreau notes, "I saw at once how, probably, the Indian jugglers had imposed on their people and on travellers, pretending to hold coals of fire in their mouths." This natural phenomenon—one clearly as rich in signification for Thoreau as the melting bank in *Walden*—prompts him at first to mock American Indian spirituality but then to admit his susceptibility to awe in the presence of the wood's "ring of light": "I little thought that there was such a light shining in the darkness of the wilderness for me" (*MW* 180). In true transcendental fashion, Thoreau appropriates messianic prophecy from the gospel of John by suggesting that one focus on rotting wood rather than the biblical God incarnate.[45] As Thoreau's testimony to "the light that dwells in rotten wood" accumulates (*MW* 182), he literally becomes "the voice of one crying in the wilderness, Make straight the way of the Lord."[46] No longer the Poet who follows the way of the woodsmen and Indian to uncover the significance of Nature, Thoreau now prophecies a greater revelation to come. This section of the essay ends with a string of sentences on the limits of Thoreau's insight: he calls himself "a believer," who has "much to learn of the Indian, nothing of the missionary" (*MW* 181) and admits, "Long enough I had heard of irrelevant things," knowledge of which "evaporates completely." He then leaves the reader with the image of this revelatory light extinguished, admitting, "I kept those little chips [of wood] and wet them again the next night, but they emitted no light" (*MW* 182). Relinquishing his authority as mediator, Thoreau acknowledges his need for the wisdom of "Indian jugglers."[47] In the final essay of *The Maine Woods*, American Indians emerge as models for the Poet, the Poet learns the limits of his insight, and a third possibility for the intermediary dawns.

The Indian as Intermediary

Fuller and Thoreau never denied their dependence on actual American Indians to authenticate their journeys and narratives. After imagining a savage presence at Niagara, Fuller declares that seeing American Indians camping on the river St. Clair, "gave me the first feeling that I really approached the West" (*SL* 80). Her excursion to Mackinac and her research while in Chicago and at the Harvard library show the extent to which Fuller pursued knowledge of American Indians to sharpen her understanding of the land to which she made her pilgrimage. Likewise, Thoreau's hiring of guides and writing of the Indian Books, begun by the time of "Chesuncook," leave no doubt that he believed American Indian culture, and more specifically that which survives from the precontact period, would be central to a richer understanding of Nature. Roy Harvey Pearce hypothesizes that upon death Thoreau believed that, "Savages, in their humanity and their thought, in their harmony and their wholeness, might guide men into the happiness proper to civilization." [48] For Fuller and Thoreau, records of travels in the American frontiers required an informed encounter with American Indians independent, or at least aware, of widespread stereotypes. Yet, as I have suggested in the previous pages, both resisted the idea of American Indians as facilitators of encounter and authorities on the relationship of humanity to Nature.

Fuller and Thoreau's use of the text and Poet as intermediaries in their travel narratives leads them briefly to consider the American Indian as the best candidate for bridging the difference between Euro-Americans and American Indians, revising the literary moving encounter to reflect their formulation of transcendental mediation. Fuller moves from harsh depictions of degraded and impoverished American Indians, as well as distrust of commentary by Jane Johnston Schoolcraft, to a vision of an American Indian leader-intellect who will preserve American Indians. During his three Maine trips, encounters with Indian guides, and composition of the essays, Thoreau comes to see the American Indian response to a rapidly changing society and environment—their negotiation of cultural difference, political tensions, and contested property—as a model for the transcendentalist. In these ways, Thoreau and Fuller entertain what so many nineteenth-century Euro-American authors reject: the possibility of American Indians as model intermediaries, as authoring forces in the context of Indian-white relations.

Although Fuller argues that Jane Johnston Schoolcraft cannot claim an objective perspective, in other passages of *Summer on the Lakes* she appears drawn to liminal figures, including contemporary American Indians. Her long review of the memoir of the Seeress of Provorst considers the life of Frederica Hauffe, who hovered between the living and the dead. More specifically, it contemplates the "peculiar inward life" of a woman who, upon marriage, the death of a spiritual guide, and a crippling fever, comes to live on the "atmosphere and nerve communications of others" (*SL* 152, 157). When Fuller considers "George Guess [Gist]," or Sequoyah, the inventor of the Cherokee alphabet, she notes "that his face had an oriental cast" and, further, that Hauffe's face did as well. Assuming the oriental quality as arising in an earlier social-cultural stage, Fuller proposes their features to be the result of "intellect dawning through features still simple and national" (*SL* 208). Gist and Hauffe are able to bridge disparate spheres—living and dead, literate and oral cultures—because they are positioned somewhere between the barbarous and the civilized stages and between the simply emotive and the intellectual. Moreover, Fuller suggests in chapter 6, "The historian of the Indians should be one of their own race, as able to sympathize with them." She turns to John Ross, the Cherokee leader who had led an organized resistance to removal, because his mind is "enlarged and cultivated" and "his eye [is] turned to the greatness of the past, rather than the scanty promise of the future" (*SL* 210).[49] The driving force for American Indian civilization is the educated

American Indian who is situated between cultures. "Could their own intelligent men be left to act unimpeded in their behalf," she declares, "they would do far better for them than the white thinker, with all his general knowledge." Yet they are not, and Fuller laments that the promise of the Cherokee is "now lost forever" (*SL* 212). In the end, Indian extinction pervades even Fuller's inspired vision of an American Indian intermediary.

Thoreau, in contrast, resists the language of doom. In "Allegash and East Branch," he depicts Joe Polis as possessing an almost ideal blend of cultural commitments and practices, placing him in direct contrast with Thoreau's previous guides: Louis Neptune breaks his word to go on a drinking binge, prompting Thoreau to declare, "We thought Indians had some honor before" (*MW* 78), and Joe Aitteon appears simply ignorant of what Thoreau believes to be his culture. Joe Polis has also been informed by Euro-American culture; he is an active Christian who insists on observing the Sabbath: he is a savvy social critic who travels to New York, Boston, and other cities; he has a net worth of six thousand dollars; and he has pursued Euro-American education in the hope of retaining his property (*MW* 193–95, 197, 162, 293). But Polis proves an effective ethnographic informant for Thoreau, who praises the authenticity of Polis's accent, his singing of Indian songs (in direct contrast to Aitteon's poor performances), his ability to "talk" with the musquash, and his skill at tracking (*MW* 169, 179, 206, 276–77). As a child, Polis learned much of what he knows from an old American Indian, but he admits that others do not have that opportunity and knowledge is being lost (*MW* 235). In "The Allegash and East Branch," Thoreau clearly comes to respect Polis for his knowledge but also for the way in which he retains his American Indian culture while living squarely in the political and economic systems of the contemporary United States.[50]

Thoreau's admiration for Polis leads him to replace the culture's incessant lament for the inevitably disappearing Indian with a celebration of American Indian linguistic resources. Polis's economic independence enables him to move freely between the wilderness and the city; this Indian intermediary adapts to Euro-American society and retains the language and much of the cultural practice of American Indians.[51] Thoreau, then, proposes that the Indian, degraded or otherwise, is not fated to disappear—after all, many live and work in Maine—but just as tragically for Thoreau, Nature and the American Indian language that holds the key to understanding Nature are endangered. This threat to humanity's understanding of Nature leads Thoreau to declare, "The Anglo American . . . cannot converse with the spirit of the tree he fells—he cannot read the poetry and mythology which retire as he advances" (*MW* 229). Dismissing the concept of the retreating Indian, Thoreau envisions a Natural world most completely understood by American Indians as obliterated by Euro-American settlement. Polis models a form of mediation that would stave off environmental and linguistic destruction.

Polis appears to share qualities with Thoreau, so much so that Gura suggests Polis functioned for Thoreau as a "Representative Man."[52] Polis acts, for example, as a self-ordained critic of Euro-American culture, arguing that Euro-Americans are "too fast," criticizing the prominent orator Daniel Webster as rude, and recounting his resistance to a Catholic priest who attempted to close a Protestant school for Indians (MW 197, 252–53, 293–94). Polis's ability to manipulate language and rhetoric suggests an additional affinity with Thoreau. Refusing to address his employers by name and sarcastically responding to Thoreau's and Hoar's condescending use of rhetorical questions, Polis shows an awareness of how linguistic practice contributes to unequal relations (MW 167, 289). As Thoreau seeks to purify vocabulary and rhetoric, Polis resists the dilution of his own language—just as he retains a "wild" affinity with Thoreau. Toward the end of the essay, Polis challenges Thoreau to a race, and Thoreau's subsequent scramble while toting a full load of greasy dishes humanizes the serious narrator. "O, me love to play sometimes," Polis laughs, and Thoreau quips, "I bore the sign of the kettle on my brown linen sack for the rest of the voyage" (MW 286). When Polis refuses to declare his happiness upon coming home—"It makes no difference to me where I am," he explains—Thoreau notes with approval that "there was no relenting to his wildness" (MW 296). Indeed, Polis's comment resonates with Thoreau's famous pronouncement, "I left the woods for as good a reason as I went there." Thoreau finds in his guide evidence of the life to which he aspires.[53]

With their emphasis on the role of the Poet and the power of the text to mediate between the ME and NOT ME, *Summer on the Lakes* and *The Maine Woods* forward the transcendental project of inspiring readers to commune with Nature. Fuller and Thoreau find that the American Indian's own intuition may be brought fruitfully to bear on overarching questions of Nature's spiritual resources in addition to the dilemma of Indian-white relations. For these reasons, the Indian-white encounter as constructed in the age of sentiment enriches Fuller's and Thoreau's respective perceptions of their authorial projects as well as of the lands in which they travel. They, in turn, revise the travel narrative to suit these projects. Although Fuller and Thoreau do not fully transcend the myth of the doomed Indian, their engagement with both the moving encounter and the idea of correspondence prompts them to consider a future inclusive of, rather than vacated by, American Indians.

6

"Sorrows in excess!"

The Limits of Sympathy in the Ethnography of George Catlin,
Jane Johnston Schoolcraft, and Henry Rowe Schoolcraft

In the antebellum period, the trans-Mississippi movement of explorers, survey-
ors, agents, settlers, and others and the subsequent impact of this activity and its
attendant ideology on the American economy and culture created a blending of
what we might identify as scientific and artistic pursuits or, more specifically, empirical and aesthetic expressions. The Lewis and Clark Expedition (1804–6) initiated a period of increased exploration of the territories and of related scientific
and literary developments. The often indistinguishable objective and subjective
responses to the overwhelming fact of "the West" and its Native inhabitants had
to do, at least in part, with the emergence of self-consciously American culture
and letters in the period, the creation of professional writers and scholars and
audiences to support them. The natural and social sciences in this period were
indebted to an imperialism that "understood itself primarily as a cultural project
involved in naming, classifying, textualizing, appropriating, exterminating, de-
marcating, and governing a new regime," but they also identified and celebrated
as American the unique and exceptional, practicing a form of "science exoti-
cism."[1] In an age of romanticism, scientific and artistic acts intertwined as both
took their energy from the pursuit of the unique and exceptional. Authors and
artists of this period pursued a distinctively national culture through the expression of individual vision stirred by the moving encounter with sublime American nature and her Native children but also informed by scientific catalogues of
natural and human features. American Indians proved common subject matter
for science and art because their "savagery" and their historical decline and "disappearance" required the distance of objective observation and the intimacy of
sympathetic exchange. From this context emerged antebellum ethnography, a
science concerned with cultural, social, and linguistic practices of the races as
recorded by an increasingly professionalized class of government employees and
curious travelers.[2]

The moving encounters in literature by such authors as Lydia Maria Child,

James Fenimore Cooper, William Gilmore Simms, Henry David Thoreau, and Margaret Fuller, with their focus on an intermediary's sympathetic observation of American Indians as communicated to a curious audience, may be seen as contributing and responding to early ethnography. More generally, early ethnography bears marks of sentimentalism, which performed a particular and important role in the antebellum considerations of the West. The scientific pursuit of knowledge through observation depended on the senses in much the same manner as the sentimental intermediary depended on knowledge of the heart, and feeling readily served as a sixth sense. Ethnographers like Henry Rowe Schoolcraft and George Catlin created scientific knowledge and produced what many would call artistic representations on paper and on canvas by using an empiricism that was framed, if not infused by, their sentimental relationships. Henry Rowe Schoolcraft collaborated with his first wife, Jane Johnston Schoolcraft, whose mother was Ojibwe and whose father was Scotch-Irish. Jane's talents as a translator and poet and the Schoolcrafts' marital relationship deeply informed Henry's earliest writings (indeed, many of these are best considered collaborations). Catlin traveled to American Indian communities up and down the Mississippi and Missouri Rivers and beyond, and the individual American Indians whose portraits he gathered taught him the rewards and dangers of an ethnographer's pursuit. Working in the nascent science of ethnography, Catlin and the Schoolcrafts developed methodology attuned to the affective as well as the natural "fact." When Brian Dippie differentiates between Henry Rowe Schoolcraft and Catlin in terms of their attention to Native humanity—"For Catlin the Indian was both an idea, a noble savage with all the virtues and flaws the phrase implied, and a human being; for Schoolcraft, the 'representative of a *condition*'"—he neglects Schoolcraft's lifelong composition of poetry and his earliest writings in collaboration with his wife, and he overemphasizes the stability of Catlin's sympathetic narrative.[3]

Works by George Catlin, Jane Johnston Schoolcraft, and Henry Rowe Schoolcraft, with their analyses of subjects' affections and rhetorical pathos, suggest that sentimentalism infused early ethnographic texts. Catlin's *Letters and Notes on the Manners, Customs, and Conditions of North American Indians* (2 vols., 1841) and Indian Gallery and the Schoolcrafts' manuscript writings of the 1820s and 1830s—particularly their early manuscript journal, *The Literary Voyager, or Muzzeniegun* (1826–27)—rely on and recreate moving encounters, proclaiming affective understanding of American Indians and calling for reader sympathy.[4] At the same time, these authors establish through their professional practices and their works what they determine to be the necessary distance between Euro-Americans and American Indians. Catlin's conviction that the "primitive Indians" of the Far West would be preserved only through their continued separation from Euro-Americans ultimately undermined his attempt to mediate between the two groups. Henry Rowe Schoolcraft's desire to examine Indian emotions caused him to consider his own and to develop a means of controlling danger-ous, overwhelming sentiment—an action complicated by his marital and work-ing relationship with Jane Johnston Schoolcraft, who similarly analyzed and managed affections through composition. Henry Rowe Schoolcraft and Catlin desired intimate knowledge of American Indians but found that knowledge too unwieldy and too volatile for comfort. An attention to moving encounters in the works of Catlin and the Schoolcrafts and their participation in the larger dis-course of sentimentalism suggests that America's obsession with sympathy, like its new emphasis on "objective" physical measurements, contributed to the codi-fication of racial difference in the antebellum period and to the related rejection of Indian sovereignty and rights.[5]

Science and Race in the Antebellum Period

Ethnography arose within the framework sentimental culture but drew energy from the development of racial science. Before exploring the emphasis on feeling in Catlin's and the Schoolcrafts' ethnography, we must consider the relationship between race and scientific empiricism in the antebellum period. In the years 1812–42, the work of what was once known as "natural philosophy" was relo-cated to the college or university, divided into subfields, and generally taken out of the realm of popular activity. George H. Daniels writes, "The sum of all these changes was the creation in the early nineteenth century of an esoteric body of knowledge called 'science.' As one would expect, the term 'scientist' was also coined at this time to refer to those who had previously been designated 'natural philosophers.'" Still, scientific work was not wholly removed from the grasp of the masses; public lectures on scientific topics proliferated in these years to the point that science and entertainment were not always readily distinguishable. The science developed and promulgated in antebellum America was dependent on "pure Baconianism—collection, description, and classification."[6] In this for-mative period, empiricism stood at the center of American science, and energy was spent on observation, collection of data, and classification.

Descriptions of the American Indians, African Americans, and other minori-ties within the multiracial nation and territories proved central to the creation of a distinct scientific tradition in the antebellum United States.[7] In particular, a cadre of racial scientists sought to uncover the origins of the races and debated the viability of two theories: monogenism, or single origin, which connected racial difference to environmental adaptations, and polygenism, or multiple ori-gins, which challenged accounts of a single creation. Because American science developed in the context of the debate over slavery and growing sectionalism and reflected the struggle over biblical literalism and historical determinism, its attention to racial classification received widespread attention. By the 1840s a substantial group of scientists, many of them from or working in the South, promoted polygenism, despite Judeo-Christian scriptures, and came to be known as the American School of science. These men pursued quantified descriptions of biological racial difference and focused their energy on the measurement of biological specimens, such as skulls, brains, and hair, that they felt provided hard evidence of Euro-American or white superiority and of uncommon ancestry.[8] The most prominent figure of this school was Samuel George Morton, whose *Crania Americana* (1839) became the standard bearer of American racial science. To write the volume, Morton amassed, measured, and compared a large quantity of skulls, concluding that the American Indian cranial capacity, thus brain size, thus intelligence, is less than that of the Caucasian as the result of postdiluvian adaptation. (In fact, Henry Rowe Schoolcraft included an essay by Morton in volume 2 of his *Historical and Statistical Information Respecting the History, Condition and Prospects of the Indian Tribes of the United States*, though he had harsh words for racial scientists espousing polygenism.)[9] In the hands of Morton and his many disciples, who mustered the concepts of biological species and adaptation to show how and why the "noble savage" would fade away, the narrative of the doomed Indian became the subject of biology as well as history.[10]

When American scientists collected samples and theorized racial origins, they implicitly modeled what Dana D. Nelson calls the "normalcy" of the Caucasian race. The ability of the scientist to see, with God-like vision, the origins of racial difference and the hierarchy of racial types established the superiority of the scientists' own racial category and its function as the standard of rational, civilized humanity. The activity of science, with its emphasis on accurate records and the dissemination of research through professional journals, underscored the act of writing itself as the most reliable sign of human reason and social progress. After all, "without writing, no *repeatable* sign of the workings of reason, of mind, could exist." Racial scientists posited the superiority of literate (or, perhaps, hyperliterate) races and cultures, all the while participating in a culture of letters.[11]

Ethnographers who examined American Indian life established their professional and racial authority through the act of writing (as the very name of their profession indicates). In fact, literacy was the subject as well as the tool of ethnography as the author analyzed what many believed to be the impeding effects of illiteracy on American Indian culture. Rather than focus on physiological difference and biological origins of the races, ethnography took the cultural, social, and linguistic practices of those races as its subject matter. Analyzing "living" data, not physical remains, ethnographers by necessity sought direct encounters with subjects and assistance from American Indian autoethnographers,[12] and they employed imagination and empathy in their interpretation of American Indian domestic life and social relations. The ethnographers' need to observe living subjects as well as inanimate artifacts lent immediacy to the task: their work, they declared time and again, must be finished before the demise of American Indian culture and Indians themselves. Additionally, the imperative that ethnographers come face-to-face with their subjects was a source of pride and of anxiety. While they could tout their brave adventuring as a form of public service—they sought out and preserved a fleeting savage life, after all—they faced the possibility of being implicated in that savage life. Ethnographers' sympathy for their subjects needed to be sufficient to the task of collecting data but not so strong as to make their analysis of that data dubious. Catlin embraced the role of a sentimental intermediary between American Indians of the Far West and Euro-American audiences back east, only to find himself, and in particular his artistic medium, a source of suspicion among both groups. Henry and Jane Schoolcraft applied a model of Christian marriage to their collaborative ethnography, but as their marriage declined, Henry questioned whether they too were guilty of the emotional excesses he observed among American Indians. Departing from contemporary racial scientists by focusing less on the biological component of historical determinism and more on the contribution of American Indians' affective qualities to historical change, these early ethnographers were soon caught between the two worlds they attempted to bridge.

George Catlin's Full-Bodied Empiricism: Overcoming Euro-Americans' "distrustful distance"

George Catlin, like Henry Rowe Schoolcraft, came to ethnography through other professional pursuits. Unable to achieve prestige in the art community, Catlin painted portraits and miniatures in New York City and later in Philadelphia during the 1820s. Then, in the summer of 1830 a new artistic opportunity presented itself: Catlin was hired to accompany General William Clark as he negotiated the Treaty of Prairie du Chien and to paint American Indians at Fort Leavenworth in northern Kansas. Catlin went on four more western excursions between 1832 and 1836—up the Missouri River, into the southwest territory, over the length of the Mississippi River, and across the Great Lakes region—and visited the infamous incarcerated American Indian leaders Osceola (Seminole) and Black Hawk (Sauk). On each of these trips, Catlin collected artifacts and portraits of western tribes for the purposes of gaining federal patronage and popular success. Also to this end, Catlin published a series of letters in the New York *Commercial Advertiser* during and just after his travels, and after 1836 he displayed his portraits and artifacts in "Catlin's Indian Gallery," a traveling exhibition and lecture series he took first to American cities and then to London and the rest of Europe. The gallery included more than five hundred paintings of American Indians (portraits and communal scenes) and western landscapes as well as a wealth of American Indian artifacts, including costumes, weapons, crafts, and even a Crow tipi. In 1840, Catlin began collecting and editing his letters to form *Letters and Notes on the Manners, Customs, and Conditions of North American Indians*, a work appearing serially in England and America then published in two volumes in 1841. In the letters and then the book, Catlin expressed his anger over the degradation of American Indians at the hands of fur companies and the U.S. government. Because of his outspoken views, the quality of his paintings, and bad luck, Catlin never landed a significant government commission and spent most of the rest of his life, at home and abroad, trying to make his Indian Gallery profitable.[13]

Letters and Notes tells the story of Catlin's professional development, not his professional failures. Letter 1 is a retrospective introduction that provides an overview of his project and an account of its genesis. Catlin reports that while he was working in Philadelphia, presumably sometime between 1821 and 1825,[14] a visit by "a delegation of some ten or fifteen noble and dignified-looking Indians, from the wilds of the 'Far West'" quickened his artistic pulse. The men were, Catlin remembers, "arrayed and equipped in all their classic beauty,—with shield and helmet,—with tunic and manteau,—tinted and tasselled off, exactly for the painter's palette!" His reported decision upon seeing the delegation initiates an extended description and defense of Catlin's professional calling:

> Man, in the simplicity and loftiness of nature, unrestrained and unfettered by the disguises of art, is surely the most beautiful model for the painter,—and the country from which he hails is unquestionably the best study or school of the arts in the world: such I am sure, from the models I have seen, is the wilderness of North America. And the history and customs of such a people, preserved by pictorial illustrations, are themes worthy the life-time of one man, and nothing short of the loss of my life, shall prevent me from visiting their country, and of becoming their historian. (*LN* 1:2)

Catlin's use of superlatives shows a retrospective enthusiasm. In this account, his urban moving encounter with "these lords of the forest" convinces him of the existence in the American West of an aesthetic paradise worthy an artist's total commitment. There, Catlin affirms, the subjects and their surroundings are naturally noble and attractive; there the inhabitants have an unrecorded culture and are, as Catlin, like so many of his peers, emphasizes, "rapidly passing away from the face of the earth" (*LN* 1:3).

Catlin's determination did not make him the first American artist to paint American Indians, nor was he the only artist of the Indian in the period of removal. Following passage of the Civilization Fund Act of 1819, the federal government began to collect portraits and information about American Indians, sending draftsmen on expeditions and hiring artists, most prominently Charles Bird King, to paint portraits of all American Indian delegations visiting Washington, DC.[15] Catlin emphasizes in Letter 1, however, that he determined not to paint the delegations visiting eastern cities but instead to visit American Indians in their homes and paint them where they stood, in his estimation, as the quintessence of artistic and historical subjects. More specifically, he explains, he felt he must go to the American Indians of what he names as the Far West ("the prairies and Rocky Mountains"), for the degraded American Indians of the frontier (the western region in which Euro-Americans and American Indians co-exist) are akin to "a basket of *dead game,*—harassed, chased, bleeding, and dead" (*LN* 1:10). In Letter 9, from the upper Missouri River, Catlin further contrasts the Far West with the frontier. In the latter space, American Indians are a "tainted class" who reside in "the most pitiable misery and wretchedness of savage degradation" because they have been exploited by greedy Euro-Americans. But the *"classic West,"* Catlin affirms, is home to "these uncontaminated people" for whom, he says, "I would be willing to devote the energies of my life" (*LN* 1:60). Catlin's beloved subject is the untainted American Indian in his natural environment, and the purity of the American Indian and his region depends on the absence of Euro-Americans. Catlin insists that he heads to the Far West to record images of American Indians and landscapes whose virtues are preserved through isolation from Euro-Americans.

Catlin, of course, appreciates the paradox of pursuing Indians he believes safest in isolation, admitting that while the distance between the East and the Far West safeguards American Indians, it also strengthens the prejudice of eastern Euro-Americans who create and support destructive policies. Catlin declares in Letter 1: "I am fully convinced, from a long familiarity with these people, that the Indian's misfortune has consisted chiefly in our ignorance of their true native character and disposition, which has always held us at a distrustful distance from them; inducing us to look upon them in no other light than that of a hostile foe" (*LN* 1:8). Catlin seeks to encounter American Indians because he is convinced he should and can help rectify this ignorance and subsequent violence. He will overcome the "distrustful distance" at which Euro-Americans psychologically and emotionally keep American Indians by bridging physical distance between them, approaching American Indians sympathetically, collecting accurate information and artifacts, and ultimately providing for Euro-Americans a strategically vicarious experience of the moving encounter.

In the account of his response to the delegation in Philadelphia and in his description of the Far West, its inhabitants, and Euro-Americans' ignorance of them, Catlin establishes for himself the vital role of sentimental intermediary, and secondarily the profession of ethnographer-painter. Catlin declares that he will figuratively open the Far West to scientists, historians, philosophers, and the American public through "a literal and graphic delineation of the living manners, customs, and character of an interesting race of people, who are rapidly passing away from the face of the earth" and "a very extensive and curious collection of their costumes, and all their other manufactures," all gathered by a man who approached his subject "with feelings to meet feelings" (*LN* 1:3, 4, 8). This three-part approach (recording, collecting, feeling) springs from Catlin's full-bodied empiricism, a method of ethnographic observation incorporating scientific, artistic, and sentimental techniques. Catlin asserts that he will overcome the "distrustful distance" by collecting and presenting to Euro-Americans scientific evidence, compelling portraits, and sympathetic accounts that, taken as a whole, will recreate for them the experience of direct encounter. At the same time, he will preserve the American Indian culture—though not American Indian sovereignty—by insisting on limited, controlled encounters by intermediaries like himself who do not ply their subjects with alcohol or meet them with guns.[16]

Letters and Notes treats not only with the future of American Indians but also with that of George Catlin, artist. During the period when Catlin supposedly reacted so strongly to the visiting American Indians, he was particularly frustrated by his professional limitations, the necessity of painting portraits to earn money and the public denigration he suffered at the hands of fellow artists in the National Academy of Design in New York. This opening story operates as a creation or origin myth for the lengthy text, as well as Catlin's subsequent professional life, and according to William H. Truettner it appears to be fictional.[17] But this possibility does not detract from the work that the myth performs: the construction of Catlin's sentimental intermediary role and his concept of the Far West. Catlin's emphasis on first-hand understanding of American Indians allows him to discount the work of others ("he who takes the Indian for his theme, and cannot go and see him, finds a poverty in his matter that naturally begets error" [*LN* 2:7]) and to claim authority for himself and his gallery. However, when Catlin justifies his intermediary role by pointing to the violence and degradation of the frontier, he inadvertently reveals the limitations of the moving encounter. Like Natty Bumppo of *The Prairie*, Catlin of *Letters and Notes* operates as both a translator of culture and the harbinger of destruction; his activities inexorably lead to the misunderstanding and destruction they are meant to circumvent.[18] Intending to bridge the "distrustful distance" between American Indians and Euro-Americans, Catlin never abandons the belief that geographic distance is a necessity and throughout *Letters and Notes* appears to admit that even a sympathetic observer cannot avoid contributing to the violence between American Indians and Euro-Americans.

For Catlin, his ability quickly and accurately to record the faces, costumes, objects, and natural environment of American Indians resulted in a useful collection for scientists as well as for average spectators. Letter 1 emphasizes that Catlin's sample is representative and of sufficient scope: he declares that he has "visited forty-eight different tribes"; made 310 portraits of American Indians and 200 paintings of villages and their customs, "(containing in all, over 3000 full-length figures)"; and compiled "a very extensive and curious collection of their costumes, and all their other manufactures, from the size of a wigwam down to the size of a quill or rattle" (*LN* 1:4). Catlin's attention to representativeness and reproducibility is clear throughout the work; he often promises that particular items he has mentioned appear in the gallery for others' analysis.[19] His concern with collecting artifacts and samples creates a burden during his excursions, but

Catlin perseveres. In Letters 54 and 55 he details his groundbreaking journey to the Red Pipe Stone Quarry at Côteau de Prairies where, against the protest of "a rascally band of the Sioux," he collects samples of the sacred red pipe stone that would be named catlinite (*LN* 2:166). Catlin concludes the account with a footnote declaring that Benjamin Silliman's *American Journal of Science* has presented an analysis "made by Dr. Jackson of Boston, one of our best mineralogists and chemists ... who pronounced it, '*a new mineral compound*'" (*LN* 2:206). *Letters and Notes* makes clear that Catlin's artistic pursuit is wedded to a scientific one and that his active collection of artifacts and data improves Euro-Americans' understanding of as well as their aesthetic appreciation for the American Indians and geography of the Far West.

Catlin's occasional criticisms of science target its use of theory without consideration for human expression. He focuses on the linguists and natural scientists he believes foolishly pursue the origins of American Indians while neglecting "their actual existence, their customs." The racial scientists are unwilling to leave the safety of their studies, which leads to the neglect of field data, and Catlin satirizes their questions by imagining a discussion between a "votary of science" and "his red acquaintance":

> 'You white man, where you come from?'
> 'From England, across the water.'
> 'How white man come to see England? how you face come to get
>   white, ha?'   (*LN* 2:230)

The ridiculousness of this Indian's interrogation undermines the pursuit of racial analysis to the exclusion of sympathetic understanding of living communities.[20] Catlin will humbly admit that he is not adequate to the task of theorizing racial origins, but asserts that he can offer more significant information and advice for the progress of science: "I have travelled and observed enough amongst them [American Indians], and collected enough, to enable me to form decided opinions of my own; and in my conviction, have acquired confidence enough to tell them, and at the same time to recommend to the Government or institutions of my own country, to employ men of science, such as I have mentioned, and protect them in their *visits* to these tribes, where 'the truth, and the whole truth' may be got" (*LN* 2:237). Only when scientists encounter living American Indians, not just American Indian skulls (notice the emphasis Catlin places on "*visits*"), will they develop an accurate and just knowledge of American Indian life.

An implicit criticism of the scientific practice of collecting Native remains—a practice of which Catlin was guilty—underlies the description of a Mandan gravesite and its mourners in Letter 12. The site, called "the village of the dead," includes hundreds of scaffolds whereon corpses lie until the structures decompose, at which time the bones are buried and the skulls placed in a large circle.[21] Although Catlin is careful to describe this interment process, his interest rests largely with the mourning practices surrounding it, for "if he [the traveler] will give attention to the respect and devotions that are paid to this sacred place . . . he will learn, at least, that filial, conjugal, and paternal affection are not necessarily the results of civilization" (*LN* 1:89). The extremity of emotion shown by mourning family members, Catlin is convinced, "will wring tears from his [the traveler's] eyes, and kindle in his bosom a spark of respect and sympathy for the poor Indian, if he never felt it before" (*LN* 1:90). Thus the Mandan village of the dead stands as one of the most moving sites in Catlin's travels and writings.

In his description of the Mandan's funeral rites, Catlin focuses on the mourners' interactions with the skulls and creates a strong contrast between their reverence for the remains and scientists' objective study of bones. *Letters and Notes* appeared only two years after Morton's *Crania Americana*, but unlike the skulls the latter work analyzes, the skulls at the Mandan village of the dead are "objects of religious and affectionate veneration" individually identifiable by the faithful mourner (*LN* 1:90). Catlin refers to the circles of skulls in the village of the dead as "Golgothas," alluding to "the place of the skulls" where Christ was crucified but also (inadvertently, most likely) using the same nickname of Morton's impressive collection of skulls at the Academy of Natural Sciences: "the American Golgotha."[22] Catlin encounters the Mandans and, rather than simply measuring their skulls, records the significance of those skulls to the survivors. The letter concludes with the telling comment that though the skulls would be "a very interesting study for the craniologist and phrenologist," the Mandan's emotional attachment to them would make it "a matter of great difficulty (if not impossibility) to procure them at this time, for the use and benefit of the scientific world" (*LN* 1:91). The Mandan Golgotha provides Catlin with a glimpse of American Indian humanity, and Morton's Golgotha a measure of their degradation as justified by science: the inevitability of American Indian extinction "can be easily proved—we have a civilized science that can easily do it, or anything else that may be required to cover the iniquities of civilized man in catering for his unholy appetites" (*LN* 1:260).[23] Science at present, suggests Catlin, works as the handmaiden of violent cultural and geographic imperialism, and he wishes to avoid such complicity. For all his sympathy at the Mandan village of the dead, however, Catlin nonetheless collected skulls and other sacred artifacts like pipe stone to exhibit for profit at the conclusion of his sojourn among the American Indians.

Insisting that the lack of Euro-Americans', and particularly scientists', affective knowledge of American Indians causes that "distrustful distance" between them, Catlin fills *Letters and Notes* with sympathetic observations of American Indians in their domestic, familial, and communal settings and roles. In so doing he creates a series of moving encounters. He repeatedly shows that direct contact with American Indians in the Far West allows him, and his audience through him, to sympathize with the subjects: "There is no difficulty in . . . finding him [the Indian] an honest and honourable man; with feelings to meet feelings, if the above prejudice and dread can be laid aside, and any one will take the pains, as I have done, to go and see him in the simplicity of his native state, smoking his pipe under his own humble roof, with his wife and children around him, and his faithful dogs and horses hanging about his hospitable tenement" (*LN* 1:8–9). But the majority of Catlin's audience does not and will not enter the American Indian community and home and thus depends on Catlin to interact sympathetically with American Indians on their behalf. Both *Letters and Notes* and the Indian Gallery arrange images of American Indian homes and domestic scenes with the effect of simultaneously providing methodical descriptions of American Indian culture and placing the audience in thrilling, vicarious contact with American Indians. In *Letters and Notes*, Catlin writes about purchasing a Crow tipi, includes a print of it, and reports that he will be "transporting it to New York and other eastern cities" for display (*LN* 1:44). Truettner notes that the tipi appeared at the gallery display in London's Egyptian Hall, "beautifully decorated with a series of hunting and battle scenes, and around this the artist had arranged, perhaps on screens, several thousand Indian costumes, weapons, and domestic utensils." [24] Catlin's placement of artifacts around the tipi indicated a thorough scientific collection and produced the effect of encounter (as seen in fig. 1). Similarly, Catlin's portraits, which in his own words were "as large as life" (*LN* 1:223), lined the walls of any room in which the gallery was displayed. Logically arranged in rows and columns according to tribal and regional categories, the paintings surrounded the viewer with a sea of American Indian faces—an experience akin to Catlin's depictions of "the gaze of the wild group that is continually about me" (*LN* 1:191). The gallery and *Letters and Notes*, and the commentary on the gallery in *Letters and Notes*, provided the audience with an array of scientific knowledge and the illusion of thrilling contact with the American Indian world. [25]

Catlin's written description of the Mandan lodge is a particularly effective example of a moving encounter in antebellum literature. The ethnographer celebrates it as "one of the most picturesque scenes to the eye of a stranger, that can possibly be seen" with its "graceful (though uncivil) conversational, garrulous, storytelling and happy, though ignorant and untutored groups, that are smoking their pipes—wooing their sweethearts, and embracing their little ones about their peaceful and endeared fire-sides" (*LN* 1:83). Plate 46 (fig. 2), depicts just this, with reclining Mandans in conversation around a communal fire, and emphasizes Catlin's perspective and the audience's through him. And in Letter 14, he writes that he has purchased from the Mandans "articles of dress and ornament . . . which I intend to exhibit in my Gallery of Indian Paintings, that the world may examine them for themselves" (*LN* 1:101). Through this construction of moving encounter in text and display, Catlin is able to prove that "it would be untrue, and doing injustice to the Indians, to say that they were in the least behind us in conjugal, in filial, and in paternal affection" (*LN* 1:121).

FIG. 1. Plate 22 [His Majesty visits Catlin's Gallery, the Louvre], from George Catlin, *Notes of Eight Years' Travels and Residence in Europe, with His North American Indian Collection*, vol. 2 (3rd ed., 1848).

FIG. 2. "Interior of a Mandan lodge," from George Catlin, *Letters and Notes on the Manners, Customs, and Conditions of the North American Indians*, vol. 1 (4th ed., 1844; repr., New York: Dover, 1973).

Like other Euro-American authors of "the Indian," Catlin depicts American Indians in domestic situations in order to examine their emotions and dramatizes their familial relationships in particular by dwelling on their mourning practices. His portrayal of the latter, however, complicates what in other works appears to reinforce the tragic, fated disappearance of the American Indian. For example, Catlin writes of American Indians for whom his portraits preserve the precious memories of dead loved ones, including the daughter of the Sioux chief Black Rock, to promote the vitality and accuracy of his art (*LN* 1:224n).[26] His striking description of Sioux bereavement for an infant resonates with Black Hawk's declaration in *Life* that, among the Sauk people, "The mother will go alone to weep over the grave of her child!"—affirming her humanity and defending her right to reside on land in which her loved ones are interred.[27] Plate 232 of various "Sioux cradles" includes a "*mourning cradle*," and Catlin describes in the accompanying letter the mother's practice of filling the cradle of a recently deceased infant with black feathers, "So lasting and strong is the affection of these women for the lost child," Catlin emphasizes, that the mother tends this item as if it were a child for the entire period of mourning (*LN* 2:133). In sentimental antebellum America, where the death of a child was a popular subject for evoking strong emotions, Catlin's illustration of the mourning cradle is a clear attempt to create sympathy for the American Indian mother who feels the death of a child as deeply as the white mother—if not more deeply.[28]

Catlin's emphasis on full-bodied empiricism and references to infant death and domestic scenes demonstrate his investment in sentimental knowing and his insistence as intermediary on a scientific method incorporating sympathy. Yet the limits of the moving encounter—the sense that sympathy will ultimately fail and the distance between spectator and spectacle will persist—readily appear. In Letter 27, Catlin tells of "a very aged and emaciated" Puncah who is abandoned by his tribe as they depart for buffalo hunting. Catlin's response is to luxuriate in emotion: "I lingered around this poor old forsaken patriarch for hours...to indulge the tears of sympathy which were flowing for the sake of this poor benighted and decrepit old man....I wept, and it was a pleasure to weep, for the painful looks, and the dreary prospects of this old veteran....In this sad plight I mournfully contemplated this miserable remnant of existence" (*LN* 1:216). Like the reader of Cooper's Leatherstocking Tales or the spectator of an Indian melodrama, Catlin passively but intentionally watches a tragic death that he might experience "pleasure," and the reader of *Letters and Notes* watches over his shoulder. When Catlin mourns at the hilltop grave of Sergeant Floyd of the Lewis and Clark expedition he again embraces melancholy as if pleasurable and finds that tragedy readily leads to sympathy: "Stranger!" he cries out, "oh, how the mystic web of sympathy links my soul to thee and thy afflictions! I knew thee not, but it [thy tale] was enough" (*LN* 2:4). This, however, is a grave of a peer, another white man seeking encounters in the Far West, and soon the limits of Catlin's sympathy stand revealed. Within a page of this account, Catlin mentions his visit to the grave of the Omaha chief Black Bird, who was, in accord with his dying wishes, buried on his horse, and Catlin pulls the chief's skull from the tall mound through a hole made by a "ground hog" (*LN* 2:6). The impulse to collect specimens overwhelms sympathy. The contrast between his responses to *"Floyd's grave"* and *"Black Bird's Grave"* represents a textual moment when Catlin, unawares, reveals his implication in the racial science he condemns.

Yet Catlin's closing criticism of pleasurable sympathy eclipses his pleasurable experience at the old man's grave. As in Letter 1, in Letter 58 Catlin attacks Euro-Americans for dwelling on historical (i.e., dead) American Indians rather than on living ones, declaring that the plight of the latter "lays an uncompromising claim upon the sympathies of the civilized world." He then proceeds, in no uncertain terms, to dismantle the present inactive form of Euro-American sympathy: "If the great family of North American Indians were all dying by a scourge or epidemic of the country, it would be natural, and a virtue, to weep for them; but merely to sympathize with them (and but partially to do that) when they are dying at our hands, and rendering their glebe to our possession, would be to subvert the simplest law of Nature, and turn civilized man, with all his boasted virtues, back to worse than savage barbarism" (*LN* 2:224). As he does throughout the text, Catlin uses the dual meanings of "civilized" and "barbarism" to expose the hypocrisy and greed behind Western imperialism. And although he argues throughout *Letters and Notes* that sympathy, created by encounter, will correct this, in the end he acknowledges, perhaps because he has demonstrated, that sympathy rarely persists beyond the first release of tears.

Catlin's Cautionary Tale

As the opening letter of *Letters and Notes* emphasizes, not everyone should act as Catlin does; his distaste for the "degraded" American Indians of the frontier leads him to fear similar cultural mixing in the Far West, and his knowledge of hostile American Indians leads him to fear for his life. According to Catlin, the reason he must head to the Far West, where Euro-Americans have yet to settle, is that Euro-American presence endangers American Indians. Commerce on the frontier, overseen by "traders and sellers of whiskey," debases American Indians (*LN* 2:83). Further, weapons, pathogens, alcohol, and armed conflict make the frontier a lethal environment; in Catlin's estimation the process of frontier settlement runs, "White men—whiskey—tomahawks—scalping knives—guns, powder and ball—small-pox—debauchery—extermination" (*LN* 1:99). If American Indians meet Euro-Americans by traveling east, the situation is no better, for "an Indian is a beggar in Washington City" and "contend[s] with the sophistry of the learned and acquisitive world, in bartering away his lands" (*LN* 1:85). Catlin supports his focus on the Far West and his criticism of American attitudes toward

American Indians by naming the dire consequences of encounter for American Indians.

Catlin repeatedly points out the danger that contact with American Indians poses to him. He tells the reader, "[My portraits] will be found in my INDIAN GALLERY, if I live, and they can be preserved until I get home." (*LN* 1:54). Catlin's fear of his early death is justified, for he and his companions are threatened by illness, hostile American Indians, prairie fires, and even buffalo. Catlin takes on the singular and isolating role of the intermediary; "I broke from them all,—from my wife and my aged parents,—myself my only adviser and protector" (*LN* 1:3). His obvious sacrifice for performing the role of intermediary makes his actions and his professional skills more impressive and encourages the audience to appreciate his collections as the products of a singular, selfless pursuit. In the final entry of *Letters and Notes*, Catlin offers himself as the model for successful and ethical study of American Indians. Not government or business officials, he argues, "but the humble biographer or historian, who goes amongst them [Indians of the Far West] from a different motive, *may* come out of their country with his hands and his conscience clean, and himself an anomaly, a white man dealing with Indians, and meting out justice to them; which I hope it may be my good province to do with my pen and my brush, with which, at least, I will have the singular and valuable satisfaction of having done them no harm" (*LN* 2:225). All this leads Catlin to a particular solution to the Indian Question. Just as Catlin's attitude toward scientific collection alters over the course of *Letters and Notes*, his acceptance of the Indian's doom disappears by the final letter, in which he encourages historians and artists to follow in his footsteps. If a Euro-American layperson will travel among American Indians, or at the very least review the best sources on them, Catlin asserts, he "will find enough to enlist all his sympathies, and lead him to cultivate a more general and intimate acquaintance with their true character" (*LN* 2:249). Christian missionaries should visit the American Indians of the Far West, who will be receptive to the religion because they have not developed "a burning sense of injustice, the most deadly and thwarting prejudices" (*LN* 2:244). In concluding his series of accounts, Catlin promotes full-bodied empiricism and the intermediary's re-creation of sympathetic encounter as the solution to the Indian Question. His sentiment-inflected ethnography is the best method for civilizing as well as studying American Indians.

Catlin's endorsement of minimal contact and lasting relationships challenges the logic of the moving encounter that concludes with dissociation. Yet the sense of tragedy creeps back into *Letters and Notes* through Catlin's reflection on the dangers posed to the intermediary in a time of aggressive settlement and civilization efforts. In his day, Catlin's literal sympathy with the American Indians angered many Euro-Americans, especially Southerners, and resulted in widespread attempts to discredit his work. Although Schoolcraft originally endorsed *Letters and Notes* and praised the Indian Gallery as "one of the best means, perhaps, of awakening sympathy for the race," he soon turned against Catlin, even writing to Congress to detract from Catlin's work.[29] Not surprisingly, Catlin defended himself by highlighting the sacrifices he made to come into direct and sympathetic contact with American Indians: "Even though some of them [my stories] should stagger credulity, and incur for me the censure of those critics, who sometimes, unthinkingly or unmercifully, sit at home at their desks, enjoying the luxury of wine and a good cigar, over the simple narration of the honest and weather-worn traveller (who shortens his half-starved life in catering for the world), to condemn him and his work to oblivion . . . merely because he describes scenes which they have not beheld, and which, consequently, they are unable to believe? (*LN* 1:5–6). Distrustful armchair ethnographers and racial scientists, Catlin charged, could not believe what was true because they lacked compassion for the sacrificing traveler and his subject matter.

Catlin responded to detractors through the story of Wi-jún-jon, or Pigeon's Egg Head, as well. Wi-jún-jon was selected by a federal Indian agent to represent the Assiniboine for a trip to Washington, DC, in the winter of 1832. "Dressed in his native costume, which was classic and exceedingly beautiful," he was the star of the entourage. After a year's travel in "the giddy maze" (*LN* 2:196), Wi-jún-jon returned to his community "with a complete suit *en militaire*, a colonel's uniform of blue, presented to him by the President of the United States, with a beaver hat and feather, with epaulettes of gold—with sash and belt, and broad sword; with high-heeled boots—with a keg of whiskey under his arm, and a blue umbrella in his hand." Only after a half hour of "mutual gazings" did Wi-jún-jon and his family and community recognize one another, Catlin claims (*LN* 1:56). Weeks later, when Catlin saw Wi-jún-jon again, his wife had cannibalized his clothing (she made herself leggings from the tail of his coat), his whiskey was gone, and he was held "in the estimation of his tribe, to be an unexampled liar" (*LN* 1:67). Catlin writes, "He was denominated a *medicine-man*"; moreover, "he was denominated the very greatest of medicine; and not only that, but the '*lying medicine*'" and the extremity of his magic won him execution (*LN* 2:199). In Letter 54, Catlin expresses sympathy for the tragic figure of Wi-jún-jon and interprets his plight for his traveling companion, Batiste: "We may call it a 'caution;' for instance, when I come to write your book, as you have proposed, the fate of this poor fellow, who was relating no more than what he actually saw, will *caution* you against the *imprudence of telling all that you actually know*, and narrating all that you have *seen*, lest like him you sink into disgrace for telling the truth" (*LN* 2:200). Catlin told this "parable" to audiences of the Indian Gallery and displayed Wi-jún-jon's scalp in anticipation of incredulity. Wi-jún-jon, an intermediary for the Assiniboine, had been doubted, though his reports were accurate, and his death was his people's loss. Catlin told Wi-jún-jon's story and displayed his portraits and remains to convince his audience of their loss should they doubt their own intermediary.[30]

FIG. 3. George Catlin, *Wi-jún-jon, Pigeon's Egg Head (The Light) Going to and Returning from Washington* (1837–1839), oil on canvas, 29 x 24 in. (73.6 x 60.9 cm). Smithsonian American Art Museum, Washington, DC. Gift of Mrs. Joseph Harrison, Jr. 1985.66.474.

Despite Catlin's rhetorical use of Wi-jún-jon's story as a defense of his profession, it contained for him a significant warning about the corrupting elements of mediation. Indeed, his painting *Wi-jún-jon, Pigeon's Egg Head (The Light), Going to and Returning from Washington* (fig. 3) underscores Wi-jún-jon's degradation after encountering Euro-American culture but before he encountered hostility at home. The canvas is divided in two, with full-length portraits of Wi-jún-jon on either side, before going to Washington on the left and after his return on the left. The returning Wi-jún-jon fits the description of the degraded Indian of the frontier whose bastardized clothing and alcohol consumption make him

APPENDIX—C.

CHARACTER.—(Page 256.)

Original.	Secondary.	Original.	Secondary
Handsome	Ugly	Warlike	Peaceable
Mild	Austere	Proud	Humble
Modest	Diffident	Honest	Honest
Virtuous	Libidinous	Honourable	Honourable
Temperate	Dissipated	Ignorant	Conceited
Free	Enslaved	Vain	Humble
Active	Crippled	Eloquent	Eloquent
Affable	Reserved	Independent	Dependent
Social	Taciturn	Grateful	Grateful
Hospitable	Hospitable	Happy	Miserable
Charitable	Charitable	Healthy	Sickly
Religious	Religious	Long-lived	Short-lived
Worshipful	Worshipful	Red	Pale-red
Credulous	Suspicious	Sober	Drunken
Superstitious	Superstitious	Wild	Wild
Bold	Timid	Increasing	Decreasing
Straight	Crooked	Faithful	Faithful
Graceful	Graceless	Stout-hearted	Broken-hearted
Cleanly	Filthy	Indolent	Indolen
Brave	Brave	Full-blood	Mixed-blood
Revengeful	Revengeful	Living	Dying
Jealous	Jealous	Rich	Poor
Cruel	Cruel	Landholders	Beggars

FIG. 4. Appendix C from Catlin, *Letters and Notes*, vol. 2.

not civilized but pathetic. Appendix C of *Letters and Notes* (fig. 4), which compares the "Original" and "Secondary" (or frontier) characteristics of the Indian, "reproduce[s] in tabular form" the before-and-after portrait of Wi-jún-jon: Handsome/Ugly, Temperate/Dissipated, Straight/Crooked, Graceful/Graceless, Ignorant/Conceited, Long-lived/Short-lived, Sober/Drunken, Increasing/Decreasing (*LN* 2:266)[31] Because this painting was widely circulated and made manifest Catlin's and others' description of the noble versus degraded Indian, it has become one of his most famous representations, finding its way into many texts, from Margaret Fuller's criticism of Schoolcraft's translations in *Summer on the Lakes* (1844) to the cover of Robert F. Berkhofer's *White Man's Indian* (1978), where it illustrates the imperialist perception of American Indians.

A closer look at the painting suggests that it treats the role of the intermediary in addition to the situation of the frontier American Indian. Wi-jún-jon on the left represents Catlin's noble Indian of the Far West, literally stepping out of an earlier Catlin canvas ("Wi-jun-jon, Pigeon's Egg Head (Assiniboine)," Plate 28 in *Letters and Notes*), with his detailed and authentic costume. He moves left in the panel (his left leg is even bent) toward a background image of the White House, carrying a pipe in anticipation of peaceful negotiations. He does not move toward the viewer—we see his face in profile as he looks undaunted and perfectly suspended between there and here. Nearing the site of the U.S. government, Wi-jún-jon embodies his nation as the White House embodies the young republic; yet on the right he has come to represent not political authority but cultural bastardization and disempowerment. Returning from Washington, Wi-jún-jon resembles nothing so much as the minstrel Zip Coon, much like the "true Indian dandy" Thoreau observes in *The Maine Woods*, who masquerades as a member of another class and race and in the process forfeits his masculinity.[32] With this odd ensemble, his locks and earrings, his aquiline nose, and his strikingly red skin, Wi-jún-jon does not look like those U.S. representatives he has met or those he has traveled to represent; encounter on behalf of others has made him an absurd figure.

Looking at both sides of the painting simultaneously, one notices that, for the most part, items of the one culture correspond to items of the other—the head dress with the feathered top hat, the jewelry with the epaulettes, the pipe and cigar with the pipe and the umbrella, the dress of a tribal leader with a military uniform—as if to embody his alteration in material items. However, notable exceptions and emendations result in the effeminate appearance of the figure on the right. The fan on the right also visually echoes the headdress, and the umbrella the phallic pipe. The alcohol bottles lack a visual parallel all together; they stick out of his back pocket as particularly alien and superfluous to this confused Indian, for Catlin did not include in this portrait the broad sword of his written account and of his original sketch. Wi-jún-jon on the left is authentic Indian, on the right, tainted; on the left he is manly, on the right, effeminate. The line down the center of the painting represents the distance of space and time and a division of the subject, which Catlin refers to as "this plight and metamorphose" (*LN* 1:56). Wi-jún-jon, in encountering U.S. authority, has been split between cultures and lost his manhood. The layout of this image emphasizes that the "returning from Washington" Wi-jún-jon has turned from himself, making membership in either the Native or the non-Native communities impossible. After moving between worlds, he finds himself on the outskirts of both.

Catlin's fascination with Wi-jún-jon's story contributes to a negative assessment of his own ethnographic practice. Wi-jún-jon's story-telling or "lying" is interpreted by his people as medicine, which Catlin insists, "means *mystery*, and nothing else" (*LN* 1:35). Catlin accuses the medicine men he meets of manipulating superstition to gain control over the community, taking credit when their magic works, blaming "the will of the Great Spirit" when it does not (*LN* 1:39). This markedly un-sympathetic attitude regarding American Indian spiritual practice does not keep Catlin from taking advantage of his own status as "medicine man" among the Indians, the access it gives him to portrait sitters. Letter 55, in which Catlin gives the fullest account of Wi-jún-jon and his fatal "medicine," begins with the story of Mah-to-tchee-ga (Little Bear) and the deadly feud Catlin's portrait of him created among the Sioux. While Catlin painted a profile view of Mah-to-tchee-ga, chief of the Hunkpapa band (see fig. 5), Shon-ka (the Dog), chief of the Caz-a-zshee-ta band, hurled a related insult: *"Mah-to-tchee-ga is but half a man"* (*LN* 2:190). Afterwards, Caz-a-zshee-ta killed Mah-to-tchee-ga in a duel, shooting away half his face and beginning a series of retributive strikes (*LN* 2:191). At a subsequent council, many Sioux argued for the execution of Catlin because, in the words of one, his *"medicine* is too great " (*LN* 2:193). Warned by a federal Indian agent, Catlin did not stop the next time he passed the Sioux encampment, and he noted that the portrait was "the last picture that I painted amongst the Sioux" (*LN* 2:194, 2). Unable fully to translate his technology into Sioux culture, Catlin found that his "medicine" worked beyond his control and placed him in grave danger.

Catlin justified his pursuits as intermediary by defining the Far West, insisting on the necessity of encounter to understanding American Indians, emphasizing the private, domestic, familial, and sentimental aspects of American Indian life, and underscoring the mutual danger of contact to Indians and whites in the Far West. However, as the parable and portrait of Wi-jún-jon and Catlin's association with medicine men implied, his mediation between whites and Indians placed him in danger and saved no one. Called a "white medicine man," Catlin found himself associated with American Indians he deemed liars and with Euro-American showmen who manipulated audience superstition and whose arts the rational and educated easily dismissed (*LN* 2:193). Catlin, after his ethnographic travels from 1832 to 1836, spent the rest of his life touring with his Indian Gallery and seeking in vain a purchaser for it. *Letters and Notes* contains the promotion of his work and his tragic knowledge of its failure. Catlin wished to overcome the "distrustful distance" between Euro-Americans and the American Indians of the Far West but discovered in that distrust an uncanny understanding of the mutual dangers of the moving encounter.

FIG. 5. George Catlin, *Mah-tó-che-ga, Little Bear, a Hunkpapa Brave* (1832), oil on canvas, 29 x 24 in. (73.7 x 60.9 cm). Smithsonian American Art Museum, Washington, DC. Gift of Mrs. Joseph Harrison, Jr. 1985.66.84.

Familial Collaboration in Jane Johnston Schoolcraft and Henry Rowe Schoolcraft's Early Writings

Henry Rowe Schoolcraft was neither an artist nor a showman but a government man whose study of American Indians was always calculated to capture the attention of his superiors. Yet like Catlin, Schoolcraft struggled with the personal consequences of an ethnography attentive to American Indian emotion, and more specifically, an endeavor that implicated him in an American Indian family. As the federal Indian agent at Michilimackinac from 1822 to 1841, Schoolcraft spent his time at Sault Sainte Marie and Mackinac Island, Michigan, attempting to establish federal control over a volatile territory and to study the "primitive" language and culture of the local and visiting American Indians.[33] He received American Indians visiting the agency, distributed goods, participated in negotiations and administered treaties, challenged the influence of British fur traders in the area, and led exploratory trips for resources. In addition, notes William M. Clements, Schoolcraft was "the first professional student of American Indian cultures," recording languages, stories, rituals, and domestic practices of the American Indians of the Lake Superior Region, particularly the Ojibwe.[34] Beginning in 1821, Lewis Cass, the territorial governor of Michigan who would go on to serve as the secretary of war under President Jackson from 1831 to 1836, requested that agents in the territory collect such information on the grounds that, to civilize the American Indians, the government must understand their moral and intellectual condition as readily revealed through a systematic consideration of their language and everyday practices. Further, Cass argued, federal agents' objective recording of American Indian ways would help preserve the culture of a people fated to die off. Schoolcraft's initial study of the language and practices of the Ojibwe and other tribes was prompted by the imperial desire to convert American Indians and by the myth of their disappearance.[35]

Schoolcraft's many ethnographic works contain important information about American Indians, embody the imperial project in particular ways, and as Joshua David Bellin details, communicate a "theory of a mythic mind in thrall to its own symbolic code[, which] shaped anthropology into the next century."[36] Schoolcraft's works also deserve study as influential sources of information for nineteenth-century American literature. By widely disseminating the oral literatures he collected and by composing numerous poems on American Indians, Schoolcraft made a remarkable contribution to the national literary scene and the popular conception of American Indians. In 1839, he established his national reputation with *Algic Researches*, and throughout the 1830s and 1840s he published hundreds of articles and poems on American Indians in periodicals and more than twenty volumes of collected material.[37] His greatest achievement as an author was the six-volume *Historical and Statistical Information Respecting the History, Condition and Prospects of the Indian Tribes of the United States*, illustrated by Captain Seth Eastman, which appeared from 1851 to 1857 (though with inconsistent titles). By the time Schoolcraft died in 1864, his popular writings and ethnographic studies had directly affected the work of Washington Irving, Francis Parkman, William Gilmore Simms, Henry David Thoreau, and Henry Wadsworth Longfellow.[38]

Through his literary activities, Schoolcraft established an additional purpose for the collection of American Indian traditions: the control of primitive emotion through composition. Schoolcraft's formulation of this task may be seen in particular in two manuscripts from the first decade of his ethnographic career that provided material for later work: *The Literary Voyager, or Muzzeniegun*, a journal produced in collaboration with Jane Johnston Schoolcraft and the Johnston family from 1826 to 1827 that was a key source for *Algic Researches*, and *An Essay on the Indian Character In Four Parts*, a long poem Schoolcraft first showed to Governor Cass in 1828 and later distributed to peers and the public in various forms and under various titles. In the former, the production of knowledge and the composition of poetry is a family act; the journal is suffused with Johnston family information both personal and applicable to other families of the region. In the latter, Schoolcraft portrays an American Indian family whose loving relationships suggest that Euro-Americans and American Indians share a common ground emotionally with regard to familial attachments but are radically different in their ability to control attendant emotions. Thus, in Schoolcraft's formative ethnographic writings, family is the helpmate and subject matter but a source of anxiety too. Schoolcraft controls emotion through writing, carefully and objectively recording the nature of relationships within his family and within "the Indian family" and by modifying American Indian stories for a Euro-American audience. His ethnography adopts the structure of the moving encounter and he the role of sentimental intermediary, developing through poetry as well as prose an ethnographic method that humanizes and sets apart the American Indians in sentimental terms.[39]

Governor Cass praised Schoolcraft for providing the most accurate and detailed responses to his inquiries and attributed this success to his "very favorable opportunities, which are afforded you by your communication with the amiable family," the Johnstons of Sault Sainte Marie.[40] The daughter of the famous leader Waubojeeg, Susan Johnston (Ozhaguscodaywayquay), like her husband, was prominent in the political and economic activities of the Sault Sainte Marie area. As the Johnstons' tenant, Schoolcraft depended on their expertise as he embarked on a study of the Ojibwe language. He wrote in a July 28, 1822, entry in his *Personal Memoirs*, "My method is to interrogate all persons visiting the office, white and red, who promise to be useful subjects of information during the day, and to test my inquiries in the evening by reference to the Johnstons, who, being educated, and speaking at once both the English and Odjibwa [*sic*] correctly, offer a higher and more reliable standard than usual."[41] In 1823, Schoolcraft married Jane Johnston and, as Michael T. Marsden puts it, won "a permanent position among the Indians and the traders of the Northwest."[42] Susan's position within the Ojibwe tribe and her eldest daughter Jane's knowledge of Ojibwe language and stories—as well as the expertise of the other Johnston children—meant that Schoolcraft could attend ceremonies otherwise off-limits to Euro-Americans and record in detail Ojibwe stories, despite the fact that he had difficulty learning the language.[43] In 1822, Schoolcraft felt compelled to defend the shift of his scholarly attention from Indian language to "fictitious legendary matter": "The fact, indeed, of such a fund of fictitious legendary matter is quite a discovery, and speaks more for the intellect of the race than any trait I have heard.... What have all the voyagers and remarkers from the days of Cabot and Raleigh been about, not to have discovered this curious trait, which lifts up indeed a curtain, as it were, upon the Indian mind, and exhibits it in an entirely new character?" (*PM* 109). Schoolcraft determined that the existence of such stories among the American Indians was the surest proof of intelligence and humanity; he placed himself in the company of two famous explorers of America but, in a sense, made his ability to "discover" greater than theirs.[44] Thus, Schoolcraft justified his new direction not through any professional shortcoming but by arguing that Euro-Americans could come closest to understanding and to sympathizing with the Indian mind through the study of oral traditions. The curtain he lifted was that of insurmountable difference, and he did so by attending to the "fanciful" and "wild" stories surrounding him as a white man among Indians, for they showed the Indian to be "a man capable of feelings and affections, with a heart open to the wants, and responsive to the ties of social life," a discovery he proclaimed "amazing" (*PM* 196).

Governor Cass appreciated this focus on stories, and soon Schoolcraft shared his findings with others interested in American Indians through publications and circulated manuscripts.[45] From December 1826 to April 1827, he created the hand-written *Literary Voyager*, which included local news, Ojibwe stories, commentary on American Indian languages, and poems and which he circulated among his neighbors at Sault Sainte Marie and among his peers in Detroit and various eastern cities.[46] Although Schoolcraft was the official editor of the *Literary Voyager*, the family authored the periodical collectively: Jane Johnston Schoolcraft contributed poems and translations of Ojibwe stories and history, including that told to her by Susan Johnston, and John Johnston supplied essays and poems. Schoolcraft had initially determined to study the language and lore of the American Indians in pursuit of professional recognition, but the *Literary Voyager* made his project a family activity as well. Four of the thirteen extant issues (numbers 2, 3, 4, and 13) relate the history of Susan's father, Waubojeeg, cementing the connection between Ojibwe history and Johnston family history.

An even more striking familial aspect of the *Literary Voyager* is its commemoration of William "Willy" Henry Schoolcraft, the Schoolcrafts' first son, who died unexpectedly at the age of two on March 13, 1827. The fourteenth issue (March 1827) is devoted entirely to the beloved child, including an extended obituary and a poem by his father, a sonnet by his mother, a poem by his grandfather Johnston, and even a laudatory letter from the attending physician. It may seem odd to some that a magazine filled with Ojibwe history and narratives would focus on a boy who, Schoolcraft emphasizes, had "a face of the purest Caucassian [*sic*] whiteness, eyes with the brilliancy of a polished diamond, auburn hair, and features of the sweetest amenity of regularity" (*LV* 144). However, Schoolcraft's professional duties became intertwined with family commitments, and what he began as a favor to Cass quickly developed into a personal pursuit.

Jane Johnston Schoolcraft's acknowledged contributions to the *Literary Voy-*

ager provide insight into the sentimental origins of Henry Rowe Schoolcraft's ethnographic and literary projects. Jane had an unusual upbringing. The oldest daughter and her father's favorite, she often accompanied John Johnston on his trips abroad and as a result attended school in Dublin for three or four months (though her parents were responsible for the bulk of her schooling).[47] The Johnston children's English educations were paired with American Indian educations; their revered mother continued to speak only the Ojibwe language with her children and taught them Ojibwe history and traditions. Jane Johnston's biographer, Marjorie Cahn Brazer, suggests that, as a result, "[Jane] shared the enlightened white man's patronizing pity for these demoralized [Ojibwe], but her own pride in her heritage reached back from the contemporary scene to her illustrious ancestors."[48] When she met Henry, Jane possessed admirable attainments and a historical appreciation for the customs of her mother's people. She quickly became a sentimental intermediary for her husband, the aspiring Indian agent, who could encounter Ojibwe culture in the safety of his own family.

Today we remember Jane Johnston Schoolcraft as an early ethnographer and poet who made essential contributions to the *Literary Voyager* and to Henry Rowe Schoolcraft's subsequent publications and whose work appeared in Anna Brownell Jameson's *Winter Studies and Summer Rambles in Canada* (1838). In a study of American Indian historians of this period, Maureen Konkle emphasizes that the recovery of Jane's poetry and her historical and ethnographic writings has been impeded by Henry's "effacement" of her contribution to his work. She argues convincingly that "Schoolcraft's transformation of the knowledge provided by his wife's family into evidence of Indians' difference, inferiority, and impending disappearance quite literally supported colonial control," particularly as Henry provided Cass and others with authoritative arguments in favor of removal.[49] What remains unexplored in Jane and Henry's early ethnographic collaboration is the extent to which Henry's use of Jane's compositions signals a marriage in which the wife readily submitted to the husband's control in the name of Christian morality, echoing the individual's submission to God.

In a passage dated 1823, Jane declares her intellectual and moral deference to Henry through the words of Portia in *The Merchant of Venice*:

> . . . the full sum of me
> Is sum of something; which to term in gross,
> Is an unlesson'd Girl, unschool'd, unpractis'd:
> Happy in this, she is not yet so old
> But she may learn; & happier than this,
> She is not bred so dull but she can learn;
> Happiest of all, is that her gentle spirit
> Commits itself to yours to be directed
> As from her lord, her governor, her king.

Schoolcraft, who "made his career on his wife's stories," as Konkle asserts, established his methodology through marriage to a Christian poet and translator who considered him her "king."[50] Henry's appropriation of Jane's work indicates not simply his belief in Euro-American intellectual and cultural superiority but also the couple's mutual vision of a sentimental marriage in the service of the husband's calling and mutual practice of sentimental authorship in the service of personal devotion. When it came to the relationship between Christian faith and marriage, Jane had the example of her mother to guide her. Like other Ojibwe women who married Euro-American men in this period, Susan Johnston did so in the context of Christian conversion; prior to her engagement, writes Jacqueline Peterson, Susan had a vision of a "guardian spirit" in the form of a white man who assured her he would save her from a destructive fire, and after her marriage she was baptized. While the Christian, patriarchal marriage was an institution of colonialism—part of the *"ideological assault"* that altered American Indian women's gender roles and deprived them of economic, political, social, and sexual power—that familial model was a part of her maternal inheritance as well.[51]

The *Literary Voyager* is the only Schoolcraft text that directly and specifically acknowledges Jane's contribution, although *Algic Researches* lists her as a translator. The issues of the journal attribute sixteen items to Jane or one of her personae, Rosa and Leelinau. Two poems are attributed to "Jane Schoolcraft" and eight to Rosa; one Ojibwe story is attributed to Jane under her Native name (Bame-wa-wa-ge-zhik-a-quay) and five to Leelinau. In particular, Jane's use of the pseudonyms allows her to write in at least two distinct modes. The figure of Rosa, in Jeremy Mumford's words, is "dignified, sentimental, and virtuous"; Henry assures the reader that "her lines...possess chasteness in the selection of her images, united to a pleasing versification" (*LV* 5).[52] Not necessarily chaste or in verse, Leelinau's writings stand in contrast to the controlled sentiment of Rosa's. Rosa adapts romantic poetry to the station of a civilized American Indian woman, and Leelinau presents to the Euro-American audience the alien culture of the Ojibwe by translating stories.

Moving beyond the contrast between Rosa and Leelinau, one finds a similar tension even within Jane's Rosa persona. The name Rosa, given to Jane-as-poet, animates the liminal status of a mixed-blood or métis author in this period. Jane's identity as an Ojibwe and Scotch-Irish woman results in odd poetry reflecting at once her interest in her mother's culture and "her reading of the English poets, especially those of the pre-Romantic and Romantic periods."[53] In "Invocation: To My Maternal Grandfather On Hearing His Descent From Chippewa Ancestors Misrepresented," Rosa adamantly declares her grandfather Waubojeeg was not Sioux using a five-stanza poem with an abbaccdd rhyme scheme (*LV* 142–43). Another Rosa poem proudly declares itself "By an *Ojibwa Female* Pen," underscoring the rarity of such an author and implying an Indian context for a poem otherwise generically romantic (*LV* 8). Poet Rosa displays an inner tension and compromise between the expression of emotion and Christian submission to God's will. In "Resignation," "Lines Written Under Affliction," "Lines Written Under Severe Pain and Sickness," and the poems dealing with Willy's death, Rosa draws on her faith to formulate a stoic response to physical and emotional hardship (*LV* 26–27, 84–85, 97, 153, 157–58). In the first of these, she confides, "How hard to teach the heart, opprest with grief, / Amid gay, worldly scenes, to find relief," only to continue, "But Faith, in time, can sweetly soothe the soul, / And Resignation hold a mild control." (*LV* 26–27). Rosa seeks emotional comfort in Faith and the control of emotions through Resignation to (presumably) God's will. Likewise, as the poet of virtuous sentiment, she reveals her own submission to a marriage that places her solidly in the domestic realm. In an untitled poem, the poet of natural beauty thinks of her husband as he "Glides down the Mississippi dark," where "nature's charms [are] in rich display," and asks, "Say, do thy thoughts e'er turn on home? / As mine to thee incessant roam" (*LV* 156). Rosa cannot hide her appreciation for the Mississippi valley, yet she makes no suggestion of traveling to it. She doubly contains her romantic impulse within loving thoughts of her husband and the verse expressing those thoughts.

The *Literary Voyager* gives us a direct indication of Henry Rowe Schoolcraft's conception of the proper marital relationship. In the first issue, Henry meditates on the submission of woman to man through union in a fabricated Indian legend, "The Vine and Oak." In this version of a common Victorian allegory, a vine asks an oak to bend over and support it, and the oak tells the vine that they would both be better served by the vine's twining around the oak where it stands. When the vine complains, "But I wish to grow *independently*," the oak instructs, "It is impossible that you should grow to any height *alone*, and if you try it, the winds and rain, if not your own weight, will bring you to the ground. Neither is it proper for you to run your arms hither and yon, among the trees. The trees will begin to say—'It is not my vine—it is a stranger—get thee gone, I will not cherish thee.' By this time thou wilt be so entangled among the different branches that thou canst not get back to the oak; and nobody will *then* admire thee, or pity thee" (*LV* 20). In response, the vine submits and "both grew and flourished happily together." This "allegory in the manner of the Algics"[54] instructs the reader on the natural relationship, biological and social, between man and woman, a relationship often linked metaphorically to the relationship between sinner and God and between American Indian and missionary or agent: woman submits to man, the believer to faith, and the savage to civilization. As Rosa's poems dramatize the submission of one to another for the good of both—the submission of American Indian ancestry to Euro-American expression, the submission of sentiment to Christian stoicism, and the submission of wife to husband—Henry's "The Vine and Oak" repeats this lesson in the so-called manner of the Indian. In a move strikingly parallel with Rosa's use of traditional European poetic form to defend her Ojibwe heritage, Henry produced a highly stylized form of American Indian legend to convey the values of sentimental culture.

Returning to Leelinau, we discover translated or, perhaps more accurately, transfigured Ojibwe stories that dramatize the dire consequences of the Indian's failure to control his strong emotion. Although "only one of these stories fits the sentimental model" as Konkle points out,[55] all of the stories do speak to a sentimental Euro-American culture with its interest in and apprehension regarding the unwieldy American Indian—the same culture that consumed William Gilmore Simms's tales of star-crossed Indian lovers. Three of the four legends attributed to Leelinau concern the transformation of children into animals as the result of physical and emotional abuse. "The Origin of the Robin" tells the story of a young man whose proud father insists he fast for twelve days, ignores the omen of his son's bad dreams, and then suffers the consequence: his son becomes a robin (*LV* 37–39). Abandoned by his siblings, the orphan of "The Forsaken Brother" turns into a wolf (*LV* 93–96). And "Origin of the Miscodeed" recounts how a young maiden is transformed into the Miscodeed tree during an attack on her home in which her parents are killed (*LV* 122–24). In a fourth legend recorded by Leelinau, "Moowis, The Indian Coquette," a young woman who denies the sexual advances of a man falls in love with a suitor made of "dirt," or feces (*LV* 56–57). While "Moowis" and the other tales may, as Konkle suggests, point toward Jane's faithfulness to traditional sources despite the overarching sentimentalism of *The Literary Voyager*,[56] when read in the context of the journal they suggest that the excess of emotion degrades Indians, making animals of innocent victims and filth-lovers of frigid women. In this way, Rosa's poems and Leelinau's tales bear related messages: encounter and union must lead to repression and control.

Thus Jane Johnston Schoolcraft's acknowledged contributions to the *Literary Voyager*, distinguished by her pseudonyms, insist on the necessity of containing emotion and yielding to the family structure and to God.[57] The liminal figure of Rosa—at once an American Indian and a Euro-American, a romantic poet and a submissive Christian—demonstrates through her poetry the necessity of allowing one half of the tension to control the other. The romantic Leelinau recounts Ojibwe stories easily read as allegories of the danger of uncontrolled passion, a danger to which Henry would eventually link the figure of Leelinau. Jane's pieces suggest that even a culture of sentiment must ensure that emotion is regulated, just as the institution of marriage requires the husband to check the wife and national progress requires the Euro-American to civilize the American Indian.

Civilizing Sentiment in Henry Rowe Schoolcraft's
An Essay on the Indian Character

The connections traced in the preceding discussions among sentiment, marriage, the family, and imperialism become clear in a manuscript by Henry Rowe Schoolcraft from the late 1820s. In 1828, Schoolcraft sent Governor Cass a lengthy poem on the traits of American Indians that he claimed had been under composition for "upwards of two years." Cass expressed appreciation for the poem, declaring, "the parts of Indian character are the most natural I have yet seen in poetry or prose."[58] Although neither Schoolcraft nor Cass mention the title of the poem in their correspondence, it was, no doubt, a draft Schoolcraft had begun in 1826 and with which he would continue to tinker through the early 1850s, titling it variations on *An Essay on the Indian Character* or *The Man of Bronze*. Of the approximately fifteen distinct drafts, fragments, and outlines extant, the most complete manuscript of the poem is an eighty-page bound copy bearing the title *An Essay on the Indian Character. In Four Parts*, a likely candidate for the version Cass saw in 1828. This manuscript is a crucial statement of Schoolcraft's formative thoughts on the study and civilization of the American Indian. The poem declares that the Indian character is family oriented but emotionally unstable, and in this light, the best model for the civilizing project is the marriage of Ethwald and Leelinau, otherwise known as Henry and Jane Schoolcraft.[59]

Why did Henry choose to versify his assessment of Indian character? His use of rhymed couplets in iambic pentameter suggests his childhood education included Enlightenment poetry of eighteenth-century Britain, with its emphasis on human reason as well as sensibility. Poetry, then, demonstrated his education and his professional aspirations, both as an agent (after all, he showed the poem to Cass) and as an author. He and Jane also entertained themselves by composing poetry, as Henry emphasizes in *Personal Memoirs*.[60] Ultimately for the Schoolcrafts, poetic composition embodied civilized life—gentlemanly activity and feminine moral authority; Henry noted, "Poetry is to literature, what woman is in life—it charms & sooths, and is never admired but when advocating virtue."[61] Just as through poetry Jane drew a parallel between her wifely and Christian duties, Henry associated his roles as Christian husband and Indian agent. In 1826 he wrote, "[The Indian's] very position—a race falling before civilization, and obliged to give up the bow and arrow for the plough—is poetic and artistic. But he had no sustained eloquence, no continuous trains of varying thought. It is the flash, the crack of contending elements" (*PM* 256). Further, in an essay titled "Poetic Development of the Indian Mind," Henry emphasizes that the "the pensive—the reminiscent" nature of Indian verse means, "if poetry is ever destined to be developed in such minds, it must be of the complaining and plaintive, or the desponding cast" (*HIS* 3:327, 328). Through the transcription and analysis of oral traditions in prose and in verse, Schoolcraft made poetry from the po-

etic traits of American Indians, claiming authority in the face of their impending ruin.

The four parts of *An Essay* proceed from Schoolcraft's analysis of American
Indian culture to his plans for civilizing it. Part 1 brings the readers into a moving
encounter, encouraging them "the houseless, homeless Indian to survey" and
describes at length the Indian's love of war and fame. Part 2, in response, emphasizes Indians' humanity as seen through their softer emotions of love and friendship, which suggest they are not truly without homes. Schoolcraft then considers
in part 3 the difficulties of civilizing Indians in the light of their supposed disdain
for husbandry. The poem concludes with an account of Ethwald and Leelinau's
courtship and a rousing call to adjust civilizing efforts with reference to Indian
nature—to "Go, teach the Ind[ian] to triumph over time." As the final four lines
suggest, Schoolcraft has an optimistic vision of the resulting conditions:

> Peace, peace shall reign! And rosy health delight,
> Contentment charm, and competence invite,
> And every season, spring succeeding spring,
> Augment the welfare of the tribes I sing.

The title of the poem suggests the poet's interest in descriptive ethnography,
and its execution confirms the central task of forever altering the character
described.

In particular, Schoolcraft identifies the Indians' indulgence in emotion as a
primary target of civilizing efforts, for what prompts the Euro-Americans' sympathy seals American Indians' doom. In part 2 of *An Essay*, Schoolcraft, like
Catlin, locates sentiment in familial relationships, but he takes great pains to distinguish between the Euro-American and the American Indian family. He begins
by describing a warrior with "pious grief" who mourns a fallen comrade and
vows revenge for his death. Next he watches as, "In softer strains deep, tremu-
lous & wild, / The Indian mother wails her infant child." Then, he eavesdrops
on the painful departure for war of a brave who reassures his lover, "I live for
thee, for thee shall I expire." Finally, and appropriately for a Schoolcraft composition, he paints for us a domestic scene: "Around his frugal fire, the father
draws, / The little groupe to whom his words are laws." Each of these emotion-
laden moments humanize American Indian subjects by placing them in situations similar to those experienced by Euro-American readers and reverenced for
their poignancy (mourning for a friend or child, parting from a lover, instructing
a child).[62] However, as soon as *An Essay* establishes the humanity of American
Indians through moving scenes, it reemphasizes their primitiveness through an
interpretation of the father's instruction, which takes place through storytelling.
In this way, Schoolcraft's poem exhibits what Bellin describes as a foundational
ethnographic tenet: "that myth was essentially different from history, that it
could not be comprehended—embraced or assessed—by historical means."[63]

According to Schoolcraft, American Indian oral culture, essentially fluid, casts even the most loving father and attentive children into moral darkness. "Tradition," Schoolcraft explains in *An Essay*,

> thus, draws out her motley chain [of legend],
> And when it sunders, fancy forms again
> Till grown to monstrous bulk, link blends with link,
> And in one maze we see the fabric sink
> Another fabric rises to its stead
> (As once the fabled hydra teemed with head.)

As one teller after another alters the stories, the stabilizing force of common history is lost. In its place arises a messy conglomeration of disparate worldviews. Schoolcraft sums up: "Each [storyteller] building on the ruins of the fall, / Till doubt and darkness settles upon all." Thus the father's best intentions to entertain and instruct his children through storytelling contribute to American Indian ignorance. The lack of a written record in American Indian culture translates into historical and moral instability, for "Truth flies the land, where letters never thrive." The Indian's paternal act that at first seems familiar now appears utterly monstrous, for legend must be submitted to the pen if its moral content is to be stabilized. Whereas Catlin imagines the ethnographer saving American Indians from the devastating effects of contact with the worst of Euro-American culture, Schoolcraft, in painstaking rhymes, shows how only through the mediation of Euro-American writing will the Indians be saved.

The rest of part 2 of *An Essay* meditates on the emotional instability of a culture bereft of the written word. We learn that the sentimental Indian at the graveside readily becomes the barbaric savage when endangered: "No spark of pity lingers in his heart, / No warm compunction—no relenting start!" Though Schoolcraft insists that these hot-headed people are "the wayward sons of Adam still!" his primary goal is to convince us that their emotions and moral judgment are erratic; the Indian, he tells us, "flits a feather, through life's airy dance, / Wrong oft through ignorance, & right through chance." Schoolcraft easily moves from the moral pitfalls of a culture with an exclusively oral record to those of a culture overly indulgent in emotion. He seems to warn that a people who pander to the emotions of the lover, parent, and child require writing to stabilize those individuals' strong responses to turmoil. In this view, the central, overwhelming trait of Indian character is the inability to write. From this springs the motley stories and the vengeful nature. The Indian, Schoolcraft says, "loves, hates, joys, fears, sorrows in excess!"

Ultimately, Schoolcraft suggests, recording and analyzing oral traditions is a moral imperative for those who wish to "civilize" American Indians. As he argues throughout his work, only the ethnographer can stabilize American Indian history and culture—and through them actual American Indians. The description of an insubstantial American Indian history appears in the first issue of the *Literary Voyager* (*LV* 6), and in 1835 Schoolcraft warned readers of the *Literary and Theological Review* that "the gossip and the historian" are indistinguishable in American Indian culture.[64] By the time he compiled the first volume of *Historical and Statistical Information* in 1851, Schoolcraft confidently linked the creativity of American Indian stories to the instability of American Indian history: "Whenever it is attempted, by the slender thread of their oral traditions, to pick up and re-unite the broken chain of history...their sachems endeavor to fix attention by some striking allegory to incongruous fiction; which sounds, to ears of sober truth, like attempts at weaving a rope of sand" (*HSI* 1:13). Schoolcraft's ethnography was intended to record a fleeting history and culture and, in the process, to aid the government's understanding of American Indians. But part 2 of *An Essay* gives it an additional task. The reason the Indian resists "civilization" is that he, like his stories, is "forever changing, yet fore'er the same." The ethnographer's recording of stories will tie off the "motley chain" of oral culture, will cement that "rope of sand," and preserve it as an unchanging artifact. This, in turn, will create a stable source for Indian morality and thus halt the Indian's wild swing between overwhelming love and furious passion—the emotional extremes that drive away the sympathetic Euro-American and end emotional intimacy. *An Essay* reveals Schoolcraft's evolving conception of ethnography to be a civilizing force in and of itself.

Schoolcraft's vision of emotional extremes being stabilized by the written word is a complicated one with which he apparently wrestled. As early as 1827, in the aftermath of Willy's death, he doubted whether even a family immersed in a literate culture could avoid emotions that overwhelm reason and morality. Printed in that fourteenth issue of the *Literary Voyager* is an extract of a letter Henry wrote Jane nine days after the death, making sense of their son's death as retributive: "God saw that we had erected an idol in our hearts, and to the end, that we might fix our attention with less intensity upon sublunary objects, transferred him, to that bright, eternal sphere." (*LV* 150).[65] The Schoolcrafts' love for their son had overwhelmed their love for God, and they had worshiped an idol like common savages. Even as he edited this issue dedicated to Willy, Henry seemed to question whether any amount of writing could temper parental love of this quality.

Further, as Scott Michaelsen has suggested, the story "Leelinau, or the Lost Daughter" in *Algic Researches* indicates that by 1839 Henry had reconsidered his personal and professional relationship with Jane and, like Catlin, considered whether his intimacy with American Indians came at too high a cost. The ethnographer adapted an Ojibwe story regarding "a girl who prefers a spiritual presence to an earthly spouse" into one that, like "Moowis," recounts a girl's disruptive resistance to marriage.[66] In Henry's version, Leelinau habitually visits the sacred but feared grove of pine trees, the Manitowak, which make her "dissatisfied with the realities of life" and "disqualify her for an active and useful participation in its duties."[67] When the son of a neighboring chief requests her hand in marriage, Leelinau's parents ignore her objections, and she runs away to a tree fairy. Allowing her melancholia and her sentimental attachment to nature to override her ties to human society, and rejecting any compromise between her duty to her parents and her fondness for the Manitowak, Leelinau literally fades into the forest. Thus Henry associates Jane, who had used Leelinau as a pseudonym in the *Literary Voyager*, with an Indian woman who refuses to submit her emotions to reason and herself to marriage and, as a result, loses human company and her very humanity.[68]

Such a reading of "Leelinau" supports scholars' accounts of Henry's increasing alienation from Jane and the Johnstons after his religious awakening in the late 1830s and subsequent involvement in the Presbyterian Church as an elder.[69] Schoolcraft spent additional time away from his family in the 1830s. In those years he led an expedition to the source of the Mississippi, published a narrative of the trip, negotiated various treaties, became the superintendent of Indian affairs for Michigan, and published his most famous collection of tales and observations, *Algic Researches* (which, again, reprinted Jane's legends without attributing them directly to her).[70] Seen another way, Henry rededicated himself to the politics of "civilizing" the American Indian, the profession of ethnography, and the extension of evangelical Christianity even as Jane's illness and addiction to laudanum led her to an early death in 1842. Moreover, Henry subsequently obscured his sentimental and professional relationship with his wife.

While the Schoolcrafts' writings and biographies suggest that Henry came to distrust his and Jane's ability productively to channel sentiment, part 4 of *An Essay* indicates that Henry, just before this busy decade, held up his marriage as a model for relations between man and wife and between Euro-America and Native America. To clarify how civilizing efforts need to be adjusted, Henry offers another "Leelinau" story, but this time the character of Leelinau refers directly to Jane and the story concerns her education and subsequent relationship with her husband. According to the poem, Leelinau, a beautiful young woman "from Ojeeg's warrior line," learns under the attentive tutelage of her Scotch-Irish father to "restrain the passions & improve the mind / To gain her maker's and her father's love." Her studies, then, work alongside her religious and familial faith to make Leelinau a paragon of feminine virtue. Key to her virtue is the careful balancing of "Books" and the "silent walk" in the woods, as well as "the prayer" and the "evening hymn." When she meets Ethwald, an intellectual and "stoic," her refinement wins his heart and drives him to create "frank, unvarnish'd lays, or lines resembling these," a reference to *An Essay*. Henry concludes with a catalogue of Leelinau's virtues, the declaration of Leelinau and Ethwald's marriage, and the moral: "Youth is the season when the yielding breast / Is moulded, formed, directed, and imprest." Leelinau/Jane represents at once the perfectly equipped wife and the perfectly civilized métis woman, and her accomplishments stem from careful reading, composition, prayer, and family devotion. In the 1820s, Schoolcraft uses her life as well as her works as inspiration, suggesting the essential contribution Jane made to his work and to ethnography more generally in this formative period.

Despite their marital rift in the 1830s (or, perhaps, because of it), the treatment of the affective lives of American Indians and the poets' marriage in *An Essay* remained relevant to Schoolcraft for decades. Schoolcraft culled at least one shorter poem from *An Essay* for his 1830 collection, *Indian Melodies*, and a year later he published a gift book titled *The Souvenir of the Lakes* that concludes with a poetic message titled "To a Young Lady Under Severe Sickness and Depression" by "H. R. S."[71] Then in 1833, Schoolcraft recited a version of *An Essay* to the Algic Society, an American Indian research and benevolence society he helped found that included such illustrious members as Lyman Beecher, Benjamin Silliman, Noah Webster, and Francis Scott Key.[72] Two proposed tables of contents found in his papers suggest that Schoolcraft planned to include a version of the poem in a never-published volume of his collected poetry. Most strikingly, Schoolcraft returned to the poem almost a decade after Jane's death and his subsequent marriage to South Carolinian slavery apologist Mary Howard. In December 1851 Schoolcraft sent a draft of the poem to William Cullen Bryant, asking whether he should publish this piece by a man named William Hetherwold. Despite Bryant's sage advice not to seek publication of the poem—for no one had heard of Hetherwold, he explained, and the poem was in the fashion of "some twenty or thirty years since"—Lippincott, Grambo, and Company published *The Man of Bronz: A Poem on the Indian Character. In Six Books* by William Hetherwold in 1852. Extant copies include only one book of the poem's intended six; one wonders whether the latter were expunged because of the portrayal of the relationship between "Ethwald" and "Leelinau."[73] The development of the poem indicates that though Schoolcraft obscured Jane's authorship, he never wholly abandoned the foundational role of their marriage (metaphorically and actually) in his professional life. Through their family-infused ethnography, Schoolcraft found a method for containing the "primitivism" of American Indian culture and American sentimental culture.

Ethnography and the Moving Encounter

Like George Catlin, Henry Rowe Schoolcraft believed American Indians would never be known unless Euro-Americans met them in their homes and attended to their emotional lives. Also like Catlin, Schoolcraft held that a fuller understanding of American Indians would be necessary before a successful solution to the Indian Question could be established. There the two men parted methodologically, with Schoolcraft focusing on American Indian language and stories as manifesting the essence of the American Indian character and Catlin practicing a full-bodied empiricism to recreate encounter for popular and scientific audiences. These two early ethnographers' investment in the sentimental culture's desire to experience (if only vicariously) physical proximity and emotional intimacy with American Indians led them to new knowledge with scientific and political purposes, information that would help the young nation create a better plan for incorporating (or more accurately, divesting and acculturating) its aboriginal inhabitants. At the same time, their moving encounters led both to question the prudence of seeking emotional intimacy with American Indians— intimacy appearing, like the American Indians, potentially treacherous and certainly fleeting.

For Catlin, the danger of a sympathetic encounter with American Indians did not lie in unfettered emotion but in violence, in the brutal acts moving encounters prompted among American Indians and in the professional community he rejoined back east. In his mind, he became another Wi-jún-jon, degraded and destroyed by sympathetic contact that alienated him from his own people. For Henry Rowe Schoolcraft, ethnography performed a civilizing role by controlling and stabilizing what he perceived to be the excesses of American Indian emotion. Jane Johnston Schoolcraft provided essential materials for her husband's scholarship and a model for the civilized American Indian, uplifted through her Christian devotion and wifely submission. The Schoolcrafts' marriage and common poetic and ethnographic pursuits, they believed, were touchstones for proper professional and moral behavior as well. As that relationship deteriorated in the 1830s, it perhaps provided an allegory for Henry's fear of unrestrained emotion and the unrecorded Indian. As I argue in the next chapter, Mary Howard Schoolcraft, Henry's second wife, used the story of her husband's first marriage to recalibrate the family model he employed in his ethnography and to appropriate intimacy between American Indians and Euro-Americans for the purposes of Southern slaveholders. The sympathetic contact Henry Rowe Schoolcraft and George Catlin sought appears to have established their professional identities and unsettled their self-conceptions, resulting in the desire to perpetuate Indian-white separation. To read their early works is to understand the interplay and interdependence of science and sentiment at the origins of American ethnography and the failure, in this context, of the moving encounter to represent sustained, respectful relations between Euro-Americans and American Indians.

7

Restoring the Noahic Family

The Three Races of America in Mary Eastman's *Aunt Phillis's Cabin*
and Mary Howard Schoolcraft's *The Black Gauntlet*

Henry Rowe Schoolcraft required extensive assistance when he compiled the six-volume *Historical and Statistical Information Respecting the History, Condition and Prospects of the Indian Tribes of the United States* in the 1850s because of a series of paralytic strokes he suffered beginning in 1848. Captain Seth Eastman, the primary illustrator for the work, performed many of the necessary office duties. The collaborators' wives also took part in the massive undertaking. Mary Eastman, who had published her own volume of ethnographic sketches in 1849, tirelessly promoted her husband for the job, and Mary Howard Schoolcraft, Henry's second wife, served as her husband's amanuensis.[1] A shared advocacy of their husbands' careers and respective contributions to the ethnographic literature of the period are not all these two women had in common. Both were Southerners who believed in the necessity of slavery and promoted their opinions in proslavery novels that reclaimed the sentimental familial vision of Harriet Beecher Stowe's *Uncle Tom's Cabin; or, Life among the Lowly* (1852) for the patriarchal slave culture.[2] The intersection of the Indian Question and the Slavery Question in Mary Eastman's *Aunt Phillis's Cabin; or, Southern Life as It Is* (1852) and Mary Howard Schoolcraft's *The Black Gauntlet; A Tale of Plantation Life in South Carolina* (1860) clarifies further the mutual dependence of sentimental and ethnographic discourses in the antebellum period and the interplay between sympathetic and empirical impulses in the moving encounter. Indeed, Mary Howard Schoolcraft revises not only the most famous abolitionist novel but also the early ethnographic collaboration of Henry Rowe Schoolcraft and Jane Johnston Schoolcraft.

As I argue in the previous chapter, foundational ethnographic works by Henry and Jane Schoolcraft reflected a sentimental culture's preoccupation with familial attachments, its fascination with sympathy in the presence of difference, and its fear that the moving encounter between American Indians and Euro-Americans would unleash unwieldy and even destructive emotions. Their ethnographic writings revealed their literary aspirations, but, more important, the works influenced contemporary belles lettres. Most notably, Henry Wadsworth Longfellow borrowed freely from Henry Rowe Schoolcraft's works for his *Song of Hiawatha* (1855), and Schoolcraft in his subsequent *Myth of Hiawatha* (1856) and published poetry showed his desire to capitalize on the literary as well as scientific market for his wares.[3] For Mary Howard Schoolcraft and Mary Eastman, ethnographic and sentimental discourses converged in their common conception of race as a family issue, broadly and complexly conceived, and likewise led to literary authorship. Like many authors in the antebellum period, including William Gilmore Simms, these authors were concerned with the origin and characteristics of racial difference in the larger human family, the impact of race on the structure of the individual family, or basic social unit, and the role of race in the construction and maintenance of the national family. As Lucy Maddox notes, "To figure the nation as a family, especially in an era in many ways uncritical of patriarchy, is to depoliticize questions of power and to naturalize social and political hierarchies."[4] As Southerners, ethnographers, and wives of federal employees (an army captain and a former Indian agent/congressional historian, respectively), Eastman and Schoolcraft described the United States as a benevolent patriarchy in which white women were naturally situated between their male partners and the childlike minorities both tended.

Complicating Schoolcraft and Eastman's familial vision was their common struggle to accept their mixed-blood stepchildren. Seth Eastman, during his first tour of duty at Fort Snelling and before his marriage, lived with a Sioux woman who bore him a daughter. The extent to which Mary Eastman had a relationship with her stepdaughter, Nancy, while residing at Fort Snelling in the subsequent decade is somewhat unclear; however, her writings leave sufficient evidence that she frowned on mixed-race families. Mary Howard Schoolcraft was horrified by her husband's previous marriage to a mixed-blood woman and by the existence of their children. She includes in *The Black Gauntlet* a ruthless account of his "squaw" wife and their reportedly debased offspring. Not surprisingly, Mary Eastman and Mary Howard Schoolcraft defend the paternalistic institution of slavery through ethnographic observations of American Indians and African Americans and through the portrayal of families (actual and figurative) endangered by challenges to the racial hierarchy.

Encounters between "The Three Races of America"

Simms, Eastman, and Schoolcraft were not the only antebellum authors to link the Indian and the Slavery Questions through familial models; in a period when federal Indian policy and the defense of slavery were characterized by paternalism, a number of works considered the relative position of the nation's two "dependent" races. Comparisons of the races from this period included empirical observations informed by attention to the affections, reflecting the rise of ethnography and the popularity of sentimental literature. In a convergence of scientific and affective discourses, catalogues of physical and cultural differences were complemented with details of the races' emotional displays, including and especially in the context of familial relations. The comparisons often reinforced a hierarchy based on the individual's ability to control the public displays of emotion (as seen in Simms's short stories as well as Henry Rowe Schoolcraft's ethnography): American Indians were stoical, though likely to erupt in violent emotion, especially when drinking; African Americans indulged their emotions, and in particular their pride, through frivolous displays that end when the slave is reprimanded; and Euro-Americans observed members of both groups with sympathetic judgment, determining how best to rein in excessive emotion and cultivate productive, appropriate feelings among these inferiors. The centrality of the family to considerations of race went above and beyond the issue of direct biological inheritance and emphasized emotional bonds and emotional differences in need of classification and management. The patriarchal family, with its structure based on the presumed superiority of the husband/father and the primal emotional bonds of its members, was a model for proper relations among the races. As seen in this literature, the family, in either its ideal or its dysfunctional state, provided a ready symbol for the multiracial nation in the antebellum period.[5]

Examples of moving encounters that include an African American participant abound in antebellum literature, but few are richer than those found in Alexis de Tocqueville's *Democracy in America* (1835) and Martin R. Delany's *Blake; or, The Huts of America* (1861–62) because the authors of these works self-consciously draw on the common intersection of the family and racial hierarchy in contemporary literature and practice a sentiment-informed ethnography. In the final chapter of the first volume of *Democracy in America*, "The Present and Probably Future Condition of the Three Races that Inhabit the Territory of the United States," Tocqueville emphasizes the oppression African Americans and American Indians have experienced at the hands of Euro-Americans and theorizes why "they do not amalgamate, and each race fulfills its destiny apart."[6] To illustrate he recounts a scene he claims to have witnessed while traveling near Creek territory in Alabama, a moving encounter between an American Indian woman, an enslaved African American woman, and a Euro-American girl in which the relations of mother and child are perverted by the presence of racial hierarchy. An Indian woman enters the woods, holding the hand of "a little white girl of five or six years, whom I took to be the daughter of the pioneer" and "followed by a "Negress." Tocqueville proceeds to evaluate them as representatives of the races, reflecting the period's keen interest in the details of a "doomed" American Indian culture. He writes, "A sort of barbarous luxury set off the costume of the Indian; rings of metal were hanging from her nostrils and ears, her hair, which was adorned with glass beads, fell loosely upon her shoulders; and I saw that she was not married, for she still wore that necklace of shells which the bride always deposits on the nuptial couch. The Negress was clad in squalid European garments" (*DA* 335). Tocqueville pays careful attention to the Creek woman's "costume," the metal rings, beads, and shells decorating her person and indicating her social status. In contrast, he defines the "Negress" by her lack of authentic African culture (she wears European castoffs), and he does not mention the white child's dress. As spectator and as the intermediary for the reader, Tocqueville naturally adopts the stance of the ethnographer.

The actions and demeanor of the representative Euro-American and her American Indian and African American attendants suggest the emotional, familial-based relationships among the three races. Tocqueville continues:

> All three came and seated themselves upon the banks of the spring; and the young Indian, taking the child in her arms, lavished upon her such fond caresses as mothers give, while the Negress endeavored, by various little artifices, to attract the attention of the young Creole. The child displayed in her slightest gestures a consciousness of superiority that formed a strange contrast with her infantine weakness; as if she received the attentions of her companions with a sort of condescension. The Negress was seated on the ground before her mistress, watching her smallest desires and apparently divided between an almost maternal affection for the child and servile fear; while the savage, in the midst of her tenderness, displayed an air of freedom and pride which was almost ferocious. (*DA* 335–36)

Tocqueville's ethnographic observation proves highly sentimental, for he measures the differences among the three females primarily through their displays of affection, which he proposes point to the natural attachments among them. Their interactions betray the correlation between their relative positions of power and their emotional responses to one another—whether their love is mixed with condescension, fear, or ferocity. Even as a child, the Euro-American has an innate sense of her authority, of her right to be mothered (to benefit from her status) and her obligation to receive their attentions (noblesse oblige). The representative African American is not the caretaker for the young mistress but, it seems, a fawning supplicant. The American Indian woman, in all her "barbarous luxury," leads and caresses the child, demonstrating affection for the representative of civilization but apparently refusing the abject pose of the slave. Tocqueville writes earlier in the chapter, "The servility of the one dooms him to slavery, the pride of the other to death" (*DA* 335). In the Creek territory, the American Indian woman's resistance to slavery and what Tocqueville believes to be her manifest fate makes her a source of volatility as well as a noble attendant for the Euro-American.

For this reason, Tocqueville's observed encounter among the three races of America ends because of the ferociousness of the American Indian's "freedom and pride." Once the American Indian woman becomes aware of Tocqueville's presumptuous gaze, he writes, she "suddenly rose, pushed the child roughly from her, and, giving me an angry look, plunged into the thicket." Tocqueville's moving encounter ends when the pride of the American Indian woman sends her headlong back into the woods and away from the influences of civilization, a passage similar to one in Margaret Fuller's *Summer on the Lakes* when an Indian, indignant that he has been made the subject of a white man's gaze, hastily departs.[7] Tocqueville derives a clear lesson from the scene: "a bond of affection here united the oppressors with the oppressed, and the effort of Nature to bring them together rendered still more striking the immense distance placed between them by prejudice and the laws" (*DA* 336). Through observation of this moving encounter, Tocqueville concludes that natural affection brings together the three races but unnatural, institutionalized bias will overwhelm this bond just as it has precluded "amalgamation."[8]

Tocqueville exaggerates as well the segregation of the races in this period, overlooking, for example, sexual relations between masters and slaves and the many relationships between American Indians and African Americans, including that of master and slave.[9] Delany's *Blake* returns to the scene of moving encounter among the three races of America but with an eye on the artificial suppression of strategic familial alliances among the races. In chapter 20, "Advent among the Indians," a fugitive slave and revolutionary named Henry Blake visits Mr. Culver, the chief of the united Choctaw-Chickasaw nation and a slave owner, to assess his support for a hemispheric slave revolt. Culver's white brother-in-law, Dr. Donald, takes offense when Blake questions why Culver would hold twenty slaves and snaps, "We have had enough of that!"[10] A fight ensues between Donald and Culver's nephew, Josephus Braser, "an educated young chief and counselor among his people" who plays gracious host to Blake (*B* 85). Braser quickly asserts that Donald's refusal to let Blake speak points to his desire to assert control over both groups: "He'll make the Indians slaves just now, then Negroes will have no friends." He then orders Donald, despite Culver's protests, to be silent. This encounter of the three races does not end with a proud American Indian plunging into a thicket to escape the Euro-American's observation and civilization. Instead, Delany depicts a controlling Euro-American reverting to explicit racism in the face of American Indian authority—and then leaving: "Donald stood pale and trembling before the young Choctaw born to command, when receiving no favor he left the company muttering 'nigger!'" Donald has married into the Choctaw-Chickasaw nation on false pretenses (we learn that he seeks money, not love), and his inability to submit to the family bonds because of his racism proves it. Carver tells Blake, "Now you see . . . the difference between a white man and Indian holding slaves. Indian work side by side with black man, eat with him, drink with him, rest with him and both lay down in shade together; white man even won't let you talk!" (*B* 86). With reference to marriages between American Indians and African Americans, especially among the Seminole people, Carver proceeds to urge Blake, "You see the vine that winds around and holds us together. Don't cut it, but let it grow till bimeby, it git so stout and strong, with many, very many little branches attached, that you can't separate them." Racial equality arises from community and marital relationships, and Carver and Blake form an allegiance when they make equality a common goal for their peoples. Carver has another lesson for his guest, one compatible with Blake's long-term plans: " 'If you want white man to love you, you must fight im!' concluded the intelligent old Choctaw" (*B* 87). When white racism prohibits true affection between Euro-Americans and African Americans, Euro-Americans and American Indians, violence is the only option. The close relationship between maternal love and ferocity in Tocqueville's representative Indian makes sense from Delany's perspective, and Indian pride does not necessitate Indian death.

For Mary Howard Schoolcraft and Mary Eastman, an allegiance between American Indians and African Americans in pursuit of equal communal relations among the races is simply not acceptable. Indeed, in refutation of what we might call Tocqueville's historical analysis and Delany's social philosophy, these authors insist that the servility of the African American and the foolish pride of the American Indian are natural traits, and relations among the three races should follow the familial model without creating interracial families. The white parent nurtures the Indian and African children.

The suggestive connections between the act of ethnographic observation, honed on American Indian subjects, and proslavery formulations of Euro-American paternalism as seen in Eastman's and Schoolcraft's works arises in part from Southern slaveholders' interpretation of Genesis 9.20–27, which relates the story of Noah's curse against Canaan. In this passage, Noah becomes drunk from the wine of his vineyard and lies naked in his tent. Upon seeing his father unclothed, Ham tells his brothers, Japheth and Shem, who then carefully cover their father with a garment and avoid looking at his nakedness. When Noah awakes and learns what has happened, he judges Ham's actions and curses Ham's son, Canaan:

> And he said, Cursed *be* Canaan; a servant of servants shall he be unto his brethren.
> And he said, Blessed *be* the Lord God of Shem; and Canaan shall be his servant.
> God shall enlarge Japheth, and he shall dwell in the tents of Shem; and Canaan shall be his servant.[11]

As Thomas Virgil Peterson and Stephen R. Haynes argue in their respective exegetical histories of this passage, the account of Noah differentiating among his sons and condemning his grandson provided antebellum Southerners with a religious, ethnographic, and familial explanation for African slavery and Euro-American colonialism. Few refuted the popular understanding that Japheth was the progenitor of the Europeans, Ham of the Africans, and Shem of the Asians and, by extension, the indigenous North Americans. According to Haynes, Southern readers found in this story "an egregious violation of honor"—an example of a child disobeying the fifth commandment ("Honour thy father and thy mother," Exodus 20.12) and, moreover, publicly shaming his father.[12] A culture that sought in the Bible a model for a godly society discovered in Genesis an explanation for racial hierarchy and a justification of it. This explanation maps the hierarchy of the patriarchal family onto the diversity of the human race (unlike polygenism, the theory that racial distinctiveness resulted from multiple creations, which most Southerners rejected but many racial scientists accepted by mid-century). In addition, it preserves biblical literalism and weds the study of racial hierarchy to a social vision.

For all of these reasons, Genesis 9.20–27 played a prominent role in proslavery writings; as Theodore Weld famously commented (and as Peterson and Haynes emphasize), "This prophecy of Noah is the *vade mecum* of slaveholders, and they never venture abroad without it."[13] Harriet Beecher Stowe directly addressed the prominent use of scripture in the twelfth chapter of *Uncle Tom's Cabin*. A clergyman who looks upon a group of recently acquired slaves but still maintains that slavery is a benevolent institution comments, "It's undoubtedly the intention of Providence that the African race should be servants,—kept in low condition.... 'Cursed be Canaan; a servant of servants shall he be,' the scripture says." Hearing this, another man quips to the slave trader, "See what 't is, now, to know scripture." He continues, "If y'd only studied yer Bible, like this yer good man, ye might have know'd it before, and saved ye a heap o' trouble. Ye could jist have said, 'Cussed be'—what's his name?—and 't would all have come right." As Stowe does so often in the novel, she follows sarcasm with biblical sincerity; the scene ends with the intervention of a second clergyman who observes, "'All things whatsoever ye would that men should do unto you, do ye even so unto them.' I suppose ... *that* is scripture as much as 'Cursed be Canaan.'"[14]

Undeterred by Stowe's mockery of the slaveholder's exegetical skills or by the specter of an American Indian and African American allegiance, Eastman and Schoolcraft continued to refer to the relationships among Noah's sons and their descendents in their literary defenses of slavery. The biblical story informed Eastman's call to correct improper relations among members of the national family, to restore the subservience of African Americans but also the paternal and maternal care Euro-Americans owe them. Schoolcraft referred to Genesis 9:20–27 in her attack on "amalgamation," an unusual theme for a proslavery novelist to take up but one necessitated by her desire to discredit Jane Johnston Schoolcraft's personal and professional relationship with her husband.[15] Eastman and Schoolcraft drew on their experiences writing ethnography or assisting their husbands with ethnographic work and found in Genesis 9: 20–27 a model for uniting the ethnographic and the sentimental defenses of slavery while attacking the viability of racial intermarriage. As Martin Delany insisted, such appeals to a "natural" family order grounded in patriarchal Christian tradition ironically suppressed the actual familial relationships among the three races of America.

From *Dahcotah* (1849) to *Aunt Phillis's Cabin* (1852)

Mary Henderson Eastman grew up in Virginia and Washington, DC, and in 1835 she married Captain Seth Eastman, a Maine-born drawing instructor, in West Point, New York. In 1841, Seth Eastman was transferred to Fort Snelling, in future Minnesota Territory, where he served as commander of the post until 1848. While living at Fort Snelling, Mary Eastman studied the language and traditions of the Dakota Indians who came regularly to the fort and whose portraits her husband painted. After the Eastmans return to the East, she published *Dahcotah; or, Life and Legends of the Sioux around Fort Snelling*, a collection of oral traditions, customs, and her commentary, illustrated with lithographs of Seth's paintings. Eastman followed this moderately successful publication with the popular *Aunt Phillis's Cabin*, which sold eighteen thousand copies in a few weeks. Writing to help support a large family, she went on to publish three other collections of American Indians materials. Eastman's defense of slavery deserves reconsideration in the light of her ethnographic work.[16]

Like Henry Rowe Schoolcraft's *Algic Researches* before it, Eastman's *Dahcotah* is not simply a collection of American Indian oral traditions and customs. The work is united by what at first appear to be two highly contradictory themes: romantic but ill-fated courtships between noble, beautiful Dakota youths and shocking accounts of hardships faced by Dakota women, including spousal abuse and starvation. But Eastman's introduction and subsequent commentary make clear the connection between thwarted love and what she describes as the pitiable situation of Dakota women: the future of all American Indians, Eastman insists, depends on the restoration of proper relations within the American Indian family through the intervention of the Euro-American Christian woman. Eastman offers herself as the exemplar of the latter even as she creates for the reader a literary moving encounter with the women she tends. Though warned that Dakota women "were filthy and troublesome," she emphasizes, "yet I could not despise them: they were wives and mothers—God had implanted the same feelings in their hearts as in mine."[17] Her belief in the comparability of their emotions, grounded in the universality of familial attachments, produces in Eastman deep sympathy. The Dakota women, she writes, seem "so unused to sympathy, often comparing their lives of suffering and hardship with the ease and comfort enjoyed by the white women, it must be a hard heart, that could withhold sympathy from such poor creatures" (D 7). Portraying women who often "go into the pathless prairies to weep" (D 157), Eastman solicits readers' tears so long withheld. Their common familial ties but disparate living conditions should cause Euro-American women to work on behalf of American Indian women.

Similar emotions and family relationships, however, do not produce a desire for social equality. Rather, Eastman stirs sympathy to prompt a *maternal* intervention in the lives of Dakota wives and mothers. "The Dahcotah Convert" begins with Hiatu-we-noken-chah's challenge to a missionary wife: "Why has he [the Great Spirit] made the white woman rich and happy, and the Dahcotah poor and miserable?" (*D* 52). "Could it be," Eastman asks, "that the Creator had balanced the happiness of one portion of his children against the wretchedness of the rest?" We discover that this is not true, for the missionary's wife recalls a time before ministering to American Indians when "she only wept with others when they sorrowed" (*D* 53); however, since moving with her husband she has lost all but one of her children and finally left the surviving child in the care of friends so she might follow her husband further on his "path of duty." To fulfill her true responsibilities as wife and mother this seemingly privileged woman ironically has had to forfeit her home and her children. "The Dahcotah looked in astonishment," Eastman writes, "at the grief which for a few moments overcame the usual calmness of her kind friend; and . . . she wondered why, like her, she should shed bitter tears." The missionary wife's sacrifice means that her sympathy is now grounded in similar experience, sanctified by the transference of her role as mother from her own children to the Dakota woman. Her sacrifice, that is, allows her to teach a central, converting lesson: "God afflicts all his children" (*D* 54).

American Indians and Euro-Americans, children of God, belong to one human family but not to common earthly families—a crucial stipulation in Eastman's work. In *Dahcotah*, she renounces Indian husbands' treatment of their wives only to emphasize the ridiculousness of racial intermarriage; when a Dakota man proposes they marry, Eastman scoffs, telling him "that I did not fancy having my head split open every few days with a stick of wood" (*D* 9). Her rejection of a literal union between savage and civilized was likely a deeply personal response to her husband's previous relationship with Wakan inajin win (Stands Sacred), a daughter of Mahpiya Wichasta (Cloud Man), and their daughter, Mary Nancy Eastman (Stands Like a Spirit), who was born in 1831. Seth left Fort Snelling in January 1832, returning in 1841 with Eastman, whom he had married in 1835.[18] Mary Eastman's knowledge of this stepdaughter is not confirmed, though historians speculate the two women could not have avoided one another. "Mary Eastman must have been aware of Nancy," Brian Dippie asserts, "but in her writings based on life at Fort Snelling she never mentioned her, though she did name Man in the Clouds [Cloud Man]. Nancy died in 1858, sparing Mary Eastman the embarrassment of public disclosure"—at least, he adds, until the publication of autobiographical writings by Charles Alexander Eastman (Ohiyesa), Nancy's last son.[19] Rena Neumann Coen has identified one letter written by the army surgeon at Fort Snelling on January 16, 1848, that suggests Eastman not only knew of Nancy but reluctantly called on her to assist the family when they were all stricken with scarlet fever. The lack of commentary Eastman left concerning her relationship with Nancy, paired with Coen's evidence that "in the crisis of her daughter's illness, it was Nancy to whom Mary turned for help," suggests

Eastman, at best, grudgingly acknowledged the place of her mixed-blood step-daughter in the Eastman family.[20] In *Dahcotah*, she clearly avoids the subject of mixed-race families on the frontier and embraces a different model for acculturating American Indians: the maternal authority of Euro-American women.

Euro-American women's maternal sympathy, sacrifice, and instruction contrasts directly with a masculine response to what Eastman defines in a closing passage as the plight of the Dakota women:

> He, in the halls of legislation, decides when the lands of the red man are needed—one party makes a bargain which the other is forced to accept.
>
> But in a woman's heart God has placed sympathies to which the sorrows of the Dahcotah women appeal. Listen! for they tell you they would fain know of a balm for the many griefs they endure.

Eastman continues by repeating the basis of her and her female readers' sympathy for these pleading women. "Like us," she emphasizes, "they pour out the best affections of early youth on a beloved object. Like us, they have clasped their children to their hearts in devoted love. Like us, too, they have wept as they laid them in the quiet earth" (*D* 177). Not masculine negotiations for sovereignty and land rights but feminine sympathy and assistance will soothe the pain of these American Indian women. Though Eastman's emphasis on conversion as the ultimate goal of her sympathy may disappoint us as "anticlimactic" and "ethnocentris[t]," not to mention costly, such converting amelioration is consistent with a nineteenth-century evangelical Christian worldview, the same held by Jane Johnston Schoolcraft.[21] The missionary sacrifices his children and his wife's happiness to his duty, just as God afflicts the missionary. Jane Tompkins's famous observations about *Uncle Tom's Cabin* apply to *Dahcotah*: it is "the story of salvation through motherly love," "a narrative aimed at demonstrating that human history is a continual reenactment of the sacred drama of redemption."[22] Eastman's contrast between feminine sympathy and masculine legislation confirms that the woman sacrifices not to improve the physical or political situation of American Indians but to act in accord with God's will and thereby to save souls.

Joshua David Bellin likewise draws on Tompkins's analysis of Stowe's famous novel to illuminate the sentimentalism of *Dahcotah*, which, he argues, "subtly modifies the very idea of an absolute frontier between peoples, illustrating instead how Indian and white women's stories intersect to tell a common encounter." But what Bellin identifies in *Dahcotah* as an "interracial communion of hearts" that leads to a unified response to patriarchy may be alternatively described as feminine solidarity in the context of their common submission to masculine authority.[23] Tellingly, the white woman of *Dahcotah* differs in one crucial way from her Indian sister: in submitting to her husband—and more generally to the rule of Man—she submits to God. That is, her suffering represents the choice of a Christian adherent rather than the fate of the squaw drudge, and any common voice of feminine protest is finally overwhelmed by the sense that the white woman has embraced her divinely ordained burden. Empathy serves a divine, converting purpose, ideally bringing both the white heart and Indian heart in line with God's.

Eastman writes *Aunt Phillis's Cabin* three years later, transferring her Christian, feminine program of amelioration and acculturation for the Dakota women to the context of the Southern plantation. From her explication of Genesis 9.20–27 in the introduction through her many examples of families strengthened by the institution of slavery, Eastman provides an emotional and legal context for a human family in which Indians and blacks are children—again, rather than partners—of kindly white parents. Noah's curse of Canaan was justified, Eastman emphasizes, because Ham's was "an act of a child dishonoring an aged father," and "had he been one after God's own heart, we would not have been guilty of such a sin." [24] As God curses Ham's descendents for the dishonoring of his father, so Eastman criticizes the abolitionists for undermining the natural hierarchy of the family, for allowing their sympathy with slaves to convince them of racial equality. "The application made by the Abolitionist of the golden rule is absurd," she writes: "it might then apply to the child, who *would have* his father no longer control him; to the apprentice, who *would* no longer that the man to whom he is bound should have a right to direct him. Thus the foundations of society would be shaken, nay, destroyed" (*APC* 19). During the Revolution, and prior to abolitionism, she emphasizes, "Our country was then like one family" (*APC* 21). Abolitionist confusion rends apart the national family, and Eastman again offers herself as a meliorating intermediary.

The Southern patriarch of *Aunt Phillis's Cabin*, Mr. Weston, finds social disorder, or inversions of hierarchical relationships, when he travels to Washington, DC, and he blames abolition as its cause. On Pennsylvania Avenue, "the great bazaar of America," he sees young and old, congressmen and the President, and representative American Indians and African Americans. But the treatment the last two receive signifies something is wrong. Observing, Tocqueville-like, "people of every shade and hue," Mr. Weston narrates to his daughters: "And see! there are a number of Indians, noble-looking men, and a white boy throwing a stone at them. I wish I had the young rascal." Immediately the Westons spy "a colored man, sauntering along in an impudent, dont-carish manner," with an expression that seems to say, "Who says I am not as good as anybody on this avenue; Mr. Fillmore, or any one else?" (*APC* 231–32). But when the well-dressed black man bumps into a visiting white Philadelphian, he finds himself knocked down to the pavement, which delights the Westons. Later, after her husband recounts the scene, Mrs. Weston declares, "This is the effect of Abolition" (*APC* 233). Previously, the Westons' son, attending college in New England, has likewise asserted the racial hierarchy in the face of abolitionist-produced confusion. He tells an argumentative peer, "we have as good a right to our *property* as you to yours—we each inherit it from our fathers" (*APC* 133). For him, the Euro-American ownership of Indian land and enslavement of African Americans are equally justified, for they represent the patriarchal inheritance of New England and the South, respectively.

As in *Dahcotah*, Eastman brings women's concerns and maternal sympathy to the fore, particularly through two autobiographical chapters in which the charming Southern wife of an army officer eloquently defends the institution of slavery.[25] At "a military station at the North," Mrs. Moore has fashioned a pleasant home and entertains a group of officers with charm and wit (*APC* 51). Mrs. Moore has two African servants: Polly, who has been manumitted but is uncomfortable with her new status, and Susan, a former runaway whom Mrs. Moore has taken in. One of her guests, the "ultra Abolitionist" Mr. Kent, chastises Mrs. Moore for encouraging Susan to return to her former master and mistress (*APC* 54). In response, Mrs. Moore criticizes Kent and other abolitionists for not aiding slaves after they have escaped. Kent's response demonstrates the abolitionists' heartlessness and shirking of duty: "If I see a man with his hands and feet chained, and I break those chains, it is all that God expects me to do; let him earn his own living" (*APC* 66–67). This contrasts directly with Mrs. Moore's treatment of Susan, whom she takes on as employee. Like Eastman's description of the Dakota women of Fort Snelling, the argument between Mrs. Moore and Mr. Kent elucidates Eastman's promotion of white women's commitment to ameliorate the sufferings of black and red children. Mrs. Moore, the sympathetic white mother, directs the reincorporation of the daughter of social disorder, a victim of abolitionists' confusion and deceit. As the missionary wife instructs Hiatu-we-noken-chah on the proper submission to God, and as Eastman corrects the savagery of Dakota husbands, Mrs. Moore stresses the proper relationship between slave woman and mistress.

Eastman's emphasis in *Aunt Phillis's Cabin* on the relationship between the white mistress and her black female charge underscores the moral authority of the white woman within an evangelical context and her unique and potent bond with the woman of color. Just as Bellin traces a potentially subversive (but ultimately contained) alliance between Euro-American and American Indian women in *Dahcotah*, Minrose C. Gwin argues that "loving bonds formed between white and black women in *Aunt Phillis's Cabin* create female community and female power," and that white women characters like Mrs. Moore are able to create and defend moral households only by countering and correcting the "male evil or male silliness" around them.[26] However, Eastman's *Dahcotah* and *Aunt Phillis's Cabin* always place white women's intervention on behalf of women of color within the larger context of a racially hierarchical patriarchy. In *Dahcotah*, Eastman reports but does not challenge the lack of sympathy in the "halls of legislation"; she does not seek to change the law (this would be inappropriate and Stowe-like), only to provide its subjects the emotional and spiritual support that is inherently extralegal. In *Aunt Phillis's Cabin*, Mrs. Moore establishes domestic and moral order within the military setting with her chintz, fans, piano, and work basket and within the greater national setting through her employment and moral instruction of Susan, whose rebellion has irreparably harmed her previous mistress. Like other Southern domestic novelists of this period, Eastman asserts feminine morality in support of an established order: that of Southern, slaveholding patriarchy.[27]

The Gauntlet of "Amalgamation"

Eight years after the publication of *Aunt Phillis's Cabin*, Mary Howard School-craft echoed Eastman's defense of slavery and use of familial ethnography in *The Black Gauntlet* (1860). In response to the growing rift between the Schoolcrafts and Eastmans over the rights to Seth Eastman's illustrations and his compensation, Schoolcraft may have consciously copycatted her former friend in the pursuit of extra income. The poorly written book was not at all popular, however, and she lost money on the venture.[28] *The Black Gauntlet* records another parallel between the women's lives: their husbands' relationships with American Indian women. As discussed in the preceding chapter, Henry Rowe Schoolcraft's first wife was Jane Johnston Schoolcraft, whose father, John Johnston, was a Scotch-Irish trader and whose mother, Susan Johnston (Ozhaguscodaywayquay), was the daughter of the Ojibwe leader Waubojeeg. Jane died in 1842, and two of their children, Johnston (John) and Jane (Janee), survived to adulthood. Mary Howard Schoolcraft, coming from a South Carolina family of planters and owning at least twenty slaves at the time of their wedding, strongly disapproved of her husband's previous marriage. *The Black Gauntlet* includes a thinly veiled portrait of her husband that praises his ethnographic work yet also presents his first family as a warning against so-called amalgamation. Calling the novel "an autobiographical narrative, in the thinnest possible disguise," Chase and Stellanova Osborn go so far as to replace character names in excerpts from the novel with those of Jane, Waub-ojeeg, Janee, John, Mary, and Mr. Schoolcraft.[29] Like Mary Eastman, Mary Howard Schoolcraft defends the paternalistic institution of slavery through ethnographic observation of American Indians and African Americans and the dramatization of an immediate and a national family endangered by challenges to the racial hierarchy.

The Black Gauntlet's "Dedication to Henry Rowe Schoolcraft, LL.D." establishes the relationship between Schoolcraft's defense of slavery and her marriage to a prominent ethnographer. Schoolcraft begins the dedication by addressing Henry as "Ne na baim," which she glosses as "Indian word meaning my husband."[30] Placing the book immediately in the context of her husband's career and her support of it, especially after a series of paralytic strokes incapacitated him, the dedication moves from their shared study of American Indian language to the natural submission of Eve to Adam to the proper relationship of the races. Her response, then, to abolitionists' descriptions of slave abuse is to highlight the sanctity of marriage: "I grant that slavery, and marriage, and many other institutions of God, are used by Satan to culminate sin, and to torment the human heart; but shall we therefore abolish marriage, because it has been abused?" (BG viii). She makes clear this link between the abuse of marriage and that of mastery later in the novel when she asserts that a Southern wife "would be utterly scorned for her *negrofied* vulgarity, if she entertained, or was suspected, even of a penchant for her husband's young white overseer" (BG 239; emphasis mine). Beginning with the dedication, *The Black Gauntlet* uses the author's relationship with "Ne na baim" as a model for marriage and her husband's first marriage as a warning against betrayal of the racial hierarchy. Not surprisingly, then, Schoolcraft had copies of the dedication printed for advertisement purposes.[31]

Like Eastman, Schoolcraft includes in her novel an analysis of Genesis 9:20–27 in terms of both filial disobedience and ethnographic explanation. The devout planter, Mr. Wyndham, hosts a group of Northern ministers who have come to South Carolina for the Baptist Association meeting. On Sunday night, "excited about the respectable negro Christians they had just communed with,...[the men] sat up nearly half the night, talking over the developments of plantation life in the South" (BG 86). In addition to asserting that fugitive slaves brought agricultural skills to "the Creeks, Cherokees, Choctaws, and Chickasaws," the men review scientific and biblical evidence of the inferiority of Indians and Africans (BG 94). The Reverend Mr. Joab Beecher comments, "The ethnologist tells us that Ham is the father of the black race, Shem of the red race, and Japheth of the white race. If so, is not the above prophecy exactly fulfilled? for do not we palefaces dwell in the tents of Shem on this American continent, and is not Canaan our servant?" (BG 98). The ethnologist's interpretation of scripture treating filial disobedience secures the argument. The ethnologist represents, of course, the novelist's husband, Henry Rowe Schoolcraft. By the time he published the volumes of *Historical and Statistical Information* in the 1850s, Henry had come to reject a racial science that explained the existence of distinct races through polygenism, or multiple creations, for an account of savagery as a result of perpetual decline.[32] In the late 1850s, Henry also drafted a literary treatment of the link between the sons of Noah and the history of American Indians. "The Book of Ed, or Chronicles of Shem" recounts the degenerated state of "the sons of Shem" when "the sons of Japheth" arrived in America and the efforts of the sons of Japheth to civilize the sons of Shem, all in scriptural form. A brief excerpt is telling: "It grieved the heart of Japheth to see this lost people—so long strayed away & [*indecipherable*] from the place that one knew them, and more than all, grieved it him, that they had forgotten God, & set up & clung to Gods of their own imaginations, wind & matters of earth, perverting then ancient rites & customs

& singing songs to daemons & devils. And Japheth commenced to teach them."[33] "The Book of Ed" recounts the Revolutionary War and the migration of the sons of Shem "to Appalachia beyond Jordan" and then to "the land of Promise, west of Jordan." As Henry brought his account of frontier conflict and removal policy into conformity with his religious worldview, he made American history a new testament, perhaps intentionally echoing Joseph Smith. Henry provided the very blend of religious and scientific explanation that Mary Howard Schoolcraft praised in *The Black Gauntlet*, and she, in turn, enshrined him in her novel.

The Black Gauntlet criticizes the marriages of John and Susan Johnston and Henry and Jane Schoolcraft as deviations from Noah's prophecy through her portrayal of the relationships between the Earl of Nottingham and Mud-wa-wa-ge-si-co-gua and Roland Walsingham and an unnamed "Pocahontas wife" (*BG* 495).[34] An overwhelmed Nottingham "rashly consented to this dangerous amalgamation of races, so that [with] the romance of one of England's Anglo-Saxon sons—one of the descendents of Japheth whom divine prophecy had lifted far above his brothers, Shem and Ham, forever—we find this nobleman's aristocracy culminating in his marriage with a genuine North American Indian squaw" (*BG* 492). The imagination of Walsingham, who is a poet and intellectual, becomes "electrified with the idea of another edition of the far-famed Pocahontas," and he is "charmed to discover that she not only wrote the tenderest wild poetry, but that pride of her race had excited her to perfect herself in the study of Indian language" (*BG* 493). The romantic view of the Indian and, in Walsingham's case, an appreciation for their mutual artistic and linguistic interests cause these men to break with biblical prophecy, to dwell alongside the daughter of Shem rather than simply to take her father's tent.

The prophecy and the ethnographic "truth" of Genesis 9:20–27 subsequently clarify the natural limits of affectionate familial relations among the races. Mrs. Walsingham dies from illness brought on by opium addiction and leaves behind two children, Jefferson and Lenora (i.e., John and Janee Schoolcraft), who neither trust nor love their father. Moreover, they do not show respect for his subsequent wife, Musidora, whose identity as a Southern belle links her to the author. Through crime and drug use, Jefferson "finally brought his father to the grave from remorse, that he had made so suicidal an experiment as to amalgamate in marriage with a race as inferior to his own as an ape is to a Napoleon Bonaparte, or a Skenandoah is to an African cannibal negro (Mumbo Jumbo.)" (*BG* 498). Schoolcraft undermines her own racist analogy through what is an apparent inversion of the final two terms, for surely Skenandoah, an Oneida leader who assisted American troops in the Revolutionary War, represents the American Indian who does not resist civilization.[35] Thus her treatment of Walsingham's "suicidal experiment" muddles rather than clarifies a racial hierarchy in which she includes an ape, a European emperor, an American Indian ally, and a human flesh eater (Mumbo Jumbo indeed!).

Jane Johnston Schoolcraft had been fluent in the Ojibwe language, and Mary Howard Schoolcraft's jealousy of her husband's first wife apparently extended even to the part Jane played in his early work as translator and poet. Perhaps this jealousy was compounded by the fact that Henry continued to mythologize the figure of his first wife and their early collaboration through her pseudonym Leelinau—despite the couple's marriage troubles in the decade prior to Jane's tragic death in 1842. Henry first mythologized his marriage to Jane in the 1820s through the story of Ethwald and Leelinau included in the final part of the long poem *An Essay on the Indian Character in Four Parts*, and in 1840 he ensured that Jane would live on in Michigan history by using "Leelanau" for one of the twenty-eight Michigan counties he named.[36]

In addition, an unpublished poem apparently from the period of Henry's marriage to Mary does suggest that even as he obliterated official records of Jane's contribution to his ethnographic work, Henry continued to mull over and idealize their early relationship. In "Illula, The Pride of the Lakes," labeled "by the author of Geehale," a narrating young scholar praises his mixed-blood maid from Michilimackinac, despite public disapproval of his first marriage.[37] The narrator emphasizes in canto 1 that his love has personal consequences: "The world's esteem I forfeit, lose or miss / Because she is society's antithesis, / Of Indian blood"—even though he has been "forgiven the trace" of Indian blood in his own family (apparently an alteration in Henry's genealogy). His relationship with Illula nonetheless bears fruit as he acquires the key to the Indian mind:

> Yet did my Indian alliance ope a vein
> Of Indian lore, that showed the hunter mind,
> Coil within coil, compacted in the brain
> Hiding in deep concealment all confined,
> The hopes, fears[,] thoughts, wisdom of the Indian mind.

"Illula" clearly recounts the Schoolcrafts' early collaboration, and Henry returns to celebrate their partnership. Much of the manuscript is difficult to read, especially from canto 7 on, but the later fragments contain an intriguing plot: after the untimely death of his beloved Illula, the Orpheus-like narrator journeys to the "Indian paradise" to retrieve her. While there he speaks with "Hiawatha" and other spirits and receives comforting words:

> Thy coming hath been heralded, & all,
> Thy thoughts impondered been, and kindly read,
> And she thou wishest kindly to recall
> To life below, and quiet [*illegible*] thy father's hall
> For scenes of woe & death—know it was love sincere
> Of the Great Spirit, that drew her from that ball,
> Of tears & misery, for a welcome here,
> And she will guide thy footsteps, through this happy sphere.

Enfeebled and dwelling on his own mortality, Henry apparently imagined a heavenly reunion with Jane, who would be restored to her proper role of moral helpmate. The poem complicates accounts of the Schoolcrafts' alienation as Henry seems to have recognized Jane's essential role in his lifetime of ethnographic pursuits. Surely this galled Mary if she read the poem. *The Black Gauntlet* eliminates all possibility for a postmortem reunion.

Mary Howard Schoolcraft had a contentious relationship with her stepchildren Janee and John Johnston Schoolcraft, which had at least as much to do with her disdain for "half-breeds" as with their negative response to the new woman of the house. In 1855, much to her stepmother's dismay, Janee married Benjamin Screven Howard, Schoolcraft's half-brother, of which Schoolcraft wrote, "My anguish was so great that my high souled, morally elevated, & idolized brother was to be connected to that hateful Indian race, that it seemed, death to every ambition, every hope &c." Her anguish was compounded by the fact that John Eckerd, the family friend who conducted the ceremony, had the previous spring attempted to persuade her slave, Polly, to run away.[38] Schoolcraft's belief that both sides of the family were disintegrating because of the willful disregard of the Old Testament separation of the races creates a novel seething with bitterness. Through *The Black Gauntlet*, Schoolcraft (as narrator and as represented by the character of Musidora) takes up the role of "true" wife for Henry Rowe Schoolcraft in a country confused by the abolitionists' lies. Indeed, she concludes the dedication to Henry with the assertion that, if they are forced to retreat to the natural world, "I could now be contented to live alone with *you* surrounded with books, in a wigwam, in the Oke-fe-no-ke Swamp, among the birds, the flowers, and the wild beasts" (*BG* x). In this pastoral image she, not Jane Johnston Schoolcraft, assists Henry and establishes the proper balance of sentiment and ethnography. Submissive to her husband and certain of racial superiority, she declares herself the appropriate partner for his study of the races—and for all eternity.

Restoring the Family

Mary Eastman's work in *Dahcotah* and her subsequent collections of American Indian materials insist on a gender division within efforts to "civilize" American Indian populations. The long-suffering Euro-American woman will tend to the long-suffering American Indian woman, teaching her the power of sympathy and the necessity of submission to God's will, which requires submission to the will of the husband and the legislator. The influence of Eastman's white female characters emerges from and is circumscribed by their domestic and maternal roles; they do not challenge the decisions made in the public sphere but tend the female victims of those decisions. The closing paragraphs of *Aunt Phillis's Cabin*, which take on Stowe directly, illustrate Eastman's philosophy vividly:

She [Stowe] asks the question, "*What* can any individual do?" Strange that any one should be at a loss in this working world of ours.

Christian men and women should find enough to occupy them in their families, and in an undoubted sphere of duty.

Let the people of the North take care of their own poor.

Let the people of the South take care of theirs.

Let each remember the great and awful day when they must render a final account to their Creator, their Redeemer, and their Judge. (*APC* 279–80)

The Virginia-born author of the most popular anti–Uncle Tom novel had no trouble identifying her "undoubted sphere of duty" during the Civil War. In 1864, as her husband and son fought in the Union Army, Eastman published *Jenny Wade at Gettysburg*, a celebration of another woman who sacrificed herself literally within her sphere.[39]

In *The Black Gauntlet* Mary Howard Schoolcraft attacks abolition but also her husband's early formulation of a sentimental ethnography and his marriage and collaboration with Jane Johnston Schoolcraft. Schoolcraft links her sacrifice as Henry's nurse and amanuensis and her distress as a reluctant stepmother back to her husband's first marriage and his ambitious travels. Her proslavery novel declares the wife's submission to the husband as helpmate, and it revises their story to reflect the reinstatement of proper relationships within the family. The novel concludes with the fictional restoration of Schoolcraft's (or rather, Musidora Walsingham's) happiness, which had been destroyed by abolitionists' zeal and her stepchildren. In this account, the slavery debate ends as the country splits amicably into "the United States South, and the United States North," Mr. Walsingham (that is, Henry Rowe Schoolcraft) finds a cure for his paralysis in "the far-famed medicinal springs of Germany," his mixed-blood daughter and her husband, Musidora's brother, become "most excellent" and repentant Christians, and the Walsinghams, reconciled with Musidora's siblings, return to South Carolina (*BG* 568–69). Musidora's moral integrity pays off, but in real life Mary Howard Schoolcraft did not enjoy such resolution. She spent the war unhappily in Washington, DC, as her stepson, John, and her adopted son, Charles, fought for the Union. Henry died in 1864 after years of physical deterioration, leaving Schoolcraft impoverished.[40] Dippie, points out, however, that the funeral oration for Henry must have offered some comfort to the author of *The Black Gauntlet*, for it distinguished between the assistance Jane Johnston Schoolcraft and Mary Howard Schoolcraft provided their husband: according to the speaker, Jane had been his "handmaid and interpreter" while Mary has been "providentially sent to him to be his associate in the higher mission of giving a scientific form and literary finish to the results of his former explorations."[41]

The explanation of racial difference slaveholders derived from Genesis 9.20–27 depended on the primal betrayal of the family order and subsequent divinely sanctioned punishment. The discourses of scriptural literalism, racial science, ethnography, sentimental literature, evangelicalism, and Southern patriarchy converged in this overdetermined story of a son's rebellion and a father's punishment. Rather than hearkening back to a prelapsarian relationship between man and wife to describe the basic structure of society, those who used this scripture to defend slavery insisted that the authority of the father and the bonds of his family had been and continued to be threatened from within. The Noahic defense of slavery arose within the context of a vigilant and suspicious Southern paternalism that moved rapidly between compassion and reprimand, that described the white patriarch's punishment of his subjects as benevolent. The racial hierarchy dependent on a familial model necessitated emotional bonds and physical separation between the races, appropriate for a family battling the destructive tendencies of its juvenile members. For Schoolcraft and Eastman, the scriptural assertion that a disciplinary or corrective love held together the human family must have seemed perfectly apt. Both women were haunted by amalgamation in their own families and the challenge it posed to what they saw as the racial order. Like the Noah of Southern accounts, they set out to correct the sins of the members of their immediate families and the broader human family.

8

Staging Encounters and Reclaiming Sympathy through Indian Melodramas and Parodies, 1821–1855

American playwrights and theaters produced a surprising number of dramas treating relations between Euro-Americans and American Indians during the first half of the nineteenth century, and particularly in the 1820s and 1830s at the height of the debates over the Indian Removal Act of 1830.[1] Many of these were melodramas, or "intense emotional and ethical drama[s] based on the manichaeistic struggle of good and evil," that allied the Indians and the young nation in the interest of the good.[2] In recent years, scholars have pointed out that one cannot assume the Indian melodrama was received as an argument for removal but that in the age of Jackson the noble savage was perhaps more readily seen as a representative tragic hero.[3] Certainly American Indian subject matter, and more specifically the myth of the doomed Indian, proved essential to the creation of a peculiarly American theater that promoted republican virtues. The most popular Indian melodrama of the period, John Augustus Stone's *Metamora; or, The Last of the Wampanoags*, which premiered in New York in 1829, is a good illustration. The preface declares, "To-night we test the strength of native powers, / Subject, and bard, and actor, all are ours—." In this "native" production, the Indian leader Metamora, a noble savage extraordinaire, saves the white heroine from a panther, fights vicious Puritan elites, defends his beautiful wife and baby son, and finally dies cursing his killers. The white actor Edwin Forrest's thrilling portrayal of this noble savage's heroism—a loud and physical performance that struck audiences as breathtakingly authentic—helped secure his fame and fortune.[4] *Metamora*, like many of the Indian melodramas, offered audiences an admirable, sympathetic, indigenous "ancestor" who predicted the rise of the nation and modeled virtue even as he declared, in word and in death, the inevitable disappearance of American Indians.

Antebellum Indian melodramas cannot be reduced either to blunt expressions of U.S. imperialism or to uncomplicated examples of cultural nationalism. In a period when the Indian Question dominated national life, these dramatic portraits of citizenship forced audience members to compare their relationship to the United States with the historical relationship of American Indians to their own nations, entities devalued or denied in Jacksonian America. Critics have traced the ways in which Indian melodramas recorded the struggle to form a national identity within a society that oppressed racial and ethnic minorities—the ways in which these dramas, as Susan Scheckel has it, "provided an imaginative space for Americans to confront the moral principles that defined and, at times, threatened to undermine the legitimacy of national identity." [5] Teresa Strouth Gaul, for example, traces how Indian melodramas incorporated and responded to the emergent fields of ethnography and racial science and to the frequent visits of American Indian delegations to eastern cities. Thus, antebellum Indian melodramas reflected the literal convergence of Euro-Americans and American Indians in urban spaces as well as in the territories. While most audience members may not have associated such performances with the debates in Congress or the legal arguments in the Supreme Court, they must certainly have responded to them as another venue for observing the American Indians whose future was wedded to both the expansion and the moral health of the nation. Staging moving encounters that oscillated between underscoring and surmounting divisiveness between peoples, Indian melodramas accomplished a broad range of cultural work with respect to the two people's national identities and political future. [6]

Indian melodramas' sentimental treatments of the nation's literary, historical, and scientific narratives made them highly intertextual and self-reflexive—and subject to revision and parodic treatment. For this reason, they have much to teach us about the interplay between race and sympathy in nineteenth-century theater. In *Playing the Race Card*, Linda Williams argues that *Uncle Tom's Cabin*, the novel and the many performances it spawned on stage and on film from 1851 through the early twentieth century, should be seen as "the inauguration of an extended cycle of racial melodrama seeking to give 'moral legibility' to race." Williams, that is, considers Stowe's abolitionist novel and the related productions to be the first in a long line of melodramatic works that chronicle "the gaining of rights through the recognition of injury." I suggest instead that the American racial melodrama—its narrative "ultimately concerned with a retrieval and staging of virtue through adversity and suffering" [7]—appeared at least three decades earlier in the works of such playwrights as Stone, George Washington Parke Custis, Lewis Deffebach, and Mordecai Manuel Noah. The sentimental theatrical exploration of the Indian Question necessarily impacted and was, in turn, impacted by similar explorations of slavery and the place (or lack thereof) for free blacks in the nation. The re-creation and production of Indian-white encounters in antebellum Indian melodramas signified more than a development in an indigenous

American theater or a dramatization of removal ideology; these melodramas contributed to a malleable narrative of racial differentiation and inclusion based on volatile sympathy.

To explore just how complicated this narrative could be, I look first at the staging of Indian-white encounter in selected melodramas and then turn to three theatrical responses, beginning with Louisa Medina's 1838 adaptation of Robert Montgomery Bird's *Nick of the Woods, or The Jibbenainosay; A Tale of Kentucky* (1837). Bird's historical romance overtly reacts to James Fenimore Cooper's historical romances, particularly the Leatherstocking Tales (1823–41), which were also regularly adapted for the stage in this period.[8] Just as Bird's "Indian hater" work challenges Cooper's rendering of a sympathetic intermediary, Medina's *Nick of the Woods* challenges the melodramatic use of the moving encounter, strategically altering the plot of Bird's text in the process. More specifically, Medina restages victimhood, transferring nobility and suffering from Indian characters to white characters. John Brougham's parodies in the subsequent decades contain inversions and juxtapositions that expose the absurdity of stage Indians and Euro-Americans' questionable sympathy with them. His *Metamora; or, The Last of the Pollywogs* and *Po-Ca-Hon-Tas, or, The Gentle Savage* foreground the violence of encounters between American Indians and Euro-Americans through an emphasis on the long tradition of colonialism in North America. Medina's and Brougham's divergent revisions of the Indian melodrama arose within an antebellum theater culture that repeatedly brought to life literary and historical encounters between various groups and privileged the emotional, spectacular staging of racialized victimhood. Indian melodramas and parodies of them suggest that the moving encounter was a crucial vehicle for theatrical considerations of the role of sympathy in national life during the antebellum period.

Staging Encounters

As discussed in the preceding chapters, authors in the role of sentimental intermediaries portrayed and recreated for their audiences negotiations between indigenous and conquering peoples. Likewise, through Indian melodramas, playwrights and performers staged emotionally charged moments of Indian-white encounter, both producing them on stage and causing them to happen in public. In *Theatre Culture in America, 1825–1860*, Rosemarie Bank argues that "culture is not only or even exclusively metaphoric, a figure standing for something else, but is itself taken as constitutive of the relationships that we find circulating in and among the many universes of antebellum America."[9] Accordingly, Indian melodramas, like Catlin's Indian Gallery and displays of American Indians at Barnum's American Museum, created public encounters between Euro-Americans and (theatrical) Indians, illustrating dramatic sympathy on the stage and prompting it in the audience. When we read these dramas, then, we should consider not only the depiction of encounter and sympathy among the characters but also those moments when characters, particularly the Indians, confront audience members, directly eliciting and even challenging the intended sympathy.

Such direct appeal to audience emotion in the context of moral conflict is a staple of melodrama in the antebellum period. According to Peter Brooks, melodrama then and now concerns the "moral occult," or the clear manifestation on stage of good and evil, despite the ambiguous morality of post-Revolutionary Western culture. "If emotional and moral registers are sounded," Williams explains, "if a work invites us to feel sympathy for the virtues of beset victims, if the narrative trajectory is ultimately concerned with a retrieval and staging of virtue through adversity and suffering, then the operative mode is melodrama."[10] The sentimental culture of antebellum American naturally embraced the melodramatic display of personal and national virtue as best expressed through characters' and audience members' emotional responses. Actors addressed audiences directly and employed "a highly conventional system of poses and gestures which physicalized states of emotion for the audience"—these were visual and aural cues for the audience members to aid their interpretation of the melodramatic morality play—and in turn, audience members helped control what and who performed. Gender served a crucial role in the moral occult, as male characters displayed national virtue and the female characters rewarded them with love and domestic bliss.[11] As mentioned earlier, race became part of the melodramatic vocabulary; dramatists used the sentimental impulse toward Euro-American paternalism (and maternalism) at home and abroad and a "romantic racialism" that "asserted the moral superiority of feeling over intellect, of affection, docility, and patience over Anglo-Saxon coldness, will, and impetuosity." Overall, as Jeffrey D. Mason emphasizes, "the fundamental currency of interaction between audience and performer was sympathy—the seed of the sentimental vision."[12] Actors and their spectators directly engaged one another in a public staging of morality.

The central Indian characters of these melodramas function as objects or ideal practitioners of sympathy much as American Indian characters do in the work of Lydia Maria Child or as the American Indian autobiographers do in their narratives, though to different ends. Joyce Flynn notes that Indian dramas often centered on one of two famous American Indian figures from colonial history or mythology that were central to the literature and iconography of the period.[13] The first common plot concerned a tragic Indian leader and his bloody, futile resistance to white settlement, someone like Metacom, alias King Philip, who played a pivotal role in the 1675–76 war between New England colonists and Algonquin Indians. Stone's *Metamora* is the most famous example. The second common plot for Indian melodramas recounted the sacrifice of a young Indian woman for European colonizers, a story included in John Smith's *The Generall Historie of Virginia, New England, and the Summer Isles* (1624) in which Smith famously claims that Pocahontas intervened in his execution. George Washington Parke Custis's *Pocahontas; or, The Settlers of Virginia* (1830) was one particularly successful staging of the story.[14] As these character-centered plots suggest, Indian melodramas presented the duality of the noble savage—dignified and uncivilized, peace-loving and warmongering, loving and hating, resistant and malleable, commanding and submissive, attractive and terrifying—through recognizable, gendered forms.

The most notable actions of the noble, resistant leader are his direct condemnation of whites as a group, his judgment of their actions as immoral, and his curse of their future actions. In his closing speech, Metamora declares, "My curses on you, white men! May the Great Spirit curse you when he speaks in his war voice from the clouds! Murderers! The last of the Wampanoags' curse be on you! May your graves and the graves of your children be in the path the red man shall trace!...Spirits of the grave, I come! But the curse of Metamora stays with the white man! I die! My wife! My Queen! My Nahmeokee!"[15] Even as he announces his intention to wage bloody war on the whites, or spends his dying breath conjuring violence, the tragic Indian leader prompts sympathy by highlighting the heartless actions of his enemies and remaining true to his victimized kin (here, Metamora's wife). He is, in short, "an idealized hero who embodie[s] sentimental values."[16] In striking contrast, the Pocahontas figure recognizes and praises the innate superiority of the whites and their culture, even to the point of disowning blood relations for a family of civilized and benevolent whites. This clarity of moral vision arises from her acceptance of Christianity and prompts her to intervene on behalf of the white victim. Custis's heroine, staying the hands of Indians who would club John Smith to death, declares: "Cruel king, the ties of blood which bound me to thee are dissever'd, as have been long those of thy sanguinary religion; for know that I have abjur'd thy senseless gods, and now worship the Supreme Being, the true Manitou, and the Father of the Universe; 't is his almighty hand that sustains me, 't is his divine spirit that breathes in my soul, and prompts Pocahontas to a deed which future ages will admire."[17] She demonstrates to all an ideal sympathy that brings Christian enlightenment to the American Indians and produces mutual affection between them and Euro-Americans. Thus the Indians in these dramas engage audience sympathy directly and at times exhibit for Euro-Americans the benevolent emotion for which they should strive.

The passages quoted above, particularly Pocahontas's praise for the Supreme Being, demonstrate how the Indian's curse and blessing of the whites often involves prophecy. Through prophecies, Indian characters reinforce the historical narrative of white ascendance and Indian decline in a way that directly acknowledges the world of the audience; they link the coming conclusion of the drama to the moral condition of the spectators and their nation in the present. Werner Sollors even argues that on stage "the Indian speech functions as the departing chieftain's last will and testament to his paleface successors and resembles a parent's last wish for his child." [18] Custis's *Pocahontas* concludes with prophecies by the princess's father, Powhatan, who is swayed by his daughter's intervention, and Matacoran, the vengeful warrior. The latter, like Metamora, prophesies the immortality of his criticism and the sympathy and admiration of future generations: "Now that he [Matacoran] can no longer combat the invaders he will retire before them, even to where tradition says, there rolls a western wave. There, on the utmost verge of the land which the Manitou gave to his fathers, when grown old by time, and his strength decay'd, Matacoran will erect his tumulus, crawl into it and die. But when in a long distant day, posterity shall ask where rests that brave, who disdaining alliance with the usurpers of his country, nobly dar'd to be wild and free, the finger of renown will point to the grave of Matacoran." The grave he imagines, like that of Natty Bumppo on the prairie, represents the memory of a man but also a time when the ascendancy of Euro-American society was far from manifest. Matacoran exits with Smith's praise, and the king, "looking thro' a long vista of futurity, to the time when these wild regions shall become the ancient and honour'd part of a great and glorious American Empire," offers commentary that is part prophecy, part prayer, and in the tradition of the dramatic epilogue, part request: "may we hope that when the tales of early days are told from the nursery, the library, or the stage, that kindly will be received the national story of POCAHONTAS, OR THE SETTLEMENT OF VIRGINIA." [19] The prophecies of the Indian melodrama announce the impact of the staged encounter on the audience—it will stir sympathy confined to the context of colonial history and its tumuli—and proclaim a national story of ascendance. The theatrical Indian reaches across time and the boundary between fact and fiction through what Patrick Brantlinger has identified as "proleptic elegy," overcoming the longstanding tension between native and colonizer and confirming the sad but irresistible tale of the Indian's disappearance. [20]

Moving encounters abound in other Indian melodramas prominent in their day but not often read in our own, such as Mordecai Manuel Noah's *She Would Be a Soldier; or, The Plains of Chippewa* (1819), a staple of the Jacksonian stage but an unusual Indian melodrama because of its nineteenth-century setting. Notably, Edwin Forrest performed the role of the Indian chief to great praise, which contributed to his later determination to play the role of Metamora. [21] Noah's melodrama takes the American victory at the Battle of Chippawa in 1814 as its historical basis but primarily focuses on the white, star-crossed young lovers, Lenox and Christine, who become romantically involved as the former cares for the latter while he recovers from war wounds. Christine's father, Jasper, arranges for her to marry a wealthy yokel, Jerry, and as a result, Christine runs off disguised as a boy to find Lenox at the front. Christine comes to believe Lenox has been untrue and enlists, and her subsequent actions in camp result in the accusation of mutiny and the sentence of death. Ultimately, of course, Lenox discovers Christine's true identity, and the couple is reunited. The subplot of this melodrama involves a noble Indian chief who discloses the effeminate foppery of a British captain and his French manservant. Captured by the Americans, the Indian chief curses his foes who "rose like wolves upon us, fired our dwellings, drove off our cattle, [and] sent us in tribes to the wilderness, to seek for shelter." Within a few lines, however, the chief's curse becomes praise for his American captors and their Christian mercy. Excusing his earlier "unjust anger," the Indian chief requests, "Protect our warriors and wives; guard their wigwams from destruction; soften their prejudices and remove their jealousies." [22] Through the mercy shown by his captors, this Indian leader drops his complaint and issues a call for the benevolent civilization of his people, echoing the shift in U.S. Indian policy in the years after the War of 1812. He adopts the stance more readily associated with the Indian princess and revises his sympathy-inducing narrative.

Lewis Deffebach's *Oolaita; or, The Indian Heroine* (1821) also follows the plight of lovers thwarted by parental wishes; however, unlike Christine and Lenox of *She Would Be a Soldier*, Oolaita and Tullula are Indians and do not experience a happy ending. Oolaita is a heroine because of her faithfulness to Tullula (she commits suicide believing she must marry another) and because of her sympathetic intervention in the stabbing of a young white woman, Eulelia. Oolaita kneels before Eulelia after saving her life and explains that, though she is neither Christian nor educated, "the Great Spirit, who loves the Indian as he loves the whiteman, gave me a feeling heart as well as you." Having established her equality with reference to emotion, Oolaita further asserts, "Though Oolaita's skin were black as night, her soul is pure and spotless as the snow." Oolaita demonstrates for the audience, then, appropriate sympathy between the races, and soon she does the same for her father, King Machiwita of the Sioux. At first Machiwita will not sympathize with the white captives, asking sarcastically, "Who can extend to wretches vile as they the hand of friendship?" But when Oolaita offers her life for theirs and draws on his parental feelings by threatening, "as the infant clings unto its mother, so will I cling to thee till mercy is pronounced," Machiwita declares, "Enough, enough—this aged heart will melt." Oolaita proves to the audience the moral and affective equality of Indians, a point confirmed when the noble Tullula, speaking in blank verse, tells the white man who has attempted to kill him: "through your life remember this great truth— / The Indian too can pity and forgive." [23] Yet the young Native woman is done for. Demonstrating sacrifice in the name of true love and in the name of Indian conversion to Christianity, the Pocahontas figure dies after converting father and spectators to sympathy and admiration.

Three years before he wrote *Pocahontas*, Custis penned *The Indian Prophecy, A National Drama* (1827), a three-scene drama based on an installment of *Recollections and Private Memoirs of Washington* that Custis had published in the Alexandria *Gazette* in 1826.[24] The grandson of Martha Washington, and George

Washington's foster son, Custis was well positioned to contribute to the hagiography of the first President. According to the installment, in 1772 Washington and his attendants met up with a party of Indians while exploring territories around the Kanawha River. Washington's men were alarmed because "the savage, driven farther and farther back, as the settlements advanced, had sufficiently felt the power of the whites, to view them with fear, as well as hate."[25] Yet this party of Indians included a "Grand Sachem" who sought Washington after having seen him at the Battle of the Wilderness in 1755. Refusing to smoke with Washington, the Grand Sachem declared that Washington had been protected from their bullets in battle and that he was marked to become "the Chief of Nations" (IP 6). *The Indian Prophecy* stages an encounter between the audience and the prophesying Indian and declares the crucial role of sympathy, as learned through formative colonial conflict, in the future of the nation.

Like *She Would Be a Soldier*, *The Indian Prophecy* envisions a pastoral nation made safe through resistance to traditional patriarchal rule, the merciful sympathy of Euro-Americans, and the incorporation of the feminine, acculturated American Indian. Custis precedes the prophecy, the occasion and the climax of the drama, with a reversal of Indian-white captivity and hostility. In the first scene, we meet an eighteenth-century Pocahontas, Manetta, the daughter of the great Indian chief Menawa. Manetta has fled her father and her culture for the rustic hut of a benevolent white couple, Captain Woodford and his wife, Maiona. Maiona's devotion to Menawa lies in direct contrast to her previous experience among American Indians: when Maiona was a young child, Indians killed her family and held her captive until Woodford (also held captive) helped her escape. When the curtain lifts, Manetta sits before a rustic hut studying the Bible with Maiona and flanked by a spinning wheel. She declares her happiness in this home "where you have taught me the benefits of civilization, the blessings of faith, and how to be good and happy" (IP 9), and Maiona reminds herself, "her affectionate attachment deserves everything at my hands" (IP 11). As suggested by their surroundings and activities, the women represent the good life; in the words of Woodford, Manetta and Maiona are "plain unsophisticated children of nature" whose "native innocence of heart" secures their patriarch's happiness (IP 22). Each is a new form of indigenous woman who establishes the national ideal through work, faith, family, and resistance to fashion, a woman quite similar to Jane Johnston Schoolcraft as idealized by Henry Rowe Schoolcraft in *An Essay on the Indian Character*. Before the prediction of Washington's and the nation's ascendance, Custis offers an example of republican virtue secured through domestic captivity.

Custis further emphasizes the plantation of civilizing virtue on the continent through a series of predictions made by members of Washington's party and the nation's father himself. "The mother country," declares one attendant, "should embrace, with arms of parental fondness, this child of promise; for rely upon it, although America is yet but in the infancy of her being, she will hereafter be clothed with a giant's power" (*IP* 27). Immediately following the prediction, Washington and the audience meet this child of promise incarnate, the Woodfords' young son who, Washington declares, "will, one day or other, outstrip his Indian neighbours in the chase, and in war" (*IP* 28). Talk of war blends easily with this vision of the blessed babe as Woodford reveals that the young one has a name "which calls forth the best feelings of love, admiration, and gratitude in my heart... *George Washington*" (*IP* 29). The future of the nation in battles, industry, virtue, and even the arts lies with the new generation, a suggestion emphasized through the allusion to George Washington Parke Custis's epiphany in this, his first drama. Finally, Washington predicts "that the day will arrive, when the boasted forces of Europe, led by gallant and illustrious commanders, will be discomfited, fly, or surrender before the warlike prowess of the land" (*IP* 31), clearing the way for Menawa's speech. The anticipated prophecy of the Great Chief, even if grounded in past hostility, will confirm and authenticate the confidence of the nation's parents.

The kind acts of whites and the influence of their religion have transformed Menawa as they have transformed his daughter. When first introduced, Menawa explains to the Woodford family and Washington's company, "Menawa is changed; good man missionary has been here, (*pointing to his heart,*) good man has changed Menawa" (*IP* 25). The missionary's transformation of Menawa's heart signals the end of resistance and curses, the beginning of acculturation and praise. After a brief prank in which Menawa is introduced to a hunter in the guise of Colonel Washington, Menawa singles out Washington in the crowd and declares he has "much to say" before dying (*IP* 34). Misunderstanding Menawa's urgency, the group is befuddled by his rejection of the calumet, drink, and food. Exasperated, the Great Chief declares, "Fathers, children, listen to Menawa. He will speak for the last time. It is here, (*pointing to his heart.*)." The knowledge and faith in the converted heart that Menawa again indicates—the "something here, which bids him speak in the voice of Prophecy"—confirm the greatness of Washington and the embryonic nation. "Listen!" Menawa insists again, "*The Great Spirit protects that man, and guides his destiny.* He will become the Chief of Nations, and a people yet unborn, hail him as the Founder of a mighty Empire!" (*IP* 35). Menawa dies dramatically after finishing his prophecy, and the curtain falls. His prophecy concerns whites on stage and whites in the audience as it affirms a future in which (admittedly belated) right feeling will strengthen a united republic. The presence in *The Indian Prophecy* of praise, complaint, and prophecy, and of various sympathetic and sympathizing acts, produces a complex vision of a nation that achieves unity through affection but rejects, through displays of tremendous feeling, the representative of Indian sovereignty. The Pocahontas, or the Christianized female, survives, but the Metacom, the resistant leader or mournful prophet, dies.

Reclaiming Sympathy

Not all audience members believed an American Indian's heart could be transformed or that the nation in reality or symbolically rested on the sympathetic
intervention of the American Indian maiden. As Richard Drinnon and Richard
Slotkin trace, and as I discuss in an earlier chapter on William Gilmore Simms,
texts portraying and justifying bloody retaliation against American Indians, even
to the point of genocide, emerged in the 1830s in direct response to the proliferation of historical romances, poetry, nonfiction prose, and dramas promoting
sympathy for American Indians.[26] Robert Montgomery Bird's Indian-hater romance, *Nick of the Woods, or The Jibbenainosay; A Tale of Kentucky* (1837), includes
this straightforward denouncement of sentimental portrayals:

> Such is the red-man of America, whom courage,—an attribute of all lovers of
> blood, whether man or animal; misfortune,—the destiny, in every quarter of the
> globe, of every barbarous race, which contact with a civilized one cannot civilize;
> and the dreams of poets and sentimentalists have invested with a character wholly
> incompatible with his condition. Individual virtues may be, and indeed frequently
> are, found among men in a natural state; but honor, justice, and generosity, as char-
> acteristics of the mass, are refinements belonging only to an advanced stage of
> civilization.[27]

The work's title refers to the central character, a Quaker named Nathan
Slaughter who has emigrated from Pennsylvania to Kentucky. Unbeknownst
to himself or to the other characters, Nathan doubles as the Jibbenainosay, or
Nick of the Woods, a devil that brutally kills Indians at night, leaving their chests
maimed with the mark of a cross. Nathan-as-Jibbenainosay enacts revenge
against Wenonga and his Shawnee band, the reader learns, not simply because
they massacred his neighbors, the Ashburn family, but because Wenonga and his
men murdered Nathan's family years before in Pennsylvania and left Nathan to
recover from a brutal scalping. The central plot of the romance takes place in
1782 and concerns the noble Virginian Captain Roland Forrester and his cousin,
Edith Forrester, who have been swindled of their rightful inheritance through
the machinations of an evil lawyer, Richard Braxley. The young couple enters
the Kentucky wilderness in search of a new life only to find their tireless enemy
and his conspirator, Abel Doe, hostile Indians, and tales of the Jibbenainosay, as
well as the sympathetic and generous family of "Colonel" Tom Bruce and an
assortment of amusing frontier types. Calling *Nick of the Woods* "probably the
most successful novel about the Indian wars in the Upper Ohio," Gordon M.
Sayre points out that the climax of Bird's most famous work is based on a 1782
attack by Kentucky militiamen on a Shawnee village in southwestern Ohio.[28] In
response to Cooper, Bird spins a more vengeful fiction from the violence of the
Ohio Valley.

Through Nathan Slaughter, Bird parodies Cooper's Leatherstocking, or Natty

Bumppo, a character who, as I argue in Chapter 2, embodies the sentimental intermediary and the belief that peaceful co-existence of Euro-Americans and American Indians based on sympathy is, finally, doomed to fail. "In contrast to Leatherstocking, Cooper's 'man without a cross,'" writes Slotkin, "Bird makes it plain that Nathan bears a cross and also exhibits by his behavior a psychological cross between Indian and Christian. Both these crosses are figured in the one he carves in the flesh of his victims." [29] Not only does Bird reject the concept of a Leatherstocking with the ability to bridge and blend the Indian and Christian worlds, he casts his Nathan as a victim of foolish sympathy as promoted within Quakerism. In literature of the period, Quakers, James Emmett Ryan explains, are "angelic representations of an unrealizable social ideal," or "Americans who are morally correct and yet insufficiently equipped to wrestle with modernity." Bird employs this literary figure of the Quaker to indicate the pitfalls of sympathy, not just the threat of American Indians' violent actions but also the threat to the human psyche posed by "the radical fissures in [the Quaker's] moral condition." One who is unwilling to defend his family on the frontier may quickly be overtaken by devilish bloodlust.[30]

Bird had tried his hand at melodramas, writing such plays as *The Gladiator* (1831) and *Oralloossa, Son of the Incas* (1832), both of which won competitions sponsored by Forrest, and revising *Metamora* at Forrest's request; however, Bird was frustrated by the poor compensation he received from Forrest and stopped writing plays.[31] It took another author to bring Bird's most popular romance to the stage. Louisa Medina's adaptation opened on February 5, 1838, at the Bowery Theatre, where Medina's husband, Thomas Sowerby Hamblin, was manager. In this adaptation, careful alterations in Bird's antisympathetic revision of the Cooperian frontier romance produce an implicit attack on the conventions of Indian melodrama.[32] More specifically, Medina transforms the standard heroes of the Indian play, the tragic Indian leader and the mediating Indian princess, whitewashing the moral exemplars and objects of sympathy before killing them off.

In Medina's dramatization, Telie Doe is described as "a white Indian's daughter"; her father, Abel Doe, has aligned himself with the evil Indians, Piankeshaw and Wenonga, and the white villain, Braxley.[33] Her willingness to intervene repeatedly on behalf of noble whites, despite her father's hostility toward them, makes Telie a new Pocahontas. In act 1, she whispers to the sleeping Roland Forrester that he should take the lower ford to avoid an ambush and halts Braxley, Doe, and Piankeshaw as they approach to kill Roland (*NW* 75–76). She then serves as their guide for the remainder of the drama, mediating much like her famous predecessor. Medina makes Telie the actual lost child of Major Forrester (*NW* 93)—a final revelation, unique to the theatrical version, that confirms the parallel between the royal Indian princess and this child of the British martial aristocracy. But, as with Powhatan's daughter and other melodramatic heroines, Telie's nobility inheres naturally, as evidenced by her prophetic dreams concerning Edith's fate and by her "moral sensitivity," "the essential criterion of rank" in early melodrama.[34] Roland insists, "Sweet girl, were you fathered by a fiend, your virtues would redeem him" (*NW* 84). In particular, Telie repeatedly shields the Forrester cousins, her cousins, from physical harm, beginning when she saves Roland's life at the battle of James's River (as recounted in act 2, scene 3). In acts 2 and 3, Telie guards Edith and Roland from direct threats by Braxley, echoing Pocahontas's physical intervention on behalf of John Smith. At the close of the drama, when Braxley fires on Roland, she intercepts the bullet, despite Roland's wavering faith in her.

Medina's *Nick of the Woods* has no room for the eloquent, resistant, noble, and heartfelt Indian of theater, fiction, poetry, and Native protest literature and oratory. Wenonga's crude motivations are matched by his crude speech; before engaging Roland in battle, for example, he declares, "Ha! The pale-face! I am Wenonga, the Black Vulture of the Shawnees. I am Wenonga, and have no heart!" (*NW* 85). Medina replaces a character like Menewa of *The Indian Prophecy*, who indicates the influence of his heart, with the heartless Wenonga, and in her adaptation of Bird's characters for the stage, depicts two white men as having the contradictory characteristics of the noble savage and a savage hatred for all Indians. Just as Telie (Indianized briefly and by association only) replaces the Pocahontas figure, so Captain Ralph Stackpole and Nathan Slaughter (Indianized by antisocial or anticivilization behavior) stand in for Metacom.

Colonel Tom Bruce sums up the incongruity of Stackpole: he is "a captain of horse thieves," but "being all fight, there's no one can equal him" (*NW* 68). He is simultaneously a deviant enemy of civilization and a brave defender of it, "a ring-tailed squealer" who, as Constance Rourke notes in her classic study of such comic types in American culture, took on the characteristics of the Indian he "conquered" and the land he "ravaged."[35] Though Roland declares himself "not in the habit of joining hands with savages and horse thieves," Ralph ferociously insists, "I'm a gentleman, and my name's fight!" (*NW* 72), again emphasizing the antithetical union of civilized and savage characteristics. Roland changes his mind about Ralph shortly thereafter when the roarer saves a child from a panther through excellent marksmanship, an act reminiscent of Metamora's killing a panther in defense of Oceana. In response Roland pleads, "I ask pardon, Captain Stackpole, for my rude words to you. Give me your hand; you are a bold and worthy man, and I am proud to take it." Yet the worthy Ralph appears unable to pause with his bragging long enough to take his comrade's hand, and the exasperated Roland declares, "What a strange medley of the bully and the hero is that man!" (*NW* 73). Like "King" Philip, "Captain" Ralph holds a dubious title of distinction; he challenges the property rights of the local settlers (in this instance, horses); and he readily subdues the wild beast on their behalf. The strange medley of the bully renegade and heroic defender marks Bird's revision of Cooper's Leatherstocking and Medina's comic adaptation of the melodrama's romantic Indian leader.

The noble savage's characteristics in Nathan Slaughter are less comic, their inner tensions contributing to Medina's highly critical analysis of the sentimental stage Indian and the audience's eager encounter with him. Whereas Ralph Stackpole is "the man for a massacre" (NW 72), "Bloody" Nathan Slaughter is the innocent victim of unprovoked violence inexplicably unwilling to partake of primal vengeance. Reminding others repeatedly of the violent acts Indians have committed and the inevitability of violence in the frontiers, he echoes Noah's Indian Chief's sad complaint, Menawa's heartfelt submission to Euro-American ascendance, and Metamora's stoic acceptance of death. That is, by accepting his violent fate, Nathan reiterates the tragic complaints and prophecies of the stage Indian from the position of the beleaguered white settler. Nathan tells Ralph, "You scent the trail that is laid on the earth for blood, blood, blood! I have seen rivers of it flowing, warm and gushing; but that was before this solid earth was builded [sic], and men were men, not ravening tigers. I have seen—but you'll tell nobody?—peace, peace, peace!" (NW 74). This opening speech—delivered by a man "dressed in sheep skins, and a staff in his hand"—echoes Metamora's prophesying but with a distinct visual and aural undertone of a new John the Baptist (indeed, he precedes the advent of Jibbenainosay). Medina, like Bird before her, corrects the direction of white sympathy and asks whether the sentimental Indian princess, leader, or prophet does not represent a racial fiction rather than evidence of affective commensurability between whites and (historical) Indians.[36]

Medina extends her disapproval of the sentimental Indian to its white consumers, the theatrical audience, by fracturing Nathan's psyche more overtly and more permanently in the adaptation. In Bird's essentialist worldview, one Medina heightens for the stage, Indians are violent savages, appropriately labeled by Stackpole as "red niggers" (NW 87). An individual, and by extension a culture, who refuses to engage brutal inferiors in combat is illogical, even insane. In the play, Nathan's adamant pacifism does not stem from Quaker faith but solely from the fact that "his wits are unsettled" (NW 74); thus Medina portrays resistance to frontier violence, whether by characters or by the audiences watching them, as pathological and in need of correction. For this reason Medina's Nathan Slaughter, unbeknownst to the other characters, is actually Reginald Ashburn, a settler presumed dead after a gruesome attack on the scene of his wedding, when, in Colonel Bruce's words, "the brute Injuns rushed in, burnt the house, murdered them all and took their scalps," including that of "the bride, the pretty Alice!" (NW 71).[37] The Indians robbed Ashburn of family, home, sanity, and identity, and in this sense he was murdered along with this young bride. The lesson resembles that repeated in the historical romances and short stories of Simms: one must respond to Indians with appropriate military force (as embodied by Colonel Bruce and, in exaggerated yet admirable form, Ralph Stackpole) to avoid the psychic and physical harm of their reign of terror.

Appropriately for a melodrama, Medina makes Nathan's duality and psychological struggle apparent from his first appearance. In his first speech (quoted earlier), Nathan struggles to hide his history and to repress his pursuit of bloody vengeance. Dressed in sheepskins, Nathan symbolizes both a prophet and a disguised and hungry wolf, a fact Stackpole observes as he demands, "Off with your lamb skins, you bloody-mouthed cur" (*NW* 74). Striking the belligerent Ralph Stackpole, Nathan cries, "Ha, ha, ha! The cry is up and shouts are loud for vengeance! Strike! Kill! Slay! Blood—blood! No peace—no peace!" (*NW* 75). Whereas Nathan's contradictory impulses manifest themselves in Bird's romance through Nathan's unintended injury of others, the seizure brought on by his recitation of his painful history, his transformation before attacking Wenonga's village, and his gruesome murder of Wenonga,[38] in Medina's play the instability of Nathan's character is primary to his depiction in all of his scenes. Ashburn's fate—to become the wolf in sheep's clothing—conveys the affective and psychic danger of the white man's encounter with the Indian and the misrepresentation of that encounter in sentimental works. For this reason, the drama emphasizes at once the viciousness of the Indians and the necessarily savage response of otherwise civilized white frontiersmen. While attacking Piankeshaw, a self-described "creeping panther," Nathan-as-Jibbenainosay declares, "Dog of an Indian, red skin, red wolf, die!" (*NW* 77), and as he grapples with the murderous Wenonga he cries, "Die, thou human wolf, infuriate tiger, die! Die!" (*NW* 95). Nathan, like the audience, represses his intense desire to kill, but that natural inclination for revenge emerges in a virulent form, and unnatural passivity quickly leads to atavistic aggression. The sympathetic and passive audience of *Metamora* feels as the noble Indian even while retaining civilization; in *Nick of the Woods*, the white victim occasionally becomes his enemy in the extreme, exhibiting raw savagery as the Jibbenainosay.

The quick transitions between Nathan's warring sides and the eruption of incendiary violence are key to the spectacle of Medina's drama. The iconic scene of *Nick of the Woods* celebrates the wild savagery of Nathan in Jibbenainosay dress as he is *"precipitated down [a] cataract in a canoe of fire"* (*NW* 87). Fittingly, as the drama concludes, Medina overtly reunites the fragments of this central character (which the Dramatis Personae lists as "Nathan Slaughter, alias Reginald Ashburn, alias The Jibbenainosay") by dispensing with the Jibbenainosay costume. Act 3, scene 1, foreshadows this development as Nathan, Roland Forrester, and Ralph Stackpole make plans for rescuing Edith from Indian captivity. Nathan decides to sneak into the camp wearing Ralph Stackpole's Indian disguise (a *"blanket and head-dress"*), telling Ralph, "Strip the clothing off the wolf; 'twill serve to free the lamb" (*NW* 90). Though here the wolf is Ralph and the lamb Edith, Nathan also describes how stripping the Jibbenainosay will allow him to free or abandon the peaceful persona of Nathan. Thus in act 3, scene 4, after denouncing the wolfish Wenonga, Nathan *"throws off Indian disguise"* and declares, "And with thy dying glance behold the fearful fiend, the Jibbenainosay, in Reginald Ashburn! Ha, ha, ha! Mother, sister, wife—at last ye are revenged!" (*NW* 95). Ashburn, shattered by the violent attack belying sympathetic encounter, had become a vengeful ghost and a repressed fool. Phoenix-like, he now emerges from the flames of the Jibbenainosay and the sheepskins of Nathan to claim his and the audience's proper, embodied revenge.

Bird's *Nick of the Woods*, true to the form of the historical romance, closes with a domestic vision, the reunion of families, and prophecy of future peace. The Forrester cousins finally receive their rightful inheritance and return together to their Virginia home, but not before they bestow some of their new wealth on Telie Doe, who soon after marries Dick Bruce. The Bruce family continues to thrive in Kentucky, but Ralph Stackpole and Nathan Slaughter do not remain with them. Stackpole eventually trades horse thieving for navigating the Salt River and is "transformed into a Mississippi alligator," a fitting end for the comic ring-tailed roarer. Nathan (who is not Ashburn in this version) disappears entirely, perhaps fleeing the locals' knowledge of his story and violent revenge, and certainly abandoning Roland and Edith's proposal that he join them in Virginia. Like Natty Bumppo at the close of *The Pathfinder* (1840), though in a much more dramatically violent context, Nathan sees no place for himself in the new national home. He remains in the woods because "there is none left to look upon me with smiles and rejoicing,—none to welcome me from the field and the forest with the voice of love—no, truly, truly,—there is not one,—not one." [39] Though Nathan's rejection of Roland and Edith's offer extends the tragedy of the Indian's victim, the romance's closing pages move from bloody revenge with the burning of an Indian village to the peaceful fruits of colonial war, happy and productive marriages.

In adapting the historical romance to the melodramatic stage, Medina clarifies the moral to be derived from Nathan Slaughter's/Reginald Ashburn's fractured psyche and Telie Doe's noble interventions on behalf of the Forresters by inverting the Indian melodrama's final moments; the play ends with the moving death of the Indian's victim, rather than the Indian victim, and a white heroine's renunciation of earthly marriage, rather than the intermarriage of white colonist and Indian princess. Moreover, Medina rejects even the paternalism (or maternalism) of the proslavery, pro-removal literature exemplified by Mary Eastman's *Dahcotah*; in this drama, Indians have no place in the human family. As the drama concludes, events reveal Nathan and Telie's actual, honorable identities just before their spectacular deaths, confirming their status as white rewritings or corrections of the Metacom and Pocahontas figures. Telie discloses that she is the long-lost daughter of Major Forrester, whose inheritance is in question, and she proves her noble lineage by sacrificing her life for Roland in the final scene.

Just after this, Ashburn enters dragging Wenonga's body, and Colonel Bruce exclaims, "'Tis Reginald Ashburn!" The public revelation strikes Ashburn like a bullet, and he collapses into Bruce's arms, dying shortly thereafter. Even his final words indicate the wolfishness of Indian murderers: "That was indeed my name, ere hell-hounds seared my brain and turned my blood to fire" (*NW* 96). Indians indiscriminately victimize white families, not vice versa, and the white acceptance or adoption of Indian culture springs from and contributes to an ongoing cycle of savage retribution. Ultimately, Medina replaces Bird's vision of domestic bliss in the Kentucky woods with a Manichean vision of heavenly and hellish domesticity. Dying in the arms of Roland, the man she once hoped would marry her, Telie (like Nathan in Bird's romance) emphasizes her exclusion from an earthly home but acceptance into a spiritual one: "This earth, though full of joys to others, to me had no sacred ties of love.... Oh, happy flight! I wing my way midst songs of joy! 'Tis transport—ecstasy—'tis sweet oblivion!" (*NW* 95–96). As Ashburn dies in the arms of Colonel Bruce, the head of the community that has belittled the misunderstood man, Ashburn spies his "long-lost home" and exclaims, "My Alice awaits me there—my fair, my lovely bride. I come, I come, I come!"[40] Though these final lines of the play indicate heavenward movement, the final tableau includes the hellish destruction of Indian homes. According to the stage directions, seven characters are arranged across the stage, Ashburn lies in the center, and in the background *"The wigwams are burning"* (*NW* 96). This melodrama reinterprets the genocide so often lamented in other Indian melodramas as necessary, conclusive retribution that sends white victims and Indian aggressors to their respective, opposing spiritual homes. Medina suggests that the ambiguity of the Cooperian intermediary and the melodramatic encounter between white audience members and stage Indians springs from a national disorder or affliction in need of diagnosis. Inspired by Bird, she inverts and then eliminates the characters of the racial melodrama.

A "Per-Version" of the Indian Melodrama

Modern literary critics and historians are not the first to interrogate the encounters Indian melodramas afforded audiences and the violent renunciations of encounter as formulated by Bird, Medina, and others. John Brougham, a popular Irish comedian-actor-playwright who immigrated to the United States in 1842, parodied Indian melodramas, whose popularity was on the wane, in *Metamora; or, The Last of the Pollywogs* (1847) and *Po-Ca-Hon-Tas, or, The Gentle Savage* (1855). These plays—one a "burlesque," the other an "extravaganza"—lampoon the absurd contradictions and gaps in performances so closely linked to the Indian Question, Jacksonian citizenship, national historiography, and the development of an American theater through attention to the melodramas' ethnographic context, racial mimicry, historical inaccuracy, and fashionable nature. Moreover, their attention to stereotypes leads to an association of violence not with natural enmity or historical progress but with an imperially motivated land grab. These two parodies characterize the irrepressible emotions and violence of Indian-white encounter, and more specifically, Indian bloodlust, as ridiculous and meaningless, except insofar as they originate with Euro-American greed. Arriving in the United States at the close of the Second Seminole War (1835–42) and writing during the Mexican-American War (1846–48) and a period of increasing violence over the extension of slavery into the territories, Brougham was well positioned to join the backlash against the romanticized Indian, and unlike Medina, irreverently to highlight national pageantry's dependence on ethnic and racial caricatures and Euro-Americans' exploitation of the peoples caricatured. Through the inversions and juxtapositions central to parody (of the original and the copy, past and present, high and low, noble and base, white and Other) Brougham exposes the absurdity of Indian melodramas even as he fishes for raucous laughter. The popularity of these plays suggests Brougham struck at the heart of the moving encounter.[41]

"Parody," writes Simon Dentith, "includes any cultural practice which provides a relatively polemical allusive imitation of another cultural production or practice." This incisive description allows parody a broad range of targets, making it particularly useful for the analysis of nineteenth-century burlesques and extravaganzas whose aesthetic mimicry, social commentary, and humor are difficult, if not impossible, to separate. Through "ironic inversion," what Linda Hutcheon identifies as a central feature of parody, Brougham's plays criticize a culture engaged in the construction of racial, ethnic, gender, and economic hierarchies.[42] Such parodic work was common in the theater of mid-nineteenth-century United States, and Great Britain as well; the overlapping comic forms of burlesque and extravaganza contained ludicrous treatments of high culture, popular dramas, theatrical practices, and current events, and combined absurd imitation with biting satire through spectacle and music.[43] Brougham's works are fundamentally inversive: *Metamora*, labeled a burlesque, caricatures Stone's play and Forrest's performance, and *Po-Ca-Hon-Tas*, an extravaganza, consists of a series of absurdist variations on the Indian melodrama and the Pocahontas myth through musical performances, minstrelsy, incessant punning, and blatant anachronism. Robert C. Allen points out that Brougham's parodies of Indian melodramas reach beyond the meta-theatrical humor of other mid-nineteenth-century burlesques, for they "struck at the larger issue of their hypocritically romantic representation of Native Americans."[44] Brougham parodies a genre that favors historical Indians over contemporary ones, unsuccessfully repressing the connections between colonial imperialism and removal policy.

Whereas Indian melodramas drew on ethnography's narrative of human progress, Brougham's parodies appropriately lampoon the socioracial categorization of American Indians as transitional types—barbarous/savage, semi-civilized, and civilized—employing the discourse of a "low other" "to call into question the right of higher discourses to determine the vertical order of culture to begin with." [45] Just as melancholic Ishmael of *Moby-Dick* uses book terminology to classify whales, Brougham retools scientific categories to describe accurately his spoof of a revered cultural form, labeling *Po-Ca-Hon-Tas* a "Semi-Civilized and Demi-Savage Extravaganza." More to the point, his pun on the tribal name Wampanoag in *Metamora; or, The Last of the Pollywogs* points to the ridiculous reduction of human dignity within racial classification. These stage Indians are strange critters—at once fish and amphibians—that "have wriggled through their race." [46] In this context, and in the words of Metamora, the narrative of racial progression may be divorced from value judgment and the label transferred to whites:

> The red man's fading out, and in his place
> There comes a bigger, not a better, race.
> Just as you've seen the squirming Pollywog
> In course of time become a bloated frog.   (M 123) [47]

The triumphant race does not possess biological or cultural superiority; it simply acquires a surfeit of power and land. Accordingly, puns in *Metamora* associate skin color solely with political alliances and conspiracies: Metamora notes that whites have "changed the Indian's native hue" through alcohol, "making the red man blue" (M 111), and the prophet Kantshine declares, "The Smiths have with the Joneses met, and Brown, / Jones, Black, and White, to pull the red man down" (M 119). In an era when scientist and poet alike described "natural" racial progression, Brougham's puns underscore the dehumanizing effect of biological determinism.

Brougham's use of the term *pollywog* to lampoon Stone's Wampanoag leader predates the British racial slur *wog*, "a vulgarly offensive name for a foreigner," especially East Indians and Pakistanis. In fact, when Brougham uses disparaging slang in *Metamora*, it concerns another issue he targets in the play: that of political corruption. According to Laurence Oliphant's *Episodes in a Life of Adventure* (1887), *pollywog*, like *filibuster*, was an insulting name for a politician in the United States at least as early as 1854. [48] Brougham's parodies regularly attack political corruption; in particular, his 1857 *Columbus El Filibustero!!* boldly lampoons the continent's revered "discoverer" as the tool of greedy monarchs to censure United States imperialism in the territories and in Latin America. Again, his description of American Indians as pollywogs is ironic, for the term more fittingly describes their white enemies whose only lament is "I wish we had some more on 'em to fleece" (M 110). Whereas Stone's Metamora is presented a tragic Jacksonian hero, Brougham emphasizes the hypocrisy of such comparisons and the corruption at the heart of antebellum politics, no matter how the nation conceives of its imperial actions. The U.S. politician is no noble Indian to be revered and mourned but a slippery opportunist whose amorphous, pollywog character stems from a clash between public ideals and private scheming.

Metamora and Po-Ca-Hon-Tas drive home Brougham's criticism of racial progression and political corruption by underscoring, in ways typical of the nineteenth-century burlesque, the literary or theatrical, rather than the ethnological or historical, basis for the Indian melodramas and their employment of sympathy. In this period, burlesques regularly referred to contemporary theatrical culture, "dispers[ing] meaning by implicating the play in an extensive network of references and cross-references."[49] In the Dramatis Personae of Metamora, the title role is described as "a favorite child of the Forrest" (M 101), referring to the actor who made the drama famous, and in Po-Ca-Hon-Tas, Smith describes Powhatan as speaking and looking like his predecessor: "Like Metamora both in feet and feature, / I never met-a-more-a-musing creature!" (P 139). The hero of Metamora scolds another character for forgetting his lines, refers to the "Howard Athenaeum audience" and the delivery of his own "exit speech," and discovers he has mistakenly spoken lines from "the Lady of the Lake" (M 113, 120, 123). In Po-Ca-Hon-Tas, the heroine recalls reading "Napoleon's life in Harper's magazine," and Smith borrows "the words of that black wight Othello" (P 136, 129). Brougham's Indians and their tormentors directly challenge the authenticity of staged encounters by flaunting their status as theatrical constructions.[50]

The reference in Po-Ca-Hon-Tas to Shakespeare's Othello, a classic often parodied in nineteenth-century minstrel performances, is one of many allusions to theatrical blackface in the play. Powhatan longs for a minstrel show when Smith first arrives, and the stage directions and song titles indicate the chorus members "give themselves Ethiopian airs" at least twice (P 128, 136).[51] Reflecting the ascension of the stage adaptation of Uncle Tom's Cabin as the premier racial melodrama of the age and, equally important, the South's association of the Indian and the Slavery Questions, Brougham associates moving situations in Po-Ca-Hon-Tas with abolitionism. For example, upon first meeting Smith, Pocahontas inquires, "Are you a fugitive come here to seek / A railway, underground?" (P 138), and in an argument with Powhatan, she declares, "The king who would enslave his daughter so, / Deserves a hint from Mrs. Beecher Stowe!" (P 142). Foregrounding minstrelsy and abolitionism in this extravaganza of "Old Virginny" (P 119), Brougham wins laughter through anachronism but also acknowledges that colonials established slavery on the continent and made slaves of their American Indian enemies—and moreover that contemporary proponents of slavery like Simms and Mary Howard Schoolcraft proposed that Indians, like enslaved Africans, submit to the rule of the white patriarch.[52] By highlighting the literary and theatrical sources of the melodramatic Indian, Brougham ultimately reminds the reader of the persistent exploitation of racial Others in the United States despite spectacular stagings of sympathy.

Brougham incorporates the wide variety of ethnic types that appeared on the antebellum stage and provides a hodgepodge of competing "American" cultures rather than an example of a unifying national myth. In *Metamora*, one of the sachem's compatriots is Old Tar, *"Indian Interpreter, from the Junk, half savage, half sailor,"* who displays the nautical language and rustic ways of the typical stage mariner (*M* 101). Tar demonstrates urban multiculturalism when he reports that Metamora's degraded but eloquent compatriot, Whiskee Toddi, has "gone in the lager bier line in New York," abandoning such "blarney" as oratory (*M* 108). In *Po-Ca-Hon-Tas*, Powhatan, often played by Brougham himself, praises smoking with a song about his "dhudieen," or clay pipe, "by a wily Paddy whack sent" (*P* 124), and the Dutchman (i.e., Deutschman) Rolfe, a character far removed from Pocahontas's historical spouse, belts out a Tyrolean song in a thick accent, expressing his wish that Virginia's landscape turn into sausages, sauerkraut, and beer (*P* 145). The very songs of this extravaganza, adapted from such popular tunes as "Widow Machree," "Pop Goes the Weazle," and "Hark 'tis the Indian Drum," suggest a proliferation and hybridity of races and ethnicities; one exchange is sung "In the Anglo-Italiano Style," another in "Hibernoso affettuosamente," and song types include an "Inter-Aria Nigroquae," and *"A Scotch Indian march"* (*P* 128, 143, 136, 151). Given the plurality of peoples in the antebellum United States, and the proliferation of racial and ethnic performances, the melodramatic pursuit of a single, coherent *native* American culture is misguided, even ludicrous. Brougham's parodies offer instead a playful celebration of the antebellum period's many cultures and the related chaos of the stage.[53]

Further, the parodies insist that the attempted appropriation of *Native* American culture leads only to a comical, commodified Indian. *Metamora* acknowledges the commercialized noble savage through a reference to "Indian Vegetable Pills" (*M* 118), and *Po-Ca-Hon-Tas* gives credit for its props ("crowns, war-clubs, Indian pipes, and other regalia") to "Mr. Timmany, and his aids," or New York's Tammany Hall (*P* 115). Most damning of all is the lengthy prolegomena to *Po-Ca-Hon-Tas* in which Brougham parodies Henry Wadsworth Longfellow's *Song of Hiawatha* in a one-hundred-line fragment of "The Song of Pocahontas," an epic poem supposedly discovered in "the contents of a wallet found in the vest pocket of the man in armor, dug up near Cape Cod, ... written by a Danish Poet, the Chevalier Viking, *Long Fellow* of the Norwegian Academy of Music, who flourished Anno Gothami, 235." Longfellow's liberal adaptation of Henry Rowe Schoolcraft's collection of American Indian mythology and use of the meter of the *Kalevala*, a Finnish national epic, does not escape Brougham's critical attention. The fragment, he declares, has a "peculiar *Finnish*" and an "inscrutable" nature (P 119, 141). Brougham uses the meter of *Hiawatha* as he further plays on the antebellum significance of Pocahontas and John Smith's home colony:

> Ask you—How about these verses?
> Whence this song of Pocahontas,
> With its flavor of Tobacco,
> And the Stincweed—the Mundungus,
> With its pipe of Old Virginny,
> With the echo of the Breakdown,
> With its smack of Bourbon whiskey,
> With the twangle of the Banjo;
> Of the Banjo—the Goat skinnet,
> And the Fiddle—the Catgutto,
> With the noisy Marrowbonum.   (P 119) [54]

By associating Longfellow's composition with the instruments of black-face minstrelsy (banjo, fiddle, and bones), Brougham underscores the venerable poet's red-face minstrelsy and denies the authenticity of this national epic and hero, Hiawatha, whose very name reflects the poet's manipulation (Longfellow replaced the name of the Ojibwe culture hero Manabozho with that of the founder of the Iroquois Confederacy). At the same time, Brougham suggests that traces of the mimicked culture permeate the epic, only in degraded form, like the poor tobacco known as stinkweed or mundungus. Longfellow, like the medicine salesperson and the fraternal society member, readily manipulates supposedly essential and certainly romantic qualities of American Indian culture to promote white consumption of "the Indian," but any truly Native quality has been distorted or perverted. By combining disparate literatures and developing a stilted meter, Longfellow has unknowingly initiated a burlesque. [55]

The noble savage of melodrama, as well as historical romances, poetry, and artwork, appeared vibrant and dying, angry and submissive, demonstrating at once a valiant defense of his people and a noble submission to the narrative of racial progression. Playwrights like Custis, Deffebach, and Stone and performers like Forrest drew on these paradoxical characteristics and actions of "the white man's Indian" to induce audience interest and sympathy and to claim American Indians for eternal art rather than national membership. As Stone's Metamora declares shortly before his death, "We are destroyed—not vanquished; we are no more, yet we are forever." Responding to the emergence of female burlesque troupes in August 1869, Richard Grant White wrote that burlesque "forces the conventional and the natural together just at the points where they are most remote, and the result is absurdity, monstrosity." [56] This is exactly what Brougham's parodies do, highlighting the distance between stage conventions and expected human behavior by having the Indian hero move rapidly and illogically between the two. In lines almost identical to those in Stone's original, Metamora of the Pollywogs declares that he has "been very yielding, like the willow, / Drooping o'er the streamlet's gentle billow," but that he is also "the rock / That does the tempest's rage and lightening mock" (*M* 109).[57] Simultaneously compliant with his white enemies and fixed in this determination to kill them, the savage leader repeatedly proves self-defeating. Having killed a weasel that frightened Oceana, Metamora declares, "He died like a Pollywog. He had to go, / Whether he liked the principle or no," but in the next breath highlights white guilt: "His death you'll have to answer for; one more / To the black list of injuries we bore, / Since the first white man trod upon our ground" (*M* 104). He spares Oceana and her father rather than break his promise, an act he admits is "absurd" (*M* 117), then gracefully accepts his own child's death declaring, "If fate had not come first, I should have had, / With my own knife, to slay the gentle lad" (*M* 121). Brougham depicts the actions of the Puritan enemies as similarly illogical— Vaughan declares, "He spared our lives, and 'tis but right we should / Kill off his squaw to show our gratitude" (*M* 118)—yet strategic in the context of warfare. Metamora's concluding rejection of the doomed Indian and of the whites' short-lived sympathy with him is entirely appropriate. Rather than submit like Stone's hero to the Euro-American aesthetic, this Metamora rises from the dead and declares, "Confound your skins, I will not die to please you!" (*M* 124). The para-doxical stage Indian finally refuses to meet audience expectations.[58]

Indians and their inevitable, thrilling deaths were central to Euro-Americans' creation of historical narratives, a fact Brougham does not overlook. Accounts of Indian-white relations provided visions of alternately utopic and deadly de-finitive colonial relations, and representations of Indian eloquence infused his-torical narrative with affirming prophecies and sublime language. Brougham's parodies undermine these historical contributions, questioning their signifi-cance and basis in fact. Most directly, *Metamora* rejects white claims of having fairly bought the land (*M* 104, 106, 110), and *Po-Ca-Hon-Tas* exposes the distance between George Bancroft's account of the Indian maiden's marriage to John Rolfe and dramatizations of Pocahontas's romantic attachment to John Smith (*P* 139–40, 155).[59] In *Metamora*, Brougham resists glorifying colonial genocide by highlighting the construction of the Pollywog's "fate" and simplifying Metamora's dream of conquest: "Pile after pile of dead I sent to sleep, / Their red scalps streaming in a gory heap" (*M* 107). Brougham empties Indian prophecy of the sublime and relocates it in an urban environment, turning Kaneshine's vision in Stone's *Metamora* of "a panther wounded and dying in his thick red gore"[60] into Kantshine's drunken vision of a "poor benighted pig" rooting for food in gutter and then fleeing (*M* 119). Finally, in these parodies Brougham purposely twists the "Indian" names of melodrama into humorous commentary on, at one level, the syllabic transcriptions of American Indian names into English and, at another, social evils. In *Po-Ca-Hon-Tas*, we find, among others, the Indian messenger Kreem-Fay-Sloon, medicine men such as Kod-Liv-Royl and Sas-Sy-Pril, and the pretty schoolgirls Dah-Lin-Duck, O-You-Jewel, Luv-Lie-Kreeta,

Oso-Char-Ming, and Lum-Pa-Shuga. In *Metamora*, Puritans Lord Fitzarnold and Goodenough become Lord Fitzfaddle and Badenough, and the Pollywog cast includes Whiskeetoddi, Anaconda, Tapiokee, and Pappoose. Brougham's parodies revise traditional historical narratives, particularly as they are adapted to the forms of the historical romance and the melodrama, and their stock characters, revealing a primary but hidden motivation for such works: to reassure Euro-Americans they act with the best intentions and respond with purest hearts. Smith declares in *Po-Ca-Hon-Tas*, "Be sure I'll make the best of this bad story, / To *gild* our *guilt* we've but to call it glory" (P 131).

Brougham, like Stone, Custis, Noah, Deffebach, and Medina, wrote for a theater culture one might describe as taking a pollywog form because it blended European theatrical genres with American themes and characters, incorporated a patchwork of ethnic types, responded to the demands of a diverse audience, and absorbed multiple modes of popular entertainment, including historical romances by such authors as Cooper and Bird. In *Po-Ca-Hon-Tas* and *Metamora*, Brougham recognizes the parodic potential in the contradictory traits of both the genre of melodrama and the figure of the noble savage and compiles a hodgepodge of theatrical and literary forms to call attention to the absurdity of staged encounters. The title-page description of *Po-Ca-Hon-Tas* hints at this strategy:

> An Original
> Aboriginal Erratic Operatic Semi-Civilized and
> Demi-Savage Extravaganza, being a Per-Version of Ye Trewe
> And Wonderrefulle Hystorie of Ye Rennownned
> Princesse.   (P 115)

Original and imitative, erratic and operatic, somewhat civilized and somewhat savage, revisionary to the point of perversion, or even generic obliteration, and wonder-full by way of the true and historical, Brougham's *Po-Ca-Hon-Tas* and *Metamora* strip bare the politics of a waning genre and its representation of doomed Indians and national sympathy. Through puns, anachronism, dramatic contradictions, and minstrelsy and ethnic performance, these parodies prompt the audience to laugh at the tenuous constructions of the antebellum stage and to reflect on the often violent negotiations of North America's constitutive peoples. We could do worse than to read Brougham's burlesques as enlightened Per-Versions of the antebellum moving encounter.

CONCLUSION

Moving beyond Sentiment or Cynicism

Parodies of the moving encounter like those found in John Brougham's burlesques continued to undermine portrayals of Indian-white sympathy as the nineteenth century progressed. According to one version of nineteenth-century literary history, the sentimental Indian was eventually eclipsed by the warlike, degraded Indian because of the rise of literary realism and the bloody conflicts of the Far West, from Little Big Horn to Wounded Knee. Authors, the narrative goes, rejected the former figure as a construct with no basis in fact. In this account, Mark Twain bests James Fenimore Cooper with his Goshoot Indians ("They deserve pity, poor creatures; and they can have mine—at this distance. Nearer by, they never get anybody's.") and his analysis of the Leatherstocking Tales' (il)logistics.[1] In Twain's hands, the encounter between American Indians and Euro-Americans is an occasion not for emotional exchange but for trickery and brutality. As his incomplete "Huck and Tom among the Indians" makes clear, Euro-Americans are subject to deception because literature's sentimentalized Indians mask the savagery of actual American Indians, who are capable of unspeakable acts, including the murder of a defenseless frontier family and the kidnapping and assumed rape of the daughter and heroine, Peggy. In *Adventures of Huckleberry Finn*, Twain sinks a symbolic Southern steamboat called the *Walter Scott*, connecting the murderous game of Southern "honor" to the romantic nationalism of Sir Walter Scott's historical fiction. Similarly, though more overtly, in "Huck and Tom among the Indians" he blames Cooper's Leatherstocking Tales for the boys' misplaced trust in the local Indians.[2] Here Indian-white convergence on the frontier does not produce temporary intimacy that models a national or spiritual ideal; instead, encounter signifies the clash of base cruelty and starry-eyed naiveté. Moreover, the mediating author (Cooper) has failed in his role, neither depicting sincere emotion nor protecting his audience.

Twain's incomplete novel of "lighting out for the Territory" and his criticism of Cooper do not tell the whole story. Just as Twain's sinking of the *Walter Scott* did nothing to deter the rise of the plantation novel and nostalgia for an imaginary Southern past in the late nineteenth century, his roasting of the American Scott did not halt the creation of literature treating American Indians in sympathetic terms or using the apparent demise of the Indian to prompt the benevolence of the white. In this period, for example, Helen Hunt Jackson composed literature of political protest in the tradition of Lydia Maria Child by exposing the deleterious effects of federal Indian policy first through the nonfiction work *A Century of Dishonor* (1881) and then through the novel *Ramona; A Story* (1884), with which she hoped to "do for the Indian a thousandth part of what Uncle Tom's Cabin did for the Negro." Her depiction in *Ramona* of a beleaguered American Indian man, driven to insanity by a series of dispossessions, and his tragic mixed-blood wife did more to spur a vast tourist trade, however, than to promote the cause of the California Mission Indians. Readers nostalgic for California's "romantic-but-vanishing ranchero lifestyle" flocked to the region looking for traces of Ramona's world.[3] Nonetheless, Jackson's reform work inspired organizations like the Women's National Indian Association, the Indian Rights Association, and the Lake Mohonk Conference to take up the cause of the Mission Indians and, among other things, to push for the passage of the Dawes General Allotment Act of 1887 and other "civilizing" laws. Perhaps had Jackson lived past 1885, she would have come to question her literary method and these political goals, as American Indians lost millions of acres in land holdings through allotment.[4]

American Indian autobiographies attentive to the language of familial relations and emotional identity continued to appear in the post–Wounded Knee period, and their authors continued to face readers' judgments of their authenticity. In autobiographical writings, Charles Alexander Eastman (Ohiyesa, Santee Sioux), the grandson of Seth Eastman and Wakan inajin win (Stands Sacred), and Gertrude Bonnin (Zitkala-Ša, Yankton Sioux) describe the moving encounter as psychologically traumatic. Born and raised in American Indian communities, educated in Euro-American schools, and as adults asked to represent American Indian culture for Euro-American audiences, Eastman and Bonnin recorded their experiences as cultural brokers who, with varying degrees of success, negotiated and even promoted a "civilizing" process they nonetheless found deeply problematic. In *From the Deep Woods to Civilization* (1916), Eastman describes his pursuit of Euro-American education beginning at the age of fifteen as the "warpath" set before him by his determined father. Having admitted that his service as the doctor at Pine Ridge Indian Agency in the aftermath of the Wounded Knee massacre "was a severe ordeal for one who had so lately put all his faith in the Christian love and lofty ideals of the white man," Eastman in subsequent pages defiantly declares that despite white hypocrisy, "we Sioux are now fully entrenched, for all practical purposes, in the warfare of civilized life." Like Black Hawk, Eastman offers himself, the representative Native, as a model of morality for a "civilized" society threatened by its own greed.[5] Bonnin's autobiographical essays, which appeared in the *Atlantic Monthly* in 1900 and were later collected in *American Indian Stories* (1921), elicit reader sympathy in a manner similar to

William Apess's *A Son of the Forest*, recreating the child's experience of encounter with the Other and emphasizing the hypocrisy of Christian Euro-Americans who support policies of coercive acculturation and dispossession. "Like a slender tree," Bonnin concludes, "I had been uprooted from my mother, nature, and God. I was shorn of my branches, which had waved in sympathy and love for home and friends. The natural coat of bark which had protected my oversensitive nature was scraped off to the very quick."[6] Alienated from her natural environment and community and deprived of compassion, Bonnin seeks in her essays to restore sympathy rather than announce its demise. She and Eastman, like American Indian autobiographers before them, provided audiences the rare American Indian perspective on the impact of "civilization" efforts.

Euro-American actors continued to perform in "redface" in the late nineteenth and early twentieth centuries, and American Indians continued to harness curious audiences to their own ends. The cynicism of Twain and the protest of Eastman, Bonnin, and others existed alongside public stagings of nostalgia for an American Indian past and a national identity in the present, including Buffalo Bill Cody's popular Wild West Show and Hiawatha pageants—dramatizations of Longfellow's *The Song of Hiawatha* often performed by American Indian actors and in American Indian languages, despite the triumphant arrival of the white missionary at the conclusion of the epic. "If it seems jarring that Native people would gravitate toward performances of a script that rendered them absent," writes Michael D. McNally of the Hiawatha pageants, "it suggests the intriguing possibility that some considered the pageants a field wherein they could assert their presence in consequential, if subtle ways."[7] Sitting Bull did just this when he toured with Cody's Wild West Show in 1885, and in the early twentieth century accomplished American Indian musicians, including boarding-school students, drew audiences with presentations of Native culture and of cultured Natives (Bonnin herself collaborated on an opera titled *The Sun Dance* and recited *Hiawatha* for audiences).[8] American Indian authors and political leaders who lectured about Native progress toward civilization often strategically employed traditional attire to capture audiences. Eastman, for example, emphasized, "It was not until I felt that I had to a degree established these claims"—that is, claims to American Indians' many gifts and admirable traits—"that I consented to appear on the platform in our ancestral garb of honor." Performances of Indianness continued to draw spectators as they had in the antebellum period, and American Indians persisted in "playing Indian" to their own ends.[9]

Moving Encounters traces the close link between the discourses of doom and sympathy in antebellum literature of the Indian Question and the malleability of a figure that symbolized the promise (however fleeting) of a sustained relationship between Natives and non-Natives. When Brougham's burlesques and Melville's *The Confidence-Man* express distrust of sentimental representations and explicit justifications of violence against American Indians, they emphasize two dichotomies initiated by the moving encounter: the melodramatic Indian versus the parodic Indian and the sentimental approach to Indian-white relations versus the cynical one. These dichotomies, like that of Cooper's good and bad Indians, persisted through the end of the nineteenth century and continue to inform the critical debate over the motives of sympathy in the antebellum period—and in our own. But we need not resign ourselves to embracing either a sentimental or a cynical approach to the portrayals and performances of Indianness in U.S. culture. As the preceding chapters show, the history of the moving encounter figure, and in particular its use by American Indian activists and removal apologists alike, suggests that the image of white-Indian exchange and sympathy has been revised and refigured according to contemporary concerns. Rather than reject all sentimental treatments of the Indian in this period as complicit with the ideology of removal, we should consider how images of mediation between non-Natives and Natives may be harnessed in the name of both cultural pluralism and American Indian sovereignty.

In closing, then, I wish to jump ahead to the present to consider one of the most successful revisions of the moving encounter and its associations with the doomed Indian myth and ethnographic analysis. Since opening September 21, 2004, on the National Mall in Washington D.C., the National Museum of the American Indian (NMAI) has actively adapted the institution of the museum to presentation of an American Indian–composed history and a celebration of living American Indians. The NMAI is the result of legislation passed November 28, 1989, which also funded the George Gustav Heye Center in New York and the Cultural Resources Center outside of Washington, DC, a facility designed to house the museum's collections responsibly.[10] Through exhibits that foreground the mediating role of Native peoples (who select and design museum content), the NMAI requires non-Native visitors to come face-to-face with contemporary American Indians and to acknowledge that the relationship between the Native and non-Native does not end when the latter walks out the museum door.

Those charged with the task of designing the building and the exhibitions of the NMAI spent years consulting Native peoples of the Americas in an effort to synthesize, as best they could, a vision for the new museum. The director, W. Richard West Jr., summarizes what they learned: "First, while acknowledging our deep past, Native peoples want to be seen as communities and cultures that are very much alive today. Second, we want the opportunity to speak directly to museum visitors through our exhibitions and public programs, and to describe in our own voices and through our own eyes the meanings of the objects in the museum's collections and the importance in Native art, culture, and history. And third, we want the museum to act in direct support of contemporary Native communities."[11] The dual emphasis on representing Native communities as neither done for nor dead and on enabling the communities to "speak directly to museum visitors" is at the heart of the NMAI's revision of the typical museum presentation of "the Indian." Native peoples become the mediators for sustained intercultural encounters with the complementary goal of strengthening Native communities. In a review of the museum, Amanda Cobb argues that by "changing what has historically been a cabinet of curiosities into a community-centered gathering place for the celebration of living cultures," the NMAI becomes "an exercise of what filmmaker and scholar Beverly Singer (Santa Clara) calls 'cultural sovereignty.'" This exercise of cultural sovereignty, Cobb continues, enables expressions of national sovereignty in the communities' individual displays throughout the three permanent exhibitions. "For Native Americans," she writes, "the NMAI—a Smithsonian institution—promotes *Native American national identities*. For non-Native Americans, the NMAI provides a real chance to consider what those national identities mean in the context of American identity." [12] The ability of Native peoples to speak directly to visitors through the NMAI displays produces intertwined assertions of cultural and national sovereignty.

The NMAI contains three permanent exhibitions titled Our Universes: Traditional Knowledge Shapes Our World; Our Peoples: Giving Voice to Our Histories; and Our Lives: Contemporary Life and Identities. The second of these, Our Peoples, comments directly on the history of American Indians' representation in museums and other areas of popular culture—what I would call the material and textual recreation of Native culture for non-Native consumption—through a display that combines paintings by George Catlin with modern video. A print narrative adjacent to the display tells the viewer of Our Peoples that "the history of this hemisphere is written in the lives of Native people" and encourages her or him to "think of the exhibition as an excavation site, where evidence that has been buried, ignored, and denied is finally brought to light." [13] The viewer immediately faces seventeen framed and numbered portraits from Catlin's Indian Museum hanging side-by-side in rows as they would have in Catlin's display but interspersed with three vertical plasma screens of approximately the same size on which plays a video presentation. The actor and director Floyd Favel (Cree) walks from screen to screen, handling relevant materials and interacting with museum staff as he tells spectators "about history and about the past—two different things." [14] Covering the sources of various American Indian stereotypes in everything from classroom history lessons to popular films, he also includes praise for Catlin and Heye who, despite their failings, created and collected objects important to contemporary Native versions of American Indian history. Nonetheless, Favel's narrative emphasizes how, through the NMAI, "a history-loving people stripped of their own history" now presents its own history or account of the past. He concludes by emphasizing that the NMAI "has a point-of-view, an agenda" and encouraging visitors to view the museum with "respect" as well as "skepticism." "Explore this gallery," he urges, "*encounter* it." This modern adaptation of Catlin's Indian Gallery expropriates the nineteenth-century artist's images and his full-bodied empiricism for thriving, modern American Indians who pursue their own ideological goals.

The vast majority of visitors to the NMAI are non-Native, and in the light of this fact, the "new" Indian Gallery in Our Peoples borrows from and transforms Catlin's use of the intermediary. Like American Indian autobiographies, the display offers an American Indian rather than a Euro-American guide to American Indian life. Favel visually moves among the pictures and between the pictures and the NMAI, bridging the cultural-historical narratives of American Indians and non-Indians and introducing the Smithsonian visitor to a museum philosophy and format that has been a source of frustration for early non-Native reviewers.[15] The presence of a revised Indian Gallery in this portion of the exhibition acknowledges the museum's debt to Catlin and to others who collected American Indian materials in the nineteenth century even while articulating the negative legacy of nineteenth-century ethnography, with its voracious appetite for objects and information and its oppressive language of extinction.[16] In this way, the last museum on the National Mall continues the process of critiquing and refashioning the trope of Indian-white encounter and the promise of productive, mutually respectful relationships based on sympathy and political equality. To ask visitors to encounter the NMAI's evidence—the living and breathing American Indians who reside in a variety of communities and nations across two continents—is to appeal to the heart as well as the head. The display rejects the doomed Indian and doomed sympathy, and instead expresses hope that one day intimacy may be used truly to overcome prejudice, political injustice, social inequality, and all the legacies of colonialism.

In his remarks at the Grand Opening Ceremony of the NMAI, West declared the museum an icon of emotional as well as intellectual understanding: "It is a symbol for the hope, centuries in the making, that the hearts and minds of all Americans, beyond this museum and throughout the Americas, will open and welcome the presence of the first peoples in their history and in their contemporary lives" and, moreover, "that understanding and respect make possible the true cultural reconciliation that until now has eluded American history."[17] The NMAI transforms the trope of moving encounter between Natives and non-Natives—a figure crucial to the development of the very museum displays it seeks to correct—into an expression of cultural and national sovereignty. Sympathy, it appears, need not be doomed or dooming but can, when grounded in historical and cultural contexts, be the means for achieving sustained understanding and respect.

NOTES

Introduction

1. "Civilization Fund Act. March 3, 1819," in *Documents of United States Indian Policy*, ed. Francis Paul Prucha, 3rd ed. (Lincoln: U of Nebraska P, 2000), 33.

2. Throughout this book I use multiple pairs of terms: *Euro-American* and *American Indian, white* and *Indian*, and *Native* and *non-Native*. In general, I use the first pair when discussing the historical groups, the second when describing a widespread conception or depiction of those groups, and the third when including African Americans and members of other "racial groups" in the discussion. Exceptions do exist; for example, I use the phrase *Indian-white encounter* to describe both the actual and the depicted contact between these groups. I use *race* advisedly throughout the book, recognizing that this term, so important to society in the antebellum period and today, is a social and scientific construct.

3. Overviews of removal policy and the image of the paternal President and doomed Indian in this period include Michael Paul Rogin, *Fathers and Children: Andrew Jackson and the Subjugation of the American Indian* (New York: Alfred A. Knopf, 1975), 206–48; Brian W. Dippie, *The Vanishing American: White Attitudes and U.S. Indian Policy* (Middletown, CT: Wesleyan UP, 1982), 56–78; Francis Paul Prucha, *The Great Father: The United States Government and the American Indians*, 2 vols. (Lincoln: U of Nebraska P, 1984), 2:179–213. On this policy as it affected the Cherokee and other southern Indian nations in particular, see R. Douglas Hurt, *The Indian Frontier, 1763–1846* (Albuquerque: U of New Mexico P, 2002), 137–63.

4. For a comprehensive treatment of the discourse of extinction and its impact on antebellum literature, see Lucy Maddox, *Removals: Nineteenth-Century American Literature and the Politics of Indian Affairs* (New York: Oxford UP, 1991), 15–49. Other indispensable works on the "white man's Indian" in this period and throughout North American history include Roy Harvey Pearce's groundbreaking *Savagism and Civilization: A Study of the Indian and the American Mind*, rev. ed. (Berkeley: U of California P, 1988); Richard Slotkin's magisterial three-volume treatment of the frontier beginning with *Regeneration through Violence: The Mythology of the American Frontier, 1600–1860* (1973; repr., New York: Harper Perennial, 1996); Louise K. Barnett, *The Ignoble Savage: American Literary Racism, 1790–1890* (Westport, CT: Greenwood, 1975); Robert F. Berkhofer Jr., *The White Man's Indian: Images of the American Indian from Columbus to the Present* (New York: Vintage, 1978); Richard Drinnon, *Facing West: The Metaphysics of Indian-Hating and Empire-Building* (Minneapolis: U of Minnesota P, 1980); Susan Scheckel, *The Insistence of the Indian: Race and Nationalism in Nineteenth-Century American Culture* (Princeton: Princeton UP, 1998); Joshua David Bellin, *The Demon of the Continent: Indians and the Shaping of American Literature* (Philadelphia: U of Pennsylvania P, 2001). On displays of the American Indian body and the connections between ethnography, museums, and theatrical culture in this period, see especially Theresa Strouth Gaul, "'The Genuine Indian Who Was Brought upon the Stage': Edwin Forrest's *Metamora* and White Audiences," *Arizona Quarterly* 56.1 (2000): 1–27; Paul Gilmore, *The Genuine Article: Race, Mass Culture, and American Literary Manhood* (Durham, NC: Duke UP, 2001), 21–35, 67–96.

5. My concept of the moving encounter builds on Bellin's formulation in *Demon of the Continent* of an "intercultural literary criticism" that "sees texts as formed by, forming, and a form of encounter: fertile, contested, and multiply determined, they exist on the shifting borders, or in the

indefinite field, between peoples in contact" (6). In his account, texts of this period are encounters incarnate in that they represent products of intercultural exchange rather than the calling cards of distinct groups within a multicultural society.

6. Patrick Brantlinger, *Dark Vanishings: Discourse on the Extinction of Primitive Races, 1800–1930* (Ithaca: Cornell UP, 2003), 20. On the "static" Indian and nineteenth-century science, see ibid., 17–44; Pearce, *Savagism and Civilization*, 105–34; Robert E. Bieder, *Science Encounters the Indian, 1820–1880: The Early Years of American Ethnology* (Norman: U of Oklahoma P, 1986), 8–13. On the rhetoric of the doomed Indian in the first half of the nineteenth century, see Dippie, *Vanishing American*, 12–44; Brantlinger, *Dark Vanishings*, 45–67.

7. H. Whiting, Review of Henry Rowe Schoolcraft's *Algic Researches*, *North American Review* 49 (1839): 371–72, 372. Schoolcraft's catalogue of Indian traits appear in his "Address to the Algic Society," *Constitution of the Algic Society, Instituted March 28, 1832. For Encouraging Missionary Effort in Evangelizing the North Western Tribes, and Promoting Education, Agriculture, Industry, Peace & Temperance, among Them* (Detroit: Cleland and Sawyer, 1833), 16.

8. As Hurt explains, "By favoring removal, Jackson demonstrated his commitment to states' rights and limited federal power as well as nationalism and federally directed territorial expansion for purposes of both land and security" (*Indian Frontier*, 138). This commitment was made clear in 1832 when Jackson refused to enforce the Supreme Court's ruling in *Worcester v. Georgia* that the laws of Georgia did not pertain within the Cherokee nation. On the impact of paternalism and "the figure of the nation as a family" in the literature of this period, see Maddox, *Removals*, 170–73. Laura M. Stevens contends that benevolent paternalism in the United States was rooted in the tradition of Christian missionary work among American Indian populations with its emphasis on pity for the Indians and sympathy for their benevolent attendants. Stevens, *The Poor Indians: British Missionaries, Native Americans, and Colonial Sensibility* (Philadelphia: U of Pennsylvania P, 2004), 33. Benevolent paternalism combined with the metaphor of the "Great Father," which in the Jacksonian context, Rogin famously argues, implied a disciplinarian President (*Fathers and Children*, 3–15). Thus, an emphasis on social reform, informed by a history of Christian/national mission and an increasingly "scientific" means of categorizing human societies and races, produced an influential discourse of benevolence that Susan M. Ryan calls "a central paradigm in antebellum culture, one that provided Americans with ways of understanding, describing, and constructing their racial and national identities." Ryan, *The Grammar of Good Intentions: Race and the Antebellum Culture of Benevolence* (Ithaca: Cornell UP, 2003), 5. Richard White explores the *mutual* formation of the President-as-father image in "The Fictions of Patriarchy: Indians and Whites in the Early Republic," in *Native Americans and the Early Republic*, ed. Frederick E. Hoxie, Ronald Hoffman and Peter J. Albert (Charlottesville: UP of Virginia for the United States Capitol Historical Society, 1999), 62–84.

9. The description of 1760–1815 in this paragraph and in the following reflects Richard White's influential description of the rise and fall of Indian-white accommodation in the seventeenth- and eighteenth-century *pays d'en haut* (discussed in the next paragraph). On the demise of the middle ground between 1795 and 1815, see especially White, *The Middle Ground: Indians, Empires, and Republics in the Great Lakes Region, 1650–1815* (Cambridge: Cambridge UP, 1991), 469–523. Other works on Indian-white relations in this period have likewise explicated the rise of American hegemony in sites formerly marked by political and cultural negotiation. For example, Stephen Aron explains, "the frontier was the ground—actual and metaphorical—where European and Indian worlds met and mixed. It was the intersection where peoples came together—to trade, to fight, to procreate, to preach contrary conceptions of the good life, to restore old worlds, and to make sense of new worlds." Aron, "Lessons in Conquest: Towards a Greater Western History," *Pacific Historical Review*, 1994, 143. In the closing chapter of *Facing East from Indian Country: A Native History of Early America* (Cambridge: Harvard UP, 2001), 189–236, Daniel K. Richter focuses on the fifty years after the 1763 "campaigns of ethnic cleansing" by Ottawa war chief Pontiac and the Paxton Boys of Pennsylvania, campaigns that essentially undermined future hopes of mutual accommodation. R. Douglas Hurt focuses on the years between the Revolutionary War and the War of 1812 as the time when Euro-Americans abandoned a strategy of American Indian inclusion for one of aggressive alliances and exclusions (*Indian Frontier*, 103–36). Finally, Colin G. Calloway in his epilogue to *One Vast Winter Count: The Native American West before Lewis and Clark* (Lincoln: U of Nebraska P, 2003) concludes

that "the last twenty-five years of the eighteenth century determined the future of the American West" as the new Republic instituted policies of ethnic exclusion and acculturation (427).

10. White, *Middle Ground*, X. In an ongoing effort to understand the impact of Indian-white relations on the literature of this period, literary critics in the past decade have readily engaged with the concept of the middle ground—what Annette Kolodny describes as the reconception of "'frontier' as a locus of first cultural contact, circumscribed by a particular physical terrain in the process of change *because of* the forms that contact takes." Kolodny, "Letting Go Our Grand Obsessions: Notes toward a New Literary History of the American Frontiers," *American Literature* 64 (Mar. 1992): 3. Mary Louise Pratt's concept of the "contact zone," as detailed in her *Imperial Eyes: Travel Writing and Transculturation* (London: Routledge, 1992), has also contributed to this development. Whereas Pratt focuses on the "conditions of coercion, radical inequality, and intractable conflict" in the contact zone (6) and White on the creative collaboration that arises from stalemate in the middle ground, both replace the traditional concept of "the frontier" with that of a space in which cultural negotiation and production prevail. Through the concept of the moving encounter I emphasize instead the way in which the perceived demise of the middle ground in the early nineteenth century led to a literary figure that was often paradoxically used to announce the end of Indian-white negotiation and shared community.

11. Daniel J. Herman, "Romance on the Middle Ground," *Journal of the Early Republic* 19.2 (Summer 1999): 282. For White's discussion of the portability of the "middle ground" concept, see Richard White, "Creative Misunderstandings and New Understandings," *William and Mary Quarterly* 63.1 (2006): par. 4, http://www.historycooperative.org/journals/wm/63.1/white.html. For additional analyses of the critical (mis)uses of the "middle ground" concept, see other articles from this issue: Susan Sleeper-Smith, "The Middle Ground Revisited Introduction," 11 pars., http://www.historycooperative.org/journals/wm/63.1/sleepersmith.html; Philip J. Deloria, "What Is the Middle Ground, Anyway?," 24 pars., http://www.historycooperative.org/journals/wm/63.1/deloria.html.

12. Hurt, *Indian Frontier*, 247. Andrew R. L. Cayton and Fredericka J. Teute elaborate, "As white settlement quickly expanded into the Trans-Appalachian region, the new Republic colonized its internal frontiers by pitting the interests of Indians, African Americans, and lower-status whites against each other. Constructions of gender, racial, and status barriers, as much as physical borders, could serve as parts of imperial designs to divide peoples." Cayton and Teute, "Introduction: On the Connection of Frontiers," in *Contact Points: American Frontiers from the Mohawk Valley to the Mississippi, 1750–1830*, ed. Cayton and Teute (Chapel Hill: U of North Carolina P, 1998), 11.

13. James Fenimore Cooper, *The Last of the Mohicans: A Narrative of 1757*, ed. James Franklin Beard (1826; repr., Albany: State U of New York P, 1983), 349.

14. Ibid., 349–50. Critical discussions of *The Last of the Mohicans* abound. The most relevant for this analysis comes from Brantlinger: "No author did more than Cooper, however, to establish proleptic elegy as a generic pattern for American Literature, one that is intrinsically both racist and sentimental" (*Dark Vanishings*, 60). For more on the concluding burials of *The Pioneers* and *The Last of the Mohicans*, see Chapter 2.

15. Or, in the words of Gordon M. Sayre, such works are cathartic expressions that resolve "a wrenching moral and political ambivalence with regard to the Indian hero" as representative American Indian. Sayre, *The Indian Chief as Tragic Hero: Native Resistance and the Literatures of America, from Moctezuma to Tecumseh* (Chapel Hill: U of North Carolina P, 2005), 7.

16. As Scheckel, Renée L. Bergland, and Helen Carr all argue, the Indian of antebellum literature symbolizes the return of—or in Scheckel's account, the insistence of—the repressed colonial subject whose presence and voice challenge the nation's Enlightenment ideals and indicate postcolonial insecurity and guilt. See especially Scheckel, *Insistence of the Indian*, 3–14; Bergland, *The National Uncanny: Indian Ghosts and American Subjects* (Hanover: UP of New England for Dartmouth College, 2000), 1–22; Carr, *Inventing the American Primitive: Politics, Gender and the Representation of Native American Literary Traditions, 1789–1936* (New York: New York UP, 1996), 1–21.

17. For an illuminating discussion of the conventions of eighteenth-century British literary sensibility, one highly transferable to American sentimentalism, see Janet Todd, *Sensibility: An Introduction* (London: Methuen, 1986), 1–6. Gregg Camfield provides the Protestant context for American

sentimentalism in "The Moral Aesthetics of Sentimentality: A Missing Key to *Uncle Tom's Cabin*," *Nineteenth-Century Literature* 43.3 (December 1988): 319–45.

18. For an excellent introduction to American sentimentalism, see Mary Louise Kete, "Sentimental Literature," in *The Oxford Encyclopedia of American Literature*, ed. Jay Parini, 4 vols. (New York: Oxford UP, 2004), 3:545–54. The scholarship of sentimentalism is extensive and marked by disagreement over the mode's political efficacy and role in the public sphere, cultural and historical scope, conventions and structure, and relationship to the discourses of gender and domesticity. My consideration of sentimentalism keeps the broader critical debate in mind but draws in particular on certain key works. Two seminal (and opposing) books illuminate the relationship between sentimentalism and the changing evangelical culture of antebellum America: Ann Douglas, *The Feminization of American Culture* (New York: Doubleday, 1977); Jane Tompkins, *Sensational Designs: The Cultural Work of American Fiction, 1790–1860* (New York: Oxford UP, 1985). Philip Fisher, *Hard Facts: Setting and Form in the American Novel* (New York: Oxford UP, 1985), 87–127, situates American sentimentalism in a larger intellectual-historical context and clarifies its primary role as extending normality to those otherwise denied humanity. Shirley Samuels, ed., *The Culture of Sentiment: Race, Gender, and Sentimentality in Nineteenth-Century America* (New York: Oxford UP, 1992); and Mary Chapman and Glenn Hendler, eds., *Sentimental Men: Masculinity and the Politics of Affect in American Culture* (Berkeley: U of California P, 1999) capture the breadth of sentimentalism's cultural work, its decidedly public nature and widespread impact, and its place in the discourse of masculinity as well as its relationship to a feminized domesticity. Michelle Burnham, *Captivity and Sentiment: Cultural Exchange in American Literature, 1682–1861* (Hanover: UP of New England for Dartmouth College, 1997); Lora Romero, *Home Fronts: Domesticity and Its Critics in the Antebellum United States* (Durham: Duke UP, 1997); and Laura Wexler, *Tender Violence: Domestic Visions in an Age of U.S. Imperialism* (Chapel Hill: U of North Carolina P, 2000) treat the role of sentimentalism and, more specifically, sentimental domesticity in nation building, identifying complicity with imperialism as well as communalism. Burnham argues that sentimental literature and its language of sympathy depend on a history of intercultural exchange best captured in those textual moments when the boundary between one and the Other is crossed and implicitly erased. Finally, Glenn Hendler, in *Public Sentiments: Structures of Feeling in Nineteenth-Century American Literature* (Chapel Hill: U of North Carolina P, 2001), argues that nineteenth-century sentimentalism was public, that sympathetic identification created at once a space for public debate and a publicly oriented subject.

19. Since the nineteenth century many have charged the sentimental mode with disguising desirous spectatorship as compassionate action. See especially Marianne Noble, *The Masochistic Pleasures of Sentimental Literature* (Princeton: Princeton UP, 2000). Sayre, in his recent *Indian Chief as Tragic Hero*, goes so far as to define sentimentality as "an affective response to the suffering of another that one cannot or will not alleviate" (4).

20. James Monroe, "Message of President Monroe on Indian Removal. January 27, 1825," in Prucha, *Documents of United States Indian Policy*, 39.

21. Hendler, *Public Sentiments*, 8; Ryan, *Grammar of Good Intentions*, 19. Ryan acknowledges that the discourses of benevolence and sentimentalism "overlapped significantly" but also identifies an "antisentimental strain of antebellum benevolence" in which "commentators ... highlighted instead the risks of emotional investment and proposed elaborate, decidedly unsentimental methods for discerning which supplicants were worthy of aid" (16, 19). For more on the most common subjects and the direct address of sentimental literature, see especially Kete, "Sentimental Literature," 545.

22. Maureen Konkle, *Writing Indian Nations: Native Intellectuals and the Politics of Historiography, 1827–1863* (Chapel Hill: U of North Carolina P, 2004), 17–28. Ryan likewise argues that benevolence discourse allowed the framers of federal Indian policy "to preserve the white nation and to reproduce its most vital elements in a parallel though still subordinate form" (*Grammar of Good Intentions*, 40). See also Peter Coveillo, introduction to *Intimacy in America: Dreams of Affiliation in Antebellum Literature* (Minneapolis: U of Minnesota P, 2005), 1–23, in which Coveillo describes a nineteenth-century formulation of nationalism as emotional intimacy realized through the language of race.

23. Andrew Jackson, "President Jackson on Indian Removal. December 8, 1829," in Prucha, *Documents of United States Indian Policy*, 48.

24. Theodore Frelinghuysen, "Senator Frelinghuysen on Indian Removal. April 9, 1830," in ibid., 49.

25. Cherokee Citizens, "[Memorial of the Cherokee Citizens, December 18, 1829]," in *The Norton Anthology of American Literature*, ed. Nina Baym, 6th ed., 5 vols. (New York: Norton, 2003), B:1036. On the importance of closely analyzing the Cherokee Memorials, see Andrew Denson, *Demanding the Cherokee Nation: Indian Autonomy and American Culture, 1830–1900* (Lincoln: U of Nebraska P, 2004), 2–6. These texts, he argues, "document an effort to find an alternative to wardship as the basis for Indian-American relations" (5).

26. Here I respond most directly to Konkle and to Scott Michaelsen, who reject nineteenth-century sentimentalism and twenty-first-century interculturalism alike. Konkle, like Michelle Burnham before her, moves from "the political utility of sympathy for Indians" within nineteenth-century colonialism to a hard-hitting critique of late twentieth-century and early twenty-first-century multiculturalism (Konkle, *Writing Indian Nations*, 66). The latter, writes Konkle, places an "inordinate focus on Native difference and cultural identity, while accepting at face value the moral correctness of Native incorporation into the United States," continuing the tradition of suppressing the issue of American Indian sovereignty in favor of a sentimental preoccupation with cultural distinctiveness (7). Moreover, she argues, recent scholarly use of "concepts such as 'cultural encounters,' 'contact,' and even 'sharing' (between cultures)... downplays violence and conflict" (32). She summarizes her argument linking sympathy and multiculturalism: "If sympathy in the nineteenth century demonstrated the moral superiority of white people and elided what white people—individually and institutionally—were actually doing to Native peoples, multicultural criticism of Native American literature insists that its appreciation for the cultural difference of Indians actually demonstrates the moral superiority of universalist U.S. political values, thereby eliding not just history but, in the case of the response to Native criticism, current Native political claims. In both cases, the good feelings of white people clean up the messy details of politics and history" (35). In a related assessment of contemporary cultural criticism, Michaelsen rejects the description of the contact zone or the middle ground and intercultural exchange and instead calls the site of encounter and interaction "culture's very condition of possibility, of visibility." In this description, multiculturalism, like nineteenth-century sentimentalism, holds that "all people feel in precisely the same way," either idealizing assimilation or practicing "ethnochauvinism." Michaelsen, *The Limits of Multiculturalism: Interrogating the Origins of American Anthropology* (Minneapolis: U of Minnesota P, 1999), 38, 13, 15.

27. Like Ryan, I seek a critical method that "escape[s] the unproductive binary choice of recrimination or hagiography" (*Grammar of Good Intentions*, 192).

28. Carr emphasizes that the Euro-American of this period had an "ethnographic imagination" that "desired and fed on particularity and authenticity—at least what it took to be authenticity—but... was also highly emotionally charged" (*Inventing the American Primitive*, 17).

29. See in particular chapters 6 and 25–28 of Herman Melville, *The Confidence-Man: His Masquerade*, ed. Harrison Hayford, Hershel Parker, and G. Thomas Tanselle (Evanston, IL: Northwestern UP, 2002), in which one man collects money for the "Widow and Orphan Asylum recently founded among the Seminoles" without ever explaining just how those Seminoles were widowed and orphaned and another recounts the story of Colonel John Moredock, an "Indian-hater *par excellence*" and "a Leather-stocking Nemesis" whose mother and siblings were killed by a party of Indians and whose passion, subsequently, was "to kill Indians" (28, 149, 150, 154). On these chapters, see Pearce, *Savagism and Civilization*, 244–50; Maddox, *Removals*, 81–87.

Chapter 1. The Evolution of Moving Encounters in Lydia Maria Child's American Indian Writings, 1824–1870

1. An American Lady [Lydia Maria Child], *Evenings in New England: Intended for Juvenile Amusement and Instruction* (Boston: Cummings, Hillard, 1824), 3.

2. Lydia Maria Child, *A Romance of the Republic* (1867; repr., Lexington: UP Kentucky, 1997), 440.

Carolyn L. Karcher points out that this scene with Eulalia and Rosen is one of a series of concluding tableaux vivants "summing up the strengths and weakness of the vision *A Romance of the Republic* offers of America's destiny." Karcher, *The First Woman in the Republic: A Cultural Biography of Lydia Maria Child* (Durham: Duke UP, 1994), 526.

3. Child's American Indian writings, then, offer complex examples of what many critics have analyzed as the imperial function of familial relations and domesticity in the nineteenth century.

4. In focusing on Child's American Indian writings, I am indebted to Karcher's cultural biography, *First Woman of the Republic,* and her groundbreaking collection of Child's work, *"Hobomok" and Other Writings on Indians* (New Brunswick: Rutgers UP, 1986), which contains many of the texts discussed in this chapter.

5. Lydia Maria Child, *Hobomok, A Tale of Early Times* (1824), in Karcher, *"Hobomok" and Other Writings,* 139, 141. Hereafter cited as *H.*

6. Critics regularly note that Child's first novel does not concern itself so much with challenging Indian removal as with promoting a republic that espouses feminine virtue and freedom. See Leland S. Person, "The American Eve: Miscegenation and a Feminist Frontier Fiction," *American Quarterly* 37 (1985): 677–85; Lucy Maddox, *Removals: Nineteenth-Century American Literature and the Politics of Indian Affairs* (New York: Oxford UP, 1991), 92–103; Nina Baym, *Feminism and American Literary History: Essays* (New Brunswick: Rutgers UP, 1992), 19–35; Philip Gould, *Covenant and Republic: Historical Romance and the Politics of Puritanism* (New York: Cambridge UP, 1996), 91–132.

7. For similar insight, see Sabina Matter-Seibel's argument that "the Native Americans' claim of being part of the national family [is] supported by an emphasis on their domestic virtues." Matter-Seibel, "Native Americans, Women, and the Culture of Nationalism in Lydia Maria Child and Catharine Maria Sedgwick," in *Early America Re-Explored: New Readings in Colonial, Early National, and Antebellum Culture,* ed. Klaus H. Schmidt and Fritz Fleischmann (New York: Peter Lang, 2000), 420. See also Philip Gould's assertion that Child "reinterprets the stereotype of the 'noble savage' into a model of feminized republican manhood" who "abdicates authority within conjugal relations in the name of disinterested benevolence." Gould, "Remembering Metacom: Historical Writing and the Cultures of Masculinity in Early Republican America," in *Sentimental Men: Masculinity and the Politics of Affect in American Culture,* ed. Mary Chapman and Glenn Hendler (Berkeley: U of California P, 1999), 118.

8. While Matter-Seibel suggests that the occult operates in the novel as a constructive symbol of "the pre-Christian matriarchal world of nature" ("Native Americans, Women, and the Culture of Nationalism," 424), I see the moments described in this paragraph as ominous and decidedly unnatural, even though they lead to a loving, productive marriage. Renée L. Bergland argues that in such scenes Child specifically attacks a common metaphor for both the dispossessed American Indian and the married white woman, the ghost, though "her primary purpose in the novel is to bring white women out of spectrality." Bergland, *The National Uncanny: Indian Ghosts and American Subjects* (Hanover: UP of New England for Dartmouth College, 2000), 70.

9. Ezra F. Tawill, "Domestic Frontier Romance; or, How the Sentimental Heroine Became White," *Novel* 32 (1998): 112.

10. Child, *Evenings in New England,* 78; A Lady of Massachusetts [Lydia Maria Child], *The First Settlers of New-England: or, Conquest of the Pequods, Narragansets and Pokanokets: As Related by a Mother to Her Children, and Designed for the Instruction of Youth* (Boston: Munroe & Francis, 1829), 281.

11. Lydia Maria Child, *The Mother's Book* (Boston: Carter, Hendee & Babcock, 1831), 17. On the moral didacticism of antebellum children's literature and the elevated role of the child figure within it, see, respectively, Anne Scott MacLeod, *A Moral Tale: Children's Fiction and American Culture, 1820–1860* (Hamden, CT: Archon Books, 1975); Holly Keller, "Juvenile Antislavery Narrative and Notions of Childhood," *Children's Literature* 24 (1996): 86–100.

12. Child, *First Settlers of New England,* iv, 44. As Nina Baym has shown, the prevalent dialogue form in women-authored instructional history books of this period "figured the affective strength of the maternal as an instructional advantage over the paternal" and "counter[ed] the idea that feeling precluded intellectuality," achieving the goal of a rigorous education that induced students' moral action. Baym, *American Women Writers and the Work of History, 1790–1860* (New Brunswick: Rutgers UP, 1995), 36. Sarah Robbins includes Child in her description of New England women

authors who created the genre of "domestic literacy narratives" that "support[ed] American moth-ers' astute management of domestic literacy and, hence, of national civic virtues." Robbins, " 'The Future Good and Great of Our Land': Republican Mothers, Female Authors, and Domesticated Literacy in Antebellum New England," *New England Quarterly* 75 (2002): 572.

13. Lydia Maria Child, "Adventure in the Woods," *Juvenile Miscellany* 1.1 (Sept. 1826): 11. Karcher also discusses this tale's reversal of the captivity genre (*First Woman of the Republic*, 153–54). Etsuko Taketani mentions Child's use of the Aunt Maria persona to offer maternal instruction in *U.S. Women and the Discourses of Colonialism, 1825–1861* (Knoxville: U of Tennessee P, 2003), 18–19.

14. Lydia Maria Child, "The Adventures of a Bell," *Juvenile Miscellany* 2.1 (Mar. 1827): 24–30; "William Burton; or, the Boy Who Would Be a Sailor," *Juvenile Miscellany* 3rd ser., 1.1 (Sept. 1831): 1–46. "The Adventures of a Bell" recounts the attack of Anglo-American colonists on a French-Jesuit mission to the Norridgewock Indians during which a priest and captive Anglo boy die in the unrestrained slaughter, and the *Typee*-like "William Burton; or, the Boy Who Would Be a Sailor" concerns a young, eager sailor stranded on the Mulgrave Islands who is spared during the massacre of his shipmates because he and his friend "dealt gently with the savages" (20). He eventually re-turns to his fiancée, promising never to leave her as he did his mother, who died during his absence. "William Burton," like so many other works in the *Miscellany*, reflects what Susan M. Ryan identi-fies in this period as "the notion that white benevolence—its narratives, practices, and institutions—would produce better white people in the present and coming generations." Ryan, *The Grammar of Good Intentions: Race and the Antebellum Culture of Benevolence* (Ithaca: Cornell UP, 2003), 75.

15. Lydia Maria Child, "The Indian Boy," *Juvenile Miscellany* 2.2 (May 1827): 28, 31. The title character of "Pol Sosef. The Indian Artist" (*Juvenile Miscellany* n.s. 5.3 [Jan. 1831]: 278–84) likewise escapes the purportedly indolent habits of Penobscot men but through the intervention of Catholic school and his attraction to painting. Karen Sánchez-Eppler, in "Raising Empires Like Children: Race, Nation, and Religious Education," *American Literary History* 8.3 (November 1996): 399–425, treats such depictions of civilization efforts as akin to the religious education of white children. Taketani argues, however, that "the *Juvenile Miscellany* . . . reworks the trope of parent-child central to U.S. colonialism to call into question the way in which the Anglo-American men, who were brought to power by independence, naturalize their rule" (Taketani, *U.S. Women and the Discourses of Colonialism*, 36–37).

16. Lydia Maria Child, "Buffalo Creek," *Juvenile Miscellany*, 3rd ser., 4.3 (July 1833): 264, 271, 272. On the history of the Buffalo Creek Reservation, see Christopher Densmore, *Red Jacket: Iroquois Diplomat and Orator* (Syracuse: Syracuse UP, 1999), 106–20.

17. "Anti-Slavery Education," *National Anti-Slavery Standard*, June 3, 1841, 207.

18. Bruce Mills, *Cultural Reformations: Lydia Maria Child and the Literature of Reform* (Athens: U of Georgia P, 1994), 87–88; Karcher, *First Woman of the Republic*, 288–91. Under Child's supervi-sion, Karcher points out, the *Standard* ran pieces by such prominent authors as Frances Trollope, Caroline Kirkland, Charles Dickens, Alexis de Tocqueville, Nathaniel Hawthorne, and Catharine Beecher (273–74).

19. Karcher notes that Child's literary sketches of New York were popular with *Standard* read-ers and that *Letters from New-York* went through eleven printings in seven years (*First Woman of the Republic*, 274, 309).

20. Lydia Maria Child, *Letters from New-York*, ed. Bruce Mills (Athens: U Georgia P, 1998), 12. Hereafter cited as *LNY*. This internal struggle may have led Child to scale back the abolitionist and more radical reform statements in the letters, even omitting whole letters, when preparing the first collected volume. Bruce Mills, introduction to *LNY*, xx–xxii; Karcher, *First Woman of the Republic*, 301–2.

21. Mills, *Cultural Reformations*, 83. Child's affinity with Emerson's evolving approach to reform in "Man the Reformer" surely springs from his appeal to the Christian social ethic at the heart of the culture of sympathy. Emerson writes that "the sentiment of love" is "the one remedy for all ills, the panacea of nature." "Man the Reformer," in *Nature, Addresses, and Lectures*, ed. Robert E. Spiller and Alfred R. Ferguson (Cambridge: Harvard UP, Belknap, 1971), 158. This appeal points to what Len Gougeon describes as Emerson's steady movement toward abolition work from 1838 to the mid-1840s, as well as his defense of Cherokee land rights in an 1838 address in Concord and a letter he

sent (with ambivalence) to President Martin Van Buren and multiple newspapers. Gougeon, *Virtue's Hero: Emerson, Antislavery, and Reform* (Athens: U of Georgia P, 1990), 57–59. Child reprints "Man the Reformer" from the *Dial* in the June 10, 1841, issue of the *Standard* and then echoes and heightens this point in a letter dated September 29, 1842, in *LNY*: "The cure for all the ills and wrongs, the cares, the sorrows, and the crimes of humanity, all lie in that one word, LOVE" (123). Mills and Stephanie A. Tingley outline Child's engagement with transcendentalism, including her brother Convers Francis's Boston connections and her friendship with Margaret Fuller. Mills, *Cultural Revolutions*, 80–84, 99; Tingley, "'Thumping against the Glittering Wall of Limitations': Lydia Maria Child's 'Letters from New York,'" in *In Her Own Voice: Nineteenth-Century American Women Essayists*, ed. Sherry Lee Linkon (New York: Garland, 1997), 51–53.

22. Tingley, "'Thumping against the Glittering Wall,'" 53.

23. Lydia Maria Child, *Letters from New York. Second Series* (New York: C. S. Francis, 1845), 113.

24. For example, in a letter dated October 21, 1841, Child includes a Mississippi steamboat captain's tale of an Englishman who died on board his boat and the subsequent burial rituals performed by a sympathetic Swiss Catholic mother and daughter (*LNY* 45–46).

25. As detailed in Chapter 6, American racial science was established in 1839 with the publication of Samuel George Morton's *Crania Americana* (1839), which asserts the superiority of the Caucasian race over all others through comparisons of racially representative skulls.

26. Walt Whitman, "Crossing Brooklyn Ferry," in *Leaves of Grass: The "Death-Bed" Edition* (1892; repr., New York: Modern Library, 2001), l. 121.

27. Paul Gilmore, in *The Genuine Article: Race, Mass Culture, and American Literary Manhood* (Durham, NC: Duke UP, 2001), in addition to discussing Forrest's performance as Metamora (27–32), treats the paradoxical use of Indian display and dress in this period, arguing that such authors as James Fenimore Cooper and Washington Irving "implicitly contrast the self-identical Indian and his masculine self-sufficiency and bodily integrity with the self-objectification and commodification of a burgeoning market capitalism" (23). See also Philip J. Deloria's *Playing Indian* (New Haven: Yale UP, 1998) on how the Indian body is a model of authenticity made accessible through performance and even mimicry—the source of Child's confusion at Barnum's.

28. In *Walden*, the American Indian basket-maker, whose neighbors will not purchase his wares, echoes the conflict between Thoreau's individual expression and the literary market and justifies Thoreau's decision to opt out of capitalism: "Instead of studying how to make it worth men's while to buy my baskets, I studied rather how to avoid the necessity of selling them." Henry D. Thoreau, *Walden*, ed. J. Lyndon Shanley (1854; repr., Princeton: Princeton UP, 1971), 19. As Gilmore notes, "While the basket-selling Indian has attempted to enter into the marketplace, what he really needs to do is return to his primitive, savage past and avoid the market altogether" (*Genuine Article*, 79–80). On Thoreau's "need to erase Indians from America's economic life," see also Joshua David Bellin, *The Demon of the Continent: Indians and the Shaping of American Literature* (Philadelphia: U of Pennsylvania P, 2001), 69.

29. The *OED* reports six nineteenth-century uses of the verb *mantle*, intransitive and transitive, as: "Of the blood, a blush, etc.: to suffuse the cheeks." *OED Online*, s.v. "mantle," http://dictionary.oed.com/cgi/entry/00301503 (accessed June 1, 2004).

30. Perhaps Child's desire to emphasize the Indians' spiritual and physical transformation is why, when preparing this letter for *LNY*, she excised a closing condemnation of their willing participation in commercial culture: "If they themselves were tempted by money to prolong their stay, oh how the bleeding heart of that young chieftain will hate the yellow dust for which he sold a life so precious!" (255 n. 11).

31. Lydia Maria Child, *An Appeal for the Indians*, in Karcher, *"Hobomok" and Other Writings on Indians*, 220. Hereafter cited as *AI*. On the work's impetus, see Karcher, *First Woman of the Republic*, 553.

32. Karcher, *First Woman of the Republic*, 549, 552.

33. Karcher includes the final version of this story, "A Legend of the Falls of St. Anthony," in *"Hobomok" and Other Writings on Indians*, 203–12, and discusses these and other Indian tales Child wrote in this period in *First Woman of the Republic*, 101–25.

34. Andrea K. Newlyn, "Form and Ideology in Transracial Narratives: *Pudd'nhead Wilson* and *A Romance of the Republic*," *Narrative* 8 (2000): 55.

35. Lydia Maria Child, "Willie Wharton," in Karcher, *"Hobomok" and Other Writings on Indians*, 257. Hereafter cited as WW.

36. Karcher, *First Woman of the Republic*, 550. My reading of "Willie Wharton" draws on Walter Benn Michaels's analysis of 1920s cultural pluralist novels wherein "the essence of culture is that it cannot be reduced to either the social or the biological," that "it must be both achieved and inherited." Michaels, "The Vanishing American," in *American Literature, American Culture*, ed. Gordon Hutner (New York: Oxford UP), 1999, 570, 566; originally published in *American Literary History* 2 (1990): 220–41.

37. For example, Child playfully invokes the occult again, describing the gentle transformation of A-lee-lah and her heavy bangs through "the magical power of two side-combs ornamented with colored glass," and the narrative subsequently declares, "The conquest was complete" (WW 285).

38. Debra J. Rosenthal, "Floral Counterdiscourse: Miscegenation, Ecofeminism, and Hybridity in Lydia Maria Child's *A Romance of the Republic*," *Women's Studies* 31 (2002): 222.

39. Karcher notes the Bloomers (*First Woman of the Republic*, 551), and Rosenthal points out that "the tulip contains exotic, orientalizing, harem-type associations" ("Floral Counterdiscourse," 237).

40. On the theory of "developmentalism" in music and its link to "social evolutionary stages" and racial hierarchy at the turn of the twentieth century, see Philip J. Deloria, *Indians in Unexpected Places* (Lawrence: UP of Kansas, 2004), 201–4.

41. Lydia Maria Child, "To Charles Sumner," July 4, 1820, in *Selected Letters, 1817–1880*, ed. Milton Meltzer and Patricia G. Holland (Amherst: U of Massachusetts P, 1982), 496–97.

42. Lydia Maria Child, "The Indians," in Karcher, *"Hobomok" and Other Writings on Indians*, 290, 295, 296.

43. On the Dawes General Allotment Act see Francis Paul Prucha, *The Great Father: The United States Government and the American Indians*, 2 vols. (Lincoln: U of Nebraska P, 1984), 2:666–73.

44. Lydia Maria Child, "The Indians," in Karcher, *"Hobomok" and Other Writings on Indians*, 297.

Chapter 2. Doomed Sympathy and *The Prairie*

1. James Fenimore Cooper, *The Pioneers, or the Sources of the Susquehanna; A Descriptive Tale*, ed. James Franklin Beard (1823; repr., Albany: State U of New York P, 1980), 452; James Fenimore Cooper, *The Last of the Mohicans; A Narrative of 1757*, ed. James Franklin Beard (1826; repr., Albany: State U of New York P, 1983), 350.

2. Cooper, *Pioneers*, 452; Cooper, *Last of the Mohicans*, 347. In Andrew Newman's words, "His function in this scene [in *The Last of the Mohicans*] is as sublime translator—delivering the legacy of the Indians [rather than Indians themselves] to the futurity of America." Newman, "Sublime Translation in the Novels of James Fenimore Cooper and Walter Scott," *Nineteenth-Century Literature* 59.1 (2004): 22.

3. Kay Seymour House, *Cooper's Americans* (Columbus: Ohio State UP, 1965), 300. For Natty's discussion of his final military service, see James Fenimore Cooper, *The Prairie; A Tale*, ed. James P. Elliott (1827; repr., Albany: State U of New York P, 1985), 63–64. On General Wayne and the implications of Natty's service under him, see Gordon Brotherston, "The Prairie and Cooper's Invention of the West," in *James Fenimore Cooper: New Critical Essays*, ed. Robert Clark (London: Vision, 1985), 162–86.

4. Richard Drinnon, *Facing West: The Metaphysics of Indian-Hating and Empire-Building* (Minneapolis: U of Minnesota P, 1980), 162–63. Henry Nash Smith, in *Virgin Land: The American West as Symbol and Myth* (Cambridge: Harvard UP, 1950), writes, "[Cooper] was at once more strongly devoted to the principle of social order and more vividly responsive to the ideas of nature and freedom in the Western forest than [his contemporaries] were" (61). He continues, "The profundity of the symbol of Leatherstocking springs from the fact that Cooper displays a *genuine ambivalence* toward all these issues, although in every case his strongest commitment is to the forces of order" (62; emphasis mine). The ambivalence is registered in the figure of Natty Bumppo. Geoffrey Rans, in *Cooper's Leather-Stocking Novels: A Secular Reading* (Chapel Hill: U of North Carolina P, 1991), writes, "The radical *meaning* of Natty's life, its economy and its morality toward nature and man, is *at enmity*

with a society based on acquisition of wealth (in land or money), cupidity, and profit, and on class, exploitation, and genocide" (167).

5. Natty refers to himself as "a man without a cross" throughout *The Last of the Mohicans*. On "Hawk-eye's ritualistic insistence on blood purity and blood boundaries," see Betsy Erkkila, *Mixed Bloods and Other Crosses: Rethinking American Literature from the Revolution to the Culture Wars* (Philadelphia: U of Pennsylvania P, 2005), 14.

6. D. H. Lawrence, *Studies in Classic American Literature* (1923; London: Penguin, 1961), 62.

7. Cooper, *The Prairie*, 385. Hereafter cited as *P*.

8. David W. Noble, "Cooper, Leatherstocking, and the Death of the American Adam," *American Quarterly* 16.3 (1964): 428; House, *Cooper's Americans*, 305.

9. For example, in her reading of *The Last of the Mohicans*, Lora Romero finds that the spectacular deaths of Cooper's Indians follow the introduction of a feminine civilizing, disciplining force and register "Cooper's 'discovery' of the discipline deployed against his white men." Romero, *Home Fronts: Domesticity and Its Critics in the Antebellum United States* (Durham, NC: Duke UP, 1997), 49. Likewise, Philip Gould argues that Cooper's *The Wept of Wish-ton-Wish; A Tale* (1829) traces the implications of a benevolent sentimental manhood that "simultaneously humanizes the Native American and erases his political efficacy"; thus, the novel "recasts an ideal of sentimental manhood as a political problem." Gould, "Remembering Metacom: Historical Writing and the Cultures of Masculinity in Early Republican America," in *Sentimental Men: Masculinity and the Politics of Affect in American Culture*, ed. Mary Chapman and Glenn Hendler (Berkeley: U of California P, 1999) 121. Diane Price Herndl agrees that Cooper attacks a sentimental ideology of domesticity and feminine moral authority in *The Last of the Mohicans* but argues that he also "employs a discourse and a set of tropes developed from sentimental theory to do so," "the sentimental gaze." Herndl, "Style and the Sentimental Gaze in *The Last of the Mohicans*," *Narrative* 9.3 (2001): 261. On men and antebellum sentimental culture, see Mary Chapman and Glenn Hendler, introduction to *Sentimental Men*, 1–16.

10. Henry Nash Smith, introduction to *The Prairie; A Tale. By James Fenimore Cooper* (New York: Holt, Rinehart and Winston, 1950), ix. Wayne Fields echoes Smith: "There is no defining frame"; the prairie "provides a neutral ground where Cooper's characters are tested less for their ability to survive physically than for their ability to order their worlds and themselves." Fields, "Beyond Definition: A Reading of *The Prairie*," in *James Fenimore Cooper: A Collection of Critical Essays*, ed. Wayne Fields (Englewood Cliffs, NJ: Prentice-Hall, 1979), 94.

11. On Cooper's use of journeys by Lewis and Clark and by Long, the inspiration he drew from meeting a Pawnee chief, Petalasharoo, and his completion of the novel in France, see E. Soteris Muszynska-Wallace, "The Sources of *The Prairie*," *American Literature* 21.2 (1949); Smith, introduction to *The Prairie*, v-viii; Robert Emmet Long, *James Fenimore Cooper* (New York: Continuum, 1990), 63–64; Anne Perrin, "Opened Frontiers, Closed Deserts: The Contradictions between Source and Text in James Fenimore Cooper's *The Prairie*," in *James Fenimore Cooper: His Country and His Art*, ed. Hugh C. MacDougall, Papers from the 2001 Cooper Seminar 13 (Oneonta, NY: State U of New York College at Oneonta, 2001), 72–76, http://external.oneonta.edu/cooper/articles/suny/2001suny-perrin.html (accessed Sept. 5, 2006).

12. The Louisiana Purchase "offered [Cooper] an example of incompatible cultures compressed into one space and time more dramatically than colonial or precolonial history had allowed." Kay S. House and Genevieve Belfiglio, "Fenimore Cooper's Heroines," in *American Novelists Revisited: Essays in Feminist Criticism*, ed. Fritz Fleischman (Boston: G. K. Hall, 1982), 44.

13. William P. Kelly, *Plotting America's Past: Fenimore Cooper and the Leatherstocking Tales* (Carbondale: Southern Illinois U P, 1983), 124–27.

14. David C. Lipscomb argues that Cooper "was a gifted mythographer of national history who knew not only the tools for reading time on geographic space but also the particular history written on the map of the American frontier." Lipscomb, "'Water Leaves No Trail': Mapping Away the Vanishing American in Cooper's Leatherstocking Tales," in *Nineteenth-Century Geographies: The Transformation of Space from the Victorian Age to the American Century*, ed. Helena Michie and Ronald R. Thomas (New Brunswick, NJ: Rutgers UP, 2003), 56.

15. "Cooper's sympathetically rendered Indians served as an important vehicle through which Cooper could comment upon the cyclical nature of history and could demonstrate that history was

not simply an easy story of progress." Steven Conn, *History's Shadow: Native Americans and Historical Consciousness in the Nineteenth Century* (Chicago: U of Chicago P, 2004), 161. See 156–66 for longer discussion of Cooper's response to Heckewelder and his composition of Indian history in opposition to the emergent ethnography. On the post-apocalyptic tenor of this passage and the portrayal of human and divine judgment, retribution, and apocalypse in the novel, see Hugh C. MacDougall, " 'Their Waste Has Done It All': *The Prairie* as a Post-Apocalyptic Novel," in *James Fenimore Cooper: His Country and His Art*, ed. MacDougall (papers from the 2001 Cooper Seminar, no. 13, State University of New York College at Oneonta), 66, http://external.oneonta.edu/cooper/articles/suny/2001suny-macdougall.html; Lakshmi Mani, *The Apocalyptic Vision in Nineteenth Century American Fiction: A Study of Cooper, Hawthorne, and Melville* (Washington: UP of America, 1981), 80–89.

16. R. W. B. Lewis, *The American Adam: Innocence, Tragedy, and Tradition in the Nineteenth Century* (Chicago: U of Chicago P, 1955), 5. Natty, that is, may be called Adamic only in a postlapsarian sense.

17. Abiram tells Ishmael he once heard a traveling preacher say "that the world was, in truth, no better than a desert, and that there was but one hand that could lead the most learned man through all its crooked windings" (*P* 87). Ishmael dismisses his slave-stealing brother-in-law's momentary religious inclinations.

18. *The Prairie* contains another connection to slavery and race relations in the early nineteenth century in its allusion to the Ben Ishmaelites, a tribe of allied poor Southern whites, African Americans (fugitive and free), and American Indians who, after departing Kentucky, followed a migratory life in Indiana and Illinois from approximately 1810 to 1905. On the Ben Ishmaelites and Cooper's apparent use of them as a model for the Bush family, see Hugo P. Leaming, "The Ben Ishmael Tribe: A Fugitive 'Nation' of the Old Northwest," in *The Ethnic Frontier: Essays in the History of Group Survival in Chicago and the Midwest*, ed. Melvin G. Holli and Peter d'Alroy Jones (Grand Rapids, MI: William B. Eerdmans, 1977), 97–141. Though Cooper insists the Bush family is solely of European stock, his multiracial source contributes, I believe, to the resonance of Inez's captivity with the threat the issue of slavery in the territories posed to national union.

19. "Throughout the Leatherstocking novels, Natty serves not as a mediator, but as a frontier border guard who restricts racial interaction." Janet Dean, "Stopping Traffic: Spectacles of Romance and Race in *The Last of the Mohicans*," in *Doubled Plots: Romance and History*, ed. Susan Strehle and Mary Paniccia Carden (Jackson: U of Mississippi P, 2003), 54. Natty's translation according to the cultures and proclivities of individuals, Gordon Brotherston argues, "dismantles finally the persona he had established as *the* mediator between red and white" ("Prairie and Cooper's Invention," 174). Dean's and Brotherston's essays echo Eric Cheyfitz's analysis of the figures of civilizing translation "underwriting U.S. foreign policy" in an age of imperialism. Cheyfitz, *The Poetics of Imperialism: Translation and Colonization from "The Tempest" to "Tarzan,"* expanded ed. (Philadelphia: U of Pennsylvania P, 1997), 21.

20. Ralph Waldo Emerson, "Experience" (1844), in *Essays: Second Series*, ed. Joseph Slater, Alfred R. Ferguson, and Jean Ferguson Carr, vol. 3 of *The Collected Works of Ralph Waldo Emerson* (Cambridge: Harvard UP, Belknap, 1983), 37.

21. Donald A. Ringe, *James Fenimore Cooper*, updated ed. (Boston: Twayne, 1988), 30. William P. Kelly goes so far to suggest that, in *The Prairie*, "[Natty] has become a detached commentator on human folly, a resigned spectator who sadly observes the constant repetition of weakness and error. In that capacity, Natty advances a perspective which acquires the power of incontrovertible truth" (Kelly, *Plotting America's Past*, 119).

22. Long suggests that in the closing scene, Natty is "truly patriarchal," positioned and mediating between "civil and natural law" as represented by Middleton and Hard-Heart; however, "it is not clear if America will live up to Natty's lofty vision" (Long, *James Fenimore Cooper*, 74). Indeed, Rans convincingly argues, Natty represents a rejected ideal rather than the American or America for he "does not—cannot—animate a civilization that disparages him" (*Cooper's Leather-Stocking Novels*, 165).

Chapter 3. "Be man!"

1. Reginald Horsman, *Race and Manifest Destiny: The Origins of American Racial Anglo-Saxonism* (Cambridge: Harvard UP, 1981), 200. Mick Gidley and Ben Gidley point out, "It could be claimed that the major thrust of *United States* Indian policy (removal, reservations, extinguishment of communal ownership of land and, later, the deliberate subordination of the tribal identity of Indian individuals through 'assimilation') was originally a *Southern* policy." Gidley and Gidley, "The Native-American South," *A Companion to the Literature and Culture of the American South*, eds. Richard Gray and Owen Robinson (Malden, MA: Blackwell, 2004), 169.

2. Drew Gilpin Faust, *A Sacred Circle: The Dilemma of the Intellectual in the Old South, 1840–1860* (Baltimore: Johns Hopkins UP, 1977), 131.

3. "By 1850 four out of nine South Carolinians alive were living outside their native state, mostly in other states of the lower South. The numbers, though not the percentages, of emigrant North Carolinians and Virginians were much higher. In becoming Tennesseans, Alabamians, and Texans, these Easterners were also becoming Southerners." David Moltke-Hansen, "Between Plantation and Frontier: The South of William Gilmore Simms," in *William Gilmore Simms and the American Frontier*, ed. John Caldwell Guilds and Caroline Collins (Athens: U of Georgia P, 1997), 8. On the emergence of racial science in this period, see Chapter 6.

4. Jill Lepore, *The Name of War: King Philip's War and the Origins of American Identity* (New York: Vintage, 1998), 204. On the Augusta performance, see also Sally L. Jones, "The First but Not the Last of the 'Vanishing Indians': Edwin Forrest and the Mythic Re-Creations of the Native Populations," in *Dressing in Feathers: The Constructions of the American Popular Culture*, ed. S. Elizabeth Bird (Boulder, CO: Westview, 1996), 17; Scott C. Martin, "Interpreting *Metamora*: Nationalism, Theater, and Jacksonian Policy," *Journal of the Early Republic* 19.1 (1999): 85; Gordon M. Sayre *The Indian Chief as Tragic Hero: Native Resistance and the Literatures of America, from Moctezuma to Tecumseh* (Chapel Hill: U of North Carolina P, 2005), 122.

Other scholars have elucidated the peculiarly Southern meaning of frontier or wilderness space in this period. Richard Slotkin traces regional variations of the Daniel Boone figure, pointing out that the Southern frontiersman was a natural aristocrat, a patriarch who derived authority from "a genuine gentility of spirit, of blood." Slotkin, *Regeneration Through Violence: The Mythology of the American Frontier, 1600–1860* (New York: Harper Perennial, 1973), 462. Annette Kolodny notes that the Southern wilderness was less the pristine site of communion with nature and more the potential location for pastoral plantations. Kolodny, *The Lay of the Land: Metaphor as Experience and History in American Life and Letters* (Chapel Hill: U of North Carolina P, 1975), 131–32. Richard Drinnon argues that "the idea of the West was as much the South's as the North's, and the physical reality no less so: After all, it was a Southerner who acquired much of it through the Louisiana Purchase." Drinnon, "An American Romance in Color: William Gilmore Simms," in *Facing West: The Metaphysics of Indian-Hating and Empire-Building* (Minneapolis: U of Minnesota P, 1980), 144.

5. Nancy Grantham, "Simms's Frontier: A Collision of Cultures," in Guilds and Collins, *Simms and the American Frontier*, 106.

6. On removal in the Southeast, see R. Douglas Hurt, *The Indian Frontier, 1763–1846* (Albuquerque: U of New Mexico P, 2002), 137–63.

7. William Gilmore Simms to Henry Rowe Schoolcraft, March 18, 1851, in *An Early and Strong Sympathy: The Indian Writings of William Gilmore Simms*, ed. John Caldwell Guilds and Charles Hudson (Columbia: U of South Carolina P, 2003), 114. Schoolcraft's work eventually ran to six volumes, published between 1851 and 1857.

8. Hudson, "An Ethnohistorical View," in ibid., xxxvi, xxxviii, xxxix.

9. Guilds has done more than any other scholar to promote the study of Simms by editing numerous collections and scholarly editions and by authoring *Simms: A Literary Life* (Fayetteville: U of Arkansas P, 1992). Of particular interest in this criticism of recovery is Jay B. Hubbell, "William Gilmore Simms," in *The South in American Literature, 1607–1900* (Durham, NC: Duke UP, 1954), 572–602. Elmo Howell, "William Gilmore Simms and the American Indian," *South Carolina Review* 5.2 (1973): 57–64, provides the foundational piece for considering Simms's representation of American Indians. Three works outlining Simms's political commitments and their impact on his

authorship are Jon L. Wakelyn, *The Politics of a Literary Man: William Gilmore Simms* (Westport, CT: Greenwood, 1973); Faust, *Sacred Circle*; and Charles S. Watson, *From Nationalism to Secessionism: The Changing Fiction of William Gilmore Simms* (Westport, CT: Greenwood, 1993).

10. Thomas M. Allen, "South of the American Renaissance," review of *The Simms Reader*, edited by John Caldwell Guilds, Simms, *The Wigwam and the Cabin*, edited by Guilds, and *Early and Strong Sympathy*, edited by Guilds and Hudson, *American Literary History* 16.3 (2004): 507, 504. See also Eileen Ka-May Cheng, "American Historical Writers and the Loyalists, 1788–1856: Dissent, Consensus, and American Nationality," *Journal of the Early Republic* 23.4 (2003): 491–519. She argues, "These two imperatives—[Simms's] desire to validate political opposition and his concern with unity—were integrally related to one another" (511). Through his emphasis on regional diversity, Allen finds a justification, if you will, for the recovery of Simms's work: "The memory of heterogeneous experience synthesized into a national fantasy of homogenous union invests all of our institutions. Can Simms, unreconstructed as he is, offer any insight into these issues that would be useful to us now?" (Allen, "South of the American Renaissance," 507). Allen's answer is yes, as is mine.

11. Mary Ann Wimsatt, "The Professional Author in the South: William Gilmore Simms and Antebellum Literary Publishing," in *The Professions of Authorship: Essays in Honor of Matthew J. Bruccoli*, ed. Richard Layman and Joel Myerson (Columbia: U of South Carolina P, 1996), 126. On the popularity of *The Yemassee*, see John Caldwell Guilds, introduction to *The Yemassee: A Romance of Carolina*, by William Gilmore Simms (1835; repr., Fayetteville: U of Arkansas P, 1994), xvi.

12. Guilds, *Simms*, 36; Louis D. Rubin, *The Edge of the Swamp: A Study in the Literature and Society of the Old South* (Baton Rouge: Louisiana State UP, 1989), 61.

13. Rubin, *Edge of the Swamp*, 67. Simms also sought a role in South Carolina political life, serving in the state legislature from 1844 to 1846 and enjoying relationships with such prominent slavery defenders as James Henry Hammond, Louisa McCord, and Josiah Nott. Yet Simms resisted Southern secession until, Charles S. Watson argues, the turmoil surrounding the Compromise of 1850 "turned Simms from uneasy nationalism to militant sectionalism, a change that inevitably transformed the spirit and ideology of his literary works." Watson, *From Nationalism to Secessionism: The Changing Fiction of William Gilmore Simms* (Westport, CT: Greenwood, 1993), 72. On Simms's political involvement and relationships, see Wakelyn, *Politics of a Literary Man*, 82–84; James E. Kibler, "Simms and Louisa McCord," *Simms Review* 4.1 (1996): 46–48; William Stanton, *The Leopard's Spots: Scientific Attitudes toward Race in America, 1815–59* (Chicago: U of Chicago P, 1960), 155–56. For an overview of historians' emphasis on Simms's political life rather than his literary production, see Charles S. Watson, "The Ongoing Study of William Gilmore Simms: Literary Critics vs. Historians," *South Carolina Review* 22.2 (1990): 7–15.

14. Simms was associated with the Knickerbocker circle in the 1830s, in part because of his friendship with William Cullen Bryant, but by the 1840s he became associated with Young America. Mary Ann Wimsatt, *The Major Fiction of William Gilmore Simms* (Baton Rouge: Louisiana State UP, 1989), 34, 141; C. Hugh Holman, introduction to *Views and Reviews in American Literature, History and Fiction* by William Gilmore Simms (1845), ed. Holman (Cambridge: Harvard UP, Belknap, 1962), xxii.

15. On Simms's publication of short stories and his struggle to publish *The Wigwam and the Cabin*, see John Caldwell Guilds, "The Achievement of William Gilmore Simms: His Short Fiction," in *The Poetry of Community: Essays on the Southern Sensibility of History and Literature*, ed. Lewis P. Simpson (Atlanta: School of Arts & Sciences, Georgia State, 1972), 25–35; Guilds, *Simms*, 171–72; John Caldwell Guilds, introduction to *The Wigwam and the Cabin: Selected Fiction of William Gilmore Simms* (1845; repr., Fayetteville: U of Arkansas P, 2000), 55–56; Wimsatt, "Professional Author in the South," 128.

16. The *Knickerbocker* review was written by Lewis Gaylord Clark, with whom Simms had exchanged heated editorials from 1840 to 1841 regarding sectional literature (Watson, *From Nationalism to Secessionism*, 57).

17. Guilds, afterword to *The Wigwam and the Cabin*, 383. On the publication history of "The Two Camps," see Guilds and Hudson, "Bibliography of the Indian Writings of William Gilmore Simms," in *Early and Strong Sympathy*, 596.

18. On the assassinations, see William G. McLoughlin, *After the Trail of Tears: The Cherokees'*

Struggle for Sovereignty, 1839–1880 (Chapel Hill: U of North Carolina P, 1993), 15–17. On the Chero-kee War (1759–61), see John Oliphant, *Peace and War on the Anglo-Cherokee Frontier, 1756–63* (Baton Rouge: Louisiana State U P, 2001), 69–190; Daniel K. Richter, *Facing East from Indian Country: A Native History of Early America* (Cambridge: Harvard UP, 2001), 186–87.

19. Simms, *Wigwam and the Cabin,* 35, 32, 33. Hereafter cited as *WC.* "The Two Camps" also appears in Guilds and Hudson, *Early and Strong Sympathy,* 367–92.

20. On the narrative practice of "sentimental gaze" "that is compassionate, sympathetic, and pitying rather than controlling or desirous," see Diane Price Herndl, "Style and the Sentimental Gaze in *The Last of the Mohicans,*" *Narrative* 9.3 (2001): 273.

21. Molly Boyd points out that the stories in *WC* appeared during the heyday of southwestern humor and share some characteristics of the genre but that finally "his choice of setting, his mode of publication, his audience, his tone and material, and his purpose" distinguish Simms from prominent authors of southwestern humor. Boyd, "Southwestern Humor in *The Wigwam and the Cabin,*" in Guilds and Collins, *William Gilmore Simms and the American Frontier,* 168.

22. James Fenimore Cooper, *The Prairie; A Tale,* ed. James P. Elliott (1827; repr., Albany: State U of New York P, 1985), 82.

23. The *OED* defines *loop-hole* as "a narrow vertical opening, usually widening inwards, cut in a wall or other defence, to allow of the passage of missiles," but also notes that "[William] Cowper's phrase 'loopholes of retreat' has been used by many later writers." *OED Online,* s.v. "loop-hole, http://dictionary.oed.com/cgi/entry/50135503 (accessed May 16, 2006).

24. Sean R. Busick, *A Sober Desire for History: William Gilmore Simms as Historian* (Columbia: U of South Carolina P, 2005), xii; David Moltke-Hansen, "Ordered Progress: The Historical Philosophy of William Gilmore Simms," in *"Long Years of Neglect": The Work and Reputation of William Gilmore Simms,* ed. John Caldwell Guilds (Fayetteville: U of Arkansas P, 1988), 128.

25. Steven Frye, "Simms's *The Yemassee,* American Progressivism, and the Dialogue of History," *Southern Quarterly* 35.3 (1997): 83; Busick, *Sober Desire for History,* 4. Other treatments of Simms's philosophy of history include John Caldwell Guilds, "Simms's Use of History: Theory and Practice," *Mississippi Quarterly* 30.4 (1977): 505–11; Miriam J. Shillingsburg, "The Maturing of Simms's Short Fiction: The Example of 'Oakatibbe,'" *Mississippi Quarterly* 38.2 (1985): 99–117; Carey M. Roberts, "The Mighty River of Providence or the Secrets of Home: The Historical Theories of Simms and Bancroft," *Simms Review* 6.1 (1998): 35–43; Charles S. Watson, "Portrayals of the Black and the Idea of Progress: Simms and Douglass," *Southern Studies* 20.4 (1981): 339–50.

26. John Mayfield writes that Simms believed that in this land of violence, "a new ideal was being born, one that would favor the competitor over the patrician and mobility over place," and Busick adds that, subsequently, Simms was "as interested in the common man and woman as he was in the great men of history." John Mayfield, "'The Soul of a Man!' William Gilmore Simms and the Myths of Southern Manhood," *Journal of the Early Republic* 15.3 (1995): 487; Busick, *Sober Desire for History,* 92. On the creation of a synthesis between the patrician and the frontier hero, Moltke-Hansen writes, "Throughout this history [of the southwestern frontier] liberty contested with both tyranny and license to define the social relations of free men; the urge for new land competed with the urge to build on and cultivate one's home ground; and the traditions of the Cavalier, modified by the conditions of the frontier, shaped a distinct culture with the aid of the labor of African slaves and the infusions of various European-descended peoples—Germans, Scots, and Irish among them" ("Between Plantation and Frontier," 13).

27. Holman, introduction to *Views and Reviews,* ix. Although the first volume of the book is dated 1845, it actually appeared in 1846, and the second volume and the clothbound set appeared in 1847 (vii n. 5.).

28. Simms, *Views and Reviews,* 36. "For Simms," writes Frye, "the historical romancer is 'the true historian,' because the romancer invests a metaphysical, moral, political and perhaps a quasi-religious meaning to the events of history" ("Simms's *The Yemassee,*" 84). Shillingsburg clarifies Simms's use of "moral," which "encompasses the religious, artistic, social, and even political characteristics of a people" ("The Maturing of Simms's Short Fiction," 101 n. 9).

29. Charles S. Watson, "Simms and the Civil War: The Revolutionary Analogy," *Southern Literary Journal* 24.2 (1992): 76.

30. On Simms's novels of the Revolution, his *History of South Carolina in the Revolutionary War*, and his failed Northern tour with a lecture on South Carolina during the Revolution, see also Busick, *Sober Desire for History*, 68–87; Cheng, "American Historical Writers and the Loyalists," 510–19; James Perrin Warren, "William Gilmore Simms and the Necessity of Speech," in *Culture of Eloquence: Oratory and Reform in Antebellum America* (University Park: Pennsylvania State UP, 1999), 141–67. Cheng observes, "Seeing 'sympathy and union' emerge from bloodshed, [Simms] implied that national unity had come about not just despite such divisions but because of them" ("American Historical Writers and the Loyalists," 518).

31. Molly Boyd offers one comparison of Simms's heroes in *The Yemassee* and Cooper's Natty Bumppo that also summarizes previous comparisons in "The Southern American Adam: Simms's Alternative Myth," *Southern Quarterly* 41.2 (2003): 73–83. On the Yamassee War, see Guilds, "Historical Background," in Simms, *Yemassee*, 439–41.

32. Simms, *Yemassee*, 41. Hereafter cited as *Y*. Guilds's scholarly edition is based on the one-volume, 1853 Redfield new and revised edition, but in his textual notes Guilds comments that Simms actually "made relatively few substantive changes" (448). I use Simms's spelling for the tribe (Yemassee) rather than the now-accepted Yamassee.

33. On Craven as a Jacksonian figure, see Louis D. Rubin, "The Romance of the Colonial Frontier: Simms, Cooper, and Indians, and the Wilderness," in *American Letters and the Historical Consciousness: Essays in Honor of Lewis P. Simpson*, ed. J. Gerald Kennedy and Daniel Mark Fogel (Baton Rouge: Louisiana State UP, 1987), 119.

34. Simms, *Views and Reviews*, 32.

35. Quoted in Guilds, introduction to *The Wigwam and the Cabin*, xix.

36. In an 1845 letter to Schoolcraft, Simms writes that he has "read with exceeding interest your *Algic Researches*." William Gilmore Simms to Henry Rowe Schoolcraft, September 26, 1845, in *Guilds and Hudson, Early and Strong Sympathy*, 113. Maureen Konkle describes Schoolcraft's *Algic Researches* as "a collection of literary fairy tales with heavy-handed ethnological intrusions." Konkle, *Writing Indian Nations: Native Intellectuals and the Politics of Historiography, 1827–1863* (Chapel Hill: U of North Carolina P, 2004), 180.

37. Guilds and Hudson, "Bibliography of the Indian Writings of William Gilmore Simms," 596. "Jocassée" also appears in Guilds and Hudson, *Early and Strong Sympathy*, 178–96.

38. Hudson, "Ethnohistorical View," xlii; John D. Kerkering, *The Poetics of National and Racial Identity in Nineteenth-Century American Literature* (Cambridge: Cambridge UP, 2003), 75.

39. Peter G. Murphy, "Virtues of Romanticism in Simms's 'Jocassée: A Cherokee Legend,'" *South Carolina Review* 35.1 (2002): 43. See Chapter 6 on the Schoolcrafts' "Leelinau" and Jane Johnston Schoolcraft's use of Leelinau as a pseudonym. In one tale of star-crossed lovers similar to "Jocassée," "Legend of Missouri: or, the Captive of the Pawnee," a rash Omaha warrior fails in his attempt to rescue his lover, Missouri, from the murderous Pawnee. He departs in mourning, asking only that the Kentucky settlers who have befriended him call their new "nation" after the beautiful young woman. As in "Jocassée," the lovers' tragedy marks the land and its people indelibly, creating a presiding spirit of the place. See "Legend of Missouri: or, the Captive of the Pawnee," in Guilds and Hudson, *Early and Strong Sympathy*, 134–42. Simms published the tale four times, first in the *New York Mirror* (1832) and last in his 1854 collection *Southward Ho!* (Guilds and Hudson, "Bibliography of the Indian Writings of William Gilmore Simms," 595).

40. Guilds, afterword to *The Wigwam and the Cabin*, 385. Jürgen Hübner points out that Simms published a whopping thirty-three stories in *Godey's* and that the magazine was very popular in the South. Hübner, "William Gilmore Simms: Sectionalism and Popularity," *Southern Studies* 18.1 (1979): 43, 41. See Guilds and Hudson, "Bibliography of the Indian Writings of William Gilmore Simms," 596. "The Arm-Chair of Tustenuggee" also appears in Guilds and Hudson, *Early and Strong Sympathy*, 197–217.

41. Miriam Jones Shillingsburg, "Literary Grist: Simms's Trips to Mississippi," *Southern Quarterly* 41.2 (2003): 119. In "A New Simms Essay of 1835 and Evidence of His Earliest Trip to the Southwest," *Simms Review* 8.2 (2000): 32–42, Guilds offers evidence that Simms traveled to the region in 1819 as well.

42. William Gilmore Simms, "Miss Martineau on Slavery," *Southern Literary Messenger* 3.11 (1837):

657. The essay was reprinted widely, including as a Richmond pamphlet titled *Slavery in America, being a Brief Review of Miss Martineau on that subject*, "By a South Carolinian" (Guilds, *Simms*, 92). For a closer examination of Martineau's text and Simms's response, see Wakelyn, *Politics of a Literary Man*, 62–65. For more on the Southern defense of slavery in this period and Simms's particular contributions, see Faust, *Sacred Circle*, 112–31.

43. Simms, "Miss Martineau on Slavery," 651, 654, 650.

44. Simms, *Views and Reviews*, 138; Simms, "Miss Martineau on Slavery," 656.

45. Pauline Turner Strong, "Transforming Outsiders: Captivity, Adoption, and Slavery Reconsidered," in *A Companion to American Indian History*, ed. Philip J. Deloria and Neal Salisbury (Malden, MA: Blackwell, 2002), 339. On slavery, racial hierarchy, and the Cherokee and Creek in this period, see Theda Perdue, *Slavery and the Evolution of Cherokee Society, 1540–1866* (Knoxville: U of Tennessee P, 1979), 36–72; Katja May, *African Americans and Native Americans in the Creek and Cherokee Nations, 1830s to 1920s: Collision and Collusion* (New York: Garland, 1996), 45–51.

46. I should note that one story in *The Wigwam and the Cabin*, "Lucas de Ayllon. A Historical Nouvellette," has been read as a defense of the American Indian civilization and a condemnation of their exploitation by colonizers. This story supposedly recounts the exploits of "Velasquez de Ayllon" (actually, Vásquez de Ayllón), a sixteenth-century Spanish explorer-conquistador who made an unsuccessful attempt to establish a colony in South Carolina. In Simms's account, which is fictitious, Ayllon abducts Indians from the shores of Carolina to sell into slavery in the Caribbean by tricking the queen and her husband, Combahee and Chiquola, and many of their people, to come on board his ship, after which he sets sail. Combahee escapes but Chiquola drowns in trying. Years later Ayllon returns to capture more slaves, but Combahee, with the help of a providential storm, leads her people in a attack on the ship. Subsequently, Combahee orders Ayllon to be burned alive on a pyre of his crew's bodies. For the anticolonial reading of this bloody tale of piracy, see Peter G. Murphy, "Colonization and the American Indian in Simms's 'Lucas de Ayllon,'" *Southern Quarterly* 37.3–4 (1999): 277–82. For a discussion of Simms's inaccuracies and his dependence on "the Black Legend" of Spanish colonial atrocities, see Hudson, "Ethnohistorical View," xliv. Simms's use of a Spanish colonizer of the sixteenth century and supernatural occurrences such as the storm convert the natives into moral abstractions and the tale into a fable about greed.

47. Shillingsburg, "Literary Grist," 120–21; Guilds and Hudson, "Bibliography of the Indian Writings of William Gilmore Simms," 596. "Oakatibbé" also appears in Guilds and Hudson, *Early and Strong Sympathy*, 274–300.

48. "The Indian Student: or, Force of Nature" is found in Philip Freneau, *Poems of Freneau*, ed. Harry Hayden Clark (1929; repr., New York: Hafner, 1968), 357–59.

49. Hudson, "Ethnohistorical View," xlv.

50. Shillingsburg, "Maturing of Simms's Short Fiction." Sampson's downfall is recounted in Judges 16. I cite the authorized King James version, ed. Robert Carroll and Stephen Prickett (Oxford: Oxford UP, 1997).

51. "Caloya" first appeared in 1841, published in the Southern periodical *Magnolia*. It also appears in Guilds and Hudson, *Early and Strong Sympathy*, 218–73. Pointing to its comparison of slaves and Catawba Indians, as well as its observation of Catawba itinerancy in the 1820s, Hudson concludes, "From the point of view of an anthropologist and ethnohistorian, 'Caloya; or, the Loves of the Driver' is one of the Simms's best Indian stories" (Hudson, "Ethnohistorical View," xlvii).

52. On the Choctaw and Euro-American uses of *Mingo*, see Shillingsburg, "Literary Grist," 123; Allen, "South of the American Renaissance," 502. In a personal conversation on April 27, 2006, Moltke-Hansen mentioned the possibility that Mingo is also short for Mandingo.

53. As Allen points out, Simms excels in portraying "[failed] authority figures" ("South of the American Renaissance," 502).

54. Quoted in Hubbell, "William Gilmore Simms," 589.

55. Though Simms stresses that the loyal slaves can be trusted with arms, the Yamassee War was the last in which South Carolina colonists allowed the formation of a black militia (Perdue, *Slavery and the Evolution of Cherokee Society*, 41).

Chapter 4. Containing Native Feeling

1. For a fuller treatment of the second edition of *A Son of the Forest*, Apess's claim of being descended from Philip, and his confusion about Philip's tribal affiliation, see Roumiana Velikova, "'Philip, King of the Pequots': The History of an Error," *Early American Literature* 37.2 (2002): 311–35.

2. Review of *A Son of the Forest. The Experiences of William Apes, a Native of the Forest*, by William Apess, *American Monthly Review* (August 1832): 150. I am indebted to Maureen Konkle's reference to this review in "Indian Literacy, U.S. Colonialism, and Literary Criticism," *American Literature* 69 (1997): 483–84, n. 34, and *Writing Indian Nations: Native Intellectuals and the Politics of Historiography, 1827–1863* (Chapel Hill: U of North Carolina P, 2004), 102.

3. The reviewer makes this charge about Apess's Indian sources despite the fact that, as Velikova points out, Apess removed from the second edition a reference to the oral transmission of his family information by his grandmother. Relevant definitions of the noun *tradition* in the *OED* are 4a and 5a, with examples in 1818 and 1854 and 1851, 1872, and 1878, respectively. Both emphasize the oral aspect of tradition: "esp. by word of mouth or by practice without writing"; "(esp. orally)." Definitions 3 and 6, with examples largely from the fourteenth through the seventeenth centuries, also emphasize the oral aspect of transmission referred to as tradition. *OED Online*, s.v. "tradition," http://dictionary.oed.com/cgi/entry/50255726 (accessed June 24, 2002).

4. Review of *Son*, 149. On the extraction of Indian traditions from time to create an American myth, Joshua David Bellin writes, "The campaign for literary nationalism, in sum, was fought not only against Europe's courtly muses but against America's native mythos." Bellin, *The Demon of the Continent: Indians and the Shaping of American Literature* (Philadelphia: U of Pennsylvania P, 2001), 158. For more on the dehistoricization of American Indians in this period, see Steven Conn, *History's Shadow: Native Americans and Historical Consciousness in the Nineteenth Century* (Chicago: U of Chicago P, 2004).

5. Review of *Son*, 150; emphasis in original.

6. Nina Baym emphasizes that, while subject to the personal tastes of the individual reviewer, the review nonetheless "was directed toward readers, was conducted in constant awareness of what people were reading, and was always trying to understand the reasons for public preferences." She adds, "The reviews offer guidance and correction in a way that enables us to see what they [reviewers] thought they were guiding and correcting." Baym, *Novels, Readers, and Reviewers: Response to Fiction in Antebellum America* (Ithaca: Cornell UP, 1984) 19.

7. Michelle Burnham, "The Periphery Within: Internal Colonialism and the Rhetoric of U.S. Nation Building," in *Messy Beginnings: Postcoloniality and Early American Studies*, ed. Malini Johar Schueller and Edward Watts (New Brunswick, NJ: Rutgers UP, 2003), 140. More specifically, Burnham argues that the hybridity of such works as *A Narrative of the Life of Mary Jemison* is not necessarily subversive but arises from the antebellum act of "internally colonizing the voice and authority of a transcultural subject" in pursuit of political and cultural autonomy. Likewise, Konkle writes, "The 'inner' lives of Indians are thus always available to be judged in relation to the critics' imagined better Indian, a more complete Indian than the particular Indian at hand" ("Indian Literacy, U.S. Colonialism, and Literary Criticism," 475).

8. In this chapter I avoid describing a binary tension between a controlling Euro-American discourse and an authentic, embattled American Indian discourse, instead joining a line of criticism that describes the American Indian writings of the colonial period and nineteenth century as embodying an encounter and intermixture of two cultures. Hilary Wyss, Bellin, Gordon Sayre, and Laura Donaldson all demonstrate that we best approach early American Indian writings with the assumption that the text and its subject represent a negotiation between and even blending of cultures (in Donaldson's terms, they are "entangled") and, in as-told-to autobiography, of narrative perspectives. To abandon antebellum American Indian autobiographies as inauthentic or even compromised is to miss their encapsulation of explicit and implicit, intentional and unintentional cultural negotiations. See Hilary E. Wyss, *Writing Indians: Literacy, Christianity, and Native Community in Early America* (Amherst: U of Massachusetts P, 2000); Bellin, *Demon of the Continent*; Gordon Sayre, "Defying Assimilation, Confounding Authenticity: The Case of William Apess," *Auto/Biogra-*

phy Studies 11 (1996): 1–18; Laura Donaldson, "Making a Joyful Noise: William Apess and the Search for Postcolonial Method(ism)," in Schueller and Watts, *Messy Beginnings*, 29–44.

9. Examples of this use of *authentic* are dated 1790, 1824, and 1880. See *OED Online*, s.v. "authentic," a. 6, http://dictionary.oed.com/cgi/entry/50015034 (accessed June 26, 2002).

10. Lydia Maria Child, *Letters from New-York*, ed. Bruce Mills (1843; repr., Athens: U Georgia P, 1998), 161, 165.

11. Stephen Carl Arch, *After Franklin: The Emergence of Autobiography in Post-Revolutionary America, 1780–1830* (Hanover: UP of New England for U of New Hampshire, 2001), xi, 183. See also Ann Fabian, *The Unvarnished Truth: Personal Narratives in Nineteenth-Century America* (Berkeley: U of California P, 2000). Surprisingly, neither Fabian nor Arch includes American Indians among the oppressed whose works gave rise to the modern autobiography in America.

12. Arnold Krupat, *For Those Who Came After: A Study of Native American Autobiography* (Berkeley: U California P, 1985), 6.

13. H. David Brumble, *An Annotated Bibliography of American Indian and Eskimo Autobiographies* (Lincoln: U of Nebraska P, 1981); Brumble, *American Indian Autobiography* (Berkeley: U California P, 1988). I have not included in this list *Memoir of Catharine Brown, a Christian Indian of the Cherokee Nation*, ed. Rufus Anderson, which first appeared in 1825, because of its unusual format: the volume includes letters, diary entries, and testimonial letters. Autobiographies of acculturated American Indians include that of Okah Tubbee (1848, Choctaw), suspected of using his American Indian identity to cover his status as a fugitive slave, and those of John Tanner (1830, held by Shawnee, Ojibwe, Ottawa) and John Dunn Hunter (1824, held by Kickapoo, Osage, Kansas), famous "white Indians." On the last two, see June Namias, *White Captives: Gender and Ethnicity on the American Frontier* (Chapel Hill: U of North Carolina P, 1993), 72–78.

14. According to Gordon Sayre, "Thatcher's work saw thirteen editions by 1870, and Drake's reached its fifteenth . . . in 1880, five years after Drake's death." Sayre, *The Indian Chief as Tragic Hero: Native Resistance and the Literatures of America, from Moctezuma to Tecumseh* (Chapel Hill: U of North Carolina P, 2005), 10. For an illuminating account of white editors' autobiographical and biographical modes, using the examples of Thatcher, Samuel G. Drake, Benjamin Drake, and Patterson, see Krupat, *For Those Who Come After*, 50–52.

15. W. J. Snelling, "Life of Black Hawk," review of *Life of Mal-ka-tai-me-she-kia-kiak* [sic] *or Black Hawk, dictated by Himself*, by Black Hawk, *North American Review* 40 (1835): 68, 69. Konkle also discusses this review in "Indian Literacy, U.S. Colonialism, and Literary Criticism," 475–77. Snelling's argument that Apess's writing is not truly Indian is particularly interesting considering the assertion by Samuel Gardner Drake and the conjecture of subsequent bibliographers that Snelling and not Apess actually wrote *Indian Nullification of the Unconstitutional Laws of Massachusetts Relative to the Marshpee Tribe* (1835). O'Connell does not believe Snelling wrote *Indian Nullification*, though he concedes he may have contributed to it. Barry O'Connell, introduction to *On Our Own Ground: The Complete Writings of William Apess, a Pequot*, ed. O'Connell (Amherst: U of Massachusetts P, 1992), xliii.

16. Krupat notes these differences, however, in making an argument regarding the dialogism these autobiographies have in common. See Arnold Krupat, *The Voice in the Margin: Native American Literature and the Canon* (Berkeley: U California P, 1989), 132–201.

17. Krupat, *For Those*, 31. Joshua David Bellin argues that the discourse of *Life* "echoes the conditions of Indian-white encounter." Bellin, "How Smooth Their Language: Authenticity and Interculturalism in the *Life of Black Hawk*," *Prospects* 25 (2000): 488.

18. William Apess, *A Son of the Forest* in O'Connell, *On Our Own Ground*, 52. Hereafter cited as *S*. Regarding the appendix to *Son*: It takes up over forty pages in the O'Connell edition with, among other things, a history of Euro-American and American Indian contact and descriptions of tribal cultures. Apess also states in the headnote that for the historical information, "he is indebted in a great measure to the works of the venerated Boudinot . . . , Brainerd, Colden, and several other gentlemen," and O'Connell points out in a note, "Apess's indebtedness to Elias Boudinot's *Star in the West* (1816) is almost entire" (*S* 52).

19. Velikova, "Philip, King of the Pequots," 311–12. Konkle reveals that Samuel Gardner Drake

in the first edition of *Indian Biography* (1832), like Apess in *Son*, misidentifies King Philip's tribe as Pequot, evidence, she suggests, that "points to Drake" as the author of the 1832 review with which this chapter began (Konkle, "Indian Literacy, U.S. Colonialism, and Literary Criticism," 483–84 n. 34). If Drake is indeed the reviewer, the comparison of complaints about Apess in the review and those about Euro-American historians in *Indian Biography* is instructive. In a later work, *Biography and History of the Indians of North America*, Drake ascribes mistakes by Euro-American historians not to generally deficient cultural practice but to specific anger and prejudice. For example, Drake remarks, "It is too obvious that the early historians viewed the Indians as inferior beings, and some went so far as to hardly allow them *to be* humans." Drake, *Biography and History of the Indians of North America*, 7th ed. (Boston: Antiquarian Institute, 1837), 3:44. Apess, then, draws on a Euro-American historiography that Drake calls emotional, inaccurate, imaginative, and even prone to stereotyping; however, the reviewer in *American Monthly Review* does not assign Apess's errors to such causes.

20. Sayre, "Defying Assimilation." On Apess's response to and even revision of national historical narratives, see Anne Marie Dannenberg, "'Where, Then, Shall We Place the Hero of the Wilderness?': William Apess's *Eulogy of King Philip* and Doctrines of Racial Destiny," in *Early Native American Writing: New Critical Essays*, ed. Helen Jaskoski (Cambridge: Cambridge UP, 1996), 66–82; O'Connell, introduction to *On Our Own Ground*, xiii–xxiv; Scott Manning Stevens, "William Apess's Historical Self," *Northwest Review* 35.3 (1997): 67–84. For arguments about how Apess's narrative of religious conversion entails a critique of racism in the church and greater society, see Karim M. Tiro, "Denominated 'SAVAGE': Methodism, Writing, and Identity in the Works of William Apess, a Pequot," *American Quarterly* 48 (1996): 653–79; Arnold Krupat, *Ethnocriticism: Ethnography, History, Literature* (Berkeley: U California P, 1991), 221–29; Sandra Gustafson, "Nations of Israelites: Prophecy and Cultural Autonomy in the Writings of William Apess," *Religion and Literature* 26 (1994): 31–53; Bellin, *Demon of the Continent*, 71–97. On Apess's use of tropes and rhetoric associated with the personal narrative, including conversion, slave, and captivity narratives, see Hilary E. Wyss, "Captivity and Conversion: William Apess, Mary Jemison, and Narratives of Racial Identity," *American Indian Quarterly* 23.3 and 4 (1999): 63–82; David Murray, *Forked Tongues: Speech, Writing and Representation in North American Indian Texts* (Bloomington: Indiana UP, 1991), 49–64; Donaldson, "Making a Joyful Noise"; Bernd C. Peyer, *The Tutor'd Mind: Indian Missionary-Writers in Antebellum America* (Amherst: U of Massachusetts P, 1997), 149–52; Carolyn Haynes, "'A Mark for Them All to Hiss At': The Formation of Methodist and Pequot Identity in the Conversion Narrative of William Apess," *Early American Literature* 31 (1996): 25–44; Deborah Gussman, "'O Savage, Where Art Thou?': Rhetorics of Reform in William Apess's *Eulogy on King Philip*," *New England Quarterly* 77 (2004): 451–77.

21. See *S* 6, 12, 13, 16, 17.

22. See ibid., 12–13, 19–21, 39, 41–43.

23. O'Connell, introduction to *On Our Own Ground*, li; *S* 60–69. On Apess's use of Boudinot as a source for Irving's essay, see Sayre, "Defying Assimilation," 13; Velikova, "Philip, King of the Pequots," 319–21; Konkle *Writing Indian Nations*, 113–14. Velikova points out that Apess's use of sentimental language and tropes has a very different purpose from Irving's use of the same—Apess intends to challenge the sentimental acquiescence to removal.

24. Cheryl Walker, *Indian Nation: Native American Literature and Nineteenth-Century Nationalisms* (Durham: Duke UP, 1997), 41–59.

25. O'Connell, introduction to *On Our Own Ground*, xxxiv; O'Connell, "Textual Afterword," in *On Our Own Ground*, 312, 19–24.

26. Of the many critics who have considered Apess's strategic use of Christianity in his dismantling of racist ideology, see in particular Krupat, *Ethnocriticism*, 221–29; Gustafson, "Nations of Israelites"; Haynes "A Mark for Them All to Hiss At"; Tiro "Denominated 'SAVAGE'"; Wyss, "Captivity and Conversion"; Bellin, *Demon of the Continent*, 71–97.

27. James Everett Seaver, *A Narrative of the Life of Mary Jemison, The White Woman of the Genesee*, edited and revised by Charles Delamater Vail (1824; repr., New York: American Scenic & Historic Preservation Society, 1932), x. Hereafter cited as *N* (including additional materials in the 1932

edition). This edition by Charles Vail, like the American Scenic & Historic Preservation Society's 1918, 1925, and 1942 editions, contains a reprint of the first edition with subsequent nineteenth- and early twentieth-century appendixes and notes.

28. Accounts of Jemison's sons' deaths are found in chaps. 10, 12, and 14 of *Narrative*. Her real estate woes are reported in appendixes. Ebenezer Mix, in a chapter appended to the 1842 and subsequent editions, reports that the Seneca sold all their land on the Genesee River in 1825 and that, because of her isolation, Jemison sold her annuity and remaining land and, in the summer of 1831, "removed to Buffalo Creek reservation" (*N* 194). Further, in a chapter appended in 1877, William Clement Bryant reports, "It must be added with regret—although the circumstance harmonizes with the mournful tenor of her whole life—that this little fortune was soon after her removal to Buffalo lost through an unfortunate speculation on the part of a white man to whose custody she had confided it" (*N* 199). This "white man" was George Jemison, mentioned later in this chapter.

29. On the work's initial success, see Namias, *White Captives*, 152; Richard Slotkin, *Regeneration through Violence: The Mythology of the American Frontier, 1600–1860* (New York: Harper Perennial, 1973), 446. Namias writes, "Within the next 105 years it went through twenty-seven printings and twenty-three editions ranging from 32 to 483 pages" (*White Captives*, 152). The "Tabulation of Editions" compiled by Vail in the 1932 edition provides an overview of the many editions up through 1932 and their various contents. Namias points out that Seaver's brother, William, was "the first of many publishers to enlist 'experts' on the Jemison case and to add Indian material" (*White Captives*, 156). He produced four editions between 1842 and 1847.

30. Deborah Larsen's *The White* (New York: Knopf, 2002) is a beautiful, fictionalized account of Jemison's life that takes selected moments from Seaver's work and fills in those elements perhaps most interesting to a modern reader: the psychological trauma of captivity and an emotional, spiritual submission to (at once) Fate and Nature. Larsen claims in her acknowledgments, "Portraits of Mary, the Seneca, the blacks, the Shawnee, the whites, the French, and others in this book are not intended to re-create actual characters, races, or nations as they at one time existed" (*White*, 217); nonetheless this fictional work appears to begin with the notion that Seaver's *Narrative* contains gaps best filled by lyrical treatments of Jemison's trauma, acculturation, desire, and spousal and maternal love. PBS first aired the documentary *The War That Made America*, dir. Ben Loeterman and Eric Stange, in 2006.

31. See especially Evelyne Keitel, "Captivity Narratives and the Powers of Horror: Eunice Williams and Mary Jemison, Captives Unredeemed," *1650–1850: Ideas, Aesthetics, and Inquiries in the Early Modern Era* 5 (2000): 277. Wyss's argument that *Narrative*, like Apess's *Son*, unites the captivity and the conversion narrative to "subvert both Native and Anglo-American categories of racial identity" further complicates its generic definition ("Captivity and Conversion," 66). For treatments of the captivity narrative as a genre, see Richard VanDerBeets, *The Indian Captivity Narrative: An American Genre* (Lanham, MD: UP of America, 1984); Kathryn Zabelle Derounian-Stodola and James Arthur Levernier, *The Indian Captivity Narrative, 1550–1900* (New York: Twayne, 1993); Gary L. Ebersole, *Captured by Texts: Puritan to Postmodern Images of Indian Captivity* (Charlottesville: U of Virginia P, 1995); Christopher Castiglia, *Bound and Determined: Captivity, Culture-Crossing, and White Womanhood from Mary Rowlandson to Patty Hearst* (Chicago: U of Chicago P, 1996). For more specific considerations of acculturated white captives see J. Norman Heard, *White into Red: A Study of the Assimilation of White Persons Captured by Indians* (Metuchen, NJ: Scarecrow, 1973); James Axtell, *The Invasion Within: The Context of Cultures in Colonial North America* (New York: Oxford UP, 1985), 302–27; Namias, *White Captives*.

32. Susan Walsh, "'With Them was My Home': Native American Autobiography and *A Narrative of the Life of Mrs. Mary Jemison*," *American Literature* 64 (1992): 51. Michelle Burnham, in contrast, declares categorization of the work impossible, linking Jemison's indeterminate identity with the text's generic indeterminacy. Burnham, "'However Extravagant the Pretension': Bivocalism and U.S. Nation-Building in *A Narrative of the Life of Mrs. Mary Jemison*," *Nineteenth-Century Contexts* 23 (2001): 326. According to Seaver, Jemison's sisters renamed her Dickewamis, a name translated as "a pretty girl"; however, in the chapter appended to *Narrative* in 1877, William Clement Bryant identifies her name as "Deh-ge-wa-nus," or "The-Two-Falling-Voices," and this is the name used

in subsequent scholarship (*N* 38, 199). Either way, the work contributed to the popular sentimental treatment of Indian-white encounters in the period—specifically through its influence on such historical romances as Catharine Maria Sedgwick, *Hope Leslie; or Early Times in the Massachusetts* (1827), and James Fenimore Cooper, *The Wept of Wish-ton-Wish; A Tale* (1829)—and anticipated the emergence of American Indian autobiography in the subsequent years.

33. Axtell, *Invasion Within*, 309–311.

34. See Walsh, "With Them was My Home," 58. Chap. 8 (*N* 79–92) recounts the exploits of Ebenezer Allen.

35. Michelle Burnham, "However Extravagant the Pretension," 333. Appropriately, recent interpretations of *Narrative* have dwelt on the strength of Jemison's familial and maternal love, suggesting that the story of Jemison's relationships and domestic practices at some level subverts Euro-American racism and related imperialism (I write "at some level" because these readings have also considered the tension between Seaver's editing and the assumed presence of Jemison's "actual" words). In "With Them was My Home," Walsh describes two competing voices in the work and its appendixes, those of "assorted white male editors" and "a Seneca woman," and concludes that "a melodrama of beset womanhood segues into a tribute to departed sisters, brothers, husbands, and children" (49, 51, 54). Following Walsh and also Annette Kolodny, *The Land before Her: Fantasy and Experience of the American Frontiers, 1630–1860* (Chapel Hill: U of North Carolina P, 1984), 71–81, Susan Scheckel notes "the influence of the sentimental tradition" on Seaver's creation of Jemison-as-heroine and describes *Narrative* as "a site of cultural contestation." Scheckel, *The Insistence of the Indian: Race and Nationalism in Nineteenth-Century American Culture* (Princeton: Princeton UP, 1998), 73. Karen Oakes argues that, once traces of the sentimental tradition are identified in the text, the American Indian practices that would have informed Jemison's utterance may be identified—and so something like Jemison's actual expression may be discerned. Oakes, "We planted, tended and harvested our corn: Gender, Ethnicity, and Transculturation in *A Narrative of the Life of Mrs. Mary Jemison*," *Women and Language* 18.1 (1995): 45–51. But, as Walsh, Namias, and Scheckel point out, the sentimentality in the text may not be easily extracted; moments of emotional excess attributed to an imposing editor may very well express "the feelings she [Jemison] must have had" after losing her sons, Namias asserts, feelings "well known to women with children" (*White Captives* 177). Scheckel concludes that the description of Jemison's complete acculturation in the Seneca tribe may be doubted as much as the myth of her sustained whiteness (*Insistence*, 82–85). In the end, I suggest, Jemison's attachment to her adoptive family and to her own family may readily be viewed as stemming simultaneously from Euro-American domestic sentimentalism and from the role of women within Seneca society. On the latter, see Anthony F. C. Wallace, *The Death and Rebirth of the Seneca* (New York: Knopf, 1970), 28–30.

36. In the antebellum period, the four editions Seaver published (1842–47) were the first to add the term "White Woman" to the title, and the editor Ebenezer Mix made "new additions *in text* to the Jemison narrative [which], like Seaver's earlier insert on Hiokatoo, have a 'white' intent" (Namias, *White Captives*, 156). Thus Ezra F. Tawill argues that that, rather than challenge difference through emotion, *Narrative* "represented race as an unbridgeable difference" characterized "in terms of familial sentiment." Tawill, "Domestic Frontier Romance; or, How the Sentimental Heroine Became White," *Novel* 32.1 (1998): 102, 104. And Slotkin suggests that *Narrative* recounts Jemison's "racial degeneration" and the stories of her "degenerate and self-destructive" children (*Regeneration through Violence* 447, 449).

37. *N* xiii, 115n.; Namias, *White Captives* 185–86; Walsh, "With Them was My Home," 57.

38. Regarding Jemison's conversion by the Reverend Asher Wright, Mix reports in a chapter first added to the 1842 edition: "In the summer of 1833, she, in a peaceable and friendly manner, seceded from the pagan party of her nation, and joined the Christian party" (*N* 195). In 1918, Vail made clear in his foreword to *Narrative* the prominence Laura Wright's addition had come to have: "It is doubtful any English work presents a passage of greater dramatic elevation and pathos" (*N* h).

39. The term *autobiography* was not yet in wide circulation. According to the *OED*, it was first used in Britain's *Monthly Review* in 1797. Arch calls Matthew Carey "probably the first author to use a form of the word 'autobiography' in the title of an original work," *Auto Biographical Sketches* (1829) (*After Franklin*, 176). See *OED Online*, s.v. "autobiography," http://dictionary.oed.com/cgi/

entry/50015102 (accessed June 26, 2002). For earlier discussions of Seaver's defense of biography, see Kolodny, *Land before Her*, 72; Walsh, "With Them was My Home," 52.

40. Seaver assures readers his text is at once faithful to Jemison's experience and safe for the impressionable reader. Because "books of this kind are sought and read with avidity, especially by children," Seaver insists he has carefully shaped and arranged Jemison's narrative: "The line of distinction between virtue and vice has been rendered distinctly visible; and chastity of expression and sentiment have received due attention" (*N* v). A different conception of textual accuracy is at work here: to be effective—that is, to be affective—accounts of American Indian life and of Indian-white encounters require the hand of a sentimental editor.

41. Leonard Bliss Jr., Review of *Biography and History of the Indians of North America* by Samuel G. Drake, *North American Review* 44 (1837): 301. Like Seaver, Bliss underscores the value of the private (meaning both emotions and domestic scenes) in accounts of the doomed American Indian lifestyle. His description of an acceptable, sentimental monument helps us understand how Seaver's text could eventually lead to the erection in 1910 of a statue of Jemison at Letchworth State Park in the Genesee Valley (Namias, *White Captives*, 161–65).

42. For a discussion of Jemison, Frances Slocum, and Eunice Williams, noting the physical benefits of Jemison's and other women's captivity, see Castiglia, *Bound and Determined*, 37.

43. Quoted in Donald Jackson, introduction to *Black Hawk: An Autobiography* by Black Hawk, ed. Jackson (Urbana: U of Illinois P, 1964), 9. Information on the Black Hawk War and subsequent tour from William T. Hagan, *The Sac and Fox Indians* (Norman: U of Oklahoma P, 1958), 141–204; Jackson, introduction to *Black Hawk: An Autobiography*, 1–31; Roger L. Nichols, *Black Hawk and the Warrior's Path* (Arlington Heights, IL: Harlan Davidson, 1992); Nichols, introduction to *Black Hawk's Autobiography*, by Black Hawk, ed. Nichols (Ames: Iowa State UP, 1999), xi–xxvii. Kerry A. Trask, *Black Hawk: The Battle for the Heart of America* (New York: Henry Holt, 2006) appeared as I was completing this book.

44. Butler quoted in Nichols, *Black Hawk and the Warrior's Path*, 150. "Blackhawkiana" mentioned in Jackson, introduction to *Black Hawk: An Autobiography*, 11.

45. On Patterson, see Nichols, introduction to *Black Hawk's Autobiography*, xiv–xv. For the 1833 and 1834 title pages, see respectively, *Black Hawk: An Autobiography*, ed. Jackson; Black Hawk, *Life of Black Hawk*, ed. Milo Milton Quaife (1916; repr., New York: Dover, 1994).

46. "Black Hawk," review of *Life of Ma-ka-tai-me-she-kia-kiak, or Black Hawk* by Black Hawk, *New England Magazine* 6 (1834): 420; review of *Life of Ma-ka-tai-me-she-kia-kiak, or Black Hawk; with an Account of the Cause and General History of the Late War, &c* by Black Hawk, *American Quarterly Review* 15.30 (1834): 428. On the five editions in the first year, see Scheckel, *Insistence of the Indian*, 100.

47. Antoine LeClair, prefatory note to *Black Hawk's Autobiography*, ed. Nichols. All references to *Life of Black Hawk* are from this edition (hereafter *L*). This is a reprint of the first edition (*Life of Black Hawk*), though its title reflects that of a subsequent edition.

48. Scheckel does address the text's sentimentalism in her description of *Life* but emphasizes how it privileges the spectacle of Black Hawk over his political demands (*Insistence of the Indian*, 123). In investigating which voice dominates the text, recent criticism emphasizes the complexity of the text's composite voice. As Nichols has it, "Where the different opinions occur is over the question of whether the central voice in the account is dominated by the Indian, or the translator and editor" (introduction to *Black Hawk's Autobiography*, xix). On the savagism—its portrayal of the American Indian as a noble primitive headed for extinction—that accompanies the text's hybridity, see Krupat, *Voice in the Margin*, 152; Murray, *Forked Tongues*, 68–69; Gary Ashwill, "Savagism and Its Discontents: James Fenimore Cooper and His Native American Contemporaries," *ATQ* 8 (1994): 224. On the ways in which *Life* constructs Black Hawk as the noble savage turned cultural critic, see Mark Wallace, "Black Hawk's *An Autobiography*: The Production and Use of an 'Indian' Voice," *American Indian Quarterly* 18 (Fall 1994):481–94; Walker, *Indian Nation*, 77; Ashwill, "Savagism and Its Discontents," 218. In contrast, H. David Brumble and Timothy Sweet identify Black Hawk's task of self-vindication throughout *Life* as arising from Sauk culture, though the textual medium (which Sweet identifies as ethnographic) is Euro-American. See Brumble, *American Indian Autobiography*, 39; Timothy Sweet, "Masculinity and Self-Performance in the *Life of Black Hawk*," *American Literature* 65 (1993): 484–85.

49. Neil Schmitz, "Captive Utterance: Black Hawk and Indian Irony," *Arizona Quarterly* 48.4 (1992): 8.

50. Wallace, "Black Hawk's *An Autobiography*," 485.

51. Snelling, "Life of Black Hawk," 69.

52. "Black Hawk," *New England Magazine*, 420; "Black-Hawk War," review of *The Life and Adventures of Black-Hawk*, by Benjamin Drake, *Hesperian; or, Western Monthly Magazine* 1 (1838): 334; "Black-Hawk," *Hesperian; or, Western Monthly Magazine* 2 (1838–39): 167.

53. Review of *Life, American Quarterly Review*, 428, 445, 447.

54. Snelling, "Life of Black Hawk," 73, 79, 83.

55. Hagan, *Sac and Fox Indians*, 201, 202. For additional discussions of books on Black Hawk in the decades following his capture, see ibid.; Nichols, *Black Hawk and the Warrior's Path*, 162; Walker, *Indian Nation*, 79–80.

56. "Black-Hawk War," 327.

57. B. B. Thatcher, "Indian Biography," review of *Collections of the Maine Historical Society*, vol. 1, *North American Review* 34 (1832): 430.

58. O. W. B. Peabody, "Thatcher's Indian Biography," review of *Indian Biography*, by B. B. Thatcher, *North American Review* 36 (1833): 472–73.

Chapter 5. The Book, the Poet, the Indian

1. George Hochfield, "New England Transcendentalism," in *Critical Essays on American Transcendentalism*, ed. Philip F. Gura and Joel Myerson (Boston: G. K. Hall, 1982), 457; Ralph Waldo Emerson, *Nature* (1836), in *"Nature," Addresses, and Lectures*, ed. Robert E. Spiller and Alfred R. Ferguson (Cambridge: Harvard UP, Belknap, 1971), 37; Elizabeth A. Meese, "Transcendentalism: The Metaphysics of the Theme," in Gura and Myerson, *Critical Essays*, 510.

2. Emerson, *Nature*, 10. The brief overview of transcendentalism in this paragraph draws on the vast scholarship on the topic. Particularly important to my description here are Alexander Kern, "The Rise of Transcendentalism, 1815–1860," in *Transitions in American Literary History*, ed. Harry Hayden Clark (Durham: Duke UP, 1953), 247–314; Gura and Myerson, introduction to *Critical Essays*, xi–li; Hochfield, "New England Transcendentalism," 453–82; Barbara L. Packer, "The Transcendentalists," in *The Cambridge History of American Literature*, ed. Sacvan Bercovitch (New York: Cambridge UP, 1995), 2:329–604; Lawrence Buell, *Literary Transcendentalism: Style and Vision in the American Renaissance* (Ithaca: Cornell UP, 1973); Charles Capper, " 'A Little Beyond': The Problem of the Transcendentalist Movement in American History," *Journal of American History* 85 (1998): 502–39.

3. Hochfield, "New England Transcendentalism," 462.

4. See especially Maureen Konkle, *Writing Indian Nations: Native Intellectuals and the Politics of Historiography, 1827–1863* (Chapel Hill: U of North Carolina P, 2004), and "Indian Literacy, U.S. Colonialism, and Literary Criticism," *American Literature* 69 (1997): 457–86.

5. Roy Harvey Pearce, *Savagism and Civilization: A Study of the Indian and the American Mind*, rev. ed. (Berkeley: U of California P, 1988), 147.

6. My focus on Fuller's *Summer on the Lakes* and Thoreau's *The Maine Woods* draws inspiration from chap. 4 of Lucy Maddox's *Removals: Nineteenth-Century American Literature and the Politics of Indian Affairs* (New York: Oxford UP, 1991), which considers these texts alongside Parkman's *Oregon Trail* (1849). In contrast, Maddox focuses on how Fuller, Thoreau, and Parkman at once take "the Indian" as their subject and emphasize the nonpresence of real and admirable American Indians.

7. For biographical information on Fuller I rely on Joan von Mehren, *Minerva and the Muse: A Life of Margaret Fuller* (Amherst: U of Massachusetts P, 1994). (The details of Fuller's Great Lakes tour recounted here are found on pp. 170–77.) Important critical treatments of Fuller's oeuvre that take biography into account include Christina Zwarg, *Feminist Conversations: Fuller, Emerson, and the Play of Reading* (Ithaca: Cornell UP, 1995); Jeffrey Steele, *Transfiguring America: Myth, Ideology, and Mourning in Margaret Fuller's Writing* (Columbia: U of Missouri P, 2001).

8. For biographical information on Thoreau, I depend primarily on Robert D. Richardson Jr., *Henry Thoreau: A Life of the Mind* (Berkeley: U of California P, 1986). Joseph J. Moldenhauer, "The Maine Woods" in *The Cambridge Companion to Henry David Thoreau*, ed. Joel Myerson (Cambridge: Cambridge UP, 1995), 124–41, includes an excellent, detailed description of the Maine trips. Robert F. Sayre, *Thoreau and the American Indians* (Princeton: Princeton UP, 1977) provides the most thorough treatment of Thoreau's study of American Indians. On Thoreau's reading and his political activity, see Robert Sattelmeyer, *Thoreau's Reading: A Study in Intellectual History with Bibliographic Catalogue* (Princeton: Princeton UP, 1988); Len Gougeon, "Thoreau and Reform," in Myerson, *Cambridge Companion to Henry David Thoreau*, 194–214.

9. On the publication of *The Maine Woods*, see Moldenhauer, "Maine Woods," 128, 130–31. Of the relationship between the three essays, Philip F. Gura writes, "Read episodically, *The Maine Woods* reveals Thoreau as a budding, sometimes fumbling, anthropologist whose consecutive journeys to Maine display a gradually increasing sensitivity to the natives he sought to understand." Gura, "Thoreau's Maine Woods Indians: More Representative Men," *American Literature* 49 (1977): 372. Gura is not alone in pointing out Thoreau's developing understanding of American Indians in the collection; see especially D. M. Murray, "Thoreau's Indians and His Developing Art of Characterization," *ESQ* 21 (1975): 222–29. In a recent article, Joshua David Bellin challenges this established reading of *The Maine Woods*, arguing that "Thoreau's view of the Indians—and of his own relationship to them—held steady: their place, their culture, their identity he still took to be *his* merited birthright." Bellin, "Taking the Indian Cure: Thoreau, Indian Medicine, and the Performance of American Culture," *New England Quarterly* 79 (March 2006): 24.

10. See David S. Reynolds, *Beneath the American Renaissance: The Subversive Imagination in the Age of Emerson and Melville* (Cambridge: Harvard UP, 1988), 92–112, 484–506; Richard F. Teichgraeber III, *Sublime Thoughts / Penny Wisdom: Situating Emerson and Thoreau in the American Market* (Baltimore: Johns Hopkins UP, 1995); Paul Gilmore, *The Genuine Article: Race, Mass Culture, and American Literary Manhood* (Durham: Duke UP, 2001), 67–97, and "'The Poetical Side of Existence': Margaret Fuller, Early Mass Culture, and Aesthetic Transcendence," *ESQ* 47 (2001): 59–87.

11. Margaret Fuller, *Summer on the Lakes* (1844) in *The Essential Margaret Fuller*, ed. Jeffrey Steele (New Brunswick, NJ: Rutgers UP, 1992), 211–12. Hereafter cited as *SL*.

12. Ann Douglas, *The Feminization of American Culture* (New York: Doubleday, 1977), 259–88. Douglas's now infamous theorization of a "feminization" of American culture in the antebellum period concludes with a positive account of Fuller's "Disavowal of Fiction."

13. Discussions of Fuller's exploration of oppression, particularly in *Summer on the Lakes*, and its impact on her feminism abound. See Steele, *Transfiguring America*, 135–66; Annette Kolodny, *The Land before Her: Fantasy and Experience of the American Frontiers, 1630–1860* (Chapel Hill: U of North Carolina P, 1984), 112–30, and "Margaret Fuller's First Depiction of Indians and the Limits on Social Protest: An Exercise in Women's Studies Pedagogy," *Legacy* 18 (2001): 1–20; Zwarg, *Feminist Conversations*, 97–124; Charlene Avallone, "The Red Roots of White Feminism in Margaret Fuller's Writings," in *Doing Feminism: Teaching and Research in the Academy*, ed. Mary Anderson, Lisa Fine, Kathleen Geissler, and Joyce R. Ladenson (East Lansing: Michigan State U, Women's Studies Program, 1997), 135–64.

14. For previous work tracing Fuller's use of sentimentalism and, more specifically, her strategic use of the language of sympathy in responding to Emersonian transcendentalism and critiquing patriarchy, as well as her implication in sentimentalism's colonialist rhetoric, see Julie Ellison, *Delicate Subjects: Romanticism, Gender, and the Ethics of Understanding* (Ithaca: Cornell UP, 1990), 217–98; Sandra M. Gustafson, "Choosing a Medium: Margaret Fuller and the Forms of Sentiment," *American Quarterly* 47 (1995): 34–65; Susan Gilmore, "Margaret Fuller 'Receiving' the 'Indians,'" in *Margaret Fuller's Cultural Critique: Her Age and Legacy*, ed. Fritz Fleischmann (New York: Peter Lang, 2000), 191–227.

15. Paul Gilmore notes the connection between Fuller's appreciation for Edwin Forrest's performance as the lead in *Metamora; or, The Last of the Wampanoags* and her observation of the "theatrical" Indian, arguing that Fuller finds in the actor "a potential model of a more natural union of body and soul" ("Poetical Side of Existence," 76).

16. Margaret Fuller, *Woman in the Nineteenth Century*, ed. Larry J. Reynolds (1845; repr., New York: Norton, 1998), 26. The allusion is to Matt. 9.20–22. I cite the authorized King James version, ed. Robert Carroll and Stephen Prickett (Oxford: Oxford UP, 1997).

17. Henry D. Thoreau, *The Maine Woods*, ed. Joseph J. Moldenhauer (1864; repr., Princeton: Princeton UP, 1972), 95. Hereafter cited as *MW*.

18. Millette Shamir describes Thoreau as practicing "an alternative, contesting logic of intimacy," which is "based on physical distance rather than proximity, on concealment rather than revelation, on silence rather than speech." Shamir, "'The Manliest Relation to Men': Thoreau on Privacy, Intimacy, and Writing," in *Boys Don't Cry? Rethinking Narratives of Masculinity and Emotion in the U.S.*, ed. Milette Shamir and Jennifer Travis (New York: Columbia UP, 2002), 68.

19. Philip F. Gura, *The Wisdom of Words: Language, Theology, and Literature in the New England Renaissance* (Middletown, CT: Wesleyan UP, 1981), 123.

20. On the role of language study in dehistoricizing (and anthropologizing) American Indians in the nineteenth century, see especially Steven Conn, *History's Shadow: Native Americans and Historical Consciousness in the Nineteenth Century* (Chicago: U of Chicago P, 2004), 79–115.

21. As Paul Gilmore has it, Thoreau "proposed using museumlike methods to preserve wild Indians as a reservoir of primitiveness for overcivilized whites" (*Genuine Article*, 208 n. 78). On George Catlin's formulation of a western reserve, see Chapter 6.

22. Fuller read extensively on the American Indians, as we know from her references in *Summer on the Lakes* and from accounts of her related library studies in Chicago and at Harvard (von Mehren, *Minerva and the Muse*, 173–74, 177). Thoreau read standard works on the subject by Samuel Gardner Drake and B. B. Thatcher in his youth, and by 1850 he had begun an intensive course of study in early American Indian history (Sattelmeyer, *Thoreau's Reading*, 101–6; Sayre, *Thoreau and the American Indians*, 101–22).

23. Buell, *Literary Transcendentalism*, 190. On Fuller's and other women writers' use of the travel narrative, see Victoria Brehm, "Inventing Iconography on the Accessible Frontier: Harriet Martineau, Anna Jameson, and Margaret Fuller on the Great Lakes," *Prospects* 24 (1999): 70–71; William W. Stowe, "Conventions and Voices in Margaret Fuller's Travel Writing," *American Literature* 63 (1991): 250; Pamela Cheetwood Sellers, "Margaret Fuller's *Summer on the Lakes, in 1843*: It Is Not Good Enough Merely to *Be* Here" (Ph.D. diss., Michigan State U, 1993), 15–44; Michaela Bruckner Cooper, "Textual Wandering and Anxiety in Margaret Fuller's *Summer on the Lakes*," in Fleischmann, *Margaret Fuller's Cultural Critique*, 171–89. On Thoreau's use of the travel narrative, see Buell, *Literary Transcendentalism*, 188–207; Sattelmeyer, *Thoreau's Reading*, 47–49; Stanley Alan Tag, "Growing Outward into the World: Henry David Thoreau and the Maine Woods Narrative Tradition, 1804–1886" (Ph.D. diss., U of Iowa, 1995). Buell notes that Thoreau read at least 146 travel narratives, and Sattelmeyer concludes, "his reading of travel books is perhaps the most constant feature among his literary interests from his college years until his final illness" (*Thoreau's Reading*, 47).

24. For discussions of Thoreau's engagement with the literary market, see Steven Fink, *Prophet in the Marketplace: Thoreau's Development as a Professional Writer* (Princeton: Princeton UP, 1992); Teichgraeber, *Sublime Thoughts*, 44–74.

25. As Nicole Tonkovich argues, Fuller's researches in the library, her attempt to survey what was known about the places she had experienced first hand, had tremendous impact on the form of *Summer on the Lakes*. Tonkovich "Traveling West, Writing in the Library: Margaret Fuller's *Summer on the Lakes*," *Legacy* 10 (1993): 79–102.

26. Stowe, "Conventions and Voices," 250; Steele, *Transfiguring America*, 137. The proliferation of others' words in *Summer on the Lakes* reflects Fuller's concern with the development of a transcendental literary form that "mak[es] difficulty and dislocation *desiderata* in the experience of reading"—and that redresses the inadequacies of women's education and the oppressive conditions for women and American Indians on the frontier (Zwarg, *Feminist Conversations*, 103). See Stephen Adams, "'That Tidiness We Always Look for in Woman': Fuller's *Summer on the Lakes* and Romantic Aesthetics," in *Studies in the American Renaissance*, ed. Joel Myerson (Charlottesville: UP of Virginia, 1987), 250–51; Tonkovich, "Traveling West," 82; Steele, *Transfiguring America*, 140.

27. Adams, "That Tidiness," 256.

28. Stowe, "Conventions and Voices," 250.

29. As Colleen Glenney Boggs argues, Fuller's inclusion of translations within her works is "a methodology for relating to others without experiencing or exerting the pressures of universal genius," one that "[draws] on the sentimental register of feeling, intimacy, and relation." Boggs, "Margaret Fuller's American Translation," *American Literature* 76 (2004): 39. Clearly, the moral Fuller extracts from "Muckwa" has significance for her description of women's and American Indians' unhappy situation on the prairie and in the nation as a whole. While Zwarg (*Feminist Conversations*) argues that Fuller believes God could correct the numerous uneven relationships on the American frontier, Tonkovich ("Traveling West") and Brehm ("Inventing Iconography") both insist the tale expresses Fuller's discomfort with racial intermarriage. Like Boggs, I am concerned less with Fuller's implied moral for the tale than with a meta-narrative she develops about the proper translation of American Indian texts.

30. Jeffrey Steele notes, "In her review (*New-York Tribune*, 20 June 1845), of the works of Benjamin Disraeli (1804–81) Fuller praised his novel *Vivian Grey* (1826) for its witty, sparkling, and whimsical qualities" (*SL* 449 n. 19).

31. Susan Gilmore points out that, in her fascination with and praise for Everett's Indianized speech, Fuller actually does succumb, at least in part, to the colonial work of sentimental discourse ("Margaret Fuller 'Receiving' the 'Indians,'" 211–18).

32. Sattelmeyer, *Thoreau's Reading*, 65, 105, 58–59; Richardson, *Henry Thoreau*, 221–23.

33. On this ambivalence, see especially Ann E. Lundeberg, "Exploring the Linguistic Wilderness of *The Maine Woods*," in *Reading the Earth: New Directions in the Study of Literature and Environment*, ed. Michael P. Branch, Rochelle Johnson, Daniel Patterson, and Scott Slovic (Moscow: U of Idaho P, 1998), 165–77.

34. Henry D. Thoreau, *Walden*, ed. J. Lyndon Shanley (1854; Princeton: Princeton UP, 1971), 102.

35. Lundeberg, "Exploring the Linguistic Wilderness," 169. For a discussion of Thoreau's use of a Wordsworthian romantic sublime in this essay, see Greg Garrard, "Wordsworth and Thoreau: Two Versions of Pastoral," *Thoreau's Sense of Place: Essays in American Environmental Writing*, ed. Richard J. Schneider (Iowa City: U of Iowa P, 2000), 194–206.

36. Thoreau also found Father Sebastian Rasles's "Dictionary of the Abenaki Language" (1691–1724; published 1833) helpful during his preparation of the appendix. He began reading the dictionary in the Harvard library, February 1858 (Sayre, *Thoreau and the American Indians*, 188–89).

37. Ralph Waldo Emerson, "The Poet" (1844) *Essays: Second Series*, ed. Joseph Slater, Alfred R. Ferguson, and Jean Ferguson Carr (Cambridge: Harvard UP, Belknap, 1983), 12, 22.

38. Ibid., 8. *Summer on the Lakes*, Susan M. Levin points out, "demonstrates a certain setting of the self *against* the natural world better to explore man's position and future in that world" (emphasis mine). Levin, "Romantic Prose and Feminine Romanticism," *Prose Studies* 10.2 (1987): 189. Thoreau, Gura writes, believed "that the foundation for the 'spiritual' life for which he prayed…did not lie so much in the fact of transcendence to another sphere as in the permanence of the physical world in which he, as well as his language, was rooted" (*Wisdom of Words*, 137).

39. Refuting critics who assert that Thoreau rejected the Emersonian theory of correspondence as expressed in *Nature*, David M. Robinson writes, "Thoreau, however, found in *Nature* less a denial of the reality and specificity of the material world than a theory that gave facts significance because of their interrelations." He adds, "Idealism was for Emerson, as it was for Thoreau, a way to confirm the ever-mutating energy of the material world." Robinson, "Thoreau and Idealism: 'Face to Face to a Fact,'" *Nineteenth-Century Prose* 31.2 (2004): 33, 34. As I assert here, however, Fuller's and Thoreau's revisions of the Emersonian Poet suggest an additional emphasis on mediation within the natural world as opposed to simply the transcendence of it.

40. Emerson, *Nature*, 8.

41. Oddly enough, Fuller elsewhere suggests Jane Johnston Schoolcraft and her siblings escape the kind of bias she describes in this passage because "they have enough of European culture to have a standard, by which to judge their native habits and inherited lore" (*SL* 192).

42. Fuller writes, "Has the Indian, has the white woman, as noble a feeling of life and its uses, as

religious a self-respect, as worthy a field of thought and action, as man? If not, the white woman, the Indian woman, occupies an inferior position to that of man. It is not so much a question of power, as of privilege" (*SL* 180).

43. Anne Baker, "'A Commanding View': Vision and the Problem of Nationality in Fuller's *Summer on the Lakes*," *ESQ* 44 (1998): 73.

44. Ibid., 61.

45. See John 1.4–5: "In him was life; and the life was the light of men. And the light shineth in darkness; and the darkness comprehended it not."

46. John 1.23.

47. Bellin argues quite the opposite about this passage, that through his meditation on the phosphorescent chips "Thoreau assumes for himself the shaman's mantle" and exemplifies the Euro-American "inheritance" of Native knowledge through the Indian cure, or what Bellin identifies as the non-Native obsession with performing and imbibing American Indian spirituality ("Taking the Indian Cure," 29).

48. Pearce, *Savagism and Civilization*, 150.

49. For information on Ross and his organization of resistance to Cherokee removal, see Francis Paul Prucha, *The Great Father: The United States Government and the American Indians*, 2 vols. (Lincoln: U of Nebraska P, 1984), 1:236–39.

50. Polis's liminal state is often highlighted in critical treatments of "The Allegash and East Branch," including Moldenhauer, "*The Maine Woods*," 134–35; Sayre, *Thoreau and the American Indians*, 172–87; Gura, "Thoreau's Maine Woods Indians"; Linda Frost, "'The Red Face of Man,' the Penobscot Indian, and a Conflict of Interest in Thoreau's *Maine Woods*," *ESQ* 39 (1993): 37.

51. This portrayal of Polis contrasts with Thoreau's understanding of the basket-seller in *Walden*, as Bellin describes it: "Antebellum Noble Savagism, in sum, attempted to ensure that Indians were not simply displaced by the economy but deprived of an economic existence altogether—not merely the right to make a living but the right to exist *as* economic beings" (*Demon of the Continent*, 58). In *Maine Woods*, Thoreau finds Joe Polis to be an admirable example of someone living within the economy and in harmony with Nature.

52. Gura, "Thoreau's Maine Woods Indians."

53. Thoreau, *Walden*, 323. As Arnold Krupat writes, "And at the end of it all, his final word was Indian. So maybe even as Thoreau died in opposition, maybe his continued hope was still, as always, for reconciliation, for harmony. And so he named the only ones he knew whose relation to the world had seemed one of assent." Krupat, *Woodsmen; or, Thoreau and the Indians: A Novel* (Norman: U of Oklahoma P, 1994), 90.

Chapter 6. "Sorrows in excess!"

1. Donald E. Pease, "New Perspectives on U.S. Culture and Imperialism," in *Cultures of United States Imperialism*, ed. Amy Kaplan and Donald E. Pease (Durham: Duke UP, 1993), 22; J. L. Allen, "Horizons of Sublime: The Invention of the Romantic West," *Journal of Historical Geography* 18 (1992): 30. On the development of science in the Jacksonian United States, see especially George H. Daniels, *American Science in the Age of Jackson* (New York: Columbia UP, 1968), 6–33.

2. On the contribution of the idea of "the West" to antebellum American science and literature, see, respectively, Daniels, *American Science*, 10–12; Richard Drinnon, *Facing West: The Metaphysics of Indian-Hating and Empire-Building* (Minneapolis: U of Minnesota P, 1980). On the romantic and scientific understandings of American Indians in the antebellum period, as well as the relations between them, see Roy Harvey Pearce, *Savagism and Civilization: A Study of the Indian and the American Mind*, rev. ed. (Berkeley: U of California P, 1988), 53–236; Robert F. Berkhofer Jr., *The White Man's Indian: Images of the American Indian from Columbus to the Present* (New York: Vintage, 1978), 33–111. And on the development of ethnography in nineteenth-century America, see especially Robert E. Bieder, *Science Encounters the Indian, 1820–1880: The Early Years of American Ethnology* (Norman: U of Oklahoma P, 1986); Scott Michaelsen, *The Limits of Multiculturalism: Interrogating the Origins of Amer-*

ican Anthropology (Minneapolis: U of Minnesota P, 1999), 33–163. My use of the term *ethnography* rather than *ethnology* reflects how new these terms were in this period: "The term [ethnography] defined as 'nation description' only migrated from German into English usage in the 1830s.... The first record in English of the term 'ethnology,' with which ethnography would become inextricably linked, did not occur until 1842." Steven Conn, *History's Shadow: Native Americans and Historical Consciousness in the Nineteenth Century* (Chicago: U of Chicago P, 2004), 162.

3. Brian W. Dippie, *Catlin and His Contemporaries: The Politics of Patronage* (Lincoln: U of Nebraska P, 1990), 56. William H. Truettner also recognizes in Catlin's Indian Gallery and *Letters and Notes* a "mixture of emotion and objectivity." Truettner, *The Natural Man Observed: A Study of Catlin's Indian Gallery* (Washington, DC: Smithsonian Institution P, 1979), 74. Ultimately, the ethnography of the Schoolcrafts and Catlin, which is related to, and often located in, travel narratives, blurs the categories of early nineteenth-century romantic or sentimental and scientific travel writing that Mary Louise Pratt establishes in *Imperial Eyes*. In her discussion of Mungo Park's *Travels in the Interior of Africa* (1799) and John Barrow's *An Account of Travels into the Interior of Southern Africa in the Years 1797 and 1798* (1801), Pratt writes that, in contrast to the objectivist stance of scientific writing, "Sentimental writing explicitly anchors what is being expressed in the sensory experience, judgement, agency, or desires of the human subjects. Authority lies in the authenticity of somebody's felt experience." Pratt, *Imperial Eyes: Travel Writing and Transculturation* (London: Routledge, 1992), 76. For a comparison of Schoolcraft's and Catlin's attitudes toward American Indian oral tradition and precontact history, see especially Annette Kolodny, "Fictions of American Prehistory: Indian, Archeology, and National Origin Myths," *American Literature* 75 (2003): 695–98.

4. George Catlin, *Letters and Notes on the Manners, Customs, and Conditions of the North American Indians*, 4th ed., 2 vols. (1844; repr., New York: Dover, 1973). Hereafter cited as *LN*. (Note: The first edition of *Letters and Notes* appeared in 1841; citations are to the fourth edition reprint.) Henry Rowe Schoolcraft, *The Literary Voyager or Muzzeniegun*, ed. Philip P. Mason (1826–27; repr., East Lansing: Michigan State UP, 1962). Hereafter cited as *LV*.

5. In an "inventory" of ethnographic methods, James Clifford describes an "experiential" method akin to that which I identify in the work of Catlin and young Henry Rowe Schoolcraft. This approach "draw[s] on intuitive styles of feeling, perception, and guess work," though Clifford dissociates it from empathy. Still, Catlin's interactions with his subjects and Schoolcraft's dependence on his family associate them with what Clifford identifies as a naïve approach in which "the ethnographer accumulates personal knowledge of the field." Clifford, "On Ethnographic Authority," in *The Predicament of Culture: Twentieth-Century Ethnography, Literature, and Art* (Cambridge: Harvard UP, 1988), 36, 37.

6. Daniels, *American Science*, 38, 192. On the relationship between science and entertainment in this period, see Ellen Strain, "Exotic Bodies, Distant Landscapes: Touristic Viewing and Popularized Anthropology in the Nineteenth Century," *Wide Angle* 18 (1996): 70–100.

7. See Tzvetan Todorov, "'Race,' Writing, and Culture," trans. Loulou Mack, in *"Race," Writing, and Difference*, ed. Henry Louis Gates Jr. (Chicago: U of Chicago P, 1986), 370–80. In considering the common historical origins of racism and science, Todorov goes so far as to suggest a causal relationship: "Anyone can observe two sets of variables: on the one hand human beings differ in physical appearance, and on the other they differ in social behavior. Racism begins when one proceeds to reason that the two series cannot possibly be independent of one another; the first must vary *as* the second, or vice versa. Now, this is a typically scientific mode of reasoning, since science consists in the effort to replace chaos with order. It is therefore not surprising to discover that the advent of the natural sciences in the eighteenth century was accompanied by the appearances of the first theories concerning 'races'" (372).

8. Thomas F. Gossett, *Race: The History of an Idea in America* (Dallas: Southern Methodist UP, 1963), 58–60, 63–67. On the monogenist/polygenist debates and the various figures in them, see in particular William Stanton, *The Leopard's Spots: Scientific Attitudes toward Race in America, 1815–59* (Chicago: U of Chicago P, 1960); Bieder, *Science Encounters the Indian*; Stephen Jay Gould, *The Mismeasure of Man* (New York: Norton, 1981), 30–72; Dana D. Nelson, "'No Cold or Empty Heart': Polygenesis, Scientific Professionalization, and the Unfinished Business of Male Sentimentalism," *differences: A Journal of Feminist Cultural Studies* 11.3 (1999–2000): 29–56.

9. See Samuel George Morton, "Physical Type of the American Indians," in Henry Rowe School-craft, *Historical and Statistical Information Respecting the History, Condition and Prospects of the Indian Tribes of the United States*, 6 vols. (Philadelphia: Lippincott, Grambo & Co., 1851–57), 2:313–31. Note that this is the title of vol. 1; vols. 2–5 are titled *Information Respecting the History, Condition and Prospects of the Indian Tribes of the United States* and vol. 6, *History of the Indian Tribes of the United States: Their Present Condition and Prospects, and a Sketch of their Ancient Status*. All six hereafter cited as HIS.

10. For discussions of the scientific grounds for a doomed Indian myth, see Gossett, *Race*, 236–37; Reginald Horsman, *Race and Manifest Destiny: The Origins of American Racial Anglo-Saxonism* (Cambridge: Harvard UP, 1981), 116–57; Bieder, *Science Encounters the Indian*, 55–103; Patrick Brantlinger, *Dark Vanishings: Discourse on the Extinction of Primitive Races, 1800–1930* (Ithaca: Cornell UP, 2003), 17–44.

11. Dana D. Nelson, *National Manhood: Capitalist Citizenship and the Imagined Fraternity of White Men* (Durham: Duke UP, 1998), 125; Henry Louis Gates Jr., introduction to *"Race," Writing, and Difference*, 11.

12. On autoethnography—"instances in which colonized subjects undertake to represent themselves in ways that *engage with* the colonizer's own terms"—see Pratt, *Imperial Eyes*, 7.

13. Biographical information on Catlin from Truettner, *Natural Man Observed*; Dippie, *Catlin and His Contemporaries*. Both chronicle Catlin's long string of professional near-misses and grave miscalculations. Despite Catlin's poor judgment and bad luck, his Gallery and *Letters and Notes* had a great impact on the antebellum perception of American Indians. On the contents of the Indian Gallery, see Truettner, *Natural Man Observed*, 142–309; Truettner catalogues 607 paintings in the original Indian Gallery, 507 composed before 1837.

14. Truettner, *Natural Man Observed*, 12.

15. Dippie, *Catlin and His Contemporaries*, 13–14.

16. My description of Catlin's affect-attentive science draws on Ann Davis and Robert Thacker's analysis of artistic works by Catlin and Paul Kane: "Notwithstanding their endorsement of its general aims and methods, both had difficulty accepting the limitations of Baconian empiricism, which denied the validity of speculation beyond conclusions observable in finite factual observation," and thus, Catlin and Kane "transformed their source material to create aesthetically satisfying works." Davis and Thacker, "Pictures and Prose: Romantic Sensibility and the Great Plains in Catlin, Kane, and Miller," *Great Plains Quarterly* 6 (1986): 14. I propose that Catlin recognized sentiment and its artistic expression as essential to ethnographic empiricism.

17. Truettner, *Natural Man Observed*, 14. On Catlin's early professional frustrations, see Dippie, *Catlin and His Contemporaries*, 9–10.

18. With regard to Catlin's personal notes on Cooper's Leatherstocking Tales, Truettner also finds an affinity between the artist and Natty Bumppo (*Natural Man Observed*, 72).

19. A few examples: In Letter 27 Catlin mentions a Native woman's dress being added to the Gallery "where it will long remain to be examined," and in Letter 58, he promises that a Mandan robe he explicates "is now in my Collection; where it may speak for itself" (*LN* 1:225, 2:248). On the scientific uses of Catlin's collection (it was studied by the phrenologists George Combe and Morton, the ethnographer Lewis Henry Morgan, and the geologists Benjamin Silliman and Joseph Nicollet), see Bridget Luette Goodbody, "George Catlin's Indian Gallery: Art, Science, and Power in the Nineteenth-Century" (Ph.D. diss., Columbia U, 1996), chaps 1–3.

20. As Catlin writes in this same letter, "It is a very simple thing for the offhand theorists of the scientific world, who do not go near these people, to arrange and classify them; and a very clever thing to *simplify* the subject, and bring it, like everything else, under three or four heads, and to solve, and resolve it, by as many simple rules." He similarly comments on linguistic theories: "Several very learned gentlemen, whose opinions I would treat with the greatest respect, have supposed that all the native languages of America were traceable to three or four roots; a position which I will venture to say will be an exceedingly difficult one for them to maintain, whilst remaining at home and consulting books, in the way that too many theories are supported; and one infinitely more difficult to prove if they travel among the different tribes, and collect their own information as they travel" (*LN* 2:237, 236). Finally, Catlin includes in *Letters and Notes*—as if to challenge Henry Rowe

Schoolcraft and others directly—an appendix comparing vocabulary of English and five American Indian tribes.

21. Alfred W. Bowers describes the Mandan practice of creating skull circles (and cites Catlin's *Letters and Notes*) in his groundbreaking study *Mandan Social and Ceremonial Organization* (1950; repr., Lincoln: U of Nebraska P, 2004), 100–101.

22. Stanton, *Leopard's Spots*, 28.

23. The greatest difference between the advanced Euro-American society and the primitive American Indian society, he muses, is the ability of the former to justify theft. Catlin continues, "I say that *we* can prove such things; but an *Indian* cannot. It is a mode of reasoning unknown to him in his nature's simplicity, but admirably adapted to subserve the interests of the enlightened world" (*LN* 1:260).

24. Truettner, *Natural Man Observed*, 41.

25. My own experience at the George Catlin and His Indian Gallery exhibit at the Renwick Gallery of the Smithsonian American Art Museum (September 6, 2002, through January 19, 2003) affirmed this analysis. The curators reconstructed the gallery format, hanging the numbered paintings in rows and placing a replica Crow tipi and buffalo skin on the floor. As visitors, we were surrounded by the gaze of Catlin's numerous subjects—and we gazed back, presuming to view the range of nineteenth-century North American tribes in one journey around the room. The tipi overwhelmed the Victorian gallery with its rich carpet, velvet couches, and high ceilings, and the dwelling's open flap echoed our entry into a simulation of the American Indian world.

26. Another prominent account of Native mourning facilitated by Catlin's work comes in a note about time spent with Ha-wan-je-tah (the one horn), a Sioux chief. Catlin describes how, at a lecture given in New York, a delegation of Sioux in the audience reacted when the portrait of One Horn was displayed: "Each one placed his hand over his mouth, and gave a 'hush—sh—' and hung down their heads'" (*LN* 1:221n).

27. Roger L. Nichols, ed., *Black Hawk's Autobiography* (Ames: Iowa State UP, 1999), 42.

28. On sentimental mourning, see Karen Halttunen, *Confidence Men and Painted Women: A Study of Middle-Class Culture in America, 1830–1870* (New Haven: Yale UP, 1982), 124–52. On child mourning specifically, see John R. Gillis, *A World of Their Own Making: Myth, Ritual, and the Quest for Family Values* (New York: Basic Books, 1996), 201–21; Ann Douglas, *The Feminization of American Culture* (New York: Doubleday, 1977), 200–207.

29. Henry Rowe Schoolcraft, review of *Letters and Notes* by George Catlin, and *American Antiquities* by Alexander W. Bradford, *North American Review* 54 (1842): 283–99. On Schoolcraft's attacks on Catlin's works, see Dippie, *Catlin and His Contemporaries*, 79, 168.

30. Dippie, *Catlin and His Contemporaries*, 63. Christopher Mulvey writes about the parallel between Wi-jún-jon and Catlin: "The Assiniboine chief, Wi-jún-jon, suffered shotgun assassination for telling truths that his people thought were lies; Catlin suffered professional assassination for the same reason." Mulvey, "George Catlin in Europe," in *George Catlin and His Indian Gallery*, ed. George Gurney and Therese Thau Heyman (Washington, DC: Smithsonian American Art Museum, Norton, 2002), 84.

31. Mulvey, "George Catlin in Europe," 82. Brian W. Dippie reprints the chart from *LN, appendix C*, in *The Vanishing American: White Attitudes and U.S. Indian Policy* (Middletown, CT: Wesleyan UP, 1982) and concludes: "So a work whose first volume opened with an image of the artist and the unspoiled Indian closed by equating the noble savage, the fallen savage, and the Vanishing American" (28).

32. Henry David Thoreau, *The Maine Woods*, ed. Joseph J. Moldenhauer (1864; repr., Princeton: Princeton UP, 1972), 144. I am indebted to John Kasson for pointing out Wi-jún-jon's resemblance to Zip Coon.

33. Biographical information on Henry Rowe Schoolcraft comes from Richard Bremer, *Indian Agent and Wilderness Scholar: The Life of Henry Rowe Schoolcraft* (Mount Pleasant: Clarke Historical Library, Central Michigan U, 1987); Bieder, *Science Encounters the Indian*, 146–93; Michael T. Marsden, "Henry Rowe Schoolcraft: A Reappraisal," *The Old Northwest* 2 (1976): 153–82. Beginning in 1836, Schoolcraft was the superintendent of Indian affairs for Michigan. He lived in Detroit for much of the year but spent summers on Mackinac Island.

34. William M. Clements, ed., *Native American Folklore in Nineteenth-Century Periodicals* (Athens: Ohio UP, Swallow, 1986), xii.

35. Bremer, *Indian Agent*, 92. Pearce explains the confluence of these two motives for ethnography well: "As a government official and a humanitarian, Schoolcraft always hoped to civilize the savages. As a scientist (of a sort) he always insisted on seeing the savage objectively. If it is his objectivity which interests us here, we must nonetheless remember that it takes its quality from his hopes" (*Savagery*, 121).

36. Joshua David Bellin, *The Demon of the Continent: Indians and the Shaping of American Literature* (Philadelphia: U of Pennsylvania P, 2001), 138.

37. Philip P. Mason, introduction to *The Literary Voyager or Muzzeniegun*, xiv. Marsden calls Schoolcraft "the man most responsible for popularizing the Indian oral literature" ("Henry Rowe Schoolcraft," 162). Bellin argues that this act of popularizing Indian oral literature was culturally and territorially imperialistic: "The subordination of myth to literary history represented an effort to turn Indian claims into the absent foundation of an original literature, to create a national story out of Indian myth that left Indian myth out of the national story" (*Demon of the Continent*, 153).

38. Schoolcraft corresponded with Irving, Parkman, and Simms; George Colton ("'Tecumseh" [1824]) and Alfred Billings Street ("Frontenac" [1849]) declared their debt to him; his *Algic Researches* provided Henry Wadsworth Longfellow material for *The Song of Hiawatha* (1855); and Thoreau read widely in his oeuvre. After Schoolcraft's death, his writings influenced numerous other works, including Mark Twain's *Life on the Mississippi*. See *Henry Rowe Schoolcraft: A Register of His Papers in the Library of Congress* (Washington, DC: Library of Congress, Manuscripts Division, 1973), 5; Chase S. Osborn and Stellanova Osborn, *Schoolcraft Longfellow Hiawatha* (Lancaster, PA: Jaques Cattell, 1942); Bremer, *Indian Agent*, vii; Marsden, "Henry Rowe Schoolcraft," 167–79; James Ruppert, "Henry Rowe Schoolcraft: The Indian Expert and American Literature," *Platte Valley Review* 19 (1991): 102.

39. William M. Clements describes Schoolcraft's editorial/authorial practice, as seen in the stories he published: "The way in which Schoolcraft presented the narratives resulted in what for him was an *accurate* version of materials that were basically *literary*. Not to have made changes in them would have betrayed their aesthetic quality and made them less literary." Clements, "Schoolcraft as Textmaker," *Journal of American Folklore* 103 (1990): 183. For another critical consideration of Schoolcraft's editorial practices see Bellin, *Demon of the Continent*, 131–53.

40. Lewis Cass to Henry Rowe Schoolcraft, October 19, 1823, *The Papers of Henry Rowe Schoolcraft, 1782–1878*, 69 microform reels (Washington, DC: Library of Congress Photoduplication Service, 1966), reel 2.

41. Henry Rowe Schoolcraft, *Personal Memoirs of a Residence of Thirty Years with the Indian Tribes on the American Frontiers: with Brief Notices of Passing Events, Facts, and Opinions, A.D. 1812 to A.D. 1842* (1851; repr., New York: Arno P, 1975), 107. Hereafter cited as *PM*.

42. Marsden, "Henry Rowe Schoolcraft," 157.

43. Schoolcraft nonetheless continued to insist that language studies should play a key role in ethnography; he coined the term *Algic* to categorize most American Indians east of the Mississippi as having a common language and thus culture, and he successfully called on the Smithsonian Institution to focus its energy on linguistics. Curtis M. Hinsley, *The Smithsonian and the American Indian: Making a Moral Anthropology in Victorian America*, rev. ed. (Washington, DC: Smithsonian Institution P, 1994), 47; Henry Rowe Schoolcraft, *Algic Researches: Indian Tales and Legends*, 2 vols. (1839; repr., Baltimore: Clearfield, 1992 [both volumes included in this edition]), 1:12–13.

44. For another reading of this passage, see Bellin, *Demon of the Continent*, 135.

45. In the period prior to his first major publication, *Algic Researches*, Schoolcraft treated American Indian oral traditions in a variety of publications. His first two travel narratives, *Travels in the Central Portions of the Mississippi Valley* (New York: Collins and Hannay, 1825) and *Narrative of an Expedition through the Upper Mississippi to Itasca Lake* (New York: Harper & Brothers, 1834), contain selections of Native tales. Also, in 1835 he published "Mythology, Superstitions and Languages of the North American Indians," *Literary and Theological Review* 2 (1835): 96–121. See A. Irving. Hallowell, "Concordance of Ojibwa Narratives in the Published Works of Henry R. Schoolcraft," *Journal of American Folklore* 59 (1946): 136–53; Osborn and Osborn, *Schoolcraft Longfellow Hiawatha*, 631–45.

46. Mason, introduction to *Literary Voyager*, xv.

47. Biographical information on Jane Johnston Schoolcraft and the Johnston family comes from Marjorie Cahn Brazer, *Harps upon the Willows: The Johnston Family of the Old Northwest* (Ann Arbor: Historical Society of Michigan, 1993); A. LaVonne Brown Ruoff, "Jane Johnston Schoolcraft," in *Dictionary of Native American Literature*, ed. Andrew Wiget (New York: Garland, 1994), 295–97; Jeremy Mumford, "Mixed-Race Identity in a Nineteenth-Century Family: The Schoolcrafts of Sault Ste. Marie, 1824–1827," *Michigan Historical Review* 25 (1999): 1–23; Maureen Konkle, *Writing Indian Nations: Native Intellectuals and the Politics of Historiography, 1827–1863* (Chapel Hill: U of North Carolina P, 2004), 166–81. *The Sound the Stars Make Rushing Through the Sky: The Writings of Jane Johnston Schoolcraft*, ed. Robert Dale Parker (U of Pennsylvania P, 2007) appeared as I was completing this book. Parker corrects numerous mistakes in previous accounts of Jane Schoolcraft's biography and her contributions to Henry Schoolcraft's papers, and he catalogs the multiple versions of poems and tales that appeared in the *Literary Voyager* and elsewhere. While I have not had time to thoroughly integrate Parker's findings and analyses into this chapter—especially his detailing of various versions of texts I treat here—I have done my best to eliminate the errors Parker has uncovered in previous scholarship on the Schoolcrafts. Parker rejects descriptions of Jane as simply submissive, highlighting what he sees as her subtle challenges to Henry in their correspondence—her "artful spunk" (38)—and insists that, as a métis, she drew on a "range of femininities" (16). Nonetheless, I argue that one of the models of femininity Jane embraced is that of the sentimental wife whose (certainly artful) submissive stance is grounded in Christian faith and tradition.

48. Brazer, *Harps upon the Willows*, 179.

49. Konkle, *Writing Indian Nations*, 167. Konkle discusses Jameson's and Chandler Robbins Gilman's inclusion of Jane's stories in their works and Harriet Martineau's visit to the Schoolcrafts (179–80).

50. Jane Johnston Schoolcraft, Henry Rowe Schoolcraft Papers, Manuscript Division, Library of Congress, container 70; Konkle, *Writing Indian Nations*, 180. I am indebted to Parker for the identification of the lines as Shakespeare's. In contrast to my own analysis, he argues that if one reads the lines in the larger context of the drama, "Portia's—and Jane's—sense of submission can cut both ways" (*Sound the Stars Make*, 80).

51. Ramona Ford, "Native American Women: Changing Statuses, Changing Interpretations," in *Writing the Range: Race, Class, and Culture in the Women's West*, ed. Elizabeth Jameson and Susan Armitage (Norman: U of Oklahoma P, 1997), 57. Susan Johnston's vision quoted in Jacqueline Peterson, "Women Dreaming: The Religiopsychology of Indian-White Marriages and the Rise of a Métis Culture," in *Western Women: Their Land, Their Lives*, ed. Lillian Schlissel, Vicki L. Ruiz, and Janice Monk (Albuquerque: U of New Mexico P, 1988), 59. Of the vision, Parker writes, "I read that story as a suspect reconstruction that fits the way events turned out" (76). On Ojibwe women's relationship to Great Lawks Protestant missions in this period, see Carol Devens, *Countering Colonization: Native American Women and Great Lakes Missions, 1630–1900* (Berkeley: U of California P, 1992), 69–89.

52. Mumford, "Mixed-Race Identity," 9. A. LaVonne Brown Ruoff suggests that Jane Johnston Schoolcraft, through her multiple personae, in addition to her behind-the-scenes involvement with Henry's ethnographic and historical sketches, creates a "multiple-voiced discourse." Ruoff, "Early Native American Women Authors: Jane Johnston Schoolcraft, Sarah Winnemucca, S. Alice Callahan, E. Pauline Johnson, and Zitkala-Sa," in *Nineteenth-Century American Women Writers: A Critical Reader*, ed. Karen L. Kilcup (Malden, MA: Blackwell, 1998), 81.

53. Ruoff, "Jane Johnston Schoolcraft," 296.

54. Schoolcraft supplies this subtitle for the "legend" in the second volume of *Algic Researches* (2:243). In *Personal Memoirs*, he notes that the tales in *Algic Researches* "are, exclusively (with the exception of the allegory of the vine and the oak), wild vines, and not pumpings of my own fancy" (*PM* 655).

55. Konkle, *Writing Indian Nations*, 174.

56. Ibid., 172.

57. Jane left behind a well-organized, seventy-nine-page collection of devotional poems that declare submission to God's will and request spiritual awakening. The twenty-three-stanza "Gesthemane" is one example: "Saviour, all the stone remove / From my flinty, frozen heart, /

Thaw it with the beams of Love, / Peirce [*sic*] it with a Blood dipt dart. / Wound the heart, that wounded Thee, / Melt it in Gethsemane" (Schoolcraft Papers, container 70). Like Rosa's poems in the *Literary Voyager*, the devotional poems in Jane's papers contain a model for Christian life that also appears to describe her position as the métis wife of a Euro-American husband. Parker suggests that Jane Johnston Schoolcraft did not compose "Gethsemane" and other verses in this volume but transcribed them from a hymnal; however, he has not identified the source (*Sound the Stars Make*, 259). Even if "Gethsemane" is not an original work by Jane, it nevertheless communicates her conception of a redeemer Christ to whom the believer submits heart and soul.

58. Henry Rowe Schoolcraft to Lewis Cass, May 30, 1828, and Cass to Schoolcraft, June 4, 1828, Schoolcraft Papers, container 68. In December 1826 and October 1827, Schoolcraft reports working on a poem titled "The Man of Bronze" (*PM* 257, 276).

59. Henry Rowe Schoolcraft, *An Essay on the Indian Character. In Four Parts*, Schoolcraft Papers, container 68. The folder containing this bound manuscript (and only this manuscript) is labeled "The Man of Bronze or Portraitures of Indian Character 1828 pub. 1834" and is accompanied by the two letters between Schoolcraft and Cass cited in n. 58. Schoolcraft appears to have gotten the name Ethwald from Joanna Baillie's 1802 *Macbeth*-like tragedy; in 1840 he expresses his excitement upon receiving a letter from her (*PM* 688). Schoolcraft employed the name again in a poetic drama: Henry Rowe Colcraft [*sic*], *Alhalla, or The Lord of Talladega. A Tale of the [C]reek War* (New York: Wiley and Putnam, 1843), in which Ethwald, a Euro-American "traveller," persuades Mongazid, "an Indian Prophet and hunter," to guide him to a forbidden island on Lake Superior.

60. Henry wrote that poetic composition occupied and sharpened his mind and helped him avoid "the coarser amusements of bowling, whist, and other resorts for time-killing" (*PM* 282). See also *PM* 257, 276, 530, for Schoolcraft's justification of literary pursuits.

61. Henry Rowe Schoolcraft, Schoolcraft Papers, container 70. It appears that the word "though" was later inserted after the dash, and an indecipherable word has been added before "it charms." The used envelope on which these lines are written is postmarked New York, Oct 10, but with an indecipherable year, and addressed to "Mr. Schoolcraft, President of the Michigan Historical Society, Detroit, U. States." The society was incorporated in 1828 (*PM* 320).

62. The humanizing of American Indians through attention to their familial attachments and the focus on these attachments as promising avenues for civilizing efforts would remain a prominent aspect of Schoolcraft's work throughout his career. In vol. 2 of *Historical and Statistical Information*, within a section titled "Constitution of the Indian Family," Schoolcraft declares that the Indian's "family tie" "disarms barbarism of half its repulsiveness, and gives to this erratic and benighted branch of the species, their best claims to our sympathies and benevolence," then suggests, "the sacred tie of families, is the great fulcrum upon which the lever of hope, in doing anything to raise this people from barbarism, rests" (*HSI* 2:48, 49).

63. Bellin, *Demon of the Continent*, 134.

64. Schoolcraft, "Mythology, Superstitions and Languages," 108.

65. Bremer and Konkle cite an additional letter from Henry to Jane on November 24, 1830, as indicating the deterioration of their marriage after Willy's death. In this letter, Henry emphasizes the necessity of the wife's submission to the husband, especially because of what he considered her unorthodox and pampered upbringing (Bremer, *Indian Agent*, 111; Konkle, *Writing Indian Nations*, 178).

66. In Elémire Zolla's words, Henry "outrageously distorted" this tale. Zolla, *The Writer and the Shaman: A Morphology of the American Indian*, trans. Raymond Rosenthal (New York: Harcourt Brace Jovanovich, 1973), 151. "Leelinau, or the Lost Daughter. An Ojibwa Tale," also appeared in Schoolcraft's *The Myth of Hiawatha, and Other Oral Legends, Mythologlic and Allegoric, of the North American Indians* (1856) and both editions of his *Indian Fairy Book* (1856, 1916) (Hallowell, "Concordance," 146).

67. Schoolcraft, *Algic Researches*, 2:80.

68. Michaelsen writes, "It is hard to resist reading this text . . . as Schoolcraft's attempt to have the final word on Jane Johnston's authority, her auto-anthropology" (*Limits of Multiculturalism*, 44).

69. See Bremer, *Indian Agent*, 110–12, 153; Konkle, *Writing Indian Nations*, 178–79. Mumford and others attribute Henry's growing distance from Jane to the increasingly suspect nature of mixed-

race families in the 1830s. See Mumford, "Mixed-Race Identity," 4, 21; Jack Weatherford, *Native Roots: How the Indians Enriched America* (New York: Crown, 1991), 258–60; Bieder, *Science Encounters the Indian* 166– 67.

70. The legends reprinted from the *Literary Voyager* are "The Origin of the Robin" (titled "Iadilla, or The Origin of the Robin") and "The Forsaken Brother" ("Sheem, or The Forsaken Boy"). "Moowis, or the Indian Coquette" was first reprinted in the *Columbian Lady's and Gentleman's Magazine*, 1844. See Hallowell, "Concordance," 145, 150; Konkle, *Writing Indian Nations*, 177–78.

71. "An Indian Mother's Lament for Her Child" comes from pt. 2 of *An Essay* and appears in *Indian Melodies* (New York: Elam Bliss, 1830), 26, in *American Poetry, 1609–1900*, microfilm (Woodbridge, CT: Research Publications, 1976), reel 118. For "To a Young Lady Under Severe Sickness and Depression" see *The Souvenir of the Lakes* (Detroit: Geo. I. Whitney, 1831; rpt., Toledo: George Harrison Orians, 1939), 24.

72. Schoolcraft reports on October 12, 1833, "In accordance with a resolution passed the year previous, I recited a poetic address on the character of the race, which was received with approbation, and directed to be printed. This had been, in fact, sketched in a time of leisure in the wilderness some years before" (*PM* 449). On the membership of the Algic Society, see Algic Society, *Constitution of the Algic Society, Instituted March 28, 1832. For the Encouraging Missionary Effort in Evangelizing the North Western Tribes, and Promoting Education, Agriculture, Industry, Peace & Temperance, among Them…* (Detroit, 1833). The recitation of *An Essay* was particularly fitting because of Schoolcraft's status in the society as founder and president and the poem's mixture of ethnographic observation and a resounding call for civilization efforts. According to Chase S. Osborn and Stellanova Osborn, in 1834 George L. Whitney printed a version of the poem, titled *The Man of Bronze, or Portraitures of Indian Character, Delivered before the Algic Society at Its Annual Meeting in 1834* [sic] (*Schoolcraft Longfellow Hiawatha*, 426, 636), and two manuscript title pages for the poem in Schoolcraft's papers refer to the 1833 Algic Society address. Another entry for this work appears in *The National Cyclopedia of American Biography* (New York: James T. White & Co., 1893; rpt., Ann Arbor, MI: University Microfilms, 1967), 145. The two manuscript title pages (Schoolcraft Papers, container 68) read: "Decades on the Indian Character. A Poem. Delivered before the Algic Society, Detroit October 12th 1833" and "The Man of Bronze, or Traits of Indian Character. A poem delivered before the Algic Society and published by request of that Society." None of these titles appears, however, in *Early American Imprints, National Union Catalog Pre-1956 Imprints*, Library of Congress Card Catalog, or WorldCat.

73. On the proposed tables of contents, the poem is listed alternately as "The Man of Bronz, or Traits of Indian Character" or "The Man of Bronze; an Essay on the Indian Character," 100–pages in length (Henry Rowe Schoolcraft, Schoolcraft Papers, container 70). On the Schoolcraft and Bryant correspondence, see Frank Smith, "Schoolcraft, Bryant, and Poetic Fame," *American Literature* 5 (1933): 170–72. Hetherwold is one of Schoolcraft's many pseudonyms; an 1841 manuscript for the poem "Michilimackinac" and a collection of poems in manuscript from the 1850s are labeled "by William Hetherwold" (Schoolcraft Papers, containers 68 and 69). A March 12, 1853, statement of Schoolcraft's account with Lippincott, Grambo & Company confirms that the publisher charged him twenty dollars on December 31, 1851, for paper and printing costs to produce 250 copies of "*The Man of Bronze* [sic]" (Schoolcraft Papers, container 52, reel 40). In 1851–57, Schoolcraft had an agreement with the publisher of his *Historical and Statistical Information* to issue "one of Schoolcraft's private works concurrently with each public volume" (Bremer, *Indian Agent*, 302). More than 60 percent of the lines in the abridged poem come from pt. 1 of *An Essay*.

Chapter 7. Restoring the Noahic Family

1. On Henry Rowe Schoolcraft's illness, the selection of Seth Eastman as illustrator for *Historical and Statistical Information*, their early collaboration, and Mary Eastman's and Mary Howard Schoolcraft's contributions to their husbands' careers, see Richard G. Bremer, *Indian Agent and Wilderness Scholar: The Life of Henry Rowe Schoolcraft* (Mount Pleasant: Central Michigan U, Clarke Historical

Library, 1987), 297–99, 308; Brian W. Dippie, *Catlin and His Contemporaries: The Politics of Patronage* (Lincoln: U of Nebraska P, 1990), 178–206.

2. On the novels written in response to Harriet Beecher Stowe's *Uncle Tom's Cabin*, see Thomas S. Gossett, *Uncle Tom's Cabin and American Culture* (Dallas: Southern Methodist UP, 1985), 212–38; William Tynes Cowan, *The Slave in the Swamp: Disrupting the Plantation Narrative* (New York: Routledge, 2005), 93–110. Gossett emphasizes that, "in nearly all anti-Uncle Tom literature, the major figure is the benign and patriarchal slavemaster" whose wife is "even more kindly" (214, 218)— reflecting the importance of gender to the maintenance of the racial hierarchy. As James A. Morone has it, "The pro-slavery ranks were united on the race and gender tangle: on the place for white women, on the importance of keeping blacks on the social bottom, and—finally, inevitably—on the rigidity with which the color line had to be maintained." Morone, *Hellfire Nation: The Politics of Sin in American History* (New Haven: Yale UP, 2003) 181. Because of the place of gender in the "tangle," I find it particularly important to examine women's contributions to proslavery literature. Eastman and Schoolcraft both defend the sympathetic, maternal mistress as well as the benevolent patriarch by fictionalizing their marriages and ethnographic labors.

3. *The Myth of Hiawatha* is an 1856 revision of *Algic Researches* (1839); Henry Rowe Schoolcraft sought to capitalize on the success of Longfellow's poem and the poet's public acknowledgment of his source.

4. Lucy Maddox, *Removals: Nineteenth-Century American Literature and the Politics of Indian Affairs* (New York: Oxford UP, 1991), 171.

5. Historians and literary critics have long recognized the figure of the nation-as-family as a significant component of nineteenth-century racialist discourse. On antebellum racial paternalism in theory and in practice, see in particular Michael Paul Rogin, *Fathers and Children: Andrew Jackson and the Subjugation of the American Indian* (New York: Knopf, 1975), 165–248; Peter Kolchin, *American Slavery, 1619–1877*, rev. ed. (New York: Hill and Wang, 2003), 111–32, 139–46, 194.

6. Alexis de Tocqueville, *Democracy in America*, ed. Phillips Bradley, 2 vols. (1835; repr., New York: Vintage, 1972), 1:332. Hereafter cited in text as *DA*.

7. Margaret Fuller, *Summer on the Lakes* (1844), in *The Essential Margaret Fuller*, ed. Jeffrey Steele (New Brunswick, NJ: Rutgers UP, 1992), 138. See chap. 5 for a discussion of the passage in which an observed Indian departs in indignation.

8. Concerning Tocqueville's views on race, Cheryl B. Welch explains, "Tocqueville struggled mightily against any deterministic theory based on race, history, or biology; yet he comes close here to accepting—at the same time that he morally condemns it—the extinction of hope for populations subjected on the illusory basis of race." Welch, *De Tocqueville* (Oxford: Oxford UP, 2001) 64. Harvey Mitchell analyzes Tocqueville's treatment of the American Indian's situation in relation to the development of Anglo-American democracy, concluding that Tocqueville uncomfortably determines that Native Americans' "other notions of time and memory" place them outside of the historical development he traces, making them "a false start." Mitchell, *America after Tocqueville: Democracy against Difference* (Cambridge: Cambridge UP, 2002), 113.

9. For an overview and bibliography of scholarship on American Indian participation in plantation slavery, Black Seminole history, and the situation of freedmen in multiple American Indian communities during the nineteenth century, see Pauline Turner Strong, "Transforming Outsiders: Captivity, Adoption, and Slavery Reconsidered," in *A Companion to American Indian History*, ed. Philip J. Deloria and Neal Salisbury (Malden, MA: Blackwell, 2002), 347–49, 352–56. See also a brief description in Chapter 3.

10. Martin R. Delany, *Blake; or, The Huts of America*, ed. Floyd J. Miller (1861–62; repr., Boston: Beacon P, 1970), 85. Hereafter cited in text as *B*.

11. Genesis 9.25–27. I cite the authorized King James version, ed. Robert Carroll and Stephen Prickett (Oxford: Oxford UP, 1997).

12. Stephen R. Haynes, *Noah's Curse: The Biblical Justification of American Slavery* (Oxford: Oxford UP, 2002), 76. See also Thomas Virgil Peterson, *Ham and Japheth: The Mythic World of Whites in the Antebellum South* (Metuchen, NJ: Scarecrow and American Theological Library Association, 1978).

13. Quoted in Haynes, *Noah's Curse*, 70.

14. Harriet Beecher Stowe, *Uncle Tom's Cabin* (1852; repr., New York: Oxford UP, 1998), 129.

15. Gossett reports, "Nearly all of the proslavery white novelists from the South, however, avoided the theme of racial contamination between black and white" (*Uncle Tom's Cabin and American Culture*, 235).

16. On Eastman's time at Fort Snelling and her subsequent publications, see Rena Neumann Coen, introduction to *Dahcotah; or, Life and Legends of the Sioux around Fort Snelling* by Mary Henderson Eastman (1849; repr., Afton, MN: Afton Historical Society Press, 1995), ix–xxxi; Dippie, *Catlin and His Contemporaries*, 250–51, 258–59; W. K. McNeil, "Mary Henderson Eastman, Pioneer Collector of American Folklore," *Southern Folklore Quarterly* 39 (1975): 271–90; Elizabeth M. Tollers, "Mary Henderson Eastman," in *American National Biography*, ed. John A. Garraty and Mark C. Carnes, 24 vols. (New York: Oxford UP, 1999), 7:252–53. Her other three collections of American Indian material are *The Romance of Indian Life* (1853) (stories that first appeared in the journal the *Iris*), *American Aboriginal Portfolio* (1853), and *Chicora and Other Regions of the Conquerors and Conquered* (1854).

17. Eastman, *Dahcotah*, 6. Hereafter cited in text as *D*. Like other authors in this period—including Henry Rowe Schoolcraft, George Catlin, Lydia Howard Sigourney, and Black Hawk (in his as-told-to autobiography)—Eastman emphasizes that Euro-Americans "rarely consider the Indian as a member of a family" but that the intensity of mourning among American Indians should, in particular, cause them to reconsider (*D* 76).

18. On Mary Nancy Eastman, her parentage, and her relationship with Mary Henderson Eastman, see Coen, introduction to *Dahcotah*, xiv–xv; Dippie, *Catlin and His Contemporaries*, 387–88; Raymond Wilson, *Ohiyesa: Charles Eastman, Santee Sioux*, new ed. (Urbana: U of Illinois P, 1999), 11–13. I rely on Wilson's translation of Sioux names.

19. Dippie, *Catlin and His Contemporaries*, 388. Charles Alexander Eastman (Ohiyesa), a Santee Sioux physician and author, served at the Pine Ridge Agency during the aftermath of the massacre at Wounded Knee Creek and published such works as *Indian Boyhood* (1902), which includes a tragic description of his mother, *The Soul of the Indian* (1911), *From Deep Woods to Civilization* (1916), and *Indian Heroes and Great Chieftains* (1918).

20. Coen, introduction to *Dahcotah*, xv. Of Turner's January 16, 1848, letter to William C. Baker, Coen writes: "Turner mentioned that when scarlet fever struck Mary and the Eastman children—Virginia was seriously ill—that 'Mrs. Eastman sent for Mary [Nancy?] to come quick to take charge of the sick child and seemed willing to resign herself totally to an enemy's care and Mary [Nancy] has not neglected her charge. It was a strange scene and one which I hope will teach Mrs. E. a salutary lesson.' It is conceivable that the older woman and the young girl had exchanged some heated words or Mary may have been jealous of the affection that, according to a tradition of Cloud Man's family, Seth Eastman continued to show toward his eldest daughter. It is even possible that George Turner bore some animosity toward Mary" (xv; brackets in original).

21. Nina Baym describes *Dahcotah* in these terms: "Maneuvering between intense feelings of sympathy for the Native American plight along with guilt over white barbarism, and equally intense beliefs in Protestant Christian superiority and the inevitability of Indian disappearance, *Dahcotah* subsides in an anticlimactic call for Christianizing the remnant." Baym, *American Women Writers and the Work of History, 1790–1860* (New Brunswick: Rutgers UP, 1995) 110. In a review of the modern edition of Eastman's *Dahcotah*, Helen M. Bannan notes the book's "unabashed ethnocentrism" and declares, "I often felt insulted as I read her book." Bannan, review of *Dahcotah: Life and Legends of the Sioux around Fort Snelling* by Mary Henderson Eastman, ed. Rena Neumann Coen, *American Indian Culture and Research Journal* 22 (1998): 262, 263. Such responses to *Dahcotah* naturally clarify the distance between Eastman's nineteenth-century Christian response and that desired by a modern reader.

22. Jane Tompkins, *Sensational Designs: The Cultural Work of American Fiction, 1790–1860* (New York: Oxford UP, 1985), 125, 134.

23. Joshua David Bellin, "The 'Squaw's' Tale: Sympathy and Storytelling in Mary Eastman's *Dahcotah*," *Legacy* 17 (2000): 20, 22. Bellin later adds, "Throughout *Dahcotah* . . . Eastman's critique is deeply ambivalent: sympathy *for* and sympathy *with* coexist in uneasy tension" (27).

24. Mary H. Eastman, *Aunt Phillis's Cabin; or, Southern Life as It Is* (1852; repr., Upper Saddle River, NJ: Gregg P, 1968), 12–13. Hereafter cited in text as *APC*.

25. On the autobiographical aspects of these chapters, see Coen, introduction to *Dahcotah*, xiii–iv, in which she points out that the physical descriptions of Mrs. Moore and of her military home are very close to those of Eastman and Fort Snelling.

26. Minrose C. Gwin, *Black and White Women of the Old South: The Peculiar Sisterhood in American Literature* (Knoxville: U of Tennessee P, 1985), 39.

27. Elizabeth Moss writes: "While northern domestic fiction indicates that middle- and upper-class writers and readers may have been interested in changing their society through the integration of 'feminine' values into larger society, the emphasis in southern fiction on achieving and sustaining social and political equilibrium reveals a profound commitment to the South's existing structure." Moss, *Domestic Novelists in the Old South: Defenders of Southern Culture* (Baton Rouge: Louisiana State UP, 1992) 14. Likewise Beverly Peterson argues that Eastman's novel—and in particular the unsuccessful romance plot—demonstrates that the socially conservative vision of proslavery writers could not be brought in line with the sentimental novel's concern with "a young girl's search for love and independence." Beverly Peterson, *"Aunt Phillis's Cabin*: One Reply to Uncle Tom," *The Southern Quarterly* 33 (Fall 1994): 105.

28. Coen, introduction to *Dahcotah*, xxv; Bremer, *Indian Agent and Wilderness Scholar*, 342; Dippie, *Catlin and His Contemporaries*, 398. Schoolcraft had published a brief, nonfiction defense of slavery eight years earlier: *Letters on the Condition of the African Race in the United States* by a Southern Lady, in *Plantation Life: The Narratives of Mrs. Henry Rowe Schoolcraft* (1852; repr., New York: Negro Universities P, 1969) is a collection of four letters addressed to her brother, Gen. John H. Howard, strenuously attacking abolitionists and praising the benevolence of Southern planters. In letter 1 Schoolcraft discusses the fate of Ham, Shem, and Japheth (10–11). For more on the arguments surrounding Seth Eastman's rights to his plates, see Dippie, *Catlin and His Contemporaries*, 258–61, 388–98.

29. Chase S. Osborn and Stellanova Osborn, *Schoolcraft Longfellow Hiawatha* (Lancaster, PA: Jaques Cattell P, 1942), 610, 611–23. On the slaveholdings of the Howard family and Mary Howard Schoolcraft's relationship with her stepchildren, see Bremer, *Indian Agent and Wilderness Scholar*, 286, 308–10; Dippie, *Catlin and His Contemporaries*, 386–87.

30. Mrs. Henry R. [Mary Howard] Schoolcraft, *The Black Gauntlet: A Tale of Plantation Life in South Carolina* in *Plantation Life* (1860; repr., New York: Negro Universities P, 1969), iii. Hereafter cited in text as *BG*. For a brief overview of the novel, see Jack Weatherford, *Native Roots: How the Indians Enriched America* (New York: Crown, 1991), 259.

31. J. B. Lippincott to Mary Howard Schoolcraft, May 4,1860, Lippincott and Grambo to Mary Howard Schoolcraft, May 31, 1860, and Lippincott and Grambo to Mary Howard Schoolcraft, July 24, 1860, in *The Papers of Henry Rowe Schoolcraft, 1782–1878* (Washington, DC: Library of Congress Photoduplication Service, 1966), reel 43.

32. Richard G. Bremer writes that by the 1850s, Schoolcraft "rejected the model of cultural development which he had followed in varying degrees over the previous four decades in favor of a rigorously fundamentalist conception of human history. Thus he wrote that God had originally created man in the agricultural and not the hunter state. Therefore, the latter condition represented not the first stage along the road of human progress, but rather a declension from civilization owing to the neglect of its higher principles. . . . The Indian as savage, then, represented the end product of a process of moral degeneration. As for racial differences, Schoolcraft implied that they had resulted from a single miraculous intervention when the sons of Noah received the capacity to transmit their newly instilled ethnological types to their descendants" (*Indian Agent and Wilderness Scholar*, 324–25).

33. Henry Rowe Schoolcraft, "The Book of Ed, or Chronicles of Shem in America," Henry Rowe Schoolcraft Papers, Manuscript Division, Library of Congress, container 62. Three manuscripts of the piece are contained in this folder as well as a piece of paper that includes the title and the suggestive equation: "$1857 - 1776 = 81$."

34. "Pocahontas wife" was not a new label for Jane Johnston Schoolcraft. During the couple's visit to Washington, DC, in April 1825, curious residents viewed Jane as "the northern Pocahontas." Henry Rowe Schoolcraft, *Personal Memoirs of a Residence of Thirty Years with the Indian Tribes on the American Frontiers: with Brief Notices of Passing Events, Facts, and Opinions, A.D. 1812 to A.D. 1842* (1851; repr., New York: Arno P, 1975) 208.

35. In vol. 5 of *Historical and Statistical Information Respecting the History, Condition and Prospects of the Indian Tribes of the United States* (Philadelphia: Lippincott, Grambo & Co., 1855), Henry Rowe Schoolcraft celebrates the life of Skenandoah along with other famous American Indians, including Waubojeeg, Jane Johnston Schoolcraft's maternal grandfather, (509–18). (Note that *Historical and Statistical Information Respecting the History, Condition and Prospects of the Indian Tribes of the United States* is the title of vol. 1 only but is usually given for the work as a whole.) Elsewhere in the autobiographical plot of *Black Gauntlet*, Mary Howard Schoolcraft replaces Waubojeeg with Skenandoah.

36. William Bright, *Native American Placenames of the United States* (Norman: U of Oklahoma P, 2004), 250; "Michigan Counties," available at http://www.michigan.gov/hal/ (accessed June 9, 2005). Both sources identify the name as that of a character in Schoolcraft's work, neglecting the broader biographical significance of Schoolcraft's choice.

37. The author of Geehale, "Illula, The Pride of the Lakes," Schoolcraft Papers, container 67. Schoolcraft included his poem "Geehale" in *Indian Melodies* (New York: Elam Bliss, 1830) and printed it separately as a broadside. Schoolcraft's handwriting is extremely difficult in this manuscript of more than eighty stanzas and impossible to read in full, suggesting the poem was composed after his medical condition began to deteriorate in 1851 (Bremer, *Indian Agent and Wilderness Scholar*, 298).

38. Quoted in Bremer, *Indian Agent and Wilderness Scholar*, 310. On Eckerd and Polly, see ibid.

39. Peterson, *"Aunt Phillis's Cabin,"* 110.

40. Bremer, *Indian Agent and Wilderness Scholar*, 343–45.

41. Quoted in Dippie, *Catlin and His Contemporaries*, 401.

Chapter 8. Staging Encounters and Reclaiming Sympathy through Indian Melodramas and Parodies, 1821–1855

1. Joyce Flynn counts "nearly one hundred dramas dealing with American Indians between 1820 and 1850." Flynn, "Melting Plots: Patterns of Racial and Ethnic Amalgamation in American Drama before Eugene O'Neill," *American Quarterly* 38 (1986): 421. Eugene Jones writes that between 1800 and 1859, "at least one hundred and twenty plays featuring Native American themes and characters were written in the United States. The 1820s and 1830s were most fecund: no fewer than sixty-four Indian plays came out in those two decades." Jones, *Native Americans as Shown on Stage, 1753–1916* (Metuchen, NJ: Scarecrow, 1988), 84. For an overview of the Indian drama, including the antebellum Indian melodrama and parodies of it, see also Don B. Wilmeth, "Noble or Ruthless Savage? The American Indian on Stage and in the Drama," *Journal of American Drama and Theatre* 1 (1989): 39–78. Early analyses of the Indian melodramas (as well as poems and other popular literary genres) as communicating removal ideology include Roy Harvey Pearce, *Savagism and Civilization: A Study of the Indian and the American Mind*, rev. ed. (Berkeley: U of California P, 1988), 169–95; Robert F. Berkhofer Jr., *The White Man's Indian: Images of the American Indian from Columbus to the Present* (New York: Vintage, 1978), 86–96.

2. Peter Brooks, *The Melodramatic Imagination: Balzac, Henry James, Melodrama, and the Mode of Excess* (New Haven: Yale UP, 1976), 12. Detailed treatments of American melodrama in this period include David Grimsted, *Melodrama Unveiled: American Theater and Culture, 1800–1850* (Chicago: Chicago UP, 1968); Gary A. Richardson, "Plays and Playwrights: 1800–1865," in *The Cambridge History of American Theatre*, vol. 1, ed. Don B. Wilmeth and Christopher Bigsby (Cambridge: Cambridge UP, 1998), 250–302; Jeffrey D. Mason, *Melodrama and the Myth of America* (Bloomington: Indiana UP, 1993); Bruce A. McConachie, *Melodramatic Formations: American Theatre and Society, 1820–1870* (Iowa City: U of Iowa P, 1992). Brooks provides the clearest analysis of melodramatic conventions, though with reference to nineteenth-century French melodrama.

3. Philip Gould, "Remembering Metacom: Historical Writing and Cultures of Masculinity in Early Republican America," in *Sentimental Men: Masculinity and the Politics of Affect in American Culture*, ed. Mary Chapman and Glenn Hendler (Berkeley: U of California P, 1999), 112–24; Scott C. Martin, "Interpreting *Metamora*: Nationalism, Theater, and Jacksonian Policy," *Journal of the Early Republic* 19 (1999): 73–101; Gordon M. Sayre, *The Indian Chief as Tragic Hero: Native Resistance and*

the Literatures of America, from Moctezuma to Tecumseh (Chapel Hill: U of North Carolina P, 2005), 117–25. These works focus on Edwin Forrest's performance in *Metamora*. On Forrest's proclivity to play Jacksonian heroes, see Bruce A. McConachie, "The Theatre of Edwin Forrest and Jacksonian Hero Worship," in *When They Weren't Doing Shakespeare: Essays on Nineteenth-Century British and American Theatre,* ed. Judith L. Fisher and Stephen Watt (Athens: U of Georgia P, 1989), 3–18.

4. Prosper M. Wetmore, prologue to *Metamora; or, The Last of the Wampanoags* by John Augustus Stone, in *Staging the Nation: Plays from the American Theatre, 1787–1909,* ed. Don B. Wilmeth (1829; repr., Boston: Bedford Books, 1998), 540. After selecting *Metamora* as the winner of a contest he sponsored, Edwin Forrest continued to perform the title role for almost forty years. On Forrest's selection of *Metamora,* his performance in the title role, and the production history of the melodrama, see especially Richard Moody, *America Takes the Stage: Romanticism in American Drama and Theatre, 1750–1900* (Bloomington: Indiana UP, 1955), 93–96; Mason, *Melodrama and the Myth of America,* 23–59; Jill Lepore, *The Name of War: King Philip's War and the Origins of American Identity* (New York: Vintage, 1998), 191–226; Scott C. Martin, "Interpreting *Metamora*"; Mark Mullen, "This Land Is Your Land, This Land Is My Land: *Metamora* and the Politics of Symbolic Appropriation," *New England Theater Journal* 10 (1999): 63–87. Moody quotes Forrest's biographer, Gabriel Harrison (*Edwin Forrest: The Actor and Man* [1889]), on the matter: "So accurate had been his observations that he caught the very manner of their breathing" (96). On calls for a national drama in this period, see Walter J. Meserve, *Heralds of Promise: The Drama of the American People during the Age of Jackson, 1829–1849* (Westport, CT: Greenwood, 1986), 20–42; Christopher Bigsby and Don B. Wilmeth, introduction to *Cambridge History of American Theatre,* 1:8–19.

5. Susan Scheckel, *The Insistence of the Indian: Race and Nationalism in Nineteenth-Century American Culture* (Princeton: Princeton UP, 1998), 57.

6. For analyses of Indian melodramas as treating membership in a multiethnic, multicultural society, see especially Flynn, "Melting Plots"; Werner Sollors, *Beyond Ethnicity: Consent and Descent in American Culture* (New York: Oxford UP, 1986), 102–30. Philip Gould reminds us that playwrights and audiences of this period often pondered national membership through the display of ennobling emotions, though he emphasizes that "Stone's play...thematiz[es] the politically untenable nature of sentimental republicanism" ("Remembering Metacom," 119). Theresa Strouth Gaul suggests that the hierarchical classification of societies and races and the rise of ethnography meant that the dramas appealed to audiences who wished to see a declining people and their quaint ways reenacted by representatives of an emerging national theater. Gaul, "'The Genuine Indian Who Was Brought Upon the Stage': Edwin Forrest's *Metamora* and White Audiences," *Arizona Quarterly* 56 (2000): 1–27. On the impact of American Indian performances (on stage and in political arenas) on Indian dramas, see Mullen, "This Land Is Your Land," 72; Peter G. Buckley, "Paratheatricals and Popular Stage Entertainment," in Wilmeth and Bigsby, *Cambridge History of American Theatre,* 1:454; Rosemarie K. Bank, *Theatre Culture in America, 1825–1860* (Cambridge: Cambridge UP, 1997), 64–68; Moody, *America Takes the Stage,* 78–79.

7. Linda Williams, *Playing the Race Card: Melodramas of Black and White from Uncle Tom to O. J. Simpson* (Princeton: Princeton UP, 2001), 5, 4, 15.

8. Three of Cooper's historical romances, *The Wept of Wish-Ton-Wish, The Pioneers,* and *The Last of the Mohicans,* were variously adapted for the stage between 1820 and 1850 (Jones, *Native Americans as Shown on Stage,* 69–71).

9. Bank, *Theatre Culture in America,* 2. She further explains: "Viewed as theatre, as a performance at once earnest and assumed, true and false, accepting and contesting, liberating and oppressing, nineteenth-century American culture becomes, I think, much richer than it can be when viewed as a confining structure—as something happening inside cultural monuments (such as theatres) yet outside the bounds of history" (190).

10. Brooks, *Melodramatic Imagination,* 5; Williams, *Playing the Race Card,* 15.

11. McConachie, *Melodramatic Formations,* 112. On these acting conventions and audience responses, see also Brooks, *Melodramatic Imagination,* 47; Grimsted, *Melodrama Unveiled,* 62; Robert Allen, *Horrible Prettiness: Burlesque and American Culture* (Chapel Hill: U of North Carolina P, 1991), 55–57. With regard to the dramatization of virtue, one should note that the American melodrama evolved in the 1830s through the 1850s; as McConachie argues, melodramas focusing on the Jackso-

nian heroes of those decades slowly gave way to "moral reform melodramas" such as *Uncle Tom's Cabin* and *The Drunkard* (xii). "[The melodrama] urged men to purity, patriotism, and faith in providence," Grimsted writes, "and it promised them earthly happiness from God, home, and country; but the greatest of these was home with its cornerstone of female purity" (*Melodrama Unveiled*, 229). Richardson adds that melodramas "argued forcefully for a reassertion of abiding American ideals, ideals that by the 1840s and 1850s had become synonymous with...the ideology of sentimental domesticity for women and liberal bourgeois respectability for men" ("Plays and Playwrights," 285).

    12. Williams, *Playing the Race Card*, 57; Mason, *Melodrama and the Myth of America*, 15.

    13. Flynn, "Melting Plots," 421–22.

    14. Custis's *Pocahontas* was first produced at the Walnut Street Theatre in Philadelphia, January 16, 1830, and was followed by twelve noncontinuous performances. The 1836 revival of the drama is noteworthy for the reported but discredited attendance of John Ross and the Cherokee delegation. See Scheckel, *Insistence of the Indian*, 58–59; Bank, *Theatre Culture in America*, 66–68; Robert S. Tilton, *Pocahontas: The Evolution of an American Narrative* (New York: Cambridge, 1994), 72–74. The earliest dramatization of the Pocahontas myth was James Barker's *The Indian Princess*, which premiered in Philadelphia in 1808. On this melodrama, see Eliana Crestiani, "James Nelson Barker's *Pocahontas*: The Theatre and the Indian Question," *Nineteenth-Century Theatre* 23 (1995): 5–32; Scheckel, *Insistence of the Indian*, 45–58; Moody, *America Takes the Stage*, 86–89.

    15. Stone, *Metamora*, in Wilmeth, *Staging the Nation*, 98.

    16. Mason, *Melodrama and the Myth of America*, 23. Grimsted writes that Metamora is "an amalgam of melodramatic virtues: he was a rescuer of heroines, a doting husband, a tender father, a brave warrior in the cause of freedom, indeed, as the heroine described him, 'the grandest model of a mighty man'" (*Melodrama Unveiled*, 216).

    17. George Washington Parke Custis, *Pocahontas; or, The Settlers of Virginia*, *Representative American Plays*, ed. Arthur Hobson Quinn (1830; repr., New York: Century, 1917), 207.

    18. Sollors, *Beyond Ethnicity*, 123.

    19. Custis, *Pocahontas*, 208.

    20. Patrick Brantlinger, *Dark Vanishings: Discourse on the Extinction of Primitive Races, 1800–1930* (Ithaca: Cornell UP, 2003), 3. He identifies the "proleptic elegy" as a part of nineteenth- and early twentieth-century racial extinction discourse, an expression that is "simultaneously funereal and epic's corollary—like the epic, a nation-founding genre" (3). On the forecasting and blessing of national ascendancy in *Metamora*, see Gordon Sayre, "Melodramas of Rebellion: *Metamora* and the Literary Historiography of King Philip's War in the 1820s," *Arizona Quarterly* 60.2 (Summer 2004): 21–28.

    21. According to Richard Moody, Forrest performed the role of the Indian chief in the Albany production of Noah's play during the 1825–26 season and in a performance at the Bowery Theatre during the subsequent season. Moody, *Edwin Forrest: First Star of the American Stage* (New York: Knopf, 1960), 57–58, 67. On the popularity of the play, see Meserve, *Heralds of Promise*, 12. Meserve adds that the drama was preformed at the Bowery Theatre as late as April 22, 1845. In his introduction to the published drama, Mordecai Manuel Noah brags that it earned twenty-four hundred dollars in its first two performances. Noah, *She Would Be a Soldier; or, The Plains of Chippewa*, in *Dramas from the American Theatre, 1762–1909*, ed. Richard Moody (1819; repr., Cleveland: World, 1966), 124.

    22. Noah, *She Would Be a Soldier*, 140.

    23. Lewis Deffebach, *Oolaita, or the Indian Heroine*, in *Three Centuries of English and American Plays, 1500–1830*, ed. Henry Willis Wells (1821; repr., New York: Readex Microprint, 1954), 14, 18, 24.

    24. Beginning in 1826, Custis drew on Washington's letters and the stories told by Washington's friends and servants to compose a series of such accounts under the title *Recollections*. These appeared in various newspapers until Custis's death in 1857. In 1859, Benson J. Lossing collected them in one volume. Murray H. Nelligan, "American Nationalism on the Stage: The Plays of George Washington Parke Custis (1781–1857)," *Virginia Magazine of History and Biography* 58 (1950): 301, 306. The installment of *Recollections* on which the drama is based appears in the preface to the 1828 edition of the drama, which I cite here.

    25. George Washington Parke Custis, *The Indian Prophecy, A National Drama*, in Wells, *Three Centuries of English and American Plays*, 4. Hereafter cited as *IP*. The play debuted July 4, 1827, at the

Chestnut Street Theatre in Philadelphia and was later performed in Baltimore and Washington, though "with no startling success" (Moody, *America Takes the Stage*, 96, 97).

26. Richard Drinnon, *Facing West: The Metaphysics of Indian-Hating and Empire-Building* (Minneapolis: U of Minnesota P, 1980), 119–215; Richard Slotkin, *Regeneration through Violence: The Mythology of the American Frontier, 1600–1860* (New York: Harper Perennial, 1996), 466–516.

27. Robert Montgomery Bird, *Nick of the Woods, or The Jibbenainosay; A Tale of Kentucky* (1837; repr., New Haven: College and University P, 1967), 201–2.

28. Sayre, *Indian Chief as Tragic Hero*, 192. Dana D. Nelson likewise situates the novel in the context of the mid-eighteenth-century displacement of Delawares and Shawnees by Pennsylvania leaders and settlers—a history "elided and replaced with a mythological Other." Nelson, *The Word in Black and White: Reading 'Race' in American Literature, 1638–1867* (New York: Oxford UP, 1993), 44.

29. Slotkin, Regeneration through Violence, 514.

30. James Emmett Ryan, "Imaginary Friends: Representing Quakers in Early American Fiction," *Studies in American Fiction* 31 (2003): 192, 193, 204. See also Susan M. Ryan, *The Grammar of Good Intentions: Race and the Antebellum Culture of Benevolence* (Ithaca: Cornell UP, 2003). Ryan writes: "Within the logic of Bird's narrative, a white man's benevolence toward native people signals his complicity in the destruction of his 'true' dependents." However, she continues, "If *Nick of the Woods* is about the failure, even the idiocy, of benevolence toward Indians, it might also be read—admittedly, against the grain—as a story about Anglo-Americans' resistance to seeing the violence undergirding the benevolent claims of their contemporaries" (25). (John Brougham, discussed in the next section, might be sympathetic with this reading). In a contrasting treatment of Bird's rejection of sympathy between whites and Indians on the frontier, Dana Nelson argues that Nathan Slaughter's fatal error—his trust of the Shawnee chief who killed his family—and embattled pacifism portray local democratic fraternity as "a pre-political savagism" in opposition to national constitutionalism. Nelson, "Frontier Democracy and Representational Management," in *REAL: Yearbook of Research in English and American Literature*, vol. 18, ed. Brook Thomas (Tübingen: Gunter Narr Verlag, 2002), 227. As Paul Gilmore explains, creators of frontier romances, Cooper and Forrest, "linked the lower orders of artisans and working men with a social and cultural elite," a connection Nelson argues many considered to be detrimental to the establishment of federal authority. Gilmore, *The Genuine Article: Race, Mass Culture, and American Literary Manhood* (Durham: Duke UP, 2001), 30.

31. Grimsted, *Melodrama Unveiled*, 167–69.

32. Medina's adaptation appeared just weeks before the Bowery was destroyed by fire and nine months before the playwright's death. Hamblin successfully revived the play as *Nick of the Woods or The Renegade's Daughter* in 1839 when the theater reopened. According to Smith, the play was performed in the Northeast with John Proctor in the title role from 1843 until 1879, and it was last revived in New York in 1886. Jones notes two other 1839 adaptations of the romance, neither extant: one by George Washington Harby, performed in New Orleans, and another by J. T. Haines, performed in London. Smith mentions two British versions of the play, performed in 1841 (Edinburgh) and in 1844 (Leeds). Because multiple Cooper romances were adapted for the stage at the height of the Indian melodrama's popularity (see n. 8), adaptations of the romance greatly complemented Bird's response to Cooper's Leatherstocking. See James L. Smith, headnote to *Nick of the Woods. A Drama, in Three Acts* by L. H. Medina, in *Victorian Melodramas: Seven English, French and American Melodramas*, ed. Smith (London: Dent, 1976), 66; Jones, *Native Americans as Shown on Stage*, 74–75 n. 22, 82–83, 69–71.

33. Medina, *Nick of the Woods*, in Smith, *Victorian Melodramas*, 72. Hereafter cited as *NW*.

34. Grimsted, *Melodrama Unveiled*, 208.

35. Constance Rourke, *American Humor: A Study of the National Character* (1931; repr., New York: New York Review Books, 2004), 42.

36. My analysis augments Louise K. Barnett's reading of Indian-hater novels in *The Ignoble Savage: American Literary Racism, 1790–1890* (Westport, CT: Greenwood, 1975), 129–44. Barnett asserts: "By embracing Indian killing as an end in itself and openly avowing race murder, the atavistic Indian hater makes a mockery of the tenets of white civilization. Exemplifying the code of personal vengeance and blood sacrifice which his society claims to practice no longer, he is the logical embodiment and culmination of those dark feelings of race hatred inherent in the white conquest of

North America" (141). A close study of Medina's adaptation suggests that the mockery of moving encounters in *Nick of the Woods* (drama and novel) does not suggest ambivalence about the larger civilization project but an acknowledgment bordering on celebration of the violence westward expansion requires of a civilized people.

37. In this way, Medina combines two of Bird's characters. In Bird's romance, Nathan Slaughter's family is massacred in Pennsylvania. After he migrates to Kentucky, he witnesses the massacre of the Ashburn family but cannot intervene because Colonel Bruce, enraged by Nathan's pacifism, has confiscated his gun. See Bird, *Nick of the Woods*, 147–50, 233–34.

38. Ibid., 234–35, 263, 323.

39. Ibid., 349, 345.

40. Here Ashburn identifies the woman he had envisioned twice in act 2, the one "with a deep gash across her white breast, who beckons me to a land where sorrow is not and death cannot enter, where all is peace, peace" (*NW* 80). He declares, "See, she beckons me—she passes—she is gone! Shade of the lovely and beloved, I follow you!" (*NW* 85).

41. On Brougham's career in the United States, see Pat M. Ryan, "The Hibernian Experience: John Brougham's Irish-American Plays," *MELUS* 10.2 (1983): 33–47. For tallies of Brougham's most common performances, see Dana Rahm Sutton, "John Brougham: The American Performance Career of an Irish Comedian, 1842–1880" (Ph.D. diss., City U of New York, 1999), 374. *Metamora* premiered in 1847, and Brougham subsequently performed the title role ninety-four times. The more popular play, *Po-Ca-Hon-Tas; or, The Gentle Savage*, debuted on December 2, 1855, at Wallack's Theatre in New York. "The record of its performance in New York alone testifies to its popularity," writes Moody; "After its initial showing it was repeated at the Bowery in the following July and again at Wallack's in April of 1857. From then until its run at the Bowery Garden, from April 18 to April 23, 1881, it was revived at intervals of every few years" (*America Takes the Stage*, 105).

42. Simon Dentith, *Parody* (London: Routledge, 2000), 9; Linda Hutcheon, *A Theory of Parody: The Teachings of Twentieth-Century Art Forms* (New York: Methuen, 1985), 6.

43. As Robert C. Allen emphasizes, inversion was key to the burlesque, and "as the various forms of burlesque became increasingly loose and intermixed in the 1860s, the extravaganza came to stand for any inversive, comic, musical spectacle." Allen, *Horrible Prettiness: Burlesque and American Culture* (Chapel Hill: University of North Carolina at Chapel Hill, 1991), 102. Michael R. Booth agrees: "By the 1860s, however, plays labelled 'extravaganza' tended to be what the public understood as burlesque; they were undoubtedly 'extravagant', and the terms 'extravaganza' and 'burlesque' were used interchangeably." Booth, introduction to *English Plays of the Nineteenth Century*, 5 vols., ed. Booth (London: Oxford at the Clarendon P, 1976), 5:26. For rich analyses of the burlesque and its treatment of social and aesthetic forms, see Allen, *Horrible Prettiness*, 23–42, 101–8; Richard W. Schoch, *Not Shakespeare: Bardolatry and Burlesque in the Nineteenth Century* (Cambridge: Cambridge UP, 2002). Allen treats the emergence of female burlesque troupes in the late 1860s, and Schoch considers (primarily British) Shakespearean burlesques. On the relationship between burlesque and minstrelsy, see Claudia Johnson, "A New Nation's Drama," in *Columbia Literary History of the United States*, ed. Emory Elliott (New York: Columbia UP, 1988), 334.

44. Allen, *Horrible Prettiness*, 104.

45. Ibid., 26. Schoch writes that burlesques "do not confirm pre-existing binaries (high/low, elite/popular, legitimate/illegitimate) by inverting them, but rather explode the hierarchies on which such accustomed meanings rely" (*Not Shakespeare*, 104).

46. John Brougham, *Po-Ca-Hon-Tas, or, The Gentle Savage* (1855), in *America's Lost Plays*, vol. 11, ed. Walter J. Meserve and William R. Reardon (Bloomington: Indiana UP, 1969), 115; John Brougham, *Metamora; or, The Last of the Pollywogs* (1847), in *Staging the Nation: Plays from the American Theatre, 1787–1909*, ed. Don B. Wilmeth (Boston: Bedford UP, 1998), 121. Hereafter cited as *P* and *M*, respectively.

47. Mullen likewise argues that Brougham suggests "whites themselves have grown from the Pollywog state, a process that is clearly revealed as a kind of reptilian de-evolution.... The ending [including Metamora's resurrection and plea] is certainly comic in its effect, but comedy may have been the only way to combat the unremitting dreary seriousness of the myth of inevitable decline" ("This Land Is Your Land," 81).

48. *OED Online*, s.v. "wog," http://dictionary.oed.com/cgi/entry/50286627 (accessed January 19, 2005); Jonathon Green, *Words Apart: The Language of Prejudice* (London: Kyle Cathie, 1996), 34. Oliphant quoted in *OED Online*, s.v. "polliwog," http://dictionary.oed.com/cgi/entry/50182990 (accessed January 19, 2005). In the context of defenses of Indian policy, Brougham's use of the term *pollywog* to highlight the codification of racial types appears to prophesy later racist uses of *wog*. On the term's use as a racial slur (and its initial appearance in a work of children's literature and subsequent use in advertising), see Green, *Words Apart*, 34–35; Robert M. MacGregor, "The Golliwog: Innocent Doll to Symbol of Racism," in *Advertising and Popular Culture: Studies in Variety and Versatility*, ed. Sammy R. Danna (Bowling Green: Bowling Green State UP, 1992), 124–32.

49. Schoch, *Not Shakespeare*, 41.

50. "Brougham's satire," Mullen notes, "is therefore a reminder that the forces ranged against Native Americans were both textual and military" ("This Land Is Your Land," 81).

51. Moody goes so far as to suggest that these references "seem to indicate that the play was intended as a burlesque for the Second Part of a minstrel show" (*America Takes the Stage*, 106). *Metamora* includes the minstrel standard "Dan Tucker" as well.

52. Likewise, Stone's *Metamora* alludes to the fact that the child and possibly the wife of the historical King Philip were sold into slavery at the close of the war (Lepore, *Name of War*, 153), and Brougham's *Metamora* compares Indian vengeance with the lashing of slaves: "The spirits of the mighty Pollywog / Stretch out their cowhides long your race to flog....But hear the cry of vengeance, feel the lash, / Till, for the lands you've stolen, you've paid the cash" (*M* 114).

53. Sollors describes Brougham's parodies as containing an "irreverent mix of...polyethnic themes" (*Beyond Ethnicity*, 137). According to Flynn, Brougham's burlesques are early examples of "the drama of 'cautious cosmopolitanism,'" which portrayed multiple ethnic groups "without emphasizing any projected future merging of the groups, though limited acculturation might be indicated" ("Melting Plots," 429).

54. Contrast these lines with the original: "Should you ask me, whence these stories? / Whence these legends and traditions, / With the odours of the forest, / With the dew and damp of meadows, / With the curling smoke of wigwams, / With the rushing of great rivers, / With their frequent repetitions, / And their wild reverberations, / As of thunder in the mountains?" Henry Wadsworth Longfellow, *The Song of Hiawatha*, ed. Daniel Aaron (1855; repr., London: Everyman, 1992), ll. 1–9.

55. On Longfellow's sources for *Hiawatha*, see Daniel Aaron, introduction to *Song of Hiawatha*, xi–xii. Aaron does point out that Longfellow "was really more interested in establishing [the poem's] cousinship with the heroic poetry of the Old World...than in being ethnohistorically correct" (xii). Yet Longfellow's epic depends on readers' interest in ethnohistory (as his use of Schoolcraft indicates) and their association of American Indian material with a *native* American culture. On the "Myth of Hiawatha," and more specifically the poem's place within a broader national literature and Longfellow's use of the ethnographic work and collections of Henry Rowe Schoolcraft and George Catlin, see Helen Carr, *Inventing the American Primitive: Politics, Gender and the Representation of Native American Literary Traditions, 1789–1936* (New York: New York UP, 1996), 101–46.

56. Stone, *Metamora*, 97; White quoted in Allen, *Horrible Prettiness*, 25.

57. Compare these lines with Metamora's response to Sir Arthur's command in Stone's original: "I have been pliant—aye, very yielding like the willow that droops over the stream, but till with a single arm you can move the mighty rock that mocks the lightening and the storm seek not to stir Metamora when his heart says no. I will come!" (Stone, *Metamora*, 69).

58. Such resurrections were common in burlesques of Shakespearean plays and "endow[ed] the burlesque with an aura of unpredictability, as if tomorrow night Juliet might not be restored to life as an Ethiopian serenader but just might survive to marry Romeo" (Schoch, *Not Shakespeare*, 104).

59. Sollors notes the references to Bancroft: "The audience's laughter gives Pocahontas and Smith the power to defy not only King Powhatan but also history: they can finish the story by their own logic" (*Beyond Ethnicity*, 136).

60. Stone, *Metamora*, 94.

Conclusion

1. Mark Twain, *Roughing It*, ed. Harriet Elinor Smith and Edgar Marquess Branch (1872; repr., Berkeley: Mark Twain Project of the Bancroft Library, U of California P, 1993), 129; Mark Twain, "Fenimore Cooper's Literary Offences," in *James Fenimore Cooper: The Critical Heritage*, ed. George Dekker and John P. Williams (1895; repr., London: Routledge, 1973), 276–87.

2. On the steamboat *Walter Scott*, see Mark Twain, *Adventures of Huckleberry Finn*, ed. Walter Blair and Victor Fischer (1885; repr., Berkeley: Mark Twain Project of the Bancroft Library, U of California P, 1985), chaps. 12–13. In Mark Twain's "Huck Finn and Tom Sawyer among the Indians," in *Huck Finn and Tom Sawyer among the Indians and Other Unfinished Stories* (Berkeley: Mark Twain Project of the Bancroft Library, U of California P, 1989), Tom speaks eloquently and of course at length about Indians being "the noblest human beings that's ever been in the world" (35). After witnessing the murder of a settler family and the kidnapping of their daughter, Peggy, Huck turns to Tom and asks, "Tom, where did you learn about Injuns—how noble they was and all that?" Twain continues, in a tragicomic vein, "He turned away his head, and after about a minute he said 'Cooper's novels,' and didn't say anything more, and I didn't say anything more, and so that changed the subject" (50).

3. Helen Hunt Jackson, *The Indian Reform Letters of Helen Hunt Jackson, 1879–1885*, ed. Valerie Sherer Mathes (Norman: U of Oklahoma P, 1998), 258; Dydia DeLyser, *Ramona Memories: Tourism and the Shaping of Southern California* (Minneapolis: U of Minnesota P, 2005), x. On the novel and reader nostalgia, see particularly *Ramona Memories*, 1–30. DeLyser provides an extensive treatment of *Ramona* and the afterlife of its story, from 1884 to 1955, in various tourist attractions and landmarks of the region.

4. Valerie Sherer Mathes, *Helen Hunt Jackson and Her Indian Reform Legacy* (Austin: U of Texas P, 1990), 95–162. On the Dawes General Allotment Act, see Francis Paul Prucha, *The Great Father: The United States Government and the American Indians*, 2 vols. (Lincoln: U of Nebraska P, 1984), 2:666–73.

5. Charles A. Eastman (Ohiyesa), *From the Deep Woods to Civilization: Chapters in the Autobiography of an Indian* (Boston: Little, Brown, 1916), 32, 114, 165. Replacing the myth of the doomed Indian with an account of the deteriorating force of decadence within civilization, Eastman writes in closing, "I realize that the white man's religion is not responsible for his mistakes. There is every evidence that God has given him all the light necessary by which to live in peace and good-will with his brother; and we also know that many brilliant civilizations have collapsed in physical and moral decadence. It is for us to avoid their fate if we can" (195).

6. Zitkala-Ša [Gertrude Bonnin], "An Indian Teacher among Indians," in *Masterpieces of American Indian Literature*, ed. Willis G. Regier (1900; repr., Lincoln: U of Nebraska P, 2005), 246. For a comparison of Eastman's and Bonnin's writings in this period, as well as their participation in the Society of American Indians, see Lucy Maddox, *Citizen Indians: Native American Intellectuals, Race, and Reform* (Ithaca: Cornell UP, 2005), 126–53. Maddox also cites this evocative passage from Bonnin's "Indian Teacher among Indians" (146).

7. Michael D. McNally, "The Indian Passion Play: Contesting the Real Indian in *Song of Hiawatha* Pageants, 1901–1965," *American Quarterly* 58.1 (Mar. 2006): 106. On the Hiawatha pageants, see also Alan Trachtenberg, *Shades of Hiawatha: Staging Indians, Making Americans, 1880–1930* (New York: Hill and Wang, 2004), 86–97. On Cody's Wild West show, see Joy S. Kasson, *Buffalo Bill's Wild West: Celebrity, Memory, and Popular Memory* (New York: Hill and Wang, 2000).

8. On American Indian music and musicians in this period, see Philip J. Deloria, *Indians in Unexpected Places* (Lawrence: UP of Kansas, 2004), 183–223. Maddox treats Bonnin's *Sun Dance Opera* and musical performances in *Citizen Indians*, 152. On Sitting Bull's tour with Cody's show, see Kasson, *Buffalo Bill's Wild West*, 169–83.

9. Eastman, *From the Deep Woods to Civilization*, 188. On Eastman and Bonnin's use of traditional dress in public performances, see especially Maddox, *Citizen Indians*, 140–41, 152–53. "Understanding the extent to which Indian people were performing their histories," writes Maddox, "their successes and failures, their political appeals, and their individual and collective identities before a largely white American public is…important to understanding the nature and form of American

Indian intellectual activity from the 1890s through at least the first two decades of the twentieth century" (*Citizen Indians*, 5).

10. George Horse Capture, "The Way of the People," in *Spirit of a Native Place: Building the National Museum of the American Indian*, ed. Duane Blue Spruce (Washington, DC: National Museum of the American Indian, Smithsonian Institution, in association with the National Geographic Society, 2004), 36.

11. W. Richard West Jr., "As Long as We Keep Dancing: A Brief Personal History," in Spruce, *Spirit of a Native Place*, 56.

12. Amanda J. Cobb, "The National Museum of the American Indians as Cultural Sovereignty," *American Quarterly* 57 (2005): 489, 489, 505.

13. Paul Chaat Smith and Ann McMullen, "Making History" (text), National Museum of the American Indian, Washington, D.C., 2003. Viewed May 27, 2005.

14. "Making History" (video presentation), National Museum of the American Indian, 2004. Viewed May 27, 2005. On the logistics of this video presentation, see "Interface Media Group Partners with the National Museum of the American Indian to Produce Exhibit Programs," *iCOM: Film & Video Production & Postproduction Magazine*, Nov. 2004, http://www.icommag.com/november-2004/november-extra.html (accessed June 1, 2005).

15. Cobb summarizes three early reviews from the *New York Times* and *Washington Post* that were highly critical of the NMAI and suggests that the reviewers did not grasp the philosophy of the museum; she notes that "99 percent of the 4 million expected visitors a year will be non-Native" ("The National Museum of the American Indians as Cultural Sovereignty," 502–3, 505).

16. Noting that Catlin "represents an easy and large target" for his commercialism and racism, the NMAI director, W. Richard West Jr., emphasizes, "What Catlin shows us, perhaps unwittingly, is that the 'primitive' people he painted had long ago achieved a level of cultural sophistication and aesthetic accomplishment with which we still are coming to terms, and which continues in the new millennium through the work and art of the descendents of those whom Catlin painted." West, introduction to *George Catlin and His Indian Gallery*, ed. George Gurney and Therese Thau Heyman (Washington, DC: Smithsonian American Art Museum, Norton, 2002), 20, 22.

17. W. Richard West Jr., "Remarks on the Occasion of the Grand Opening Ceremony," National Museum of the American Indian, Washington, D.C., Sept. 21, 2005, *Smithsonian Newsdesk*, http://newsdesk.si.edu/kits/nmai/speech_west.pdf (accessed June 28, 2005).

INDEX

A native of Boone, North Carolina, LAURA L. MIELKE received a B.A. in English and philosophy from Saint Olaf College, Northfield, Minnesota, in 1997. She went on to earn an M.A. and a Ph.D. in English from the University of North Carolina at Chapel Hill, where she was awarded the William Dougald McMillan III dissertation prize in 2003. From 2003 to 2007, she served as assistant professor of English at Iowa State University, and in fall 2007 she joined the English Department at the University of Kansas. Her articles have appeared in *American Indian Quarterly*, *American Transcendental Quarterly*, *Legacy*, and *MELUS*. She currently resides in Lawrence, Kansas, with her husband and son.